Routledge
New York and London

New American Destinies

A Reader in Contemporary
Asian and Latino Immigration

Edited by

Darrell Y. Hamamoto and Rodolfo D. Torres

Published in 1997 by

Routledge
29 West 35th Street
New York, NY 10001

Published in Great Britain by

Routledge
11 New Fetter Lane
London EC4P 4EE

Book design: Jeff Hoffman

Library of Congress Cataloging-in-Publication Data

New American destinies: a reader in contemporary Asian and Latino
immigration / [edited by] Darrell Y. Hamamoto, Rudolfo D. Torres.
p. cm.
Includes bibliographical references.
ISBN 0-415-91768-9. — ISBN 0-415-91769-7 (pbk.)
1. Immigrants—United States. 2. United States—Emigration and immigration.
3. Asians—United States. 4. Latin Americans—United States.
I. Hamamoto, Darrell Y. II. Torres, Rudolfo D., 1949–
JV6465.N48 1996   96-34286
323.1'73'0904—dc20   CIP

Contents

To my parents, Joel K. Hamamoto and Joan K. Hamamoto   DYH

To Patricia, and my role model Claus Speier   RDT

Acknowledgments

A number of people have contributed directly or indirectly to the development of this volume. We would like to express our gratitude to our collegues Mario Barrera and Andy Torres for their written comments on an early version of the manuscript and for their continued support of the project. The editors are also indebted to several people who contributed to the publication of the book. Rudy Torres wishes to acknowledge Luis Arroyo, Norma Chinchilla, Antonia Darder, Robert Miles, Federico Sanchez, and Victor Valle for their support and encouragement in this project.

Darrell Hamamoto extends gratitude to his valued colleagues at UC–Davis, Peter Leung, Wendy Ho, Kent Ono. In particular, he would like to recognize Isao Fugimoto for his leadership as director of the Asian American Studies Program and Bellie Gabriel for keeping it all together. Thanks to friends: Carl Boggs, Doug Kellner, Charles Igawa, Sandra Liu, Vu Pham, and Asagiri Tomoyo.

Finally, we are grateful to Jayne M. Fargnoli, Anne Sanow, Alexandra Mummery, and Karen Deaver of the Routledge staff for their help with the preparation of *New American Destinies.*

General Introduction

The closing years of the twentieth century mark an epochal transformation in the nature of U.S. society. Nowhere is this more obvious than in the precipitous growth of the immigrant and refugee population over the past three decades. Unlike the peak years of immigration earlier in the century, when European peoples predominated, the vast majority of contemporary immigrant and refugee groups have their origins in either Asia or Latin America. According to recent Census Bureau data, Latinos and Asians will account for more than half the growth in the U.S. population every year for the next half-century. Earlier waves of immigration from Asia and Latin America (then, primarily Mexico) notwithstanding, the "new immigrants" are entering a society that is vastly different from that of their predecessors.[1]

For one, the high-wage manufacturing jobs that were once the basis of a largely middle-class society have been exported overseas, having been supplanted by skilled professions in the information economy that require specialized training through years of increasingly costly education at the post-secondary level.[2] At the lower end of the service and information economy are the legions of Asian and Latino laborers who hold ethnically typed low-wage jobs cleaning, clothing, feeding, and housing those on the other side of the widening class divide. It is the janitorial, clothing, agriculture, and construction industries that are the principal employers of immigrant workers. In extreme instances, immigrants have been found to be working under slavelike conditions.[3] On a national level, the aggressive campaign waged against ready-to-wear dress manufacturer Jessica McClintock has given wider public exposure to the rampant and routine exploitation of immigrant female workers in the garment industry.[4] But the centrality of sweatshop labor to garment manufacture attracted widespread attention only when tabloid television programs including *Inside Edition*, *Extra*, and *Entertainment Tonight* publicized the campaign of the National Labor Committee (N.L.C.) to expose the extent of the problem both internationally and domestically by naming celebrity self-promoter Kathie Lee Gifford as complicit with discount retailer Wal-Mart in marketing an eponymous line of clothing that earned her a reported $9 million in royalties during 1995.[5]

At the same time, even as the traditional industrial manufacturing base has continued to erode, the demand for highly trained technicians, engineers, and computer scientists has grown apace. Foreign-born Asians in particular have moved to fill this need and have gained high visibility in many key sectors of the allied information industries. As a group, Asian immigrants are characterized by a higher level of education and professional attainment in comparison to native-born Americans. However, the relatively high average family income reported by the U.S. Bureau of the Census (1990) conceals substantial social and economic class differences among foreign-born Asian Americans.[6]

As an example, the legacy of American military adventurism throughout Southeast Asia has had a crippling effect upon Cambodian, Laotian, Mien, "second wave" Vietnamese, and Hmong refugees resettled in the United States. In the case of these groups—strictly speaking refugees, not immigrants—the Vietnam War caused the uprooting of nonliterate, agrarian peoples and forced them into an alien environment where they would be ill-prepared to withstand the traumas of dislocation. Not the least of the problems faced by Southeast Asian refugees is the obdurate anti-Asian racism of receiving communities such as that examined by Jeremy Hein in his study of a Hmong group resettled by the federal government in the state of Wisconsin.[7]

At the opposite extreme stand the most highly educated of all contemporary immigrant groups, Indo Americans. Liberalized immigration rules, the shortage of medical professionals and engineering talent in the U.S., and blocked avenues for economic advance in the home country combined to create the large-scale entry of Indo Americans beginning in the 1970s. According to the 1990 U.S. Census, between 1980 and 1990 the Indo American population grew by 126 percent. Were the entire Indian subcontinent (including India, Bangladesh, and Pakistan) to be included in the count, their combined numbers would total 908,656. Reflecting a high level of specialized education and superior income, Indo Americans constitute 50 percent of immigrant physicians of Asian origins and are heavily represented in academia, engineering, and the mathematical sciences.[8]

Opponents of immigration led by Senator Alan Simpson (R-Wyoming), however, have more recently set their sights on skilled and professional foreign workers who in total receive 140,000 employment visas each year. Legislation authored by Simpson that would have reduced the employment-visa quota to 90,000 annually was reviewed by the Senate Judiciary Committee in March 1996 following an earlier version that was approved by the Judiciary Committee in the House of Representatives in October 1995. Simpson, who made his political reputation as an ardent foe of immigration, had strategically linked the campaign against foreign-born professionals with popular attempts at controlling the number of "illegal" entrants into the United States.[9] But bowing to pressure exerted by immigration advocates and private sector employers, the Senate Judiciary Committee later voted 12 to 6 in favor of dividing immigration reform legislation into two parts, each considering legal and "illegal" immigration separately.[10]

Unfortunately, as it concerns issues pertaining to immigration, a shared consensus among the Asian American and Latino communities plainly does not exist. Moreover, in adopting the coded distinction between legal and "illegal" immigration, a sharp—and potentially disastrous—line of division has been drawn between Asians and Latinos. While certain Asian American groups such as the Japanese American Citizens League, the National Korean American Service and Education Consortium, and the Organization of Chinese Americans, and have fought anti-immigration legislation in all its guises, others represented by U.S. Congressman Jay C. Kim (R-California) have joined such conservative bedfellows as Robert K. Dornan (R-California) and Dana Rohrbacher (R-California) in advancing the immediate interests of Asian immigrants over those of Latinos. Kim has stated that "it is an insult to law-abiding citizens and soon-to-be-citizens who patiently followed all laws and regulations to be lumped together in a bill with illegal aliens who have sneaked into this country and have knowingly and willingly broken U.S. law."[11]

Just as it is impossible to discuss the new immigration apart from fundamental changes in the world capitalist system, only through comparative theoretical and methodological approaches are the lingering effects of ethnic particularism minimized while throwing into sharp relief the patterned structural consistencies and systemic features of contemporary transnational migration. As Rubén G. Rumbaut has presciently observed, the new immigration must be understood within the context of U.S. global military, political, economic, and cultural hegemony in the post–World War II era. Control over regional economic development through the Export-Import Bank, International Monetary Fund, and the World Bank, the relative ease and low cost of transportation, the extensive reach of the U.S. popular culture industries, military occupation and repeated armed intervention, new communication technologies, and intensified transnational capital investment activity have created the conditions for the massive immigration flow of 20 million foreign-born residents who have made the United States their home as of 1990. It is evident therefore that the Asian and the Latin American countries that contributed the majority of immigrants (nine million during the 1980s alone) are inextricably linked to the postwar system of U.S. imperium.[12]

Recently, James Petras and Morris Morley have gathered and analyzed a fund of basic economic data, international investment statistics, and foreign trade information to advance a compelling argument regarding the deformed nature of U.S. global power. They conclude that a decaying "Third Word" economy is being aborn domestically while an elite stratum "grows wealthy on private services and public subsidies."[13] As military, political, and ideological power conspire to extend and consolidate the reach of U.S. global empire, the national economy continues its downward spiral and civil society descends further into breakdown and chaos. Extending the analysis of Petras and Morley, the new immigration from Asia and Latin America might be viewed as the direct outcome of the postwar advance of transnational capitalism while at the same time being symptomatic of U.S. imperial decline.

Conveniently, with mounting intensity it is the immigrant population that is being held responsible for the deteriorating domestic economy. In the early 1990s, the new nativism manifested itself in any number of anti-immigration proposals that were floated by both conservative and liberal citizens groups and politicians in the State of California. Seizing the political opportunity, California Governor Pete Wilson fought for the passage of Proposition 187 in 1994, which (along with the elimination of affirmative action at the University of California) launched a presidential campaign that nevertheless flamed-out at an early stage.[14] But for other demagogues such as presidential aspirant Patrick J. Buchanan, immigration has become the centerpiece of the mean-spirited "politics of blame."[15] In response, President Bill Clinton tapped into anti-immigration fervor by touting his record-breaking success in deporting illegal aliens. Although the number of deportees (51,100) is insignificant when compared to the estimated four to five million undocumented aliens currently residing in the United States, the Clinton Administration hoped to blunt election-year criticism by stepping up enforcement of immigration laws.[16]

It is probable that the implementation of the North Atlantic Free Trade Agreement (NAFTA) by Canada, the United States, and Mexico will simply institutionalize the already existing reality of a "binational labor market" in the U.S. Although the issue of immigration as such was not broached during NAFTA negotiations, it is anticipated that a "temporary migration hump" will add to the already large number of Mexican nationals who enter the United States each year.[17] Worsening economic conditions, political instability, and peasant uprisings in southern states such as Chiapas will continue to displace Mexicans living in rural areas, large numbers (estimates vary widely) of whom will migrate north to the United States throughout the remainder of the decade and well into the next century.

Los Angeles, the archetypal late twentieth-century "global city," boasting a foreign-born population of nearly three million souls or about one-third of the total county population, has become refuge to tens of thousands of Central Americans who began their flight to the U.S. in the 1970s.[18] The penetration of international capital and resultant economic dislocations, the war between El Salvador and Honduras, domestic political repression, and the availability of low-skill jobs in the U.S. caused a huge leap in the number of Salvadorans, Guatemalans, and Nicaraguans who joined both newly arrived *Mexicanos* and well-established Mexican American communities in the state of California.[19] Although most Americans were only dimly aware of it, U.S. foreign policy backing oppressive but compliant client regimes in Central America served to hasten the exodus north of people fleeing state-sponsored terror. For over twelve years ending in early 1992, for example, the U.S. spent more than $4 billion in El Salvador to finance a proxy war that left more than 75,000 Salvadorans dead.[20]

While the historical pattern of Mexican settlement in southwestern U.S. cities such as Los Angeles continues, the nearly century-old colonial relationship between the United States and Puerto Rico becomes further strengthened as the world economy becomes evermore closely integrated, replenishing established ethnic enclaves in New York City and New Jersey. The "circulating migration" of Puerto Ricans between the mainland and a home island economy dominated by U.S. corporations benefiting from a combination of favorable tax policies, availability of low-wage labor, and lack of regulatory controls has resulted in the anomaly of fully 40 percent of the population living outside Puerto Rico. Although formally U.S. citizens since 1917 but with limited political rights, the benefits accruing to Puerto Ricans as a result of such status have been minimal when compared to more recently arrived Latino groups such as Cuban Americans.[21]

The postrevolutionary migration of Cubans to southern Florida during the 1960s illustrates the centrality of racial identity and social class position as key determinants of immigrant success in the United States. For among all Latino groups, Cuban Americans by all objective measures — average income, level of education, occupational status, political representation — stand alone as having achieved solidly middle-class status within the larger society. The valorization of white European "Spanish" racial identity over that of Indian or African infusions and the well-educated urban professional cosmopolitan composition (*habaneros* in particular) of first-wave Cuban immigrants served them well in adapting to the new social setting. The rabid anticommunist fervor of the times further aided in the perception of Cubans as being "good" immigrants because of their explicit renunciation of state socialism led by the reviled Fidel Castro.

The mass relocation of Cuban immigrants to urban centers such as Miami provides an early example of the simmering interethnic and racial tensions that have become a persistent feature of contemporary city life. From Liberty City to Mount Pleasant to Crown Heights to greater Los Angeles, spontaneous outbreaks of violence have come about as a direct response to social discrimination, blocked access to jobs, unceasing harrassment by police agencies, and profound alienation from the the new domestic order.[22] In Miami, African American wage earners endure a poverty rate fully three to four times greater than that of non-Hispanic whites and are disproportionately represented among lower status occupations. With increasing frequency, resentment against immigrant people by members of the native-born nonwhite underclass has erupted into cataclysmic violence, occasionally at the slightest provocation.[23]

A July 1995 study released by the National Asian Pacific-American Legal Consortium reveals the extent to which anti-immigrationism has become generalized throughout society, with violent hate crimes committed against Asian Americans rising 35 percent since 1993.[24] Most recently, a 21-year-old white supremacist named Gunner J. Lindberg and his 17-year-old accomplice admitted to the January 29, 1996, murder of 24-year-old Thien Minh Ly. The victim was knifed more than a dozen times after being attacked while skating on the tennis courts at Tustin High School in Orange County, California. In a search of Lindberg's apartment, Tustin police investigators found white supremacist literature, Nazi memorabilia, and a human skull "branded with a swastika."[25]

As illustrated by the murder of Thien Minh Ly, interethnic tensions and conflict have not been confined to the central city alone. The suburban enclave of Monterey Park, California, located not far from the city of Los Angeles, has been the site of cultural and political clashes between Anglo, Latino, and Asian residents. What was once a racially segregated Euroamerican (85 percent) community in 1960, by 1990 had become 40 percent Asian, 37 percent Latino, with whites being reduced to a "minority" at 20 percent of the total population.[26] The large-scale entry of Asian immigrants from Taiwan and Hong Kong in recent years has incurred the enmity of both Latino and Anglo residents, on occasion escalating to acts of violence but at other times reaching moments of political accord and accommodation.[27] As one hopeful observer argues, after successive triumphs by interethnic alliances over "right-wing strategies of containment," Monterey Park might very well be on the way to achieving a genuine "politics of diversity."[28]

A more likely response—at least on the part of white residents—to the "darkening" of metropolitan centers such as Los Angeles, San Francisco, New York, and Chicago is the continuation of a budding demographic trend that has Euroamericans leaving for the relatively racially homogeneous states of the Intermountain West, including Arizona, Colorado, Nevada, Utah, and Idaho. Outmigration from the Northeast to "heavily white enclaves" in central Florida, Southern Appalachia, and the edge cities of the Research Triangle in North Carolina has been especially dramatic. During the years 1990–1994 alone, New York City experienced a net loss of 861,000 residents who presumably heeded the call of the "new America," leaving behind an urban way of life that George Gilder has characterized as "dirty, dangerous, and pestilential."[29]

One of the primary motives for assembling the present anthology is to bring under one cover a variety of distinct but interrelated studies that offer insight into the complex political, economic, and social forces that have combined to create the new Asian and Latino immigration. At the same time, this collection of essays is offered as a response to the failure of "culturalist" strategies to adequately theorize the often contradictory and confounding demographic revolution arising from the fundamental change in the world capitalist system at the close of the century.[30] Whether under the banner of "poststructuralism," "postmodernism," or more recently "postcolonialism," self-referential rhetoric and metaphors might be heuristically useful, but are no substitute for historical knowledge, empirical research, and politically engaged social analysis.[31] Often, the vogueish invocation of nominalist conceptual formulations such as "hybridity," "Otherness," "exilic," and "diaspora" reveal more about the sociology of knowledge production among foreign-born cosmopolitan intellectuals (i.e., immigrants!) than they do about the material processes of contemporary transnational migration.[32]

Yet it is clear, as Victor Valle and Rodolfo D. Torres observe, that a new conceptual apparatus and critical lexicon are needed for the task of grappling with the radical remaking of the social landscape, sociocultural systems, expressive forms, and political institutions in the age of a globalized "postindustrial" order.[33] Beyond the aesthetic preoccupations of the literary left, questions of public policy, political mobilization, and long-term social transformation are at stake. By way of example, in his ethnographic study of Aguilillan peasants from the Mexican state of Michoacán and their role within the U.S. economy via a "transnational migrant circuit," Roger Rouse aptly demonstrates the manner by which postmodern theoretical insights can be invested with both an empirical weight and practical importance.[34]

The new American destinies of Asian and Latino immigrants will force a radical rethinking and transformation of virtually every aspect of American culture and society in the years ahead. The opening salvos in the "culture wars" declared by conservative ideologues such as the late Allan Bloom, E. D. Hirsch, Jr., Arthur M. Schlesinger, Jr., Dinesh D'Souza, William J. Bennett, and other opponents of "multiculturalism" can be read as coded intellectual responses to the impact of modern immigration and serve as early warning signs of the struggles to follow.[35] There will be practical consequences as well, arising from intense public policy discussion and political initiatives representing every quarter of the polity on issues ranging from affirmative action to xenophobia.[36]

As it pertains specifically to women, the study of the new Asian and Latino immigration forces a "gendered" understanding of sociocultural life in all its dimensions. In addition to their participation in the labor force, the decision to migrate, family formation, patterns of settlement, and the development of ethnic enterprise are contingent upon the active participation and agency of women.[37] The "crafting of feminine identity" and the "renegotiation" of gender ideologies among immigrant women is yet another aspect of the new transnational communities in the U.S. that have been formed through the process of migration and settlement.[38] The dual responsibility of reproductive and productive work for women within specific ethnic and class locations raises the fundamental question of whether a separate conceptual framework and novel analytical strategies distinct from those applied to male migrants might be required to accurately describe, explain, and understand the immigration process in its totality.

In all, the new immigration will require a thoroughgoing theoretical reappraisal and a more nuanced understanding of interethnic patterns and race relations in U.S. society. It is certain that the traditional black-white bifurcation that still dominates both popular discussion and formal inquiry is no longer adequate to the task of mapping and traversing a plural universe formed of the seeming chaos spun by contemporary multiracial realities. As David Rieff has expressed it, with an understated simplicity that conveys neither revulsion nor celebration, "One thing we know is that the future is not white."[39] The essays represented in these pages are offered to the reader as contributions to an expanding and deepening understanding of contemporary Asian and Latino immigration in process, which by extension will lead to questions that touch at the core promise of American democracy into the approaching new century.

NOTES

1. Two-thirds of all immigrants since 1970 come from the following countries: Mexico, Cuba, El Salvador, Guatemala, Nicaragua, the Dominican Republic, Haiti, the Philippines, Vietnam, South Korea, China, Taiwan, and India.

2. As Jeremy Rifkin observes, white collar jobs also are being eliminated at a rapid rate: over three million during the past ten years, with more to follow. Although he does not specifically address the issue, the continuing displacement of jobs through technological innovation will only serve to heighten hostility toward Asian and Latino immigrants at all levels within the economy. Jeremy Rifkin, *The End of Work: The Decline of the Global Labor Force and the Dawn of the Post-Market Era* (New York: Tarcher/Putnam, 1995).

3. In the summer of 1995, a garment subcontractor in El Monte, California, was discovered to have been holding 72 Thai immigrants—mostly female—in virtual bondage. George White, "Workers Held in Near-Slavery, Officials Say," *Los Angeles Times* 03 Aug. 1995, A1, A20. Ethnic auto-exploitation in this case is seen in the sentencing of Suni Manasurangkun, a Thai grandmother known as "auntie," who ran the operation with her five sons.

   Despite having one of the more robust economies in Southeast Asia, Thailand has developed a thriving trade in illegal immigration between the United States and other advanced capitalist societies. John-Thor Dahlburg, "Smuggling People to U.S. Is Big Business in Thailand," *Los Angeles Times* 05 Sep. 1995, A1, A8, A9.

4. Gary Delgado, "How the Empress Gets Her Clothes: Asian Immigrant Women Fight Fashion Designer," in Anner, John, ed. *Beyond Identity Politics: Emerging Social Justice Movements in Communities of Color* (Boston: South End Press, 1996), 81–94.

5. Eyal Press, "Kathie Lee's Slip." *The Nation* 17 Jun. 1996, 6–7.

6. U.S. Bureau of the Census, *The Foreign Born Population in the United States*, August 1993.

7. Jeremy Hein, "From Migrant to Minority: Hmong Refugees and the Social Construction of Identity in the United States," *Sociological Inquiry* Vol. 64, No. 3 (1994), 281–306.

8. Snehendu B. Kar, Kevin Campbell, Armando Jimenez, and Sangeeta R. Gupta, "Invisible Americans: An Exploration of Indo-American Quality of Life," *Amerasia Journal* 21:3 (Winter 1995/1996), 25–52.

9. John Greenwald, "Cutting Off the Brains: Alan Simpson wants to reduce the number of imported high-tech workers. It's a troublesome idea," *Time* 05 Feb. 1996, 46.

10. Marc Lacey, "Senate Panel Opts to Split Bill on Immigration," *Los Angeles Times* 15 Mar. 1996, A1, A17.

    The U.S. House of Representatives later voted overwhelmingly for a bill that dismissed the legal-immigration restrictions advocated by exclusionists, but which would "cut public benfits for legal immigrants and make their sponsors financially responsible for their well-being." Marc Lacy, "House OKs Bill to Curb Illegal Immigration," *Los Angeles Times* Orange County ed. 22 Mar. 1996, A1.

    However, the House also approved a crucial provision of California's Proposition 187, which gives states the right to deny the children of immigrants an education. Louis Freedberg, "House Backs Key Part of Prop. 187," *San Francisco Chronicle* 21 Mar. 1996, A1, A11.

11. Quoted in Frank H. Wu, "Washington Journal: Immigrant Disaster," *Asian Week* 10 Nov. 1995, 13. The only Korean American in the U.S. Congress and himself an immigrant, Rep. Kim has been dogged by an ongoing investigation by the FBI for alleged campaign improprieties. Kim (who has never been charged with a crime) has denied knowledge of having received illegal campaign contributions from foreign companies including Hyundai Motors America, Korean Airlines, and Samsung America, each of which has admitted guilt and, have paid substantial fines for their involvement with the scheme. David Rosenzweig, "Witness Intimidation Alledged in Kim Case," *Los Angeles Times* 15 Mar. 1996, B1, B6.

12. For an incisive survey of contemporary U.S. imperial domination on a global scale, see Michael Parenti, *Against Empire* (San Francisco: City Lights Books, 1995).

    While immigrants and refugees from the Carribean are not included within the scope of these pages, Haiti has existed within the imperial reach of the United States for well over 100 years. Although there is compelling evidence to suggest U.S. complicity in the September 1991 coup against democratically elected President Jean-Bertrand Aristide, government officials were steadfast in the assertion that the 40,000 Haitians who fled the island were "economic refugees," not political refugees. See Paul Farmer, *The Uses of Haiti* (Monroe, Maine: Common Courage Press, 1994).

13. James Petras and Morris Morley, *Empire or Republic? American Global Power and Domestic Decay* (New York: Routledge), 64.

14. The so-called Save Our State (SOS) initiative, Proposition 187 would require the state to restrict public education, public health care, and social welfare programs to U.S. citizens and legal residents.

15. Robert Wright, "Who's Really To Blame?" *Time* 06 Nov. 1995, 32–37.

16. Steven A. Holmes, "Large Increase In Deportations Occurred in '95," *The New York Times* 28 Dec. 1995, A1, A10.

17. Philip L. Martin, "Trade and Migration: The Case of NAFTA," *Asian and Pacific Migration Journal* Vol. 2, No. 3 (1993), 329–67.

18. The notion of the "global city" is developed by Saskia Sassen in "The Global City: A New Frontier?" *Contention* (Spring 1994). See also Saskia Sassen, *The Global City: New York, London, Tokyo* (Princeton: Princeton University Press, 1991).

19. In contrast to Salvadorans and Guatemalans, by a slight margin more Nicaraguan immigrants settled in Florida instead of California.

20. See Mark Danner, *The Massacre at El Mozote: A Parable of the Cold War* (New York: Vintage Books, 1994).

21. Even as U.S. citizens, for example, residents of Puerto Rico cannot vote in national elections and are allowed no representation in the U.S. Congress.

22. The language of underlying ethnic and racial tensions in contemporary urban society is compellingly articulated through the lived drama of the characters portrayed by Anna Deavere Smith in *Fires in the Mirror: Crown Heights, Brooklyn and Other Identities* (New York: Anchor Books, 1993) and *Twilight: Los Angeles, 1992* (New York: Anchor Books, 1994).

23. In late December 1995, twenty-two-year-old Michael Vernon of the Bronx killed five people at a shoe store owned by a Korean American immigrant and his wife Kyong Bae, who was among those slain by the gunman who reportedly said he was "displeased with the service." John J. Goldman, "Gun-Toting Shopper Kills 5 in N.Y. Shoe Store," *Los Angeles Times* 20 Dec. 1995, A21.

24. Kenneth B. Noble, "Attacks Against Asian-Americans Are Rising," *New York Times* 13 Dec. 1995, A16.

25. Geoff Boucher and Dexter Filkins, "Police Say Suspect Organized Gangs in Two States," *Los Angeles Times* Orange County ed. 03 Mar. 1996, A15; Lily Dizon, "Tustin Man Admits to Role in Ly Slaying," *Los Angeles Times* Orange County ed. 04 Mar. 1996, A1, A10, A11.

26. José Zapata Calderon, "Latinos and Ethnic Conflict in Suburbia: The Case of Monterey Park," *Latino Studies Journal* (May 1990), 23–32.

27. Leland Saito, "Asian Americans and Latinos in San Gabriel Valley, California: Ethnic Political Cooperation and Redistricting 1990–92," *Amerasia Journal* Vol. 19 (1993), 55–68.

28. John Horton, "The Politics of Diversity in Monterey Park, California," in Louise Lamphere, ed., *Structuring Diversity: Ethnographic Perspectives on the New Immigration* (Chicago: University of Chicago Press, 1992), 241.

29. Joel Kotkin, "Beyond White Flight," *The Washington Post* National Weekly Edition, 18–24 Mar. 1996, 26.

30. In accounting for the material basis of the postmodern condition, David Harvey writes of a "post-Fordist" political economy which has given rise to contemporary sociocultural transformation. David Harvey, *The Condition of Postmodernity: An Enquiry into the Origins of Cultural Change* (Cambridge, Massachusetts: Blackwell, 1989).

31. For a critique of these post-Marxist theoretical strains from three distinct but complementary perspectives, see Steven Best and Douglas Kellner, *Postmodern Theory: Critical Interrogations* (New York: The Guilford Press, 1991); Carl Boggs, *Intellectuals and the Crisis of Modernity* (Albany: State University of New York Press, 1993); and Russell Jacoby, *Dogmatic Wisdom: How the Culture Wars Divert Education and Distract America* (New York: Anchor Books, 1995).

   See also the more focused critique on "postcolonial" criticism by Russell Jacoby, "Marginal Returns," *Lingua Franca* (September/October 1995). There are encouraging signs, however, that the trivialization of "postcolonialism" as a term of analysis has been recognized. See Aijaz Ahmad, "Postcolonialism: What's in a Name?" in Román De la Campa, E. Ann Kaplan, and Michael Sprinker, *Late Imperial Culture* (London: Verso, 1995), 11–32.

Placing it all into context, the late Christopher Lasch devotes an instructive chapter on "academic pseudo-radicalism" in *The Revolt of the Elites and the Betrayal of Democracy* (New York: W. W. Norton, 1996).

32. Sau-ling C. Wong writes forcefully of the "politically ungrounded" character of concepts such as "Asian diaspora" and the class-bound nature of the "exilic sensibility" that has come to inform much Asian American intellectual and creative expression. Sau-ling C. Wong, "Denationalization Reconsidered," *Amerasia Journal* Vol. 21, Nos. 1 & 2 (1995), 1–27.

33. Victor Valle and Rodolfo D. Torres, "Latinos In A 'Post-Industrial' Disorder," *Socialist Review* Vol. 23, No. 4 (1994), 1–28.

34. Roger Rouse, "Mexican Migration and the Social Space of Postmodernism," *Diaspora* (Spring 1991), 8–23.

35. Allan Bloom, *The Closing of the American Mind* (New York: Touchstone, 1987); E. D. Hirsch, Jr., *Cultural Literacy: What Every American Needs to Know* (New York: Vintage, 1988); Dinesh D'Souza, *Illiberal Education: The Politics of Race and Sex on Campus* (New York: The Free Press, 1991); Arthur M. Schlesinger, Jr., *The Disuniting of America: Reflections on a Multicultural Society* (New York: W. W. Norton, 1993); William J. Bennett, *The De-Valuing of America: The Fight for Our Culture and Our Children* (New York: Touchstone, 1994.

36. The link between the new immigration and the issue of affirmative action has been made by the most influential of restrictionist organizations, the Federation of American Immigration Reform (FAIR). See Mark Krikorian, "Affirmative Action and Immigration," in Martin Nicolaus, ed., *Debating Affirmative Action: Race, Gender, Ethnicity, and the Politics of Inclusion* (New York: Delta, 1994), 300–303.

37. Silvia Pedraza, "Women and Migration: The Social Consequences of Gender," *Annual Review of Sociology* Vol. 17 (1991), 303–325.

38. Amarpal K. Dhaliwal, "Gender at Work: The Renegotiation of Middle-Class Womanhood in a South Asian-Owned Business," in Wendy L. Ng et al., eds. *ReViewing Asian America: Locating Diversity* (Pullman, Washington: Washington State University Press, 1995), 75–85.

39. David Rieff, "Homelands," *Salmagundi* (Winter 1989), 65.

Immigration and Migration
A Conceptual Map

Introduction

Following World War II, the scope and character of immigration to the United States has undergone profound changes. Perhaps the most significant feature of contemporary immigration is that the majority of those entering the United States hail from either Asia or Latin America. In previous decades, immigrants were overwhelmingly of European origin. The following theoretical pieces introduce key concepts, terms, and explanatory models used in accounting for this singular shift in the regions from which immigrants originate. The legacy of colonialism, military conquest, and political-economic dependency will be advanced to explain the manner by which large-scale historical forces have brought about this transformation.

In addition to "dependency theory" and "world systems theory," among the explanatory models to be reviewed in this section is that which examines the role of domestic and international labor markets in creating and maintaining the objective conditions for immigration. But in addition to "structural" explanations that focus on labor markets, the authors variously discuss "individual" motivations shared by Asian and Latino immigrants, including the desire to unify families, procure spouses, escape political persecution, or flee from the ravages of civil war.

Chapter 1

Rubén G. Rumbaut

Origins and Destinies
Immigration to the United States Since World War II

> How curious a land is this — how full of untold story, of tragedy and laughter and the rich legacy of human life; shadowed with a tragic past, and big with future promise! . . . It is a land of rapid contrasts and of curiousty mingled hope and pain.
> —W. E. B. Du Bois, *The Souls of Black Folk*

Those apt and emotive words may serve as an epigraph for America at the end of the twentieth century, a land of rapid contrasts being again transformed by new waves of immigration that rival those of the tumultuous era before World War I. But Du Bois was describing the "Black Belt" at the beginning of the century as he traveled by train across Georgia in the "Jim Crow Car," passing by the land of the Cherokees and the Creek Indians — "and a hard time the Georgians had to seize it" — to "the centre of the Negro problem . . . of America's dark heritage from slavery and the slave trade" (Du Bois, 1989/1903:78–79). In *The Souls of Black Folk*, written soon after Africa was partitioned by European colonial powers and Puerto Rico, the Phillippines, Guam, and the Hawaiian islands were seized by the United States in the aftermath of the Spanish-American-Cuban War, Du Bois had prophesied that "the problem of the twentieth century is the problem of the color line — the relation of the darker to the lighter races of men in Asia and Africa, in America and the islands of the sea" (1989/1903:10).

Much has changed since then, mainly in the years after World War II, including the decolonization of Africa and Asia and the English-speaking Caribbean, and the dismantling of Jim Crow in the United States; but much has not, so that another preeminent African American scholar, John Hope Franklin, could "venture to state categorically that the problem of the twenty-first century will be the problem of the color line" (Franklin, 1993:5). Class, not color, had shaped the fates of the "white ethnics" — Southern and Eastern Europeans — whose arrival by the millions around the turn of the century culminated in the

From "Origins and Destinies: Immigration to the United States Since World War II" in *Sociological Forum*, Vol. 9, No. 4, 1994. Reprinted by permission of Plenum Publishing Corporation.

restrictionist national-origins laws of the 1920s (cf. Steinberg, 1989). The Great Depression and World War II thereafter combined to cut the flow of immigrants to America to its lowest point since the 1820s. But the new and rapidly accelerating immigration to the United States—from Asia, Latin America, and the Caribbean, and increasingly (though still relatively small) from Africa and the Middle East—is unprecedented in its diversity of color and class and national origins; it is changing fundamentally the racial and ethnic composition and stratification of the American population, and perhaps also the social meanings of race and ethnicity and of American identity. As were their predecessors, the new immigrants and their children are themselves being transformed in the process, and their destinies, as yet full of untold story, will bear the stamp of their diverse origins.

The stories that *are* being told in the news media of the day—particularly in the "Immigrant Belt" of global cities like Los Angeles, New York, and Miami—are full of the dramatic contrasts and the "curiously mingled hope and pain" of contemporary immigrants from all over the world who enter, with or without permission, in search of future promise or to escape a tragic past, and of the variety of ways in which the natives respond, often with alarm, to their presence. As in the past, American nativism is exacerbated during periods of economic recession. Nowhere has that been more palpable than in California in the early 1990s, where the deepest and most prolonged recession since the Great Depression, in part a product of post–Cold War cutbacks in the defense industry and military spending, coincided with the largest concentration of legal and illegal immigrants and refugees in the country. Governor Pete Wilson led other politicians of both parties in singling out the cost of providing public services to immigrants, especially in Los Angeles, as the cause of the state's budget deficit, and called for the denial of citizenship to the U.S.-born children of undocumented immigrants.

Yet in sharp contrast to the poverty and vulnerable status of many newcomers, such as laborers from Mexico and Central America and refugees from Southeast Asia, many immigrant communities throughout Southern California have thrived despite the recession. Iranians make up about a quarter of the high school enrollments in upscale Beverly Hills. In 1992 nearly 1 in 5 (19%) home buyers in Los Angeles County had a Chinese surname—although the Chinese make up only 2.7% of the country's huge population—propping up the moribund housing market and revitalizing entire neighborhoods. Some of these homes are so-called monster houses in rich suburbs for the wives and children of Taiwanese businessmen (called "astronauts" locally) who spend most of their time abroad making money. In 1993 in nearby Monterey Park—known as "Little Taipei" and as "the first suburban Chinatown"—a businessman from mainland China walked into a Taiwanese community bank, was assured by the manager that his transactions would be kept confidential from Chinese authorities, and deposited $10,000 on the spot, returning the next day to deposit another $900,000 by wire transfer. Business is booming in China's coastal provinces, and private fortunes are winding their way through Hong Kong to the United States and Canada; as a report in the *Los Angeles Times* put it, "The Gold Rush, this time, is from west to east" (Schoenberger, 1993). And the 1994 lifting of the U.S. trade embargo against Vietnam, whose rapidly growing economy is widely expected to make it the next "Asian tiger," will stimulate Vietnamese businesses throughout California, and Orange County's "Little Saigon" may come to rival the economic dynamism of "Koreatown" just to the north; already vietnamese developers and realtors in California report a growing flow of capital from Vietnam as entrepreneurs there seek safe havens for their excess cash (Kotkin, 1994). No one had imagined such an outcome when a million mostly indigent Indochinese refugees came in the years after the fall of Saigon as part of the largest refugee resettlement program in U.S. history.

Such reports, however, are less common than those that focus on undocumented immigrants, such as nannies and house cleaners for native-born affluent families (and government officials who since 1993 have discovered they had a "Zöe Baird problem"), and those who wait at busy corners throughout Southern California to be hired for day jobs—an estimated 40 sites in Los Angeles County alone: "Each year they probably complete close to a million workdays of dirt moving, tree trimming, hauling, moving, painting, yard and pool cleaning, dry-walling, plastering and tiling for the region's homeowners and small contractors. It is labor that might not get done if it weren't for migrants willing to work for $5 or less an hour" (Kelley, 1990). Several of the top economic sectors in California—especially agriculture, apparel, and construction—depend almost exclusively on immigrant labor. Still, after the massive earthquake in Los Angeles in 1994, legislation was introduced to deny assistance to foreign-born victims who could not prove their legal status. Meanwhile, on the other side of the country, the *Miami Herald* reported that just before Christmas 1993, 7 Cubans and 10 Haitians pooled their resources and sailed from the Bahamas—literally in the same boat—to Florida, where upon arrival the Cubans were duly processed by the U.S. Immigration and Naturalization Service (INS) while the Haitians were sent to detention facilities (Garcia and Cavanaugh, 1993). In 1992, the INS approved over 96% of Cubans who applied for refugee status, but less than 11% of Haitians (Immigration and Naturalization Service [INS], 1993). Color, Cold War foreign policies, and the political clout of Cuban ethnic communities in the United States have helped shape the contradictory reception accorded to recent escapees from Cuba and Haiti who make it to the United States: the Cubans, fleeing an economic crisis deepened by the 1989 collapse of the Soviet Union and a tightened U.S.-imposed trade embargo, are generally guaranteed political asylum, and under the Cuban Adjustment Act of 1966, become eligible for permanent residency a year after their arrival; the Haitians, fleeing the political terrorism of a military regime that deposed the democratically elected president in 1991, are detained and subject to deportation as economic migrants (cf. Dominguez, 1992; Stepick, 1992). Some make it spectacularly, as did a 21-year-old Cuban who in 1994 crossed 110 miles of shark-infested waters from Cuba to the Florida Keys riding a windsurfer (the second such crossing in recent years). Many do not make it at all and drown at sea.[2]

Such examples make for sensational copy, but they do humanize and illustrate memorably the extraordinary diversity of the new immigration, their motives and modes of passage to America, their contexts of exit and reception. This article is an effort to make sense of that diversity through a broad-brush sketch of the social and historical origins of immigration to the United States since the end of World War II. The focus will be on types of immigrants that comprise contemporary flows, their patterns of destination and settlement, their distinctive social and economic characteristics compared to major native-born racial-ethnic groups, and their different modes of incorporation in—and consequences for—American society.

A twofold classification of contemporary immigrants will help organize our analysis and render their diverse origins and destinies more comprehensible. First, depending on their socioeconomic status, we focus on three salient types of immigrants: professionals, entrepreneurs, and manual laborers. Second, depending on their legal-political status, we distinguish among three basic types: regular immigrants (who enter under provisions of U.S. law that favor family reunification as well as highly skilled professionals), undocumented immigrants (who enter illegally by crossing the border or overstaying a temporary visa), and refugees (or asylees, in the case of those who claim political asylum once in the United States). Each of these types is represented by several nationalities; and conversely, within a single nationality may be found individuals who represent different types (Portes and Rumbaut, 1990). In addition, these socioeconomic and legal-political statuses crisscross and combine in ways that magnify the relative social advantages or disadvantages of particular immigrant groups as they make their way in America. For example, the undocumented tend to consist disproportionately of manual laborers, whose legal vulnerability makes them in turn more economically exploitable; professionals are typically found among the first waves of refugee flows, and among "pioneer" immigrants who come under the occupational preferences of U.S. law (whereupon, once established as permanent residents or U.S. citizens, they can sponsor the immigration of their immediate family members). These and other factors—such as the extent of racial discrimination and nativist prejudice, the state of the economy, the structure and cohesiveness of families, and the presence or absence of strong co-ethnic communities in areas of immigrant settlement—form the contexts within which immigrant groups adapt and shape their diverse fates.

Changes in U.S. immigration laws—in particular the amendments passed in 1965 (fully implemented in 1968), which abolished the national origins quota system and changed the preference system to give priority to family reunification over occupational skills—have often been singled out as the principal reason for the "new immigration" and the change in its composition. But the causal effects of the Hart-Celler Act of 1965 have been exaggerated, and its most important consequences, such as the removal of barriers to immigrants from Asian and African countries (Hing, 1993; Reimers, 1985), were largely unintended. The law does matter, of course: it influences migration decisions and constitutes a key context of reception shaping the destinies of newcomers, especially their right to full membership and future citizenship. But it cannot control historical forces or determine the size or source of migration flows.

Migration patterns are rooted in historical relationships established between the United States and the principal sending countries—that is, the size and source of new immigrant communities in the United States today is directly if variously related to the history of American military, political, economic, and cultural involvement and intervention in the sending countries, and to the linkages that are formed in the process that (often unintentionally) open a surprising variety of legal and illegal migration pathways. A remarkable recent example involves the thousands of former Iraqi soldiers and prisoners of war from the 1991 Persian Gulf War who resettled in the United States as refugees. Thus, a principal argument is that immigration to the United States and the formation of new American ethnic groups are the complex and deeply ironic social consequences of the expansion of the nation to its post–World War II position of global hegemony. As the United States has become more deeply involved in the world, the world has become more deeply involved in America—indeed, in diverse ways, it has come to America.

A WORLD ON THE MOVE:
IMMIGRATION TO THE U.S. SINCE WORLD WAR II

International migration has been a major feature of the new world order that emerged from the ashes of World War II, for a complex set of reasons (Massey et al., 1993; Zolberg, 1991, 1992). Societies have become increasingly linked in numerous ways—economically, politically, culturally—and modern consumption standards (especially American life styles and popular culture) have been diffused worldwide at an accelerating rate. Transnational population movements of workers, refugees, and their families are but one of many other global exchanges of capital, commodities, and information across state borders, all facilitated by a postwar revolution in transportation and communication technologies that have reduced the costs of travel and raised expectations about opportunities abroad. In general, the patterns reflect the nature of contemporary global inequality: capital flows from rich to poor countries and labor flows from less developed to more developed regions. Also, the era since World War II—the era of the Cold War and global superpower confrontation, decolonization and the formation of new states, revolutions and counterrevolutions—has been characterized by continuing flows of refugees primarily from one "Third World" country to another (Zolberg et al., 1989). Since the disintegration of the "Second World" at the end of the 1980s and another round of new state formation, new refugee flows have been added in Europe, Africa, and elsewhere.

In asbsolute numbers, the United States remains by far the principal receiving country: the 19.8 million foreigners counted in the 1990 U.S. census formed the largest immigrant population in the world—indeed, in world history. In *relative* terms, however, only 7.9% of the 1990 population was foreign-born, a percentage exceeded by many contries and a much lower proportion than had been the case earlier in this century, as Table I makes clear. Still, net immigration accounted for 39% of total U.S. population growth during the 1980s—a proportion larger by far than any other decade in the twentieth century except for 1901–1910. The so-called foreign stock population—the two generations of immigrants plus their children born in the United States—is near an all-time high, estimated at roughly 45 million in 1990, and poised to increase much more rapidly still in the coming decades (Passel and Edmonston, 1992). Although little is known about their adaptation patterns to date, the new second generation—the children of the new immigrants—are bound to represent a crucial component of American society in the years to come (Portes and Zhou, 1993; Rumbaut, 1990, 1994).

Table 1.1 shows decennial trends in the changing size and composition of immigrant flows to the United States for the century from 1890 to 1990, using data from the two main national-level sources: the U.S. census (counts of all foreign-born persons, regardless of their legal status) and the INS (counts of persons "admitted to lawful permanent residence," who either entered the United States with an immigrant visa from abroad or were already in the United States but adjusted their status from temporary to permanent resident). The INS data do not reflect the entry of unauthorized immigrants into the United States, deaths, or emigration from the United States, which accounts for many of the discrepancies between the two data sets in Table 1. For example, the census data show an increase of some 3 million in the foreign-born population between 1900 and 1910; but INS data show 8.8 million immigrants were admitted during that decade, the largest on record. Much of this flow was initiated by active recruitment on the part of American employers, and many immigrants returened home after a few years in the United States—"birds of passage," predominantly young single men, whose movements tended to follow the ups and downs of the American business cycle (Piore, 1979).

After World War I broke out, immigration began an uneven and then precipitous decline until the trend reversed itself immediately after World War II, and has been increasing rapidly since. In the post–World War II period, legal immigration flows are more apt to be sustained by family reunification preferences in the allocation of immigrant visas and by kinship networks developed over time (Jasso and Rosenzweig, 1990) than by economic cycles and deliberate recruitment. While in the first decades of the century 67% of all immigrants were men, since 1941 the majority—55%—have been women (INS, 1991). By 1940, only 13% of immigrants were coming from Asia and Latin America and less than 13% from Europe and Canada. The pattern had been completely reversed by 1990, with 84% coming from Asia and Latin America and less than 13% from Europe and Canada (see Table 1.1).

Contemporary flows are further distinguished by sizable and increasing proportions of the following: (1) *political refugees and asylees*, beginning with the 1948 Displaced Persons Act, which first recognized refugees in U.S. law; (2) *highly skilled professionals*, who have entered variously under employment-based visa preferences, in the first waves of refugee exoduses, or under student or other temporary statuses; (3) *undocumented laborers*, whose numbers began to swell after the termination in 1964 of the Bracero Program (begun in 1942 to meet labor shortages in the Southwest during World War II, then maintained during the postwar years of rapid expansion of the U.S. economy) and also ironically after passage of the 1965 law (and after another in 1976), which placed for the first time numerical limits on legal immigration from the Western Hemisphere even as it abolished the national-origins quota system that had governed admissions from the Eastern Hemisphere; and (4) *persons entering on "nonimmigrant" visas* (university students, exchange visitors, temporary workers, and many others). These characteristics of contemporary immigration provide in part the basis for the typology of immigrants proposed above (INS, 1993; cf. Sorensen et al., 1992).

For all of the attention it has received, the 1924 Johnson-Reed Act that set preferential quotas for immigrants from northwest Europe had virtually no effect on immigration from Asia, which had already been barred in 1917 except for the U.S. colony in the Philippines; much earlier, in 1882, the Chinese had been excluded (a ban not repealed until 1943, when the U.S. and China were wartime allies), and the Japanese restricted after 1907. The 1924 law also had no effect on immigration from the Americas. Largely at the urging of American growers and ranchers, no limits were set on Western Hemisphere countries by the 1924 law: it was understood that cheap, unskilled Mexican labor could be recruited when needed, as happened during World War I and the 1920s (Vargas, 1993),

TABLE 1.1 Decennial Trends, 1890–1990, in the U.S. Foreign-Born Population (Census Data), in Legal Immigration by Region of Origin (INS Data on Admissions to Permanent Residence), and in Net Immigration Proportion of Total U.S. Population Growth[a]

Census data:
Foreign-born population

INS data: Immigration by decade and region of last residence

Census year N (1,000s)	% Foreign-born of total U.S. Population	Decade	N(1,000s)	North/West Europe and Canada (%)	South/East Europe (%)	Latin America (%)	Asia(%)	Population growth due to net immigration (%)
1900 10,445	13.6	1891–1900	3,688	44.7	51.8	1	2	20.3
1910 13,360	14.7	1901–1910	8,795	23.8	69.9	2.1	3.7	39.6
1920 14,020	13.2	1911–1920	5,736	30.3	58	7	4.3	17.7
1930 14,283	11.6	1921–1930	4,107	53.8	28.7	14.4	2.7	15.0
1940 11,657	8.8	1931–1940	528	58	28.3	9.7	3.1	1.6
1950 10,431	6.9	1941–1950	1,035	63.8	12.8	14.9	3.6	8.8
1960 9,738	5.5	1951–1960	2,515	51.8	16	22.2	6.1	10.6
1970 9,619	4.7	1961–1970	3,322	30	16.3	38.6	12.9	16.1
1980 14,080	6.2	1971–1980	4,493b	10.2	11.4	40.3	35.3	17.9
1990 19,767	7.9	1981–1990	7,338	7.2	5.3	47.1	37.3	39.1

[a]*Sources:* U.S. Bureau of the Census, *Statistical Abstracts of the United States (112th ed.), 1992, Tables 1, 5–6, and 45; U.S. Immigration and Naturalization Service, Statistical Yearbook, 1990–1992 Tables 1 and 2.*

[b]Data include 1,359,186 formerly undocumented immigrants who had resided in the United States since 1982 and whose status was legalized in fiscal years 1989 and 1990 under the provisions of the IRCA of 1986. An additional 1.7 million eligible legalization applicants, already qualified under IRCA, had not yet adjusted their status to permanent resident as of 1990 and are thus not included in this table; they are reflected in INS statistics for fiscal 1991 and subsequent years. Indeed, in 1991 a record total of 1,827,167 immigrants were legally admitted into the United States; of these, 1,123,162 were IRCA legalizes.

and again during the Bracero Program (Calavita, 1992); and that those laborers could be deported *en masse* when they were no longer needed, as happened during the 1930s and again during "Operation Wetback" in the mid-1950s (Sanchez, 1993). Similarly, the McCarran-Walter Act of 1952 (passed over President Truman's veto, who opposed it because it hampered U.S. foreign policy) basically kept the Eastern Hemisphere quota system and exempted the independent nations of the Western Hemisphere from any limits. Again at the urging of growers and ranchers, the act included a "Texas Proviso" exempting employers from sanctions for hiring illegal aliens that in fact encouraged undocumented immigration, all the more after the Bracero Program was ended in 1964. (This loophole was formally closed by the Immigration Reform and Control Act [IRCA] in 1986.)

To this general picture of post–World War II immigration flows and immigration policies need to be added the internal migration of blacks from the South to the North and West (which dwarfed the earlier Great Migration of the World War I era), and the island-to-mainland journey of Puerto Ricans (who are also not "immigrants" but travel freely as U.S. citizens by birth), since both form a key part of the labor history of the period. Labor recruitment of Puerto Ricans became widespread among employers in the Northeast during and after World War II, when cheap air travel was instituted between San Juan and New York (a one-way ticket cost less than $50). Mass immigration to New York reached its peak in the 1950s and made Puerto Ricans the first "airborne" migration in U.S. history. Net migration to the mainland during the peak decade of the 1950s (about 470,000) was higher than the immigration totals of any country, including Mexico (Falcón, 1991; Portes and Grosfoguel, 1994; Rumbaut, 1992). Puerto Ricans have since become the nation's third largest ethnic minority, after African Americans and Mexican Americans.

Although the collection of statistics on emigration from the United States was discontinued in 1957, indirect measures suggest that it has averaged over 100,000 per year since 1970, a substantial but lower proportion than had been the case in the early decades of the century; of the roughly 30 million immigrants admitted to the United States between 1900 and 1980, an estimated 10 million emigrated (Warren and Kraly, 1985). But in absolute if not relative numbers, and above all in its extraordinary diversity, the 1980s has rivaled any other decade in U.S. immigration history: nearly half (44%) of the 19.8 million immigrants counted in the 1990 census—8.7 million people—arrived during the 1980s.

Given current trends, the size of the immigrant population may well be eclipsed and its composition further diversified during the 1990s. Already, 1990 and 1991 set annual records for legal admissions—over 1.5 and 1.8 million respectively—as a result of legalizing formerly undocumented immigrants under the amnesty provisions of IRCA. The Immigration Act of 1990 (implemented in 1992) increased worldwide legal immigration limits by about 40%, to 700,000 per year through 1994 and 675,000 thereafter; of these, employment-based visas (reserved largely for professionals) nearly tripled to 140,000, and family-sponsored admissions also expanded to about half a million annually. The law also set aside 55,000 visas annually through 1994 for the spouses and children of immigrants whose status was legalized under IRCA, and 120,000 "diversity visas" for immigrants from 34 countries "adversely affected" by the 1965 law, with the lion's share going to natives of Ireland (tens of thousands of whom had overstayed their temporary visas and remained in the United States illegally in recent years). The number of temporary "nonimmigrants" admitted set a record in 1992: nearly 21 million persons, including mostly tourists and businesspeople but also over half a million foreign students and exchange visitors and their families (INS, 1993). In addition, since passage of the 1980 Refugee Act, refugees and asylees are admitted outside the regular numerical limits under *separate* ceilings determined each year by the administration and Congress. Since the end of the Cold War, refugee admissions have actually increased: in 1992 the refugee ceiling was 142,000, up from 125,000 in 1990; and the asylee ceiling has been raised to 10,000 per year, even though the number of asylum applications doubled to 104,000 in 1992.

The undocumented immigrant population has not only grown but also diversified. IRCA did not stop the flow of unauthorized migrants, despite a big drop immediately after 1986 (Bean et al., 1990); the number of apprehensions along the Mexican border increased abruptly after 1989, reaching 1.3 million in 1992, and the number of deportations grew to 1.1 million. Excluding the nearly 3 million formerly undocumented immigrants whose status was legalized under IRCA (over 2 million were Mexican nationals, followed by Salvadorans, Guatemalans, and Haitans), the INS estimated that by October 1992 the illegal resident population—consisting of "entries without inspection" and "visa overstayers"—totaled about 3.2 million, and was growing at a rate of perhaps 300,000 annually. Of that total, about 1 million were estimated to be from Mexico, 298,000 from El Salvador, 121,000 from Guatemala, and roughly 100,000 each from Canada, Poland, the Philippines, and Haiti (INS, 1992).

PASSAGES TO AMERICA:
THE NATIONAL ORIGINS OF THE NEW IMMIGRATION

Census data on the size, year of immigration, citizenship, and states of principal settlement of the 1990 foreign-born population are presented in Table 1.2, broken down by the major regions and countries of birth. For the first time in U.S. history, Latin American and Caribbean peoples replaced Europeans as the largest immigrant population in the country. Fully half of those 8.4 million immigrants came during the 1980s. Mexicans alone accounted for 22% (4.3 million) of the total foreign-born population and 26% of all immigrants arriving since 1970; Mexico is by far the largest source of both legal and illegal immigration. The Philippines ranked second, with close to 1 million immigrants and 5% of the total. Indeed, Mexicans and Filipinos comprise, respectively, the largest "Hispanic" and "Asian" immigrant groups in the United States today. Thus, while today's immigrants come from over 140 different countries, some regions and nations clearly send many more than others, despite the equitable numerical quotas provided to each country by U.S. law since 1965. Regionally, the Asian and African immigrant flows grew fastest of all, with most arriving in the 1980s; only 12% of immigrants coming in the 1980s hailed from Europe and Canada.

One pattern, a continuation of trends already under way in the 1950s, is quite clear: immigration from the more developed countries has declined over time, while from less developed countries it has grown sharply. Among the more developed countries, this pattern is clearest for Canada and most European countries, with the sharpest reductions occurring since 1960. Although traditional countries of immigration to the United States in the past, by the 1960s their prosperous postwar economies dampened the relative attraction of America. About half of all Europeans and Canadians came before 1960; many British, German, and other European scientists and professionals journeyed to America in the aftermath of the war to pursue opportunities not available in their countries—Britain alone lost 16% of its Ph.D.s between 1952 and 1961, half of them coming to the United States (Weisberger, 1994:88). Among the less developed countries, the major countries of immigration are located either in the Caribbean Basin—in the immediate periphery of the United States—or are a handful of Asian nations also characterized by significant historical, economic, political, and military ties to the United States. These historical relationships, and the particular social networks to which they give rise, are crucial to an understanding of the new immigration, both legal and illegal—and help explain why most of the less developed countries are not similarly represented in contemporary flows, as might be predicted by neoclassical economic theories of transnational labor movements.

In fact, just a baker's dozen of countries has accounted for two-thirds of all immigrants since 1970: Mexico, Cuba, El Salvador, Guatemala, Nicaragua, the Dominican Republic and Haiti in the Caribbean Basin; and the Philippines, Vietnam, South Korea, China, Taiwan, and India in Asia. Not surprisingly, the two largest source countries, Mexico and the Philippines, share the deepest structural linkages with the United States, including a long history of dependency relationships, external intervention, and (in the case of the Philippines) colonization. In both countries, decades of active agricultural labor recruitment by the United States—of Mexicans to the Southwest, Filipinos to plantations in Hawaii and California—preceded the establishment of chain migrations of family members and eventually of large and self-sustaining migratory social networks.

In the case of Mexico, the process has evolved over several generations. From California to Texas, the largest Mexican-origin communities in the United States are still located in former Mexican territories that were annexed in the last century—although other large communities stretch to Chicago and the Midwest (Vargas, 1993)—and they are today linked to entire communities on the other side of the border (Massey, 1991; Massey et al., 1987; Portes and Bach, 1985; Rico, 1992; Rumbaut, 1992). In the context of Mexico's internal economic crises in the 1970s and 1980s, big wage differentials and strong demand for Mexican labor across the 2,000-mile-long U.S.-Mexico border have acted as a magnet to attract immigrants to America. The 1993 passage of the North American Free Trade Agreement may stimulate further Mexican immigration to the United States, at least in the short term.

Unlike Puerto Rico, which also came under U.S. hegemony as a result of the 1898 Spanish-American War, the Philipines secured its formal independence dependence from the United States after World War II (symbolically, on July 4, 1946). This has since led to different patterns of immigration (Cariño, 1987). During the half-century of U.S. colonization, the Americanization of Filipino culture was pervasive, especially in the development of a U.S.-styled educational system and the adoption of English as an official language (Karnow, 1989). Today the United States is not only the Philippines' major trading partner, but also accounts for more than half of total foreign investment there and for the second largest share of income of the country's gross national product. Since the 1960s,

TABLE 1.2 Size, Year of Immigration, U.S. Citizenship, and Patterns of Concentration of Principal Foreign-Born Groups in the United States in 1990, by Region and Country of Birth, in Rank Order by how Recently Arrived[a]

Region/ Country of birth	Persons (N)	(%)	Year of Immigration to the United States				Naturalized U.S. Citizen		States of Principal Settlement		
			1980s (%)	1970s (%)	1960s (%)	Pre-1960 (%)	Yes (%)	No (%)	California (%)	New York/ New Jersey (%)	Florida (%)
Africa	363,819	1.8	61	28	7	4	34	66	18.1	22.2	4.1
Asia	4,979,037	25.2	57	29	9	5	41	59	40.2	15.7	2.3
Latin America/Caribbean	8,416,924	42.6	50	28	15	7	27	73	38.7	17.9	12.8
Europe and Canada	5,095,233	25.8	20	13	19	48	63	37	16.1	24.6	7.5
Cambodia[b]	118,833	0.6	86	14	0	0	20	80	47.5	3	1.1
Laos[b]	171,577	0.9	73	27	0	0	17	83	42	1.8	1.3
Vietnam[b]	543,262	2.7	64	35	1	0	43	57	49.9	3.9	2.4
El Salvador	485,433	2.4	76	19	4	1	15	85	60.3	10.5	2.1
Guatemala	225,739	1.1	69	22	7	2	17	83	60.2	10.7	5.1
Nicaragua	168,659	0.9	75	16	5	4	15	85	34.6	7.1	42.7
Korea	568,397	2.9	55	37	6	2	41	59	35.2	17.5	1.5
Taiwan	244,102	1.2	65	27	8	1	39	61	42.9	16.8	1.9
Iran	210,941	1.1	50	41	6	3	27	73	54.7	9.1	2.3
Haiti	225,393	1.1	61	26	11	2	27	73	1.2	45.7	36.9
India	450,406	2.3	58	30	10	2	35	65	18.6	26.4	2.7
Philippines	912,674	4.6	51	31	13	5	54	46	52.8	9.8	2.4
Mexico	4,298,014	21.6	50	31	11	8	23	77	57.6	1.3	1.3
Dominican Republic	347,858	1.8	53	27	17	3	28	72	1	79.9	6.7
Colombia	286,124	1.4	52	27	18	3	29	71	10.7	43	23.3

TABLE 1.2 continued

Region/Country of birth	Persons (N)	Persons (%)	Year of Immigration to the United States 1980s (%)	1970s (%)	1960s (%)	Pre 1960 (%)	Naturalized U.S. Citizen Yes (%)	No (%)	States of Principal Settlement California (%)	New York/New Jersey (%)	Florida (%)
Jamaica	334,140	1.7	47	33	15	5	38	62	3.4	50.2	22.1
Hong Kong	147,131	0.7	44	33	19	4	55	45	43.9	24.5	1.8
China	529,837	2.7	55	21	13	11	44	56	39.9	27.5	1.5
Japan	290,128	1.5	53	16	14	17	28	72	33.6	14.2	2.3
Cuba	736,971	3.7	26	19	46	9	51	49	6.7	15.6	67.5
Soviet Union[b]	333,725	1.7	34	17	3	46	59	41	23.2	35.3	5.3
Poland[b]	388,328	2	33	11	13	43	62	38	7.5	32.8	6.8
Portugal	210,122	1.1	25	36	29	10	44	56	17.1	23.4	1.8
Greece	177,398	0.9	13	28	28	31	71	29	9.5	32.6	5.1
United Kingdom	640,145	3.2	25	15	20	40	50	50	21.2	16.0	9.5
Canada	744,830	3.8	17	12	20	51	54	46	21	9.6	10.4
Ireland	169,827	0.9	19	8	16	57	68	32	11.1	40	4.5
Germany	711,929	3.6	11	8	22	59	72	28	14.6	18.9	7.8
Italy	580,592	2.9	5	14	23	58	76	24	8.3	44.9	4.9
Total foreign-born	19,767,316	100	44	25	14	17	41	59	32.7	19.3	8.4
Total native-born	228,942,557	100							10.2	9.6	4.9

a Sources: U.S. Bureau of the Census, 1990 Ethic Profiles for States, CPH-L-136, 1993; The Foreign Born Population in the United States 1990 CP-3-1, July 1993, Tables 1 and 3; and The Foreign Born Population in the United States: 1990, CPH-L-98, 1993, Table 13. Data on year of immigration are drawn from a 5% Public Use Microdata Sample (PUMS) of the 1990 Census, and subject to sample variability; decimals are rounded off.

b Denotes country from which most recent migrants to the United States have been offically admitted as refugees.

the Philippines have sent the largest number of immigrant professionals to the United States, particularly nurses, and a high proportion of the many international students enrolled in American universities. The extensive U.S. military presence in the Philippines—including until recently the largest American bases in the Asian-Pacific region—has also fueled immigration through marriages with U.S. citizens stationed there, through unique arrangements granting U.S. citizenship to Filipinos who served in the armed forces during World War II, and through direct recruitment of Filipinos into the U.S. navy. Remarkably, by 1970 there were more Filipinos in the U.S. navy (14,000) than in the entire Filipino navy (Reimers, 1985); and in San Diego, site of the third largest Filipino community in the United States, about half of the Filipino labor force is employed by the U.S. navy (Rumbaut, 1991).

American foreign policy, particularly the post–World War II doctrine of communist containment, is of key importance in explaining many of the most recent sizable migrations from different world regions. As of 1990, as Table 1.2 shows, the most recently arrived Asian groups were the Cambodians, Laotians, and Vietnamese, admitted as political refugees—a dialectical legacy of the U.S. role in the Indochina War (Karnow, 1991; Rumbaut, 1989). The most recent European arrivals were Soviet Jews and Poles, who also have been admitted mainly as refugees, like other groups from communist countries. From Latin America the most recent arrivals were the Salvadorans, Guatemalans, and Nicaraguans, who fled civil wars and deteriorating economic conditions in Central America in the 1980s in a context long shaped by American foreign policy (Gibney, 1991; LaFeber, 1983; Nef, 1991; Niess, 1990; Schoultz, 1992). As with Haitians, Salvadorans and Guatemalans have been denied refugee status and entered mostly without documents (although the Immigration Act of 1990 granted "temporary protected status" to many Salvadorans). Cubans, who comprise the oldest and (after Mexico) largest of Latin American immigrant groups, entered primarily in the 1960s, despite the chaotic flotilla of 125,000 *Marielitos* that began the decade of the 1980s. With the exception of the Mariel "entrants," they have been the classic example of the use by the United States of refugee policy as foreign policy (Dominguez, 1992; Pedraza-Bailey, 1985; Zucker and Zucker, 1991). In fact, it has been to "prevent another Cuba" that a variety of U.S. interventions throughout the Caribbean Basin have been justified, such as in the Dominican Republic after the assassination of Trujillo in 1961 and the U.S. military occupation in 1965, which opened key immigration pathways that over time have led to the large Dominican population in the United States (Grasmuck and Pessar, 1991; Mitchell, 1992; Portes and Grosfoguel, 1994).

Among the other leading countries of recent immigration, linkages unwittingly structured by American foreign policy and military intervention are most salient in the exodus of the Koreans in the aftermath of the Korean War and the subsequent U.S. economic and political involvement and permanent military presence in South Korea (Dudden, 1992; Kim, 1987a; Light and Bonacich, 1988). There, as in India and Taiwan, large-scale U.S. foreign aid, technical assistance, trade, and direct investment (which in India surpassed that of the United Kingdom after decolonization in 1947) helped to forge the channels for many professionals and university students to come to America (Minocha, 1987). Emigration connections forged by U.S. intervention and foreign and immigration policies are also a common denominator in the exodus of the Chinese after the 1949 revolution, and of Iranians after the 1978 revolution. Very few of the tens of thousands of students from China, Taiwan, and Hong Kong who came to the United States after World War II on nonimmigrant visas ever returned home, including an elite Chinese cohort stranded as refugees in the United States after the events of 1949 in China (Tsai, 1986). Many adjusted their status and gained U.S. citizenship via marriages or occupational connections with American industry and business, thus becoming eligible to send for family members later on, consolidating and expanding social networks that over time give the process of immigration its cumulative and seemingly spontaneous character.

Urban Destinies:
The Geography of Immigrant America Today

The impact of the new immigration on American communities is much more significant than might appear at first glance because, as in the past, immigrants tend to concentrate in urban areas where coethnic communities have been established by past immigration. Such spatial concentrations serve to provide newcomers with manifold sources of moral, social, cultural, and economic support that are unavailable to immigrants who are more dispersed. This gravitational pull to places where family and friends of immigrants are concentrated was clearly demonstrated by a recent analysis using 1980 census data for 411 countries with populations above 100,000, covering more than 90% of the national foreign-born population: it found that for every 100 immigrants in 1975, 35 new immigrants were added by 1980, whereas only 12 persons were added for every 100 natives (Enchautegui, 1992:27).

In general, patterns of concentration or dispersal vary for different social classes of immigrants (professionals, entrepreneurs, manual laborers) with different types of legal status (regular immigrants, refugees, the undocumented). The likelihood of dispersal is greatest among immigrant professionals, who tend to rely more on their qualifications and job offers than on preexisting ethnic communities; and, at least initially, among recent refugees who are sponsored and resettled through official government programs that have sought deliberately to minimize their numbers in particular localities. However, refugee groups too have shown a tendency to gravitate as "secondary migrants" to areas where their compatriots have clustered (e.g., Cubans to South Florida, Southeast Asians to California). The likelihood of concentration is greatest among the undocumented (e.g., over 25% of the 3 million IRCA applicants nationally were concentrated in the Los Angeles metropolitan area alone) and working-class immigrants, who tend to rely more on the assistance offered by preexisting kinship networks; and among business-oriented groups, who tend to settle in large cities. Dense ethnic enclaves provide immigrant entrepreneurs with access to sources of cheap labor, working capital and credit, and dependable markets. Social networks are thus crucial not only for an understanding of migration processes, but also of adaptation processes and settlement patterns in areas of final immigrant destination (Portes and Rumbaut, 1990; Rumbaut, 1991).

Over time, as the immigrants become naturalized U.S. citizens, local strength in numbers also provide opportunities for political advancement and representation of ethnic minority group interests at the ballot box (see Table 1.2 for the proportion of U.S. citizens by national origin). The median time from arrival to naturalization is eight years, though some groups such as Asian and African professionals naturalize more rapidly, controlling for length of residence in the United States. Others, such as Canadians, Mexicans, and the British have low rates of naturalization (INS, 1993). In part because of how recently they've arrived, the majority (59%) of the 1990 immigrants had not yet acquired U.S. citizenship or begun to vote in elections. Time in the United States alone does not explain why different groups become U.S. citizens at different rates, but this is an important question since, along with higher numbers and greater concentration, citizenship acquisition and effective political participation go to the heart of ethnic politics and to the ability of these groups to make themselves heard in the larger society. The research literature has shown that, among legal immigrants and refugees, the motivation and propensity to naturalize is higher among upwardly mobile younger persons with higher levels of education, occupational status, English proficiency, income and property, and those whose spouses or children are U.S. citizens (Portes and Rumbaut, 1990). Undocumented immigrants by definition remain disenfranchised and politically powerless.

Table 1.2 also lists the states of principal immigrant settlement in the United States. While there are immigrants today in each of the 50 states, just 6 states (California on the West Coast; New York, New Jersey, and Florida on the East Coast; and Texas and Illinois between the coasts) accounted for three-fourths of the total 1990 U.S. foreign-born population. A decade earlier, those same 6 states had accounted for two-thirds of the national foreign-born total, a fact that underscores the pattern of increasing concentration in just a few states and localities. California dominates the national figures, accounting for fully one-third of all immigrants in the United States (up from one-fourth in 1980), including approximately half of the undocumented; in fact, by 1990, 22% of all Californians were foreign-born, and their U.S.-born children nearly doubled that proportion. New York, New Jersey, and Florida combined for another 28% of the foreign-born in 1990, although only 15% of the native-born lived in those states.

Patterns of immigrant concentration are even more pronounced within particular metropolitan areas. By 1990, Los Angeles had become the premier immigrant capital of the world, with 2.9 million foreign-born residents (one-third of the county's huge population). The New York metropolitan area followed with 2.1 million immigrants (just over one-quarter of New York City's population), concentrated mainly in Queens and Brooklyn, then Manhattan and the Bronx. This does *not* include Puerto Ricans, who are not foreign-born, though 40% of their total mainland population of 2.7 million was concentrated in New York City. Remarkably, those two global cities together contained 5 million immigrants, 1 in 4 of the national total of 19.8 million. Orange and San Diego Countries, next to Los Angeles, added 1 million immigrants, while the San Francisco–Oakland–San Jose metropolitan area in northern California added 825,000 more. The Miami metropolitan area contained 875,000 immigrants, including the two cities with the greatest proportion of foreign-born residents in the United States: Hialeah (70%) and Miami (60%).

Moreover, as Table 1.2 shows, different immigrant groups concentrate in different states and metropolitan areas and create distinct communities within each of these cities. Asians, Mexicans, and Central Americans are heavily concentrated in California; Caribbean newcomers join European old-timers who are still densely overrepresented in New York; and Cubans and Nicaraguans are concentrated in South Florida. Among the largest contingents of recent immigrants, Miami remains the premier destination of Cubans, where they are already a majority of the city's total population (cf. Portes and Stepick, 1993), as is New York for Dominicans, Jamaicans, and Soviet Jews. Colombians and Haitians are also most concentrated in New York and Miami. Los Angeles is the main destination for Mexicans, Salvadorans, Guatemalans, Filipinos, Koreans, Iranians, and Cambodians—their communities in that city are already the largest in the world outside their respective countries—and it is the third choice of Chinese and Indians. After Los Angeles, recent Mexican immigrants have settled in largest numbers in San Diego and El Paso, Filipinos in San Diego and San Francisco, Koreans in New York and Washington, DC. The Vietnamese are concentrated in Santa Ana, Los Angeles, San Jose, and San Diego, with another major enclave in Houston. Most immigrants from China, Taiwan, and Hong Kong settle in San Francisco, Los Angeles, and New York; more Indians also settle in New York (although among all major immigrant groups Indians tend to be the most dispersed, reflecting their significantly greater proportion of professionals).

Less obvious is the fact that these concentrations often consist of entire community segments from places of origin—of extended families and former neighbors, and not just compatriots. In some cities in California and elsewhere, the links with particular towns or villages in Mexico go back generations and can be traced to the Bracero Program or earlier migration chains. In other cases, the process happens very quickly: for example, 20% of the small Salvadoran town of Intipucá was already living in the Adams-Morgan section of Washington, DC, in 1985, with an organized Club of Intipucá City to assist new arrivals (Schoultz, 1992:189). In the Detroit metropolitan area, home to the largest Arab community in North America, most Chaldeans are from the village of Tel Kaif in northern Iraq and live in Southfield; Lebanese Shiites are from Tibnin or Bent Jbail near the Israeli border and prefer Dearborn; most Palestinians are from within ten miles of Jerusalem—Christians from Ramallah, Muslims from El Bireh or Beit Hanina—and live in Livonia; Egyptian Coptic Christians are in Troy, and Lebanese Maronite Catholics on the east side (Stockton, 1994:13A).

COLOR, CLASS, AND CONTEXT

Tables 1.3 and 1.4 provide a general sociodemographic and socioeconomic portrait of the largest immigrant nationalities in the United States in 1990, compared to principal native-born racial-ethnic groups. While the effort is necessarily constrained by the nature of the available aggregate census data, the selection of variables drawn for this portrait is aimed at drawing attention not simply to individual characteristics but also to a variety of larger contexts that shape the incorporation of these groups as they make their way through the American economy and society. Table 1.3 presents basic information about the age/sex structure of the groups, fertility and selected indicators of family structure, and level of English language proficiency. Table 1.4 focuses on educational, occupational, and economic characteristics and resources of all of these immigrant groups, ranked in order of their proportion of college graduates, which may serve as a proxy for their social class origins. The overall picture drawn in Tables 1.3 and 1.4 is contrasted against the norms for the total native-born population as well as for specific groups of natives—non-Hispanic whites and blacks, Puerto Ricans on the mainland, Asian and Mexican Americans, and indigenous groups (American Indians, Alaska Natives, Pacific Islanders). Both tables dramatize the extraordinary diversity and complexity of the new immigration to the United States. In addition, though not shown in the tables, we summarize census data on self-classified "race" drawn from a 5% Public Use Microdata Sample of the 1990 U.S. foreign-born population, as a proxy for the contextual effects of racial prejudice and discrimination in the receiving society.

Most new immigrants are nonwhite: the proportion of white immigrants declined from 88% of those arriving before 1960 to 64% in the 1960s, 41% in the 1970s, and 38% in the 1980s. Black immigrants increased from 2% of pre-1960 arrivals to over 8% in the 1980s; Asians from 5% pre-1960 to 31% in the 1980s; and "other race" from 5% pre-1960 to 23% in the 1980s. This changing racial-ethnic makeup, which will change in still more complex ways due to rapidly increasing rates of ethnic intermarriage, affects primarily the leading metropolitan areas of immigrant concentration: significantly, half of all black immigrants are concentrated in the New York metropolitan area, and another 16% in Miami; half of the mestizo and Asian populations are concentrated in California; white immigrants are more dispersed, but 26% are in California and 19% in the New York–New Jersey area.

Immigrants from the Americas are the most racially mixed, with less than 45% self-reporting as white (disproportionately from Argentina and Cuba, then Colombia and Nicaragua), 13% black (most from Haiti, Jamaica and the English-speaking Caribbean, then the Dominican Republic), 1% Asian (mostly Indians from former British colonies in Guyana and Trinidad-Tobago), and over 41% identified as "other" (predominantly mixed populations of mestizos from Mexico, Central and South America; mulattoes from the Spanish-speaking Caribbean). Among African immigrants, 52% self-classify as black (of whom Nigerians and Ethiopians are the most numerous), 41% as white (the Egyptians and many South Africans), and 7% as Asian (also remnants of the Indian diaspora during British colonial rule, especially from Uganda, Kenya, and East Africa). Of immigrants from Asia, 15% self-classify as white (mainly the Iranians, Israelis, and Arabs throughout the Middle East). Virtually all Europeans and Canadians indicate they are white (98.5%).

By region of birth, very significant contrasts are apparent in the demography of the foreign-born. Europeans and Canadians, most of whom immigrated decades ago, are now a much older and rapidly aging population (median age is 53), disproportionately female (57%), with low fertility rates that match those of non-Hispanic white natives (1.8 children ever born per woman aged 35–44, which is an approximation of completed fertility); and they generally have, along with immigrants from Asia and Africa, a notably lower proportion of female-headed households and a higher proportion of children under 18 residing at home with both parents than is the case for native-born Americans. Yet immigrants from Asia include the groups with both the lowest fertility (Japanese) and the highest fertility (Cambodians and Laotians, the latter including the Hmong, the ethnic minority with the highest fertility rate in the United States). In this context, the very young median ages of the U.S.-born Asian and Mexican-origin populations (15 and 18 years, respectively), shown

TABLE 1.3 Age, Gender, English Proficiency, Fertility, and Family Contexts of Principal Immigrants in the United States in 1990, in Rank Order by Age, by Region and Country of Birth, Compared to Native U.S. Racial-Ethnic Groups[a]

| Region country of birth | Persons (N) | Age | | | Speaks English[b] | | Fertility:[d] Children born per woman 35–44 | Family Contexts[c] | |
		Median age (years)	60 years or older (%)	Gender: Female (%)	English only (%)	Not well or at all (%)		Female householder (%)	Children <18 with 2 parents (%)
Europe and Canada	5,095,233	53	40	57	45	9	1.8	10.9	86
Asia	4,979,037	35	10.6	51	8	22	2	10.7	83
Africa	363,819	34	6.2	40.7	25	5	2.2	11	75
Latin America/Caribbean	8,416,924	33	9.6	48.4	13	40	2.7	19.1	69
Italy	580,592	59	48.3	51.8	22	16	2.1	9.8	85
Poland[c]	388,328	57	46.9	52.8	20	20	1.6	11.1	83
Ireland	169,827	56	43.6	60	90	0	2.4	17.1	88
Soviet Union[c]	333,725	55	45.8	54.8	20	24	1.7	10.8	88
Canada	744,830	53	40.7	58.7	80	1	1.8	12.3	86
Germany	711,929	53	37	64.6	41	2	1.8	16.4	75
United Kingdom	640,145	50	33.9	59.8	93	0	1.8	13.9	85
Cuba[c]	736,971	49	30.1	51.6	5	40	1.8	16.2	72
Greece	177,398	49	26.6	46.2	11	20	2.1	67.4	89
China	529,837	45	25.1	50.5	3	44	1.8	8.2	87
Portugal	210,122	40	17.3	50	6	34	2.1	8	89
Philippines	912,674	39	14.7	56.7	11	7	1.9	15.1	78
Japan	290,128	38	12.5	62.6	16	25	1.6	14.7	95
Jamaica	334,140	36	12	55.2	94	0	2.2	34.6	53
Colombia	286,124	35	8.2	53.6	5	34	1.8	21.5	65
India	450,406	36	6.4	45.1	12	9	2	3.3	92

	Population								
Iran	210,941	35	9.1	41.9	8	12	1.8	7.6	86
Korea	568,397	35	8.1	57	7	30	1.8	11.1	87
Haiti	225,393	35	7.3	50.2	6	23	2.4	27.6	56
Dominican Republic	347,858	34	7.9	54.5	4	45	2.5	41.3	47
Taiwan	244,102	33	3.6	53	5	17	1.7	10.2	81
Nicaragua	168,659	30	7.1	51.8	4	41	2.5	21	66
Mexico	4,298,014	30	7	44.9	4	49	3.3	14.1	73
Vietnam[e]	543,262	30	5.3	47.4	4	31	2.5	15.3	73
Guatemala	225,739	30	4.2	48.7	3	45	2.6	19.5	66
Hong Kong	147,131	30	3.2	49.9	7	15	1.7	9.7	84
El Salvador	485,433	29	3.9	46.3	3	49	2.7	21.4	61
Cambodia[e]	118,833	29	5.1	52.4	2	43	3.3	24.3	71
Laos	171,577	27	4.9	48.3	2	43	4.2	11.9	81
Total foreign-born	19,767,316	37	18	51.1	21	26	2.3	14.8	74
Total native-born	228,942,557	33	16.7	51.3	92	1	1.9	16.1	73
Native racial-ethnic groups									
White (non-Hispanic)	188,128,296	35	19.1	51.3	94	1	1.8	11.8	80
Black (non-Hispanic)	29,216,293	28	11.6	52.8	94	1	2.2	43.2	37
American Indian/Alaskan	1,959,234	27	8.5	50.4	79	6	2.5	26.2	56
Puerto Rican	2,727,754	26	6.7	51	19	17	2.5	36.6	47
Pacific Islanders	365,024	25	6.3	49.6	69	6	2.6	18.4	68
Mexican (native-born)	8,933,371	18	5.6	49.8	35	10	2.5	21.6	69
Asian (native-born)	2,363,047	15	7.5	49.5	63	6	1.5	12.4	86

[a] *Sources:* U.S. Bureau of the Census, *The Foreign Born Population in the United States*, CP-3-1, July 1993, Tables 1 and 2; *Persons of Hispanic Origin in the United States*, CP-3-3, August 1993, Tables 1 and 2; *Asian and Pacific Islanders in the United States*, CP-3-5, August 1993, Tables 1, 2; and data drawn from a 5% PUMS of the 1990 U.S. Census, and subject to sample variability.

[b] English proficiency of persons aged 5 years or older.

[c] Children ever born per woman aged 35–44 years regardless of marital status (an approximate measure of completed fertility).

[d] Percent of family households headed by a female householder with no husband present; and of children under 18 living with two parents.

[e] Denotes country from which most recent migrants to the United States have been officially admitted as refugees.

TABLE 1.4 Socioeconomic Stratification of Principal Immigrant Groups in the United States in 1990, in Rank Order of College Graduates, by Region and Country of Birth, Compared to Native U.S. Racial-Ethnic Groups[a]

Region, country of birth	Persons (N)	Education	Labor Force and Occupation[c]				Poverty rate (%)	Income[d]	
		College graduates (%)	In labor force (%)	Self-employed (%)	Upper white-collar (%)	Lower blue-collar (%)		Public assistance (%)	Own home (%)
Africa	363,819	47.1	75.1	7.1	37	12	15.7	4.7	34
Asia	4,979,037	38.4	66.4	7.8	32	13	16.2	10.7	50
Europe and Canada	5,095,233	18.6	52.2	9.5	32	12	9.3	5.7	68
Latin America/Caribbean	8,416,924	9.1	70.7	5	12	26	24.3	11.3	37
Above U.S. average									
India	450,406	64.9	74.6	6.3	48	8	8.1	3.4	54
Taiwan	244,102	62.2	64.9	7.5	47	4	16.7	3.7	66
Iran	210,941	50.6	67.9	12	42	6	15.7	7.7	55
Hong Kong	147,131	46.8	75.1	5.5	41	7	12.7	3.5	62
Philippines	912,674	43	76.3	3.3	28	11	5.9	10.4	61
Japan	290,128	35	54.2	7.9	39	7	12.8	2.2	46
Korea	568,397	34.4	63.9	18	25	13	15.6	7.9	48
China	529,837	30.9	62.3	7.8	29	16	15.7	10.6	56
Near U.S. average									
Soviet Union	333,725	27.1	39.7	10.1	31	11	25	16.7	47
United Kingdom	640,145	23.1	57.3	8.3	40	6	6.6	3.7	69
Canada	744,830	22.1	52.1	9.5	38	8	7.8	4.8	71
Germany	711,929	19.1	54.7	9.1	33	9	7.7	4.3	73
Poland[c]	388,328	16.3	50.4	7.9	21	20	9.7	5.4	64
Vietnam[c]	543,262	15.9	64.4	5.8	17	21	25.5	26.2	47
Cuba[c]	736,971	15.6	64.1	7.3	23	18	14.7	16.2	56
Columbia	286,124	15.5	73.7	6.6	17	22	15.3	7.5	38
Jamaica	334,140	14.9	77.4	4	22	11	12.1	7.8	44
Greece	177,398	14.8	60.9	14.7	29	12	9.1	5.3	67

Nicaragua	168,659	14.6	73.1	4	11	24	24.4	8.4	26
Ireland	169,827	14.6	51.5	7.3	29	9	8.4	4.1	60
Below U.S. average									
Haiti	225,393	11.8	77.7	3.5	14	21	21.7	9.3	37
Italy	580,592	8.6	46.4	10.1	20	18	8	5.5	81
Dominican Republic	347,858	7.5	63.8	5.1	11	31	30	27.8	16
Guatemala	225,739	5.8	75.7	5.2	7	28	25.8	8.3	20
Cambodia[c]	118,833	5.5	48.4	5.2	9	23	38.4	49.5	23
Laos[c]	171,577	5.1	49.7	2.2	7	41	40.3	45.5	26
Portugal	210,122	4.6	71.6	5.1	9	36	7	8.4	62
El Salvador	485,433	4.6	76.3	4.7	6	27	24.9	7.1	19
Mexico	4,298,014	3.5	69.7	4.5	6	32	29.7	11.3	36
Total foreign-born	19,767,316	20.4	64.3	6.9	22	19	18.2	9.1	49
Total native-born	228,942,557	20.3	65.4	7	27	14	12.7	7.4	65
Native racial-ethnic groups									
Asian (native-born)	2,363,047	35.9	68.8	5.5	34	8	9.8	4.5	63
White (non-Hispanic)	188,128,296	22	65.3	7.7	29	13	9.2	5.3	68
Black (non-Hispanic)	29,216,293	11.4	62.7	2.8	18	21	29.5	19.7	43
Pacific Islanders	365,024	10.8	70.1	4.1	18	16	17.1	11.8	44
Puerto Rican	2,727,753	9.5	60.4	2.8	17	21	31.7	26.9	26
American Indian/Alaskan	1,959,234	9.3	62.1	5.8	18	19	30.9	18.6	54
Mexican (native-born)	89,333,371	8.6	67.2	4.4	16	19	24.5	13.5	54

a Sources: U.S. Bureau of the Census, The Foreign Born Population in the United States, CP-3-1, July 1993, Tables 3–5; Persons of Hispanic Origin in the United States, CP-3-3, August 1993, Tables 3–5; Asian and Pacific Islanders in the United States, CP 3–5, August 1993, Tables 3–5; and data drawn from a 5% PUMS of the 1990 U.S. Census, and subject to sample variability.

b Educational attainment for persons aged 25 years or older.

c Labor force participation and occupation for employed persons 16 years or older, upper white-collar; professionals, executives and managers; (lower) blue-collar, operators, fabricators, and laborers.

d Percent of persons below the federal poverty line, and of households receiving public assistance income.

e Denotes country from which most recent migrants to the United States have been officially admitted as refugees.

on the last two rows of Table 1.3, suggest that they consist largely of U.S.-born children of recent immigrants, and show how the higher overall levels of fertility of the foreign-born combine with high levels of current immigration to produce the rapid growth of new ethnic groups in the United States. The low fertility and low immigration of Europeans, by contrast, point to the diminution of European ethnic communities and their rapid assimilation into the "twilight of ethnicity" (Alba, 1985, 1990).

With the exception of Cubans and Jamaicans, the majority of immigrants from Latin America and the Caribbean arrived during the 1980s. As a whole, they appear to be younger, disproportionately male, with higher fertility and a higher proportion of female-headed households than non-Hispanic white natives, and significantly handicapped in their knowledge of English (40% do not speak it well or at all); but, as Table 1.3 makes clear, wide differences between nationalities are concealed at this level of aggregation. For example, the Cubans are much older and have much lower fertility; the Jamaicans and Dominicans have predominantly female populations (cf. Foner, 1987; Grasmuck and Pessar, 1991; Pérez, 1986). The Dominicans have by far the highest proportion of female-headed households (41%) and are the only immigrant nationality with less than half its children residing at home with both parents; this pattern is matched only by native blacks and Puerto Ricans, and approximated to a lesser extent by Jamaicans and Haitians. Salvadorans, Guatemalans, and Mexicans—the groups composed primarily of undocumented immigrants—are disproportionately male, much younger, with fertility rates that are the highest among all immigrant groups except for Indochinese refugees, and they also exhibit the greatest degree of English language handicaps. Yet among Latin Americans, the Mexicans, who number 4.3 million immigrants and dominate the aggregate statistics, have the highest fertility (3.3 children ever born among women aged 35–44) but also the lowest proportion of female-headed households and the highest percent of children living at home with both parents—indicators of family cohesion that belie their low socioeconomic status.

As Table 1.3 also shows, for all the alarm about the demise of the English language and the alleged lack of assimilation of today's immigrants, fully 1 in 5 (21%) speak English *only*, and another 53% speak it well or very well, although 44% just arrived during the 1980s. Only 1 in 4 do not yet speak it well or at all, and these are disproportionately the elderly (especially those in dense ethnic enclaves, such as Cubans in Miami), the most recently arrived, the undocumented, and the least educated. English proficiency increases significantly over time, and English becomes by far the preferred language of use by the second generation; this is implied by the data in Table 1.3 for the U.S.-born Asian- and Mexican-origin populations. In fact, in recent years immigrant children have been consistently the winners not only among of national science talent search contests but also of the U.S. National Spelling Bee as well (Rumbaut, 1991:225). It is the immigrants' mother tongue that atrophies over time, and quickly; this has been the pattern throughout American history—the third generation typically grows up speaking English only—and explains why the United States has been called a "language graveyard."

The Africans, who are mostly recently arrived young males, have the least difficulty with English (only 5% do not speak it well or at all, compared to 9% among the Europeans and Canadians). This is not surprising since Egypt and Nigeria alone account for

33% of all African immigration; Ethiopia, South Africa, and Ghana add another 25%; and all but Ethiopia are English-speaking countries. In fact, three-fifths (61%) of all African immigrants come from countries where English is an official language. In addition to this resource, which is key for those who come with student visas, economic and political ties have shaped their migration pathways to the United States (e.g., the United States is a principal trading partner of the main sending countries, and they include the top three African countries in U.S. direct investment; Ethiopians have entered as Cold War refugees; Egypt since the Camp David Accords receives massive U.S. foreign aid and economic and military assistance, exceeded only by israel; and while there were virtually no Somalis counted in the 1990 census, U.S. involvement in Somalia in the early 1990s could open various imigration pathways). But there are more complex reasons. The oil-rich Nigerian government in the 1970s tried to build a national university system and sent thousands of Nigerians abroad for advanced studies, but an economic crisis in the 1980s left the students abroad without funds in the middle of their studies and many failed to return. A similar situation in Ghana caused it to experience the highest "brain drain" rate of any country in Africa (Kritz and Caces, 1992:226). One irony is that Nigerians now rank with Indian and Taiwanese immigrants as the most highly educated group in the United States: nearly two-thirds of Nigerian adults over 25 are college graduates. However, many are "visa overstayers" (as I learned in 1993 from a Nigerian taxi driver with an M.A. in economic development who was finishing work on his Ph.D.). The 1990 census counted a foreign-born Nigerian population of 55,350; in 1992 INS estimated the Nigerian illegal immigrant population at between 24,000 and 30,000 (INS, 1992).

Table 1.4 stratifies all of the principal immigrant groups in the United States by their proportion of college graduates, and compares them to native racial-ethnic groups on various indicators of socioeconomic status. The foreign-born as a whole have the same proportion of college graduates (20%) as does the native-born population, as well as an equivalent rate of labor force participation and self-employment. They are, however, more likely than natives to be poor and to work in low-status jobs. But again, decontextualized data at this level of analysis conceal far more than they reveal, although that is often the level at which arguments about the supposedly "declining stock" of new immigrants are made (i.e., that relative to earlier decades, today's immigrants are less educated and more welfare dependent). By far, the most educated and the least educated groups in the United States today are immigrants, a reflection of polar-opposite types of migrations embedded in very different historical contexts. Disaggregated by region and country of birth, the huge differences among them are made clear, underscoring the fact that these groups cannot sensibly be subsumed under supranational categories like "Asians" or "Latinos." That most come from poorer nations does not mean that the immigrants themselves are poor and uneducated; on the contrary, one point that stands out in Table 1.4 is the extremely high degree of educational attainment among immigrants, especially from the developing countries of Africa and Asia—47% and 38% are college graduates, respectively—and they are well above the U.S. average in their proportion of professionals, executives, and managers.

Table 1.4 lists an upper stratum composed of sizable foreign-born groups whose educational and occupational attainments significantly exceed the average for the native-born American population. Without exception, all of them are of Asian origin—from India,

Taiwan, Iran, Hong Kong, the Philippines, Japan, Korea, and China—with recently immigrated groups reflecting the highest levels of attainment. Also in this upper stratum are several other smaller immigrant groups (not shown in Table 1.4), notably those from Nigeria, Egypt, South Africa, Kenya, Israel, Lebanon, Ghana, and Argentina. By the mid-1970s, one-fifth of all U.S. physicians were immigrants, and there were already more foreign medical graduates from India and the Philippines in the United States than American Black physicians. By the mid-1980s, over half of all doctoral degrees in engineering awarded by U.S. universities were earned by foreign-born students, with one-fifth of all engineering doctorates going to students from Taiwan, India, and South Korea alone; and one-third of all engineers with a doctorate working in U.S. industry were immigrants. These "brain drain" immigrants are perhaps the most skilled ever to come to the United States. Their class origins help explain the popularization of Asians as a "model minority" and to debunk nativist calls for restricting immigrants to those perceived to be more "assimilable" on the basis of color, language, and culture (Rumbaut, 1991).

By contrast, as Table 1.4 shows, the lower socioeconomic stratum includes recent immigrants from Mexico, El Salvador, Guatemala, the Dominican Republic, and to a lesser extent Haiti—many or most of whom are undocumented. They have higher rates of labor force participation but much lower levels of educational attainment, are concentrated in low-wage unskilled jobs, and have poverty rates as high as those of native minority groups but much lower proportions of households on welfare. Here also are less educated but less visible European immigrants from Italy and Portugal (34% of Portuguese adult immigrants have less than a fifth-grade education, compared to 1.8% of the total U.S.-born population, yet only 7% of the Portuguese are below the poverty line). And two Asian-origin groups, Laotian and Cambodian refugees, exhibit by far the highest rates of poverty and welfare dependency in the United States. Southeast Asians and to a lesser extent Chinese and Korean workers are much in evidence, along with undocumented Mexican and Central American immigrants, in a vast underground sweatshop economy that expanded during the 1980s and 1990s in Southern California. These data too debunk the stereotypes that have been propounded in the mass media as explanations of "Asian" success, and point instead to the contextual diversity of recent immigration and to the class advantages and disadvantages of particular groups.

A middle stratum evident in Table 1.4, composed of groups whose educational and occupational characteristics are close to the U.S. average, is more heterogeneous in terms of their national origins. It includes older immigrants from the Soviet Union, Britain, Canada, and Germany, and more recent immigrants from Vietnam, Cuba, Colombia, and Jamaica. However, not at all evident in Table 1.4 is the fact that *within* particular nationalities there are often also many class differences that reflect different "waves" and immigration histories. For example, while 31% of adult immigrants from China have college degrees, 16% have less than a fifth-grade education; this bimodal distribution in part reflects different patterns of Chinese immigration and enterprise between the pre-1965 *Lo Wa Kiu* ("old overseas Chinese") and the post-1965 *San Yi Man* ("new immigrants"; Wong, 1987). Desperate Haitian boat people arriving by the thousands in the 1980s and 1990s mask an upper-middle-class flow of escapees from the Duvalier regime in the early 1960s; by 1972 the number of Haitian physicians in the United States represented an incredible 95% of Haiti's stock (cf. Rumbaut, 1991). Similarly, the post-1980 waves of Cuban Mariel refugees and Vietnamese boat people from modest social class backgrounds differed sharply from the elite "first waves" of the 1959–1962 Cubans and the 1975 Vietnamese, underscoring the internal diversification of particular national flows over time.

Among the employed, the percentage of longer established Canadian and certain European immigrants in professional specialties exceeds the respective proportion of their groups who are college graduates, but the percentage of recently arrived Asian immigrants who are employed in the professions is generally far below their respective proportions of college graduates. These discrepancies between educational and occupational attainment point to barriers such as English proficiency and strict licensing requirements that regulate entry into the professions and that recent immigrants—most of them nonwhite, non-European, and non-English speakers—must confront as they seek to make their way in America. In response, some immigrants shift instead to entrepreneurship as an avenue of economic advancement and as an alternative to employment in segmented labor markets. As Table 1.4 shows, Korean immigrants are the leading example of this entrepreneurial mode of incorporation, with self-employment rates that are higher by far than any other native-born or foreign-born groups.

ARE IMMIGRANTS A COST OR A BENEFIT TO AMERICAN SOCIETY?

Entrepreneurial immigrants create jobs. For example, among Koreans in Los Angeles in 1980, a study found that 22% were self-employed, and they in turn employed another 40% of Korean workers in their business; Korean-owned firms thus accounted for almost two-thirds of all employed Koreans in the Los Angeles metropolitan area (Light and Bonacich, 1988). Similar proportions have been reported for immigrants from China, Hong Kong, and South Korea in New York City (Kim, 1987b; Wong, 1987). A panel study of Cuban refugees who arrived in Miami in 1973 showed that by 1979 21% were self-employed and another 36% were employed in businesses owned by Cubans. A subsequent survey of Mariel Cubans who arrived in Miami in 1980 found that, by 1986, 28% were self-employed and another 45% were employed by their conationals (Portes and Bach, 1985; Portes and Stepick, 1993). Indeed, the national study cited earlier of all U.S. counties with populations above 100,000 found that the larger the foreign-born population, the larger the gains in employment: immigrants added twice as many jobs to the county as natives (Enchautegui, 1992). Overall, immigrants create more jobs than they themselves fill.

There is little evidence that unemployment is caused by immigrants either in the United States as a whole or in areas of high immigrant concentration, or that immigration adversely affects the earnings of either domestic majority or minority groups (Bean et al., 1988; Borjas, 1990; Butcher and Card, 1991; Simon, 1989; Sorensen et al., 1992; but see Tienda and Stier, 1994, for an analysis of displacement effects in Chicago's inner city). To the contrary, research studies of both legal *and* undocumented immigration point to significant net economic benefits accruing to U.S. natives. To be sure, some newcomers in areas of immigrant concentration—especially the undocumented and unskilled immigrant women—are exploited as sources of cheap labor in a growing informal sector that is fueled by foreign competition and the demand for low-cost goods and services in the larger economy. In this context, the presence of a large supply of cheap labor does keep wages down: the low wages paid to immigrants who, under their precarious circumstances, are willing to accept whatever work is offered.

As a rule, the entry of immigrants into urban labor markets helps to *increase* native wages as well as productivity and investment, sustain the pace of economic growth, and revive declining sectors such as light manufacturing, construction, and apparel (New York City, Los Angeles, and Miami provide examples). An influx of new immigrant labor also has the effect of pushing up domestic workers to better supervisory or administrative jobs that may otherwise disappear or go abroad in the absence of a supply of immigrant manual labor. Less skilled immigrants typically move into manual labor markets deserted by native-born workers, who shift into preferred nonmanual jobs. And immigrant professionals, such as engineers and physicians, fill significant national needs for skilled talent and in some respects also serve as a strategic reserve of scarce expertise. For example, given declining enrollments in advanced engineering training among the native-born, the proportion of the foreign-born in these fields has grown rapidly; and foreign-born physicians have similarly performed key functions in American medical care: they have been concentrated in the less prestigious, non-university-affiliated hospitals in underserved areas that do not attract native-born physicians, especially in rural and inner-city hospitals serving Medicaid patients and the uninsured working poor, and thereby given native-born medical graduates more options in choosing jobs.

As Table 1.4 shows, the highest proportions of households receiving public assistance income are found primarily among groups admitted as *refugees* (mainly from Laos, Cambodia, Vietnam, the former Soviet Union, and Cuba). Refugee assistance programs evolved in tandem with the expansion of the welfare state in the 1960s and early 1970s (Rumbaut, 1989), and indigent persons received as refugees have the right to access public assistance programs on the same means-tested basis as U.S. citizens (legal immigrants do not, at least during their three to five years in the country). The Dominicans, whose high reliance on welfare in the New York City area is tied to a very high proportion of poor female-headed households, are the main exception. In addition, the increase in the number of elderly parents entering the United States to reunify with their children has also increased the rolls of legal immigrants eligible to receive Supplemental Security Income (the SSI program was founded in 1974 to aid indigent persons who are blind or disabled, as well as elderly Americans who do not qualify for Social Security benefits because they have not worked in the United States). Among the 10% of immigrants from China and the Philippines who receive public assistance (see Table 1.4), many are elderly SSI recipients. Because of their vulnerable legal status, the undocumented typically avoid involvement in welfare services altogether (INS, 1992; Rumbaut et al., 1988).

The costs of providing public services to immigrants—including welfare, education, and health care—have again become the focus of intensified and heated debates, particularly in states and localities of immigrant concentration such as California and Florida. Research on the fiscal impacts of different types of immigrants—legal, undocumented, refugees, IRCA legalizees—has sought to estimate both specific taxes paid by immigrants to all levels of government, as well as the specific service costs incurred by local, state, and federal governments. Such estimates are necessarily based on many assumptions. The most comprehensive and cautiously reasoned national cost-benefit assessment to date estimated that immigrants who came to the United States between 1970 and 1992 were paying a total of over $70 billion in taxes of all kinds (including FICA and a dozen other types of taxes and fees) from aggregate incomes in excess of $300 billion, more than 9% of all U.S. personal income. Subtracting from those taxes the estimated costs of all kinds for social services used by immigrants and their children—including costs borne disproportionately by state and local governments, such as primary and secondary education—indicated that immigrants entering between 1970 and 1992 generated a *surplus* of at least $25 to $30 billion (Passel, 1994; cf. Clark and Passel, 1993).

CONCLUSION

Today's immigrants are extraordinarily diverse. So is the American society that receives them. Their origins reflect the global reach of U.S. hegemony. Unlike the expanding industrial economy that absorbed the huge flows from Europe at the beginning of this century and then the smaller flows of the first two decades after World War II, since the 1970s new and much larger waves of immigrants have entered an hourglass economy that has undergone industrial restructuring and downsizing, characterized by the loss of high-wage manufacturing jobs and the growth of low-wage service jobs. This process has reduced opportunities for social mobility, particularly among the less educated, and widened the gap between rich and poor (cf. Lamphere et al., 1994). Within this changing historical and structural context, the destinies of the new immigrant groups and of the rapidly growing generation of their children born in the United States, will likely be as divergent as their origins. Internal characteristics, including their demographic structure, family organization, and social class resources, interact in complex but patterned ways with external contexts of reception—such as government policies and programs, the strength of existing ethnic communities, employer preferences in local labor markets, the color line—to mold their diverse fates in American society. In the process, as yet full of untold story, they are becoming, creatively, unevenly, its newest members.

STUDY QUESTIONS

1. What new dynamics has the racial diversity of contemporary immigration added to the questions of assimilation and diversity?

2. Does class remain a problem for immigrants?

3. How has U.S. global hegemony shaped immigration?

Notes

1. Department of Sociology, Michigan State University, East Lansing, Michigan 48824.
2. In August 1994, several months after this essay was written, over 30,000 Cubans attempted to cross the Florida Straits in flimsy rafts and inner tubes after the Castro government indicated that it would not prevent anyone who wanted to leave Cuba from doing so. The drama on the high seas climaxed several years of such increasingly desperate crossings. The Clinton administration, fearing "another Mariel," responded by interdicting the *balscros* (rafters) on the high seas and taking them to the U.S. Naval Base in Guantanamo Bay, Cuba, where they remained in indefinite detention along with over 15,000 Haitian boat people. In the process, the U.S. government reversed three decades of preferential admission and reception policies toward Cuban refugees. In a pact reached in September 1994, the Cuban government agreed to curtail the dangerous boat crossings conditioned upon the U.S. government's decision to admit 20,000 Cubans annually via regular immigration channels. Later that month, over 20,000 U.S. troops occupied Haiti to ensure the return of the Haitian president who had been ousted in the 1991 coup. The military intervention, ironically, may yet open up new pathways of Haitian immigration to America.

References

Alba, Richard D. 1985 *Italian Americans: Into the Twilight of Ethnicity*. Englewood Cliffs, NJ: Prentice-Hall.

———. 1990 *Ethnic Identity: The Transformation of White America*. New Haven, CT: Yale University Press.

Bean, Frank D., Barry Edmonston, and Jeffrey S. Passel, eds. 1990 *Undocumented Migration to the United States: IRCA and the Experience of the 1980s*. Washington, DC: Urban Institute.

Bean, Frank D., B. Lindsay Lowell, and Lowell J. Taylor 1988 "Undocumented Mexican Immigrants and the earnings of other workers in the United States." Demography 25:35–52.

Borjas, George J. 1990 *Friends or Strangers: The Impact of Immigrants on the U.S. Economy*. New York: Basic Books.

Butcher, Kristin F. and David Card 1991 "Immigration and wages: Evidence from the 1980s." American Economic Review 81:292–296.

Calavilla, Kitty 1992 *Inside the State: The Bracero Program, Immigration, and the I.N.S.* New York: Routledge.

Cariño, Benjamin V. 1987 "The Philippines and Southeast Asia: Historical roots and contemporary linkages." In James T. Fawcett and B.V. Cariño (eds.). *Pacific Bridges: The New Immigration from Asia and the Pacific Islands*: 305–326. New York: Center for Migration Studies.

Clark, Rebecca L. and Jeffrey S. Passel 1993 "How much do immigrants pay in taxes? Evidence from Los Angeles County." PRIP-UI-26. Washington, DC: Urban Institute.

Domínguez, Jorge I. 1992 "Cooperating with the enemy? U.S. immigration policies toward Cuba." In Christopher Mitchell (ed.), *Western Hemisphere Immigration and United States Foreign Policy*: 31–88. University Park: Pennsylvania State University Press.

Du Bois, W.E.B. 1989 *The Souls of Black Folk*. (1903*) New York: Bantam.

Dudden, Arthur Power 1992 *The American Pacific: From the Old China Trade to the Present*. New York: Oxford University Press.

Enchautegul, Maria E. 1992 "Immigration and county employment growth." PRIP-UI-23. Washington, DC: Urban Institute.

Falcón, Luis M. 1991 "Migration and development: The case of Puerto Rico." In Sergio Díaz-Briquets and Sidney Weintraub (eds.). *Determinants of Emigration from Mexico, Central America, and the Caribbean:* 146–181. Boulder, CO: Westview Press.

Foner, Nancy 1987 "The Jamaicans: Race and ethnicity among migrants in New York City." In Nancy Foner (ed.). *New Immigrants in New York:* 195–217. New York: Columbia University Press.

Franklin, John Hope 1993 *The Color Line: Legacy for the Twenty-First Century.* Columbia: University of Missouri Press.

Garcia, Manny, and Joanne Cavanaugh 1993. "One hope, one boat, two fates?" Miami Herald (December 19): 1A.

Gibney, Mark 1991 "U.S. foreign policy and the creation of refugee flows." In Howard Adelman (ed.). *Refugee Policy: Canada and the United States:* 81–111. Toronto: York Lanes Press.

Grasmuck, Sherri, and Patricia Pessar 1991 *Between Two Islands: Dominican International Migration.* Berkeley: University of California Press.

Hing, Bill Ong 1993 *Making and Remarking Asian America Through Immigration Policy: 1850–1990.* Stanford, CA: Stanford University Press.

Immigration and Naturalization Service, U.S. Department of Justice 1991 1990 Statistical Yearbook. Washington, DC: U.S. Government Printing Office.

———. 1992 Immigration Reform and Control Act: Report on the Legalized Alien Population. Washington DC: U.S. Government Printing Office.

———. 1993 1992 Statistical Yearbook, Washington, DC: U.S. Government Printing Office.

Jasso, Gullermina and Mark R. Rosenwsweig 1990 *The New Chosen People: Immigrants in the United States.* New York: Russell Sage.

Karno, Stanley 1989 *In Our Image: America's Empire in the Philippines.* New York: Random House.

———. 1991 Vietnam: A History. Revised edition. New York: Viking Press.

Kelley, Bruce 1990 "El Mosco." Los Angeles Times Magazine, (March 18): 10–43.

Kim, Illsoo 1987a "Korea and East Asia: Premigration factors and U.S. immigration policy." In James T. Fawcett and Benjamin V. Cariño (eds.). *Pacific Bridges: The New Immigration from Asia and the Pacific Island*: 327–346. New York: Center for Migration Studies.

———. 1987b "The Koreans: Small business in an urban frontier." In Nancy Foner (ed.). *New Immigrants in New York*: 219–242. New York: Columbia University Press.

Kolkin, Joel 1994 "An emerging Asian tiger: The Vietnamese Connection." Los Angeles Times, (April 24): M1–6.

Kritz, Mary M. and Fe Caces 1992 "Science and technology transfers and migration flows." In Mary M. Kritz, Lin Lean Lim, and Hania Zlotnik (ed.), *International Migration Systems: A Global Approach*: 221–242. New York: Oxford University Press.

LaFeber, Walter 1983 *Inevitable Revolutions: The United States in Central America.* New York: Norton.

Lamphere, Louise, Alex Stepick and Guillermo Grenier, eds. 1994 *Newcomers in the Workplace: Immigrants and the Restructing of the U.S. Economy, Philadelphia, PA*: Temple University Press.

Light, Ivan and Edna Bonacich 1988 *Immigrant Entrapeneurs: Koreans in Los Angeles, 1965–1982.* Berkeley: University of California Press.

Massey, Douglas S. 1991 "Economic development and international migration in comparative perspective." In Sergio Díaz-Briquests and Sidney Weintraub (eds.), *Determinants of Emigration from Mexico, Central America, and the Caribbean*: 14–47. Boulder, CO: Westview Press.

Massey, Douglas S., Rafael Alarcón, Jorge Durand, and Humberto González 1987 *Return to Azilán: The Social Process of International Migration from Western Mexico.* Berkeley: University of California Press.

Massey, Douglas S., Joaquín Arango, G. Hugo A. Kouaoucl, A. Pellegrino, and J. E. Taylor 1993 'Theories of international migration: A review and appraisal." Population and Development Review 19:431–466.

Minocha, Urmil 1987 "South Asian immigrants: Trends and impacts on the sending and receiving countries." In James T. Fawcett and Benjamin V. Cariño (eds.). *Pacific Bridges: The New Immigration from Asia and the Pacific Islands*: 347–374. New York: Center for Migration Studies.

Mitchell, Christopher 1992 "U.S. foreign policy and Dominican migration to the United States." In Christopher Mitchell (ed.), *Western Hemisphere Immigration and United States Foreign Policy*: 89–124. University Park: Pennsylvania State University Press.

Nef, Jorge 1991 "The politics of refugee generation in Latin America." In Howard Adelman (eds.), *Refugee Policy: Canada and the United States*: 52–80. Toronto: York Lanes Press.

Niess, Frank 1990 *A Hemishere to Itself: A History of US-Latin American Relations*. London: Zed Books.

Passel, Jeffrey S. 1994 "Immigrants and taxes: A reappraisal of Huddle's 'The Cost of Immigrants.'" PRIP-UI-29. Washington, DC: Urban Institute.

Passel, Jeffrey S. and Barry Edmonston 1992 "Immigration and race: recent trends in immigration to the United States." PRIP-UI-22. Washington, DC: Urban Institute.

Pedraza-Balley, Silvia 1985 *Political and Economic Migrants in American: Cubans and Mexicans*. Austin: University of Texas Press.

Pérez, Lisandro 1986 "Immigrant economic adjustment and family organization: The Cuban success story reexamined." International Migration Review 20: 4–20.

Plore, Michael J. 1979 *Birds of Passage: Migrant Labor and Industrial Societies*. Cambridge: Cambridge University Press.

Portes, Alejandro and Robert L. Bach 1985 *Latin Journey: Cuban and Mexican Immigrants in the United States*. Berkeley: University of California Press.

Portes, Alejandro and Ramón Grosfoguel 1994 "Caribbean diasporas: Migration and ethnic communities." The Annals of the American Academy of Political and Social Science 533:48–69.

Porters, Alejandro and Rubén G. Rumbaut 1990 *Immigrant America: A Portrait*. Berkeley: University of California Press.

Porters, Alejandro and Alex Stepick 1993 *City on the Edge: The Transformation of Miami*. Berkeley: University of California Press.

Porters, Alejandro and Min Zhou 1993 "The new second generation: Segmented assimilation and its variants." The Annals of the American Academy of Political and Social Science 530:74–96.

Relmers, David M. 1985 *Still the Golden Door The Third World Comes to America*. New York: Columbia University Press.

Rico, Carlos 1992 "Migration and U.S.-Mexican relations, 1966–1986." In Christopher Mitchell (ed.). *Western Hemisphere Immigration and United States Foreign Policy*: 221–284. University Park: Pennsylvania State University Press.

Rumbaut, Rubén G. 1989 "The structure of refuge: Southeast Asian refugees in the United States, 1975–1985." International Review of Comparative Public Policy 1:97–129.

———. 1990 *Immigrant Students in California Public Schools: A Summary of Current Knowledge*. CDS Report No. 11, Baltimore, MD: Center for Research on Effective Schooling for Disadvantaged Students, Johns Hopkins University.

———. 1991 "Passages to America: Perspectives on the new immigration." In Alan Wolfe (ed.), *America at Century's End*: 208–244. Berkeley: University of California Press.

———. 1992 "The Americans: Latin American and Caribbean peoples in the United States." In Alfred Stefan (ed.), *Americas: New Interpretive Essays*: 275–307, New York: Oxford University Press.

————.1994 "The New Californians: Comparative research findings on the educational progress of immigrant children." In Rubén G. Rumbaut and Wayne A. Cornelius (eds.), *Children of Immigrants: Theory, Research, and Implications for Educational Policy*, San Diego: Center for U.S.-Mexican Studies, University of California.

Rumbaut, Rubén G., Leo R. Chávez, Robert Moser, Shella Pickwell, and Samuel Wishik 1988 "The politics of migrant health care: A comparative study of Mexican immigrants and Indochinese refugees." Research in the Sociology of Health Care 7:148–202.

Sanchez, George J. 1993 *Becoming Mexican American: Ethnicity. Culture and Identity in Chicano Los Angeles, 1900–1945*. New York: Oxford University Press.

Schoenberger, Karl 1993 "Breathing life into Southland: Chinese immigrants boost economy." Los Angeles Times (October 4):A-1.

Schoultz, Lars 1992 "Central America and the politicization of U.S. immigration policy." In Christopher Mitchell (ed.). *Western Hemisphere Immigration and United States Foreign Policy*: 157–220. University Park: Pennsylvania State University Press.

Simon, Julian L. 1989. *The Economic Consequences of Immigration*. Cambridge, MA: Basil Blackwell.

Sorensen, Elaine, Frank D. Bean, Leighton Ku, and Wendy Zimmerman 1992 *Immigrant Categories and the U.S. Job Market*. Washington, DC: Urban Institute.

Steinberg, Stephen 1989 *The Ethnic Myth: Race, Ethnicity, and Class in America*. Second edition. Boston, MA: Beacon Press.

Stepick, Alex 1992 "Unintended consequences: Rejecting Haitian boat people and destabilizing Duvaller." In Christopher Mitchell (ed.). *Western Hemisphere Immigration and United States Foreign Policy*: 125–156. University Park: Pennsylvania State University Press.

Stockton, Ronald R. 1994 "Recognize the benefit from our Arab neighbors," Detroit News (April 3):12–13A.

Tsal, Shih-Shan Henry 1986 *The Chinese Experience in America*. Bloomington: Indian University Press.

Tienda, Marta, and Haya Stler 1994 "The wages of race: Color and employment opportunity in Chicago's inner city." Unpublished paper in review.

Vargas, Zaragosa 1993 Proletarians of the North: A History of Mexican Industrial Workers in Detroit and the Midwest, 1917–1933. Berkeley: University of California Press.

Warren, Robert and Ellen Percy Kraly 1985 *The Elusive Exodus: Emigration from the United States*. Washington, DC.: Population Reference Bureau.

Weisberger, Bernard A. 1994 "A nation of immigrants." American Heritage (February/March): 75–91.

Wong, Bernard 1987 "The Chinese: New Immigrants in New York's Chinatown." In Nancy Foner (ed.). *New Immigrants in New York*: 243–271. New York: Columbia University Press.

Zolberg, Aristide R. 1991 "The future of international migrations." In Sergio Diaz-Briquets and Sidney Weintraub (eds.). *Determinants of Emigration from Mexico, Central America, and the Caribbean*: 320–351. Boulder, CO: Westview Press.

————. 1992 "Labor migration and international economic regimes: Bretton Woods and after." In Mary M. Kritz, Lin Lean Lim, and Hania Zlotnik (eds.). *International Migration Systems: A Global Approach*: 315–334. New York: Oxford University Press.

Zolberg, Aristide R., Astri Suhrke, and Sergio Aguayo 1989 *Escape from Violence: Conflict and the Refugee Crisis in the Developing World*. New York: Oxford University Press.

Zucker, Norman L. and Naomi Flink Zucker 1991 "The 1980 Refugee Act: A 1990 perspective." In Howard Adelman (ed.). *Refugee Policy: Canada and the United States*: 224–252. Toronto: York Lanes Press.

Chapter 2

Tamar Diana Wilson

Theoretical Approaches to Mexican Wage Labor Migration

For more than half a century, rural Mexicans have moved permanently or temporarily to seek their livelihood in Mexican cities or in the United States. Permanent removal has increased the populations of all of Mexico's 31 state capitals, made Mexico City the world's largest city since 1980, and swelled the northern border cities, especially Ciudad Juárez, Tijuana, and Mexicali. The percentage of the Mexican population living in urban centers rose from 55 percent in 1965 to 72 percent in 1989 (World Bank, 1991: 265). Temporary, recurrent migration, in which household members go to rural or urban regions of higher employment or higher wages, returning periodically to rejoin household members based in the home village, is also a common pattern in Mexico. Wage labor migration to the United States usually involves crossing the border clandestinely because of the difficulty of obtaining documents conferring permission to work. Such undocumented immigration began when the border was officially closed in 1924 and persists despite the sanctions included in the 1986 Immigration Reform and Control Act against employers of undocumented workers.[1]

Whether permanent or temporary, within Mexico or to the United States, migration is mediated by networks of kin and friends who offer the migrants food, lodging, loans of money, and/or orientation to labor markets (see, on internal migration, Balán et al., 1973; Browning and Feindt, 1971; Butterworth, 1970; Kemper, 1977; Lomnitz, 1977; Ugalde, 1974; on migration to the United States, Haney, 1979; Massey, 1987; Massey et al., 1987; Mines, 1981; Mines and de Janvry, 1982; Mines and Massey, 1985; Piore, 1979;

From "Theoretical Approaches to Mexican Wage Labor Migration" from *Latin American Perspectives*, Vol. 20, No. 3, Summer 1993: pp. 98–129. Reprinted by permission of Sage Publications, Inc.

Portes and Bach, 1985; Portes and Böröcz, 1989; Portes and Walton, 1981; Stoddard, 1976a, 1976b; Tienda, 1980; Zarrugh, 1973). When residents of a rural village or rancho develop a tradition of international wage labor migration, networks composed of kin and friends enable even those with limited material resources to migrate (Durand and Massey, 1992; Massey, 1987; Massey et al., 1987; see also Dinerman, 1982; Mines, 1981; Mines and de Janvry, 1982; Portes and Walton, 1981). Prior to the development of such networks, control of economic resources is a crucial variable in determining who migrates and how far. Members of Mexican peasant households with few material resources may migrate to nearby towns or cities rather than take part in international or other long-distance migration, and the landless may more often migrate permanently (Arizpe, 1981: 643–644; Dinerman, 1982: 90; Nutini and Murphy, 1970: 95; Roberts, 1981: 38; Shadow, 1979; Stuart and Kearney, 1981; see also Pessar, 1982: 351–352).

I will review theoretical approaches to the questions of why migration occurs, where migrants go, and who migrates.

WHY DOES MIGRATION OCCUR?

There are three general theoretical approaches to the question of why migration occurs: the push-pull, the dependency, and the world-systems.

Push-Pull Theories

The push-pull, cost-benefit, utilitarian, or econometric neoclassical approach to migration takes the individual decision maker as the unit of analysis. Individuals are conceived of as "utility maximizers." "Push" or "minus" factors in the area of origin and "pull" or "plus" factors in the area of destination are catalogued, with attention being given to "intervening obstacles" such as distance or immigration laws (e.g., Borjas, 1989; Lee, 1966; Todaro, 1976). The push-pull model has been used to explain both migration within Latin America (e.g., Shaw, 1976) and undocumented migration to the United States (e.g., Frisbie, 1975; Jenkins, 1977).

Shaw (1976: 40) argues that internal migration in Latin America is induced by "economic stress" caused by an increasing number of household dependents as a consequence of declines in infant and child mortality, ecological deterioration as a result of intensive farming, and limited assets accompanied by crop failures that lead to indebtedness and insecurity. All of these stress factors are related to inequalities in land tenure (Shaw, 1976: 107; see also Schejtman, 1982). Landholdings of fewer than 5 hectares, called *minifundios*, are too small to support an average-sized family (Shaw, 1976: 26 n. 3). Farmers controlling more than 500 hectares (*latifundistas*) practice capital-intensive production that offers few work opportunities to minifundistas or landless laborers (Shaw, 1976: 26 n. 3, 46–47; see also Barkin, 1990: 19). Examining census data from 16 Latin American countries, Shaw (1976: 102) shows that an increase in either the proportion of minifundios or the proportion of land held by latifundistas is correlated with higher rates of rural out-migration. Mexico has one of the highest rates of out-migration, a high proportion of farms of fewer than 5 hectares, and a high proportion of land concentrated in farms of more than 500 hectares (Shaw, 1976: 103, Table 4). Although Shaw focuses on push factors, his data are also amenable to dependency and world-systems interpretations.

Frisbie (1975) offers a longitudinal analysis of push and pull factors in Mexican undocumented immigration based on Border Patrol arrest statistics from 1946 to 1965. The variables considered are farm wages, agricultural productivity, agricultural commodity prices, and the rate of capital investment in agriculture in both Mexico and the United States. Frisbie found that the two most important variables affecting the rate of undocumented immigration from Mexico were low farm wages and inadequate yields per hectare in Mexico, suggesting that push factors are more important than pull factors (1975: 13, Table 3). Notably, the study covers only workers employed in agriculture. There is evidence to suggest, however, that most Mexican immigrants, whether documented or undocumented, work in cities (e.g., Cockcroft, 1986a: 130; Cornelius et al., 1982: 21–22; Mines and Massey, 1985: 109; Portes, 1981b: 73).

Using Immigration and Naturalization Service (INS) apprehension statistics from 1948 to 1972, Jenkins (1977) also evaluates push and pull factors in undocumented immigration from Mexico to the United States. He concludes that migration is induced not by rising U.S. wage rates due to labor scarcity but by the increasing gap between Mexican and U.S. wage rates due to declines in Mexican real wages (Jenkins, 1977: 185; see also Barkin, 1990: 101). Jenkins (1977: 187) maintains that the Mexican rural proletariat has grown because land reform since the 1940s has fallen behind increases in population. Because capital-intensive production techniques are used on concentrated private landholdings, less labor is absorbed. The rural proletariat is supplemented by ejido holders with plots too small to eke out a subsistence who must therefore enter the labor market (Jenkins, 1977: 187). Migration is the result of a "strong push" within the Mexican economy and a "weak pull" by the U.S. economy (Jenkins, 1977: 186).

The cost-benefit, utilitarian model has been criticized for ignoring the structural and political origins of the push and pull factors confronting potential migrants (Portes and Böröcz, 1989; Portes and Walton, 1981: 25; Wood, 1982: 300).

World-Systems and Dependency Theories

Scholars using world-systems and dependency models to explain patterns of migration look at the uneven distribution of factors of production, such as industrial infrastructure and labor, and at global wage differentials. Dependency theorists stress that the movement of peoples is between two economic systems characterized by uneven development (Sassen-Koob, 1980b: 4) and by the exploitation of the less developed system by the more developed system (e.g., Cockcroft, 1986a). Although these models have usually been applied to international labor migration, they are also applicable to internal migration (Portes and Walton, 1981). Uneven regional development within Mexico has been amply documented (e.g., Cockcroft, 1983, 1986a, 1986b; Barkin, 1986, 1990; Scott, 1982).

In dependency theory, the structures that set the limits for decisions to migrate between two regions characterized by uneven development are given analytical priority. Cockcroft (1986a) uses a dependency paradigm to explain undocumented immigration from Mexico to the United States. The penetration of U.S.-based transnational agribusiness and the

Mexican government's support of commercial agriculture have led to the massive dispossession of peasant smallholders (1986a: 103; see also Hewitt de Alcántara, 1976: 101). Mexico's development pattern is generally uneven because of its dependence on and integration with the U.S. economy (Cockcroft, 1986a: 100–105; see also Herzog, 1990; Portes, 1981b: 78–79; Sanderson, 1986). Low wages in Mexico, a consequence of its dependent development, and the desire of U.S.-based agribusiness and U.S. industry for a cheap labor force have induced migration (Cockcroft, 1986a: 129–130).

World-systems theorists, rather than conceiving of international migration as occurring between an underdeveloped and a developed economic system, see migration as occurring within one overarching system undergoing constant change. This world system is characterized by uneven development both between and within nation-states and is increasingly integrated by an international division of labor (e.g., Bach, 1978; Castells, 1975; Petras, 1981; Portes and Bach, 1985; Portes and Walton, 1981; Sassen-Koob, 1980b; Sassen, 1990).

Scholars using the dependency and world-systems approaches have adopted some elements of one another's models, criticized others, and proposed new insights. There is agreement, for example, between the two schools of thought that Mexico's distorted development pattern has induced migration (e.g., Alba, 1978; Barkin, 1990; Cockcroft, 1986a; Portes, 1981b; Portes and Bach, 1985), a contention they share with push-pull theorists such as Shaw (1976) and, to some extent, Jenkins (1977). There has been increased polarization in the farm sector between commercial farms and subsistence units, accompanied by capital-intensive production technologies that have caused widespread unemployment and underemployment among the rural proletariat and semiproletariat (Alba, 1978: 505–506; see also Cockcroft, 1986a; Hewitt de Alcántara, 1976:70; Portes, 1981b: 78; Sanderson, 1986:239; Schumacher, 1981).

A classical statement of the world-systems approach to Mexican international migration is that of Portes and Bach. They maintain that "the penetration of outlying regions by capitalism has produced imbalances in their internal social and economic structures. Though first induced from the outside, such imbalances become internal to the incorporated societies and lead in time to migratory pressures" (1985: 6). Thus push-pull theories are invalid: "The pull from advanced economies is based not primarily on invidious comparisons of advantage with the outside world, but on the solutions migration represents to otherwise insoluble problems *internal* to the sending countries" (1985: 7). These statements are equally applicable to internal migration from underdeveloped rural regions within Mexico to developed urban centers where national and international capital are concentrated.

World-systems theorists tend to focus on international labor migration, stressing the ways in which an immigrant labor force contributes to higher profit rates both for capitalist enterprise and for the core capitalist subsystem:

1. Foreign workers, even if documented, are more vulnerable to exploitation by employers because of their lack of political rights. Thus, their lower wages, a consequence of their intensive exploitation (even if paid the same wage rate), contribute directly to a higher rate of profit (e.g., Castells, 1975; Jenkins, 1978; O'Connor et al., 1981; Nikoli-

nakos, 1975; Petras, 1981; Portes, 1977, 1978a, 1978b, 1981a, 1981b; Portes and Walton, 1981; Sassen-Koob, 1980b, 1978; Szymanski, 1978).

2. They can be used to undercut the organizational efforts of the domestic work force, thus holding down the general wage level (e.g., Bustamante, 1976; Castells, 1975; Cockcroft, 1986a; Jenkins, 1978; Nikolinakos, 1975; Sassen-Koob, 1981).

3. They can serve as scapegoats in times of economic crisis, deflecting hostility away from the dominant capitalist classes and diverting attention from their roles in perpetuating these crises (e.g., Bustamante, 1976; Cockcroft, 1986a; Jenkins, 1978; Portes, 1977; see also Barrera, 1979; Gomez-Quiñones, 1981; Hoffman, 1979; Mazón, 1975).

4. By filling low-paid, unstable jobs in the competitive capitalist sector, they allow these enterprises to remain competitive (Bach, 1978; Burawoy, 1975; Portes, 1981a; Portes and Walton, 1981; Sassen-Koob, 1981, 1980a).

5. Imported when needed and repatriated in periods of high unemployment, they can be used as an anticyclical mechanism for periodic expansions and contractions in the capitalists' economy (Alba, 1978; Castells, 1975; O'Connor et al., 1981; Petras, 1981; Sassen, 1990; Sassen-Koob, 1980b, 1978; see also Barrera, 1979; Hoffman, 1979; Stoddard, 1976a, 1976b).

6. They constitute cheap labor in that the costs of their reproduction and maintenance in times of unemployment are borne by the sending community (Burawoy, 1975; Bustamante and Cockcroft, 1983; Castells, 1975; Meillassoux, 1981; Nikolinakos, 1975; Portes, 1978a; Sassen-Koob, 1980b, 1978).[2]

These last two points can be expanded to cover rural-origin migrants to urban conglomerations in the context of internal migration as well. Recurrent wage labor migration by semiproletarianized peasants can be seen to subsidize capitalist enterprises and sectors wherever these are located. Meillassoux (1981), focusing on migrations internal to Africa, addresses capitalism's exploitation of the "domestic subsistence economy" by what he calls "rotating migration." He argues that the value of labor power is composed of three elements: "sustenance of the workers during periods of employment (i.e. *reconstitution* of immediate labor power; *maintenance* during periods of unemployment (due to stoppages, ill-health, etc.); *replacement* by breeding of offspring" (1981: 100). For workers fully integrated into the capitalist economy in advanced capitalist countries (or sectors), maintenance and replacement of workers takes place within the capitalist sphere of production through the provision of indirect wages or fringe benefits. When workers are paid only a direct wage for hours worked, as are rotating migrants, for example, their maintenance and reproduction takes place outside the capitalist sphere of production and within the domestic subsistence mode (1981: 102–103; for variations on this theory see Deere and de Janvry, 1979; Taussig, 1982).

What Meillassoux (1981: 111) calls "labor rents" come from that part of the worker's subsistence provided by himself or his kin within the domestic agricultural economy. Seasonal migrants, who contribute annually to agricultural subsistence production, provide a larger labor rent than do nonseasonal rotating migrants, who do not. In either case, however, the capitalist firm pays wages only to cover the immediate reconstitution of labor power. Value is transferred from the domestic mode of production to the capitalist mode of production in proportion to the goods and care invested in the worker by his kin until he can become a wage laborer, to the "market value of subsistence goods consumed by the work during his periods of unemployment spent in the domestic sector; and to the value of the goods he will consume during his 'retirement,' produced either by himself or his kin" (1981: 114). Thus, in the case of rotating migrants, capitalist profits are made up of both labor rent and surplus value. "The first derives from the free transfer of labour-power produced in the domestic economy to the capitalist sector of production, the second from exploiting the producer's labour-power bought by the capitalist" (1981: 115).

Although Meillassoux does not discuss this, migrant laborers who own small plots of land (semiproletarianized peasants) can also serve as an anticyclical mechanism in times of capitalist expansion and contraction. When employment dries up, in a phase of contraction of capitalist sectors or firms, wage labor migrants may return to their land. Alternatively, in the face of lack of work in the formal capitalist sector due either to its periodic contractions or to its absolute incapacity to absorb labor, they, as well as the rural landless proletariat who migrate permanently to the cities, may seek work in the urban informal sector (e.g., Benerfa, 1989: 182; de Janvry, 1981: 39–40; Portes and Walton, 1981: 91–94; Roberts, 1989: 51–52; see also Todaro, 1976: 29).[3]

World-systems approaches are best adapted to understanding diachronic global labor transfers from regions subjected to distorted development over time and the functions of immigrant labor in core capitalist countries. Dependency approaches aid in a synchronic understanding of how existing economic inequalities between and within nation-states lead to wage labor migration. Push-pull theories enable the researcher to understand how the large systemic changes and interpenetrations addressed by world-systems and dependency theorists are perceived and translated into decisions by individuals (members of households that they help to sustain) as to whether to migrate in search of work.

WHERE DO MIGRANTS GO?

There are three models for explaining where migrants go: the immigration-market, the stage- or step-migration, and the chain-migration.

The Immigration-Market Model

The immigration-market model, associated with Borjas (1988, 1989), attempts to answer simultaneously the questions of who migrates and where migrants go. Using a neoclassical economic approach, Borjas (1988: 5) conceives of potential migrants as "wealth maximizers" who "enter an immigration market' where different host countries reveal the costs and benefits of emigrating to each particular country, and individuals then make a decision to emigrate or not based on these comparisons" (see also Borjas, 1989: 460). This aspect of the model involves an elaboration of push-pull theories of migration.

Migrants are held to be negatively or positively selected on the basis of education or skills. Negative selection occurs when low-wage earners in the country of origin migrate to become low-wage earners in the country of destination (Borjas, 1988: 15, 1989: 469).

Positive selection occurs when migrants earn high wages in the source country and receive above-average incomes in the host country as well (Borjas, 1988: 24, 1989: 468). Individuals are also selected according to "unobserved characteristics" (Borjas, 1988: 31) related to the levels of income inequality in the countries of origin and destination. Migrants *from* countries with high levels of income inequality tend to be among the low-wage earners who are negatively selected and therefore, following the model, earn low incomes in the country to which they immigrate. Migrants *to* countries with high levels of income inequality tend to be positively selected because skilled people have greater incentives to migrate there (Borjas, 1988: 76).

Borjas's model attempts to explain the behavior of immigrants who qualify for residence visas. He argues that negative selection occurs when immigration legislation includes family-reunification provisions, giving visa priority to relatives of those legally resident in or citizens of a country (Borjas, 1988: 27–28, 1989: 470). Such provisions have been in force in the United States since 1965, for example. Negative selection occurs in this instance because "the family of the migrant that resides in the United States provides a 'safety net' that insures the migrant against poor labor market outcomes and unemployment periods in the months after migration" (Borjas, 1988: 28). "Low-ability" individuals who would not migrate to the United States without such family insurance now do so, thereby increasing the number of negatively selected migrants from the source population (Borjas, 1988: 27–28).

The immigration-market model incorporates "human-capital" arguments advanced by Becker (1962, 1975), among others. The human-capital approach maintains that (1) ability and education are positively correlated because the more able invest in more education (which may include on-the-job training and informal learning), (2) education and earnings are positively correlated, those with more skills earning more than those with fewer skills, and (3) therefore, ability and earnings are positively correlated (Becker, 1975: 85–86).[4] Tautologically, whether an individual has ability or "economic talent" is discernible by the level of his earnings (Becker, 1975: 85). (Women's work-force participation is held to have a different dynamic.) Migrants invest their human capital by seeking work elsewhere: those with the greatest ability migrate (Becker, 1975, 1962: 47; see also Sjaastad, 1962: 83). It follows that positively selected immigrants will have more education and earn more, whereas negatively selected immigrants will have fewer skills and earn less. Furthermore, if they do earn less it is simply because they have fewer skills.

There are a number of problems with human-capital arguments. What guarantees are there that the "most able" can invest in the acquisition of marketable skills or higher education, especially in rural Mexico, where some ranchos have no schools and others have only primary schools? In underdeveloped countries with high income inequality, there is even less chance for the majority to invest in education than in developed countries, where class stratification also implies unequal access to educational opportunities.

Are skills obtained and/or rewarded in one geographical location always transferable to another?

Why is it assumed that one's job is remunerated according to its "value"? Its value to whom—the employer or the consumer? Is the industry dominated by a monopoly, or is it highly competitive? Who is benefiting from the goods and services produced? Is everyone benefiting equally? Should people be paid more when more people benefit (as in the production of basic consumer goods and services) or when few benefit (as in the production of luxury items and services)?

Why is individual decision making (here human-capital acquisition) considered in isolation from the dynamics of the households of which the individuals are members and from any influence of kinship or social networks? Often one household member will have more education than others because siblings will have helped finance that education.

Finally, do owners of the means of production capture more profits the less the work force is paid? If so, it is not the skills and/or education of the workers alone that are being remunerated: rather, wages are also determined, for example, by past successes in the unionization of workers to press claims for higher wages, by minimum-wage legislation, and by the possibility of recourse to legal remedies when minimum or union-scale wages are not being paid. The reason multinationals establish subsidiaries in underdeveloped countries and move factories from regions with strong unions to regions with weak or nonexistent ones within the United States is primarily that this reduces their wage bills (e.g., Bluestone and Harrison, 1982; Sassen-Koob, 1984).

The immigration-market model can be criticized on the same and other grounds. A low-paid and thus negatively selected (according to Borjas's assumptions) labor force plays a central role in increasing profits for certain capitalist enterprises, some capitalist sectors of the economy, and the capitalist economy as a whole. The safety net provided by family members can be seen as relieving the system as a whole of the need to provide basic services to temporarily unemployed or underemployed documented immigrants. Eventually undocumented immigrants do get jobs; if they don't, they return to Mexico (e.g., Portes, 1978a). The model ignores the fact that (a) immigrants—whether documented or undocumented—usually go where they have friends or kin, and (b) because of a distorted national development that has led to lack of income-earning possibilities in their localities of origin, they may be looking for any employment at all (e.g., Stuart and Kearney, 1981).

The Stage-Migration Model

Stage- or step-migration models are usually associated with push-pull theories of migration. Ravenstein, writing at the end of the last century, is credited with having developed the first such model (Balán et al., 1973: 151; Lee, 1966; White and Woods, 1980: 34–36). His model, based on census data on migration within and among England, Scotland, and Ireland (1895) and later applied to migration patterns within and among a large number of European countries (1899), saw rural residents as moving to a nearby town undergoing "rapid growth," while migrants from more remote districts took their places in the rural settlements they had abandoned. According to Ravenstein, most migrants traveled only short distances but might move successively from place to place, describing en masse a "current of migration" flowing in the direction of the largest commercial and industrial centers (1895: 183, 198–199).

Wiest (1980) incorporates elements of a step-migration model into his dependency framework. Although not citing him, he follows Frank's (1969) conceptualization of exploitative relations that extend chainlike from core capitalist metropolises to satellite metropolises in the underdeveloped world and thence to regional centers that exploit local centers. These local centers contain large landowners and merchants who appropriate the surpluses of small peasants, and all of these together exploit the labor of the landless proletariat. Examining migration patterns from the municipality of Acuitzio, Michoacán, Wiest (1980: 41) identifies four levels of exploitation in the metropolitan-satellite structure. The first level is that of the town and the hamlet. Because of vast wage differentials, workers from Acuitzio prefer wage-labor migration to the United States over employment in local agriculture. Migrants from outlying hamlets come into Acuitzio to perform such agricultural labor (1980: 42). The displacement identified by Ravenstein from hamlets to towns as town dwellers seek work in commercial and industrial centers is apparent here despite the fact that long-distance international migration is now involved. Since agribusiness centers did not exist at the time Ravenstein wrote, he neglected to list such centers as possible magnets. The regional-municipal level of exploitation, centered on the capital city of Morelia, 30 kilometers away, takes the form not of labor use but of commercial transactions with monopolies over financing, processing, packaging, and distribution. A third level is evinced by migration to Mexico City both by upwardly mobile bourgeoisie (thus removing capital from the region) and by the poor "in a desperate search for an income source" (1980:42). The fourth level involves migration, legal or undocumented, to U.S. agribusiness centers (1980: 42).

Step- or stage-migration models can be combined with push-pull or dependency and world-systems frameworks. Little reference is made to stage-migration models in the recent literature, however, other than to deny their usefulness (e.g., Balán et al., 1973: 151).

The Chain-Migration Model

Chain migration has been defined as "that movement in which prospective migrants learn of oppurtunities, are provided with transportation and [or] have initial accomodation and [or] employment arranged for them *by means of primary relationships with previous migrants*" (MacDonald and MacDonald, 1964: 82). It has alternatively been labeled "kin-mediated migration" (Lomnitz, 1977: 61), and "network migration," the latter terms comprehending a variety of social relationships in addition to kinship (e.g., Massey, 1987; Massey et al., 1987; Mines, 1981; Mines and deJanvry, 1982; Mines and Massey, 1985; Portes and Bach, 1985; Portes and Walton, 1981). I prefer the term "network-mediated migration."

Network-mediated chain migration may be either internal or international (e.g., Banerjee, 1983; Blumberg and Bell, 1959; Boyd, 1989; Choldin, 1973; Hendrix, 1975; Jacobson, 1975; Killian, 1949; Litwalk, 1960; MacDonald and MacDonald, 1964; Tilly and Brown, 1967). Within Mexico, it has been found among Mixtec migrants to Mexico City from Tilaltongo, Oaxaca (Butterworth, 1970), and from Tzintzuntzan, Michoacán (Kemper, 1977), among migrants to Montery from a variety of sources (Balán et al., *1973*; Browning and Feindt, 1971), and among migrants to the squatter settlement of Cerrada del Condór in Mexico City (Lomnitz, 1976, 1977) and to a *fraccionamiento* (legalized settlement) in Ciudad Juárez (Ulgalde, 1974). Internationally, it has been found among Mexican immigrants to U.S. cities and agricultural communities (Durand and Massey,

1992; Haney, 1979; Massey, 1987; Massey et al., 1987; Mines, 1981; Mines and deJanvry, 1982; Mines and Massey, 1985; Portes and Bach, 1985; Portes and Walton, 1981; Stoddard, 1976a; Tienda, 1980; Wilson, 1986; Zarrugh, 1973).

Kin and friends and migrants in a variety of ways: meeting them upon arrival, providing food and lodging for a temporary period, assisting them in finding housing and work, orienting them to life in the city or town, and often constituting the primary source of continuing social relationships and moral support once the migrants have established themselves at their destination (see, e.g., Balán et al., 1973; Banerjee, 1983; Blumberg and Bell, 1959; Browning and Feindt, 1972; Butterworth, 1962; Choldin, 1973; Jitodai, 1963; Graves and Graves, 1974; Kemper, 1975, 1977; Lomnitz, 1974, 1976, 1977; MacDonald and MacDonald, 1964; Mines, 1981; Tilly and Brown, 1967; Ugalde, 1974).

Interviews with one member each of the 134 households in the *barrio* (neighborhood) of San Felipe de Real Adicional in Ciudad Juárez showed that most migrants initially stayed with relatives for up to several months. Thereafter they rented lodging and later bought lots after obtaining steady jobs (Ugalde, 1974: 24). Upon arrival in Ciudad Juárez, 54 percent of migrants received food and shelter from relatives while 10 percent received such assistance from friends (1974: Table 6). Movement in Adicional was also mediated by kin: 59 percent of the household members in the sample had relatives in other households in the barrio (1974: 39).

A sample of 904 migrants to Monterrey revealed that 84 percent had had friends or relatives there prior to migrating. Two-thirds of these migrants received some form of assistance upon arriving in the city, mainly but not exclusively from the husband's relatives (Balán et al., 1973: 159; Browning and Feindt, 1971: 60). Of those who received assistance, this took the form of provision of food and shelter for 70 percent. Notably, migrants from farm backgrounds were more likely to receive such assistance (Browning and Feindt, 1971: 60–61).

Tienda (1980: 394) found that in a sample of 822 legal male Mexican migrants interviewed at their points of entry in Texas in 1973–1974, 98 percent expected to be met by kin of friends. Seventy percent of those expecting to be met by kin indicated that these would be spouses and/or children. A reinterview with 439 persons in the original sample showed that 66.4 percent had received aid from relatives of close friends in the United States and that migrants had an average of three relatives living in the city where they resided (1980: 397, Table 3). Notably, undocumented immigrants to the United States from Mexico may show a different pattern, with wives and dependent children following husbands (e.g., Mines, 1981; Mines and deJanvry, 1982: 449; Mines and Massey, 1985: 111, 113; Reichert and Massey, 1980: 486; Wilson, 1986).

Browning and Feindt (1971: 47–48) contend that such patterns of kin reception and aid are inconsistent with the push-pull model's notion of a "migrant man," who weighs the advantages and disadvantages of migrating to a number of places and then chooses the best place to realize his aspirations. This argument tends to oversimplify the problem in conceiving of migrants as having only one place to go: where their kin are. Prospective migrants may in fact have kin and/or friends in more than one locale.

In an analysis of migration options for migrants from the village of San Andrés Zautla in the Oaxaca Valley, Uzzell (1976) points out that family members are scattered throughout localities of various sizes, from neighboring villages to Mexico City. Any of these relatives may be joined in the search for temporary work. People in the village maintain "multilocal relationships" (1976: 4). Where they go to find work and which kin and friends they call upon for aid in the migration process vary from year to year. In a study of wage-labor migration from the village of Santa María Belén, Tlaxcala, between 1900 and 1970, Nutini and Bell (1980) point to the expanding character of villagers' social networks. By 1970, Beleños had established *compadrazgo* (ritual kinship) relationships with people from 69 communities in Tlaxcala, 3 communities in the state of Puebla, in 1 community in each of the states of Hidalgo, Morelos, and Michoacán, and in Mexico City (1980: 251). It is to be expected that groups of friends within the village will have compadres or compadres of friends or kin in various locales to aid them in migration in this case. Migrants from the village of San Jerónimo, Oaxaca, also go to a number of destinations, depending in part on the stage in the family cycle and the number of dependent children that can be brought along (Stuart and Kearney, 1981). Thus, network-mediated chain migration does not necessarily mean that prospective migrants or migrant families have few options. One can postulate a "foraging pattern" (Graves and Graves's term [1974: 119]) on the part of some migrants who seek work first in one place and then in another where they have kin and friends. In retrospect this may look like step-migration to an ultimate destination.

My study of patterns of transnational migration from a rancho in Jalisco to various destinations in the United States showed that recurrent wage-labor migrants often tapped different kin on different crossings, found work in multiple locations over their working careers, and worked in more than one town or city on any particular crossing. Fifty-five percent of heads of household who migrated to a Mexicali squatter settlement from other states in Mexico had lived in at least one other population center prior to establishing themselves in that city; they sought work where there were kin or friends to aid them in this quest (Wilson, 1992).

The multilocality of community-based networks is described by Cornelius (1991). On the basis of his studies of out-migration from two communities in the Los Altos region of Jalisco, which showed wage-labor migrants from one of them going to work in 110 places in the United States, 57 of them in California, he concludes: "Social network-based migration does not necessarily tie a Mexican sending community to a single receiving area within the United States. While cases of 'specialization'—migration to a single destination—can be found, the more common pattern entails multiple migration networks leading to a variety of U.S. communities, both urban and rural" (1991; see also Cornelius, 1976).

Two subcategories of network-mediated chain migration can be distinguished: interfamilial and serial. Interfamilial chain migration (Hendrix, 1975: 539) has also been called "split migration" (Balán et al., 1973: 157; Browning and Feindt, 1971: 59) and "delayed family migration" (Banerjee, 1983: 185; MacDonald and MacDonald, 1964: 85). In this pattern the father may come alone, later sending for his wife and children and possibly his parents (Balán et al., 1973: 156; Browning and Feindt, 1971: 59). Much of migration to Monterrey, especially among migrants of rural background, is of this kind. Unencumbered by the obstacles of illegal entry and risk of deportation as in migration to the United States, 44 percent of young family men take more than a year to complete the transfer of the family group to Monterrey (Balán et al., 1973: 159). This interfamilial pattern is also typical of Tzintzuntzan migrants to Mexico City. Upon arrival, most migrants live with friends or relatives until they can find jobs and establish independent residences. Only then do they bring their wives and children to join them (Kemper, 1977). A similar pattern exists among migrants from Tilaltongo to Mexico City (Butterworth, 1970: 122). Among undocumented immigrants from an ejido in Zacatecas to Los Angeles, the family may be reunited once the head of household finds permanent employment but before he finds a separate residence (Wilson, 1986). Only after the wife has arrived and found employment is a separate residence sought.

In serial migration, migrants help other migrants, whether distant kin or friends, to come to and establish themselves in the receiving community (MacDonald and MacDonald, 1964: 85). Banerjee (1983) distinguishes this pattern, in which "destination-based contacts are extrafamilial relatives or unrelated persons known to the migrants or to their families," from "delayed family migration" (1983: 185).

In summary, migration customarily occurs to destinations where the migrant has kin or friends. Network-mediated migration can be unilocal, with the migrants going directly to one place where they return recurrently or settle permanently, or multilocal, with the migrants going to various locales where kin and friends are present over their migratory careers.

WHO MIGRATES

A number of researchers have stressed that migration is part of household survival strategies. Others have concentrated on the economic dynamics of the region from which the migrants came. Still others have related migration patterns to the class status of the household to which the migrant belongs. Many have identified social and kinship networks as important in conditioning not only where people go but also who migrates. Each of these insights will be discussed in turn.

Migration and Household Strategies

Adopting a world-systems perspective, Wood (1981: 339) defines the household as "a group which ensures its maintenance and reproduction by generating and disposing of a collective consumption fund." "Household behavior" (which can be conceived as the collective behavior resulting from the behaviors of its individual members) can be characterized by a series of "sustenance strategies" whereby the household attempts "to achieve a fit between its consumption necessities, the labor power at its disposal (both of which are determined by the number, age, sex, and skills of its members), and the alternatives for generating monetary and nonmonetary income" (1981: 339). If household consumption cannot be increased by other means, wage-labor migration (of one or more household members) will occur. In other words, migration is a strategy employed in response to structural constraints on the household's economic survival or well-being.

The household's dependency ratio is one such constraint. When the household has many working-age members, migration for wage labor is an option; when it has only one, migration may be a necessity. Insights provided by Chayanov (1986 [1966]) concerning variation in labor intensification within the household in the course of the family life cycle help to clarify when wage-labor migration from semiproletarianized or proletarianized rural households will occur. Focusing on the family-labor farm, Chayanov suggested that self-exploitation of labor occurs in response to family consumption demands. The worker increases his labor in accordance with the number of consumers in the family-household, defined as "a number of people constantly eating at one table or having eaten from one pot." The degree of self-exploitation is limited only by the drudgery of the work itself (1986 [1966]: 54, 78), and it is regulated by the family-household's dependency ratio. The dependency ratio declines as children mature and enter the family labor force: more land can then be cultivated, and the family becomes richer (1986 [1966]: 66−67). While motivation to work is induced by consumer demands, these demands are met by the efforts of all family members capable of working (1986 [1966]: 78, 60). Notably, Chayanov (1986 [1966]: 68, 60) was looking at peasant households that had unlimited access to land and did not hire labor or have members engaging in wage labor.

Chayanov conceived basic consumer demands within the household as the dynamic inducing work effort. His approach must be modified, however, to give analytic primacy to the number of producers, or workers, within a household. The more workers there are, the higher the level of welfare a household can attain. Modifying the Chayanovian model in this direction, Greenhalgh's (1985) study of farm households on Taiwan shows the importance of number of workers for a household's economic well-being. For example, "in the area of *labor*, the larger working force of complex families increases their ability to diversify the family economy and disperse workers to new economic niches" (1985: 575). The economic strategies that the family can undertake change as it moves though its life cycle (1985: 572, 575−576). Notably, family labor may be deployed in a variety of off-farm economic activities.

In migration studies little reference has been made to Chayanov, but some scholars have related migration to family life-cycle stage (e.g., Arizpe, 1982; Massey, 1987; Rengert, 1981; Stuart and Kearney, 1981; Wiest, 1973). In the village of Santiago Toxi, located 250 kilometers northwest of Mexico City, 80 percent of households have one or more members engaged in temporary wage-labor migration; 86 percent of these migrants go to Mexico City (Arizpe, 1982: 42). Over the course of the life cycles of these semiproletarianized peasant families, a pattern that Arizpe (1982: 37) calls "relay migration" emerges: "First the father migrates, and then, progressively, as the sons and daughters grow up, each migrates in turn." Daughters usually work as domestic servants from the time they are 14 until they marry between the ages of 18 and 20. Relay migration permits the family to have cash income to invest in agricultural production at each stage of the family life cycle. Arizpe notes that at least four children are needed to ensure social reproduction through wage labor migration in the village she studied; income from a fifth and sixth child means surplus income for the family in the later stages of its life cycle. Families invest in biological reproduction to ensure their livelihoods. After helping their families during the critical years, however, the majority of migrant children settle permanently in Mexico City because of land shortages in Toxi.

From examination of a sample of 855 households from two rural and two urban communities in Mexico and households in California originating in these communities, Massey (1987: 1374) concludes that as migration becomes an increasingly viable option—because of the maturation of migration networks—families increasingly incorporate it into their survival strategies. Notably, "the precise timing of migration is associated with life-cycle changes that affect the level of dependency within the household, suggesting that migration is employed in a conscious, strategic way by families during times of pressing need" (Massey, 1987: 1398).

In summary, migration depends on the internal structure of the household, especially its dependency ratio. Migration is also conditioned, however, by the household's economic milieu.

Migration, Household Strategies, and Regional Dynamics

Different regions within Mexico show variability in out-migration patterns depending upon the dynamics of the local economy. A comparative study by Roberts (1981) of four zones in Mexico—the Mixteca Baja, Oaxaca; Las Huastecas, San Luis Potosf; Valsequillo, Puebla; and the Bajfo, Guanajuato—related agrarian structures, control over resources, and migration history. In the Mixteca Baja, poor soils and traditional farming techniques keep farm incomes below the basic subsistence level. Since there are few local opportunities for wage labor and income is insufficient to risk financing circular migration to more distant regions, young villagers "often migrate permanently to cities in which networks of migrants from the local area live" (Roberts, 1981: 38). In Las Huastecas, few purchased agricultural inputs are necessary to yield a relatively high farm income. Although workers are not hired-in, about 20 percent of the household labor force is employed off-farm, mainly in agricultural work in the same or a nearby municipio. A relatively good asset position, the presence of nearby work opportunities, and the ability to utilize most household labor on-farm reduce the attractiveness of the migration option. In the more commercialized zone of Valsequillo, production is monetarized and farm incomes are low. "While households must work off-farm in Valsequillo to earn an adequate level of income, they cannot afford to undertake the substantial investment needed to support a circular migrant, and the accompanying risk that he will not quickly obtain a job and send remittances" (Roberts, 1981: 39). In the Bajfo, also a commercialized region, farm incomes are high. To diversify income sources, a portion of farm income is used to sponsor circular migration (i.e., temporary recurrent migration) to the United States. Roberts (1981: 39) concludes that analysis of these different patterns of migration suggests that "circular migration to the United States would only be undertaken by households with multiple sources of income, so as not to be too dependent upon this risky income source alone."

Motivation for migrating is thus determined by regional dynamics: the local employment opportunities, the potential for effectively using household labor on-farm or in nearby wage work, and local pay scales. Given motivation, who will migrate transnationally is influenced by the potential migrant's access to funds for his trip. Household control over sufficient resources to sponsor a member's migration to the United States is, following Roberts's argument, traceable in turn to regional dynamics. Control of resources is also affected by class status.

Migration and Class Status

Studies of transnational labor migration from rural Mexican communities have shown that initial migrants to the United States have come from propertied families rather than from among the landless or near-landless (e.g., Arizpe, 1987: 643–644; Dinerman, 1978: 489; Durand and Massey, 1992: 17–18; Massey et al.; 1987: 51–52, 61–62; Piore, 1979: 139–140; Roberts, 1981; Wiest, 1979: 87; Whiteford and Henao, 1979: 30). Members of Mexican peasant households with few material assets may migrate to nearby economic centers rather than take part in international or other long-distance migration. Landless families often migrate permanently (Arizpe, 1981: 643–644; Dinerman, 1982:90; Nutini and Murphy, 1970:95; Roberts, 1981: 38; Shadow, 1979; see also Pessar, 1982: 351–352). In other words, patterns of migration differ according to the resources that the household commands.

Three patterns of migration correlated with ownership of or access to material resources are found in the village of Villa Guerrero, Jalisco. Villagers controlling more than 500 hectares constitute 3 percent of the population but 17 percent of the migrants to Guadalajara (Shadow, 1979: 76). Migrants generally tend to be among the most affluent in the village, and 61 percent of migrants to this city, who travel there as families, remain there permanently. Only 6 percent of migrants from Villa Guerrero take part in migration for agricultural work on the coast of Nayarit; 80 percent of these are temporary seasonal migrants, and the overwhelming number (80 percent) are males (Shadow, 1979: 76). Shadow (1979: 78) notes that migration to coastal Nayarit is historically the oldest form of migration and draws the poorest individuals not only from Villa Guerrero but from the entire region.

On the rancho of Los Arboles (a pseudonym) in Jalisco, each of three landholding classes has a different type of linkage to U.S. labor markets. Householders with more than 10 hectares of agricultural land, whether ejido or private property, often hire labor during the harvest and sowing seasons while periodically engaging in wage labor migration to the United States themselves; those with fewer than 10 and (arbitrarily) more than 2 hectares usually work their land with family labor alone and enter the U.S. labor market more often; and the landless, together with those who own less than 2 hectares, form part of the rancho's rural proletariat and permanent semiproletariat.

Although how much land a household needs to exceed basic survival differs according to the number of nonworking members, ejidatarios and private property owners with more than 10 hectares are among the most affluent on the rancho. Twenty percent of the male heads of household on the rancho fall into this upper class: 90 percent of them have worked in the United States (Wilson, 1992). Rancho residents of this land classification who have migrated to work across the border can be described as intermittent semiproletarians. Semiproletarianization is the condition of peasants whose income from the land is insufficient to guarantee the survival and reproduction of their households and who must therefore make forays into the wage-labor market (Deere and de Janvry, 1981; Meillassoux, 1981). Those who have obtained an adequate land base to profit in years of average or better corn yields will make only intermittent forays into the U.S. labor market, for example, to finance the acquisition of more land, to purchase a piece of farm machinery, a truck, or other expensive commodity, or to avoid dealing with the credit banks (Wilson, 1992).

Eighteen percent of male heads of household own or control between 2 and 10 hectares of agricultural land: 78 percent of them have migrated to work in the United States. Except for those with few dependents nudging the upper limits of this landholding category, most of these heads of household will have to find supplementary income on a *regular* basis to ensure the survival and reproduction of their households. Many run small businesses on the rancho or raise livestock to supplement their income; 48 percent have crossed three or more times to work in the United States (Wilson, 1992).[6]

Heads of household with fewer than 2 hectares of land receive only supplementary use values in the form of corn from their holdings. These sub-subsistence peasants, together with the landless, include 62 percent of male household heads. They must enter the wage-labor market on a regular sustained basis, either by tapping a variety of local labor markets or by recurrent migration to the United States. Those who work locally as *jornaleros* (day laborers) in brick making, construction, or agriculture are among the poorest on the rancho. Seventy-one percent of this economically threatened class have worked in the United States, 42 percent of them three or more times (Wilson, 1992).

What landless and near-landless men in Los Arboles choose to do is partially circumscribed by their place of origin: 55 percent of male heads of household resident on the rancho were born in rural settlements elsewhere in Jalisco or in Zacatecas. Compared with the 84 percent of men born in Los Arboles with U.S. work experience, only 69 percent of those born elsewhere have such experience (a difference significant at the 0.05 level). Sixty-six percent of those in the landless and near-landless class were in-migrants to the rancho. Members of this group are poorer in both economic resources and network resources. Their offspring, however, born or brought up on the rancho, show similar rates of recurrent wage-labor migration to the United States: 45 percent of those born elsewhere have sons or daughters in the United States in comparison with 36 percent of those born in Los Arboles (Wilson, 1992).[7]

To summarize: In some communities the landless do not take part in international migration, in others they do. In some communities the poorest have different migration destinations than the more affluent; in others all classes are included in the migration stream to a specific destination. Several of the studies reviewed relate this variation to differences in material assets available to households; however, one major factor distinguishing community and class patterns of migration is the presence and strength of migration networks.

Migration and Networks

In comparing migration patterns from two villages in Michoacán, Dinerman (1982: 57–67) reveals that poor households in Huecorio are better able to support migrants than poor households in Ihuatzio because of their better-developed migration network. The network linking Huecorio and Los Angeles reduces migration risks. Ihuatuzeños view migration to the United States as riskier and more costly and migrate in greater numbers to Mexico City. Networks linking the communities of origin and destination are thus an important factor facilitating migration.

Networks based in the community of origin also constitute part of the resources tapped by potential migrants. Noting that neither the poorest nor the most affluent households in Huecorio take part in migration to the United States, Dinerman (1978: 498) contends that "the landless, those without resources to build and maintain social networks linking them to other households, those who are not prominent in community affairs and thus lack economic allies, do not sponsor immigrants." Migrants come mainly from households that engage in a variety of economic activities and have viable kinship and community networks from which they can call in their "social debts" (Dinerman, 1978: 496).

Looking at the history of migration to the United States by residents of the rancho of Altamira, Jalisco, Massey et al. (1987: 61–62) document that the first recurrent migrants to the United States during the 1940–1965 period were mainly ejidatarios seeking money to invest in agricultural production. Since then the landless have come to predominate in this migration stream. A study of the history of migration from four communities in Mexico showed that the establishment of "daughter communities" in the United States and the subsequent strengthening of networks linking the sending and receiving communities lowered the social costs of migrating. "Over time, the networks become so extensive that almost everyone has a social tie to someone in the United States, putting U.S. employment in the reach of all social classes" (Massey et al., 1987: 317). Networks thus are a variable both in the spatial distribution of migrants and in determining who migrates.

Initial migrants tend to come from families with material assets sufficient to finance a risky long-distance job search. Controlling these assets depends upon the economic dynamics in the region of origin as well as class position. As migration networks mature, however, and migration is regularized by aid extended by kin and friends in communities of destination, migrants with fewer material assets can choose the migration option, made increasingly less risky by the network. A high worker-consumer ratio within a household also makes long-distance migration of a household member less risky, since enough workers remain to guarantee household subsistence if the migrant should fail to find a job quickly.

CONCLUSION

Kearney (1991) has described "transnational communities" and Rouse (1989) "transnational migrant circuits" that result from the spatial localization of networks and the undermining of obsolescent boundaries maintained by the nation-state. As Kearney (1991: 59) points out,

> Modern capitalism has for several centuries relied in various degrees on transnational labor migration. But . . . transnational labor migration has now become a major structural feature of communities which themselves have become truly transnational. Official migration theory, i.e., migration theory informed by and in the service of the nation-state, is disposed to think of the sociology of migration in terms of "sending" and "receiving" communities, each of which has a national space. But what the ethnography of transnational migration suggests is that such communities are constituted transnationally and thus challenge the defining power of the nation-states they transcend.

The basis for the formation of the transnational community — the infrastructure that determines where people can opt to go and who can go — is kinship and friendship networks.

At the same time, national boundaries continue to play a functional role for capitalism, facilitating the superexploitation of a labor force made vulnerable by its immigrant and often undocumented status.

Recurrent long-distance migration of some family members within Mexico can be envisioned as following the same network dynamic as international migration. Permanent migration of the entire family of orientation is, however, a continuing economic strategy typical of the rural landless in Mexico (Arizpe, 1982: 44; Roberts, 1981: 38; Shadow, 1979, Table 4), although the destinations of members of any particular community or family are predictable by considering where community and/or family members can tap network aid.

Networks are of prime importance, then, in determining *where* people to to search for employment and a prominent variable in determining *who* is enabled to migrate for wage labor. *Why* people migrate, however, is determined first by macroeconomic variables leading to a distorted development, whether on the national, the regional, or the local level, and second by the way in which these variables are experienced and interpreted by people with differential access to the means of production who are directly affected by the resultant economic stress in their everyday lives.

Study Questions

1. How does the exploitation assumed in Dependency Theory affect migration?

2. What insight does the stage-migration model give for explaining differences in migration within and to the U.S.?

3. Can we develop a "profile" of who migrates within Mexican wage-labor migration?

Notes

1. The Immigration Reform and Control Act (IRCA) of 1986 granted general amnesty to undocumented immigrants who had lived in the United States continuously (with short absences permitted) since January 1, 1982, and special agricultural workers' amnesty to those who had worked in agriculture for a minimum of 90 days between May 1, 1985, and May 1, 1986. Both types of amnesty conferred documents permitting residence and work in the United States. IRCA also instituted employer sanctions, whereby employers are to be fined for employing undocumented workers at a rate that increases with each offense.

2. Bustamante (1990a, 1990b) suggests that the employer-sanctions provisions of the 1986 IRCA were designed to maintain undocumented workers as a cheap labor force, undercutting wages of other workers, and to facilitate deportations of undocumented workers in time of economic recession. In other words, employer sanctions are of greatest importance as a selectively imposed threat—to keep undocumented workers vulnerable, thus more easily exploited and deportable, and therefore susceptible to the reexportation of the costs of their maintenance in times of unemployment to the sending community and state.

3. De Janvry (1981) describes a "functional dualism" in disarticulated economics involving a subsidy of capitalist enterprise by semiproletarianized peasants and informal-sector participants. In articulated economies, workers are both producers and consumers of what is produced in the formal capitalist sector. Wages cannot be kept too low in the interests of profit

making without reducing the home market. In disarticulated economies, most products of capitalist businesses are absorbed by overseas markets or by an internal elite. Since workers have no consumer role, the primary interest of capitalist firms is to pay the lowest wage possible. "Of the two motives for [full] proletarianization of labor that exist in articulated economies, the first (reducing labor costs), but not the second (creating a home market out of rising wages) applies to disarticulated economies" (de Janvry, 1981: 36). Wages are kept low by "perpetuating the subsistence economy that partially assumes the cost of maintaining and reproducing the labor force." This subsistence economy includes both the production of commodities (food or otherwise) destined for home use by members of the semiproletarianized peasant family and intermittent employment in, and consumption of items manufactured by, the informal sector in cities.

4. Variations on the Borjas-Becker model have been offered by Chiswick et al. (1988) and, with more complexity, Simon (1991), among others. Simon's approach is the more positive toward immigration in general, although he calls for a revamping of immigration laws in the direction of inducing the most skilled to immigrate, among other ways by auctioning visas to the highest bidders. Along with Borjas, he views the family-reunification provisions of the U.S. immigration laws negatively, apart from their humanitarian value.

5. That the poorest fail to take part in international immigration even under conditions of increasing economic stress has also been shown, for example, for Irish emigration during the 1840s potato famine and the postfamine decade. Those with little or no land simply could not pay passage either to nearby England or to the more distant United States. The poorest regions in Ireland were therefore less affected by emigration than better-off ones (Cousens, 1961, 1962).

6. My study in Jalisco was partially funded by a grant from the Wenner-Gren Foundation for Anthropological Research.

7. Durand and Massey (1992), reviewing 32 community studies, identified four major variables explaining patterns of wage-labor migration from Mexico to the United States: (1) the age of the migration stream, greater age generating more mature networks that facilitate the migration of community members; (2) the position migrants occupy in the U.S. occupational-industrial structure, which affects the possibility of legalizing their status; (3) regional development factors glossed as "the position of a community within Mexico's political economy" (Durand and Massey, 1992: 34), which have an effect on whether migrants' earnings will be invested productively or in consumption; and (4) the degree of inequality of landholding in the community of origin, which conditions whether more wage-labor migrants are landless or smallholders and ejidatarios.

    The data I collected while in Los Arboles, Jalisco, fully support Durand and Massey's findings concerning the importance of the age of the migration stream as this affects the development of migration networks and the primacy of networks in facilitating transnational migration (Wilson, 1992). However, given that members of different classes have diverse motivations for migrating and distinct linkages to the U.S. economy, a fifth variable is called for: the class basis of these labor linkages.

REFERENCES

Alba, Francisco 1978 "Mexico's international migration as a manifestation of its development pattern." *International Migration Review* 12(4): 512–513.

Arizpe, Lourdes 1981 "The rural exodus in Mexico and Mexican migration to the United States." *International Migration Review* 15(4): 626–649.

————. 1982 "Relay migration and the survival of the peasant household," pp. 19–46 in Helen I. Safa (ed.), *Towards a Political Economy of Urbanization in Third World Countries.* Delhi: Oxford University Press.

Bach, Robert L. 1978 "Mexican migration and the American state." *International Migration Review* 12(4): 536–558.

Balán, Jorge, Harley L. Browning, and Elizabeth Jelin 1973 *Men In a Developing Society: Geographic and Social Mobility in Monterrey, Mexico.* Austin: University of Texas Press.

Banerjee, Biswajit 1983 "Social networks in the migration process: empirical evidence on chain migration in India." *Journal of Developing Areas* 17: 185–196.

Barkin, David 1986 "Mexico's albatross: the U.S. economy," pp. 106–227 in Norma Hamilton and Timothy F. Harding (eds.), *Modern Mexico: State, Economy, and Social Conflict.* Beverly Hills: Sage.

————. 1990 *Distorted Development: Mexico in the World Economy.* Boulder, CO: Westview Press.

Barrera, Mario 1979 *Race and Class in the Southwest: A Theory of Racial Inequality.* Notre Dame, IN: University of Notre Dame Press.

Becker, Gary S. 1962 "Investment in human capital: a theoretical analysis." *Journal of Political Economy*, suppl., 70(5): 9–49.

————. 1975 *Human Capital: A Theoretical and Empirical Analysis, with Special Reference to Education.* New York: Columbia University Press.

Benería, Lourdes 1989 "Subcontracting and employment dynamics in Mexico City," pp. 173–188 in Alejandro Portes, Manuel Castells, and Lauren A. Benton (eds.). The *Informal Economy: Studies in Advanced and Less Developed Countries.* Baltimore: John Hopkins University Press.

Bluestone, Barry, and Bennet Harrison 1982 *The Deindustrialization of America: Plant Closings, Community Abandonment, and the Dismantling of Basic Industry.* New York: Basic Books.

Blumberg, Leonard, and Robert R. Bell 1959 "Urban migration and kinship ties." *Social Problems* 6(4): 328–333.

Borjas, George J. 1988 *International Differences in Labor Market Performance of Immigrants.* Kalamazoo: W.E. Upjohn Institute for Employment Research.

————. 1989 "Economic theory and international migration." *International Migration Review* 23(3): 457–487.

Boyd, Monica 1989 "Family and personal networks in international migration: recent developments and new agendas." *International Migration Review* 23(3): 638–670.

Browning, Harley L., and Waltraut Feindt 1971 "The social and economic context of migration to Monterrey, Mexico," pp. 45–70 in Francine F. Rabinowitz and Felicity M. Trueblood (eds.), *Latin American Urban Research*, vol. 1. Beverly Hills: Sage.

Burawoy, Michael 1975 "The functions and reproduction of migrant labor: comparative material from Southern Africa and the United States." *American Journal of Sociology* 81(5): 1050–1087.

Bustamante, Jorge A. 1976 "Structural and ideological conditions of the Mexican undocumented immigration to the United States." *American Behavioral Scientist* 19(3): 364–376.

————. 1990a "Migración Indocumentada México-Estados Unidos: hallazos preliminares del Projecto Cannñon Zapata," pp. 73–85 in George Vernez (ed.), *Immigration and International Relations: Proceedings of a Conference on the International Effects of the 1986 Immigration Reform and Control Act (IRCA).* Washington, DC: Urban Institute/Santa Monica: RAND Corporation.

————. 1990b "Undocumented migration from Mexico to the United States: preliminary findings of the Zapata Canyon Project," pp. 211–266 in Frank D. Bean, Barry Edmonston, and Jeffrey S. Passel (eds.), *Undocumented Migration to the United States: IRCA and the Experience of the 1980s.* Washington, DC: Urban Institute/Santa Monica: RAND Corporation.

Bustamante, Jorge A., and James D. Cockcroft 1983 "Unequal exchange in the binational relation-ship: the case of immigrant labor," pp. 309–324 in Carlos Vásquez and Manuel García y Griego (eds.), *Mexican-U.S. Relations: Conflict and Convergence*. Los Angeles: UCLA Chicano Studies Research Center and Latin American Center.

Butterworth, Douglas 1962 "A study of the urbanization process among Mixtec migrants from Tilaltongo in Mexico City." *América Indígena* 22(3): 257–274.

———. 1970 "From royalty to poverty: the decline of a rural Mexican community." *Human Organization* 29(1): 5–11.

Castells, Manuel 1975 "Immigrant workers and class struggles in advanced capitalism: the Western European experience." *Politics and Society* 5(1): 33–66.

Chayanov, A.V. 1986 (1966) *The Theory of the Peasant Economy*. Madison: University of Wisconsin Press.

Chiswick, Barry, Carmel U. Chiswick, and Paul W. Miller 1988 "Are immigrants and natives perfect substitutes in production?" *International Migration review* 19(4): 674–685.

Choldin, Harvey M. 1973 "Kinship networks in the migration process." *International Migration Review* 7(2): 163–176.

Cockcroft, James D. 1983 *Mexico: Class Formation, Capital Accumulation, and the State*. New York: Monthly Review Press.

———. 1986a *Outlaws in the Promised Land: Mexican Immigrant Workers and American's Future*. New York: Grove Press.

———. 1986b "Immiseration, not marginalization: the case of Mexico," pp. 233–259 in Nora Hamilton and Timothy F. Harding (eds.), *Modern Mexico: State, Economy, and Social Conflict*. Beverly Hills: Sage.

Cornelius, Wayne A. 1976 *Mexican Migration to the United States: The View from Rural Sending Communities*. Cambridge: Massachusetts Institute of Technology Center for International Studies.

———. 1991 *"Los migrantes de la crisis*: the changing profile of Mexican Migration to the United States," pp. 155–194 in Mercedes González de la Rocha and Agustín Escobar Latapí (eds.), *Social Responses to Mexico's Economic Crisis of the 1980s*. La Jolla: University of California, San Diego, Center for U.S.-Mexican Studies.

Cornelius, Wayne A., Leo R. Chávez, and Jorge G. Castro 1982 *Mexican Immigrants and Southern California: Summary of Current Knowledge*. University of California, San Diego, Center for U.S.-Mexican Studies Research Report Series 36.

Cousens, S. H. 1961 "Emigration and demographic change in Ireland, 1851–1861." *Economic History Review* 14(2): 275–288.

———. 1962 "The regional pattern of emigration during the great Irish famine, 1846–51." *Transactions and Papers of the Institute of British Geographers* 28: 119–134.

Dagodag, W. Tim 1984 "Illegal Mexican Immigration to California from western Mexico," pp. 61–73 in Richard C. Jones (ed.), *Patters of Undocumented Migration: Mexico and the United States*. Totowa: Rowman and Allanheld.

Deere, Carmen Diana and Alain de Janvry 1981 "Demographic and social differentialtion among northern Peruvian peasants." *Journal of Peasant Studies* 8(3): 335–366.

Dinerman, Ina R. 1978 "Patterns of adaptation among households of U.S.-bound migrants from Michoacán, Mexico." *International Migration Review* 12(4): 485–501.

———. 1982 *Migrants and Stay-At-Homes: A Comparative Study of Rural Migration from Michoacán, Mexico*. La Jolla: University of California, San Diego, Center for U.S.-Mexican Studies.

de Janvry, Alain 1981 *The Agrarian Question and Reformism in Latin America*. Baltimore: Johns Hopkins University Press.

Durand, Jorge, and Douglas S. Massey 1992 "Mexican migration to the United States: a critical review." *Latin American Research Review* 27(2): 3–43.

Frank, André Gunder 1969 *Capitalism and Underdevelopment in Latin America: Historical Studies of Chile and Brazil*. New York: Monthly Review Press.

Frisbie, Parker 1975 "Illegal migration from Mexico to the United States: a longitudinal analysis." *International Migration Review* 9(1): 3–14.

Gomez-Quinoñes, Juan 1981 "Mexican immigration to the United States and the Internationaliza-tion of labor," pp. 13–14 in Antonio Rios-Bustamante (ed.), *Mexican Immigrant Workers in the U.S.* Los Angeles: UCLA Chicano Studies Research Center.

Graves, Nancy B., and Theodore D. Graves 1974 "Adaptive strategies in urban migration." *Annual Review of Anthropology* 3: 117–151.

Greenhalgh, Susan 1985 "Is inequality demographically induced? The family cycle and the distri-bution of income in Taiwan." *American Anthropologist* 87 (3): 571–594.

Haney, Jane B. 1979 "Formal and informal labor recruitment mechanisms: states in Mexican migra-tion into mid-Michigan agriculture," pp. 191–199 in Fernando Cámara and Robert Van Kemper (eds.), *Migration across Frontiers: Mexico and the United States*. Albany: State University of New York Press.

Hendrix, Lewellyn 1975 "Kinship and economic-rational migration: a comparison of micro- and macro-level analyses." *Sociological Quarterly* 16(4): 534–543.

Herzog, Lawrence A. 1990 *Where North Meets South: Cities, Space, and Politics on the U.S.-Mexico Border* Austin: University of Texas at Austin Center for Mexican American Studies.

Hewitt de Alcántara, Cynthia 1976 *Modernizing Mexican Agriculture: Socioeconomic Implications of Tech-nological Change, 1940–1970*, Geneva: United Nations Research Institute for Social Development.

Hoffman, Abraham 1979 *Unwanted Mexican Americans in the Great Depression: Repatriation Pres-sures, 1929-1939*. Tucson: University of Arizona Press.

Jacobson, David 1975 "Mobility, continuity, and urban social organization," pp. 358–375 in John Friedl and Noel J. Chrisman (eds.), *City Ways: A Selective Reader in Urban Anthropology*. New York: Crowell.

Jenkins, J. Craig 1977 "Push/pull in recent Mexican migration to the U.S." *International Migration Review* 1(2): 178–187.

————. 1978 "The demand for immigrant workers: labor scarcity or social control?" *International Migration Review* 12(4): 514–535.

Jitodal, Ted T. 1963 "Migration and kinship contacts." *Pacific Sociological Review* 6(2): 49–55.

Kearney, Michael 1991 "Borders and boundaries of state and self at the end of empire." *Journal of Historical Sociology* 4(10): 52–74.

Kemper, Robert V. 1975 "Social factors in migration: the case of Tzinizuntzeños in Mexico City," pp. 335–344 in Brian M. Du Tolt and Helen I. Safa (eds.), *Migration and Urbanization: Models and Adaptive Strategies*. The Hague: Mouton.

————. 1977 *Migration and Adaptation: Tzintzunitzan Peasants in Mexico City*. Beverly Hills: Sage.

Killian, Lewis 1949 "Southern white laborers in Chicago's West Side." Unpublished Ph.D. disser-tation, University of Chicago.

Lee, Everett S. 1966 "A theory of migration." *Demography* 3(1): 47–53.

Litwak, Eugene 1960 "Geographical mobility and extended family cohesion." *American Sociologi-cal Review* 25(3): 385–394.

Lomnitz, Larissa 1974 "The social and economic organization of a Mexican shantytown," pp. 135–155 in Wayne Cornelius and Felicity M. Trueblood (eds.), *Latin American Urban Research*, vol. 4, *Anthropological Perspectives in Latin American Urbanization*. Beverly Hills: Sage.

―――. 1976 "Migration and network in Latin America," pp. 133–151 in Alejandro Portes and Harley L. Browning (eds.), *Current Perspectives in Latin American Urban Research*. Austin: University of Texas Institute of Latin American Studies.

―――. 1977 *Networks and Marginality: Life in a Mexican Shantytown*. New York: Academic Press.

MacDonald, John S. and Leatrice D. MacDonald 1964 "Chain migration, ethnic neighborhood formation, and social networks." *Milbank Memorial Fund Quarterly* 42(1): 82–97.

Massey, Douglas S. 1987 "Understanding Mexican migration to the United States." *American Journal of Sociology* 92(6): 1372–1403.

Massey, Douglas, Rafael Alarcón, Jorge Durand, and Humberto González 1987 *Return to Azilán: The Social Process of International Migration from Western Mexico*. Berkeley and Los Angeles: University of California Press.

Mazón, Mauricio 1975 "Illegal alien surrogates: a psychohistorical interpretation of group stereotyping in time of economic stress." *Aztlán: International Journal of Chicano Studies Research* 6(3): 305–324.

Meillassoux, Claude 1981 *Maidens, Meals, and Money: Capitalism and the Domestic Economy*. New York: Cambridge University Press.

Mines, Richard 1981 *Developing a Community Tradition of Migration: A Field Study in Rural Zacatecas, Mexico, and California Settlement Areas*. La Jolla: University of California, San Diego, Center for U.S.-Mexico Studies.

―――. 1984 "Network migration and Mexican rural development: a case study," pp. 136–155 in Richard C. Jones (ed.), *Undocumented Migration: Mexico and the United States*. Totowa: Rowman and Allanheld.

Mines, Richard, and Alain de Janvry 1982 "Migration to the United States and Mexican rural development: a case study." *American Journal of Agricultural Economics* 64(3): 444–454.

Mines, Richard, and Douglas S. Massey 1985 "Patterns of migration to the United States from two Mexican communities." *Latin American Research Review* 20(2): 104–122.

Nikolinakos, Marios 1975 "Notes toward a general theory of migration in late capitalism." *Race and Class* 17(1): 5–16.

Nutini, Hugo G., and Betty Bell 1980 "The extracommunity and regional dimensions of the compadrazgo system," pp. 228–283 in *Ritual Kinship: The Structural and Historical Development of the Compadrazgo System in Rural Tlaxcala*. Princeton: Princeton University Press.

Nutini, Hugo A., and Timothy D. Murphy 1970 "Labor migration and family structure in the Tlaxcala-Pueblan area, Mexico," pp. 80–103 in Walter Goldschmidt and Harry Hoijer (eds.), *The Social Anthropology of Latin America*, Los Angeles: UCLA Latin American Center.

Pessar, Patricia 1982 "The role of households in international migration and the case of U.S.-bound migration from the Dominican Republic." *International Migration Review* 16(2): 342–364.

Petras, Elizabeth McLean 1981 "The global labor market in the modern world economy," pp. 44–63 in Mary M. Kritz, Charles B. Keely, and Silvano M. Tomasi (eds.), *Global Trends in Migration: Theory and Research in International Population Movements*. New York: Center for Migration Studies.

Piore, Michael J. 1979 *Birds of Passage: Migrant Labor and Industrial Societies*. New York: Cambridge University Press.

Portes, Alejandro 1977 "Labor functions of illegal aliens." *Society* 12: 31–37.

―――. 1978a "Toward a structural analysis of illegal (undocumented) immigration." *International Migration Review* 12(4): 469–484.

―――. 1978b "Migration and underdevelopment." *Politics and Society* 8: 1–48.

―――. 1981a "Modes of structural incorporation and present theories of labor immigration," pp. 279–297 in Mary M. Kritz, Charles B. Keely, and Silvano M. Tomasi (eds.), *Global Trends in*

Migration: Theory and Research in International Population Movements. New York: Center for Migration Studies.

———. 1981b "Undocumented migration and the international system: lessons from recent legal immigrants to the United States," pp. 71–83 in Antonio Rios-Bustamante (ed.), *Mexican Immigrant Workers in the U.S.* Los Angeles: UCLA Chicano Studies Research Center.

Portes, Alejandro, and Robert L. Bach 1985 *Latin Journey: Cuban and Mexican Immigrants in the United States*. Berkeley: University of California Press.

Portes, Alejandro, and József Böröcz 1989 "Contemporary immigration: theoretical perspectives on its determinant and modes of incorporation." *International Migration Review* 23(3): 606–630.

Portes, Alejandro, and John Walton 1981 *Race, Class, and the international System*. New York: Academic Press.

Ravenstein, E. G. 1885 'The laws of migration." *Journal of the Royal Statistical Society* 48: 167–227.

———. 1889 "The laws of migration." *Journal of the Royal Statiscal Society* 52: 241–301.

Reichert, Joshua, and Douglas S. Massey 1979 "Patterns of U.S. migration from a Mexican sending community: a comparison of legal and illegal migrants." *International Migration Review* 13(4): 599–623.

Rengert, Arlene C. 1981 "Some sociocultural aspects of rural out-migration in Latin America," pp. 14–26 in Oscar H. Horst (ed.), *Papers in Latin American Geography in Honor of Lucia C. Harrison*. Muncien: Conference of Latin American Geographers.

Roberts, Bryan R. 1989 "Employment structure, life cycle, and life chances: formal and informal sectors is Guadalajara," pp. 41–59 in Alejandro Portes, Manuel Castells, and Lauren A. Benton (eds.), *The Informal Economy: Studies in Advanced and Less Developed Countries*. Baltimore: Johns Hopkins University Press.

Roberts, Kenneth D. 1981 *Agrarian Structure and Labor Migration in Rural Mexico*. University of California San Diego, Center for U.S.-Mexican Studies Working Paper in U.S.-Mexican Studies 30.

———. 1984 "Agriculture development and labor mobility: a study of four Mexican subregions," pp. 74–92 in Richard C. Jones (ed.), *Patterns of Undocumented Migration: Mexico and the United States*, Totowa: Rowman and Allanheld.

Rouse, Roger C. 1989 "Mexican migration to the United States: family relations in the development of a transnational migrant circuit." Unpublished Ph.D. dissertation, Stanford University.

Sanderson, Steven E. 1986 *The Transformation of Mexican Agriculture: International Structure and the Politics of Rural Change*. Princeton: Princeton University Press.

Sassen, Saskia 1990 *The Mobility of Labor and Capital: A Study in International Investment and Labor Flow*. Cambridge: Cambridge University Press.

Sassen-Koob, Saskia 1978 "The international circulation of resources and development: the case of migrant labour." *Development and Change* 9(4): 509–545.

———. 1980a "Immigrant and minority workers in the organization of the labor process." *Journal of Ethnic Studies* 8(1): 1–30.

———. 1980b "The internationalization of the labor force." *Studies in Comparative International Development* 15(3): 3–25.

———. 1981 "Toward a conceptualization of immigrant labor." *Social Problems* 29(1): 65–85.

———. 1984 "Notes on the incorporation of Third World women into wage-labor through immigration and off-shore production." *International Migration Review* 18(4): 1114–1167.

Schejtman, Alexander 1982 "Land reform and entrepreneurial structure in rural Mexico." In Steve Jones, P. C. Joshi, and Miguel Murmis (eds.), *Rural Poverty and Agrarian Reform*. New Delhi: Allied Publishers.

Schumacher, August 1981 *Agricultural Development and Rural Employment: A Mexican Dilemma*.

University of California, San Diego, Center for U.S.-Mexican Studies Working Paper in U.S.-Mexican Studies 21.

Scott, Ian 1982 *Urban and Spatial Development in Mexico*. Baltimore: Johns Hopkins University Press.

Shadow, Robert D. 1979 "Differential out-migration: a comparison of internal and international migration from Villa Guererro, Jalisco (Mexico)," pp. 67–84 in Fernando Cámara and Robert Van Kemper (eds.), *Migration across Frontiers: Mexico and the United States*. Albany: State University of New York Press.

Shaw, R. Paul 1976 *Land Tenure and the Rural Exodus in Chile, Colombia, Costa Rica, and Peru*. Gainesville: University of Florida Center for Latin American Studies.

Simon, Julian L. 1991 *The Economic Consequences of Immigration*, Cambridge: Basil Blackwell.

Sjaastad, Larry A. 1962 "The costs and returns of human migration." *Journal of Political Economy*, suppl., 70(5): 80–93.

Stoddard, Ellwyn R. 1976a "Illegal Mexican labor in the borderlands." *Pacific Sociological Review* 19(2): 175–210.

———. 1976b "A conceptual analysis of the 'alien invasion': institutionalized support of illegal Mexican aliens in the U.S." *International Migration Review* 10(2): 157–189.

Stuart, James, and Michael Kearney 1981 *Causes and Effects of Agricultural Labor Migration from the Mixteca of Oaxaca to California*. La Jolla: University of California, San Diego, Center for U.S.-Mexican Studies.

Szymanski, Albert 1978 "The growing role of Spanish speaking workers in the U.S. economy." *Aztldn: International Journal of Chicano Studies Research* 9: 177–208.

Taussig, Michael 1982 "Peasant economies and the development of capitalist agriculture in the Cauca Valley, Colombia," pp. 178–207 in John Harriss (ed.), *Rural Development: Theories of Peasant Economy and Agrarian Change*. London: Hutchinson University Press.

Tienda, Marta 1980 "Familism and structural assimilation of Mexican immigrants to the United States." *Internatinal Migration Review* 14(3): 383–407.

Tilly, Charles, and C. Harold Brown 1967 "On uprooting, kinship, and the auspices of migration." *International Journal of Comparative Sociology* 8(2): 139–164.

Todaro, Michael P. 1976 *Internal Migration in Developing Countries*. Geneva: International Labor Office.

Ugalde, Antonio 1974 *The Urbanization Process of a Poor Mexican Neighborhood*. Austin: University of Texas Press.

Uzzell, Douglas 1976 *Ethnography of Migration: Breaking Out of the Bipolar Myth*. William Marsh Rice University Program of Development Studies paper 70.

White, P. E., and R. I. Woods 1980 "Spartial patterns of migration flows," pp. 21–56 in P. E. White and R. I. Woods (eds.), *The Geographical Impact of Migration*. London: Longman.

Whiteford, Scott and Luis Emilio Henao 1979 "Commercial agriculture, irrigation control, and selective labor migration: the case of the Tehuacan Valley," pp. 25–32 in Fernando Câmara and Robert Van Kernper (eds.), *Migration across Frontlers: Mexico and the United States*. Albany: State University of New York Press.

Wiest, Raymond E. 1973 "Wage-labor migration and the household in a Mexican town." *Journal of Anthropological Research* 29: 180–209.

———. 1979 "Implications of International labor migration for Mexican rural development," pp. 85–97 in Fernando Cámara and Richard V. Kemper (eds.), *Migration across Frontiers: Mexico and the United States*. Albany: State University of New York Press.

———. 1980 "The interrelationship of rural, urban, and international labor markets: consequences for a rural Mexican community." *Papers in Anthropology* 21(1): 39–46.

Wilson, Tamar Diana 1986 "Chain migration, household sustenance strategies, and kinship networks." Unpublished M.A. paper, University of California, Los Angeles.

———. 1989 "Wage labor migration from peasant households: modifying Chayanov." *Anthropology UCLA* 16(1): 1–23.

———. 1992 "*Vamos para buscar la vida*: a comparison of patterns of outmigration from a rancho in Jalisco and immigration to a Mexicali squatter settlement." Unpublished Ph.D. dissertation, University of California, Los Angeles.

Wood, Charles 1981 "Structural changes and household strategies: a conceptual framework for the study of rural migration." *Human Organization* 40(4): 338–343.

———. 1982 "Equilibrium and historical–structural perspectives on migration." *International Migration Review* 16(2): 298–319.

World Bank 1991 *World Development Report* 1991: *The Challenge of Development*. New York: Oxford University Press.

Zarrugh, Laura Hoffman 1973 "*Gente de mi tierra*: Mexican village migrants in a California community." Unpublished Ph.D. dissertation, University of California, Berkeley.

Chapter 3

Roger Daniels

United States Policy Towards Asian Immigrants
Contemporary Developments in Historical Perspective

The publication of figures from the 1990 United States census showed that there had been a rapid increase in persons of Hispanic and Asian birth or ancestry living in the United States. When combined with a large but relatively static African American population, these statistics helped to set off a wave of confused press speculation and "scare" stories about the country having a "non-white" majority as early as the middle of the twenty-first century. What the data actually showed was that white persons made up some four-fifths of the population, blacks about an eighth, Hispanics about an eleventh, and Asians less than a thirty-third (Table 3.1). Some of the confusion stemmed from the way in which the Census Bureau listed its figures. Many journalists and others added up all of the non-white figures to get a false total of 28.6 per cent non-white. This was a flawed calculation. All the Hispanics had already been counted in other totals: as an often ignored Census Bureau footnote cryptically reminds us, Hispanics—an amalgam that includes persons of Mexican and Central and South American heritage as well as Cubans, Puerto Ricans, Dominicans, and some other Caribbean peoples—had already been classified as either black or white. In addition, the 9.8 million persons who were classified as "other" were not of some strange race but persons who had either given "wrong" ethnic information—that is, not using the bureau's criteria—or had left the ancestry part of their questionnaires blank. In previous censuses, procedures for what the bureau calls "allocation and audit" have resulted in an eventual classification of more than 90 percent of such persons as white, and there is no reason to believe that the final result in this census will be any different.[1]

From "United States Policy Towards Asian Immigrants: Contemporary Developments in Historical Perspective" in *International Journal* XLVII (Spring 1993).

TABLE 3.1 Population of the United States by "race," 1990 Census

Race	Percentage	Millions
White	80.3	ca 200.4
Black	12.1	ca 30.2
Asian/Pacific Islander	2.9	ca 7.3
American Indian Eskimo, Aleut	0.8	ca 2.0
Other	3.9	ca 9.8
[Hispanic	8.9	22.4]

Source: United States, Census, 1990 (preliminary).

TABLE 3.2 Asian American Population of the United States, 1950−90

Year	Number
1950	599,091
1960	877,934
1970	1,429,562
1980	3,466,421
1990	7.272,662

Source: United States, Census reports.

Nevertheless, the non-white and Hispanic elements of the population were clearly growing at a faster rate than the population of the United States as a whole. Between 1980 and 1990 the total population had increased about 10 percent. For the same period the number of whites grew about 6 percent, blacks more than 13 percent. American Indians about 38 percent, the Hispanic population some 53 percent, and the Asian population more than doubled. The greater rates of increase were due largely to immigration and, in the case of some of the groups, to a higher rate of natural increase.

Although most of the scare stories were evoked by the numbers on Hispanic elements in the population, the growth of the Asian population in recent years has been spectacular, as the figures in Table 3.2 demonstrate. While some of this growth is illusory, resulting from the admission of Hawaii to statehood and the subsequent inclusion of its large Asian American population from 1960 on, the vast majority of this growth—more than 1,100 percent in four decades—consists of recent immigrants and their descendants. Emigration from Asia, historically a minuscule portion of all immigration into the United States, began to grow in statistical significance after the end of World War II. In the 1950s Asians comprised 6 percent of all legal immigrants; that percentage rose to 12 percent in the 1960s, to 34 percent in the 1970s, and to 42 per cent between 1981 and 1989.[2]

If one looks retrospectively at the data it would be only natural to conclude that, sometime after World War II, a conscious decision to increase the incidence of Asian immigrants had been taken at the highest levels of the American government. However, no such decision was taken, and it is all but certain that no one, neither official nor academic, had the slightest notion that the crucial changes effected in American immigration law between 1943 and 1965 would result in a large influx of Asians. While it would not be accurate to claim, as is often alleged about Britain's acquisition of its empire, that the changes in immigration policy were made "in a fit of absence of mind," it is nevertheless true that some of the results of those changes were undreamed of. To understand why these changes came about, we must, at least briefly, examine the evolution of American immigration policy.

IMMIGRATION POLICY TO 1952

Although Asians, almost all of whom were Chinese, were not very numerous in the United States in the late nineteenth century—constituting less than one-tenth of one percent of the population—their presence was crucial in the formation of the nation's immigration policy.[3] The first significant restriction of free immigration into the United States was the Chinese Exclusion Act of 1882, which forbade the entry of "Chinese laborers" for a period of ten years.[4] Renewed for another ten years in 1892, this ban was made permanent in 1902. Chinese were thus the first group to be excluded, and it can be argued that the 1882 act was the hinge on which all of American immigration policy turned. From that time until 1924, the once free and unrestricted immigration policy of the United States was repeatedly curtailed on economic, cultural, and political grounds.

Asians other than the Chinese were the second ethnic target. The rise of a Japanese immigrant population—72,000 by 1910, with more than 40,000 in California—created a strong demand for a Japanese exclusion act, the first calls for which had come about 1892 when there were fewer than 5,000 Japanese in the whole country. Japan's growing military power caused the American government to negotiate an executive agreement— the so-called Gentlemen's Agreement of 1907/8—which slowed but did not totally stop the immigration of Japanese. In February 1917, on the eve of American entry into World War I, Congress excluded most Asians under a "barred zone" provision, because of the Gentlemen's Agreement, pointedly did not affect Japan. Nor, in the final analysis, were Filipinos affected, as the federal courts ruled that as long as the Philippines was an American colony, its inhabitants—though not citizens—were "American nationals" and could not be excluded. Although it is too much to argue, as E. P. Hutchinson has, that the 1917 law was "an unmistakable declaration of a white immigration policy"—immigration from the Caribbean was not inhibited—it was a sign of things to come.[5]

In addition to these laws on immigration per se, the little-remarked American naturalization statutes had long discriminated against Asians. The original 1790 statute limited naturalization to "free white persons," but, in practice, dozens of Asians were naturalized in the nineteenth century. In 1868, during the first reconstruction period, the fourteenth amendment to the Constitution not only made the former slaves citizens but also provided that all persons "born . . . in the United States" were citizens; two years later, Congress passed a statute which expanded naturalization to "white persons and persons of African descent." An attempt at this time by the radical Republican senator, Charles Sumner of Massachusetts, to make naturalization color blind failed as the majority in Congress wished to deny Chinese the right of naturalization. The 1882 Exclusion Act thus specified that "no . . . court shall admit Chinese to citizenship," and it was subsequently assumed that all Asians were "aliens ineligible to citizenship."[6] The United States Supreme Court confirmed the bar in two cases in 1922 and 1923.[7]

General immigration regulation had also begun in 1882 when a small head tax was levied on each incoming immigrant to "defray the expense of regulating immigration . . . and for the care [and relief] of immigrants."[8] By 1917 American policy had created six different grounds for excluding non-Asian immigrants: certain criminals, contract laborers, persons who failed to meet certain moral standards, persons with various diseases, certain radicals, and illiterates.[9] Congress and the nation were in a pronounced nativist, that is, anti-foreign, mood in the post–World War I years that John Higham has dubbed the "tribal twenties."[10] The House of Representatives actually went so far as to vote a one-year ban on all immigration, but the Senate refused to go along. Congress did pass a one-year "First Quota Act" in 1921 and eventually extended it until 1924, when the act "To Limit the Immigration of Aliens into the United States" was passed. Both laws successfully sought to stem general immigration by imposing a relatively low cap on overall immigration and the immigration of southern and eastern Europeans—Italians, Greeks, southern Slavs, Poles, and eastern European Jews—by assigning supposedly "scientific" quotas based roughly on the ethnic mix prevailing in the census of 1890 before immigration from those groups had properly begun. Asian immigration, except for the judicially exempt Filipinos, was completely stopped by forbidding the immigration of any "alien ineligible to citizenship."

The 1924 act, which remained the basis for American immigration policy until 1965, seemed to some to bring emigration to the United States to a close. This was the reaction not only of politicians and publicists but also of the first two generations of American historians of immigration. In George M. Stephenson's *History of American Immigration, 1820–1924,* a pioneering text produced in 1926 before there was any considerable body of monographic scholarship, the narrative began by opining that the congressional curtailment of immigration had "closed a momentous chapter in American and European history," and Marcus Lee Hansen opened his seminal 1927 *American Historical Review* essay, "The History of American Immigration as a Field for Research," by speaking of the process of settlement "from its beginnings in 1607 to its virtual close in 1914."[11] Similarly, John Higham, one of the premier historians of the second generation of immigration scholars, closed his classic *Strangers in the Land* (1955) by noting that, by 1924, "although immigration of some sort would continue, the vast folk movements that had formed one of the most fundamental forces in American history had been brought to an end."[12]

While these elegiac views—Higham speaks of an "ebb tide"—are understandable, the course of American history since these works were written has meant that pronouncements about the demise of immigration are not unlike the report of Mark Twain's death, an exaggeration. The 3.3 million legal immigrants of the 1960s, the 4.5 million legal immigrants of the 1970s, and the more than 6 million legal immigrants of the 1980s make it apparent that immigration is again a major factor in American history and that the two or three decades after 1924 were a mere aberration.

Nevertheless, from 1924 until 1943 there were no significant changes in American immigration legislation although, shortly after the Great Depression began, President Herbert Hoover administratively changed the "likely to become a public charge" or LPC clause, instituted by Congress in 1882 to bar persons unable to work, into a method to keep out people who were merely without assets.[13] His successor, Franklin Roosevelt, who changed so many aspects of American life and government, never even considered instituting a New Deal for immigration. The one significant legislative change effected during the New Deal years closed the loophole that had allowed unlimited numbers of Filipinos to enter. The 1934 law that promised independence to the Philippines introduced a quota for Filipinos: the islanders were allowed fifty immigrant entries per year, half the size of any other quota, and Filipinos remained ineligible for naturalization.

We can now see that a small change instituted for reasons of international politics in 1943 was, in fact, the hinge on which American immigration policy again turned, and, as was the case in 1882, it was Chinese immigrants who were at issue. To many internationalist-minded Americans the blatant discrimination of the Chinese Exclusion Act seemed an anomaly at a time when China was an American ally in the war against Japan. Although Chinese Americans, like other Asian Americans, deeply resented the discriminatory anti-Asian statutes and provisions, the crucial impetus for the repeal of the act came not from them but from members of what can be called the white establishment. A Citizens Committee to Repeal Chinese Exclusion and Place Immigration on a Quota Basis was spearheaded by the Asiaphile New York publisher, Richard J. Walsh, the husband of the novelist, Pearl Buck. The more than 150 names on its letterhead spanned the ideological spectrum from Roger Baldwin of the American Civil Liberties Union on the left to Henry Luce, publisher of *Time, Life,* and *Fortune*, on the right. The committee's successful campaign was studied years ago as an example of "pressures on Congress." With bipartisan support in Congress led by Democrat Emanuel Celler and Republican Clare Booth Luce and a strong message from President Roosevelt, the fifteen separate statutes that had effected Chinese exclusion were repealed in December 1943. The new law was a simple one with three brief sections. Section one repealed the old laws. Section two awarded a quota to "Chinese persons," later set at 105 admissions per year. This was a global quota. A Chinese Canadian wanting to emigrate to the United States, for example, would have to find a slot within this quota. Other Asian Canadians were still inadmissible, while non-Asian Canadians were non-quota immigrants. Section three amended the nationality act to make "Chinese persons" eligible for naturalization on the same basis as other aliens.

Although President Roosevelt made it clear in two formal statements that the repeal of the acts was a good behavior prize for the Chinese people because of "their great contribution to the cause of decency and freedom" and although it did nothing at all for other Asian and Asian American groups, it was a major breakthrough and made a small hole in the dike of Asian exclusion. The hole soon helped destroy the dike. Within three years the alien Chinese wives of American citizens became eligible to enter as non-quota immigrants, the Filipino quota was doubled, and Filipinos and "natives of India" were made eligible for naturalization and the latter were given a small quota.[14] From 1945 to 1952, a period for which there were 840 Chinese quota spaces, 11,058 Chinese legally entered the United States as immigrants. Nearly 10,000 of these were women, which significantly changed the sex ratios in the hitherto heavily male Chinatowns of the United States.[15] Another 20,000 Chinese women entered between 1952 and 1960. In addition, when Mao Zedong's forces triumphed in 1949, there were some 5,000 Chinese students studying in the United States. Many, perhaps most, of these "stranded Chinese" were able to get immigrant visas and eventually became citizens. These students were the first sizable increment of what came to be called the Asian "brain drain."[16]

LIBERALIZING THE LAW 1952–65

If most of these accretional changes came about as a result of World War II politics, the general overhaul of American immigration policy in 1952 was strongly influenced by the Cold War. While the Immigration and Nationality Act of that year, also known as the McCarran-Walter Act, generally maintained the nativist quota system, it added anti-communist rhetoric and provisions including the infamous ban on issuing even temporary visitor visas to foreign scholars and artists who were even suspected of communism. The act was passed over the veto of President Harry Truman, who denounced it and the quota system it perpetuated as "false and unworthy in 1924 [and] even worse now . . . this quota system keeps out the very people we want to bring in."[17]

However, in one special sense the 1952 act was an important liberalization of immigration and naturalization law: it dropped all of the remaining bars to the naturalization of Asians and made the naturalization process color blind, as Charles Sumner had wished eight decades earlier. It also gave quotas of some kind to every nation on earth, although, to be sure, Asian quotas were still minuscule. But unlike Sumner, those who wrote the 1952 act were not devoted to racial equality, as can be seen by their treatment of black immigration from the colonial Caribbean. Although previously there had been no numerical cap on West Indian immigration, the 1952 act placed severe limits on those from islands such as Jamaica, Martinique, and Aruba, which were European possessions.[18]

The Cold War nature of the law can be seen in the discussion of the "Asia-Pacific triangle" concept that resulted in granting each Asian nation then lacking a quota—and only China, the Philippines, India, and Pakistan had quotas in 1952—an annual quota of 100, plus an additional 100 for the entire triangle to take care of persons of mixed ancestry and residents of colonial dependencies. The quotas were racial as well as national: a Chinese citizen of Great Britain who entered as a quota immigrant would still be charged to the tiny and oversubscribed Chinese quota and not the large and undersubscribed British quota.

There was objection to the "Asia-Pacific triangle" concept from both the racist right, which did not want Asians at all, and the anti-racist left, which objected to racial as opposed to national criteria. The concept's chief legislative backer, Walter Judd, a former missionary and now a Republican congressman from Minnesota who had been urging its adoption since 1947, made its Cold War context perfectly clear. He told his colleagues that proponents hoped that its adoption would "influence greatly the battle for men's minds and hearts that is going on between the two philosophies of life and government that are locked in mortal struggle in our world" while assuring them that the small size of the quotas meant "that there will not be any flooding of America with people of lower economic standards or other cultural patterns."[19]

But, as had been true of the Chinese admissions after 1943, many more Asians entered than the minimal quotas seemed to indicate was possible. Family reunification provisions in the 1952 act allowed Asians who had established citizenship or even residence in the

United States to bring in certain family members without reference to any numerical limitation. Japanese Americans were the greatest users of the citizenship provisions of the law. Once naturalized, many Japanese immigrants, almost all of whom had come before 1924, began to bring in close relatives. In addition, a growing number of Japanese women who had married members of the American Occupation forces entered the country. Thus, despite a minimal quota for Japan, more than 60,000 Japanese entered the United States as immigrants between 1952 and 1964. Members of other Asian American groups also used this process to bring in relatives, but in smaller numbers. Special provisions for refugee immigration, which had begun, belatedly, with the Displaced Persons Acts of 1948 and 1950, were extended in 1953 to some presumably anti-communist Asians. The result of these changes was that immigration from Asia began to grow both absolutely and relatively.

While that growth is often linked to the great liberalization that followed the 1965 Immigration Act—discussed below—it is important to note that the increase had already begun in the late 1940s and 1950s. Between 1951 and 1960 for example, Asian immigrants accounted for 6 percent of all legal immigration to the United States, while in the years 1961–65, before the effects of the new law kicked in, it had risen to almost 8 percent, and the trend surely would have continued even without any change in the law.[20]

However, the law did change. Calls for major changes had been fairly persistent since 1953 when a presidential commission, established by Truman in the wake of the override of his veto of the 1952 act, recommended replacing the national origins system with one that allocated visas not by nations but according to five principles: the right of asylum, family reunification, needs in the United States, needs in the "Free World," and general immigration. Whereas both the 1924 and 1952 acts had contained the same theoretical annual numerical caps—one-sixth of 1 percent of the total population, according to the 1920 census—the Truman commission proposed to keep the same percentage but base it on the most recent census: at that time this would have raised the theoretical cap from 154,000 to 251,000.[21]

To be sure, not all of the growing volume of immigration could be attributed to the 1952 law: throughout the thirteen-year life of that statute both Congress and Presidents Eisenhower, Kennedy, and Johnson earmarked certain groups, mostly refugees from communism, for special treatment. The more generous treatment of refugees was facilitated in part by provisions of the McCarran-Walter Act, even though the word "refugee"—anathema to extreme restrictionists—appears nowhere in it. An obscure provision—section 212 (d) (5)—gave the executive branch, specifically the attorney general, discretionary parole power to grant temporary admission to unlimited numbers of aliens "for emergent reasons or for reasons deemed strictly in the public interest."[22] This came to mean, in practice, that the executive branch could act—for Hungarians, for Cubans, for Tibetans, for Vietnamese—and Congress could later pass legislation regularizing that action.[23] Congress itself, at the urging of the Eisenhower administration, passed a Refugee Relief Act in 1953 authorizing the admission of 205,000 visas over and above the quota system: 3,000 of these were earmarked for refugees "indigenous to the Far East," chiefly Koreans, and 2,000 for "refugees of Chinese ethnic origin" as long as they were vouched for by the Nationalist Chinese government on Taiwan. These were the first Asian refugee admissions authorized by Congress.[24] Of course, the "stranded Chinese students" mentioned earlier were actually refugees who were granted asylum, but those terms were not applied to them.

During the Eisenhower years, despite many real changes in practice, immigration theoretically was still linked to the narrow, nativistic quota system initiated in 1921. The advent of John F. Kennedy to power raised great expectations among those interested in immigration reform. Not only did the 1960 platform of the Democratic party call for scrapping the national origins system but the nominee himself had written — or signed his name to — a book hailing the achievements of the immigrant experience.[25] However campaign remarks that Kennedy made to an audience of Japanese Americans denouncing the McCarran-Walter Act, which Japanese Americans cherished as the grantor of their right to naturalization, indicated a lack of sensitivity to Asian American issues. And, although the reforms of which Kennedy spoke and which his successor got through Congress were greatly to benefit Asian Americans, it is clear that the Democrats' attention was focused on redressing what they felt were wrongs. The party platform had denounced a post–World War I "policy of deliberate discrimination by a Republican Administration and Congress." The focus continued to be on immigration from Europe, a focus that became less relevant with every passing year (See table 3.4).

CHANGING THE RULES: THE 1965 ACT

Only in July 1963 did President Kennedy send an immigration message to Congress recommending a comprehensive series of amendments to the 1952 act concentrating "primarily upon revision of our quota system." Although the emphasis in the message was on the "elimination of past discrimination" and focused on European immigration, it did propose abolition of the Asia-Pacific triangle and would have improved the position of Asian immigrants marginally. Despite this presidential leadership, no immigration legislation had emerged by the time of Kennedy's assassination, and some supporters of immigration reform feared that it would be buried with the martyred president because his successor, Lyndon B. Johnson, unlike Kennedy, had voted to override Truman's veto of the McCarran-Walter Act in 1952. But of course President Johnson was not Senator Johnson, and the Texan quickly embraced immigration reform with an unequivocal statement in his 1964 State of the Union address.

Congress went to work on an immigration bill the following year. While it was clear that there was a majority for change, its opponents trotted out the same old arguments. The chief advocate for the status quo was Senator Sam Ervin, a Democrat from North Carolina, who insisted that the McCarran-Walter Act was not discriminatory but was rather "like a mirror reflecting the United States, allowing the admission of immigrants according to a national and uniform mathematical formula recognizing the obvious and natural fact that those immigrants can best be assimilated into our society who have relatives, friends, or others of similar background already here." What Ervin never admitted was that the "mirror" was badly distorted, like those at amusement parks, and reflected not the population of the 1960s but that recorded in the 1920 census.

The legislative history of the 1965 act is complex and cannot be considered here.[26] The meaningful debates were not about *whether* to change the old system, but about how and

TABLE 3.3 Preference Systems: 1952 and 1965 Immigration Acts

IMMIGRATION AND NATIONALITY ACT 1952

Exempt from preference requirements and numerical quotas: spouses and unmarried minor children of United States citizens.

1   Highly skilled immigrants whose services are numerically needed in the United States and their spouses and children: 50 percent
2   Parents of United States citizens over age 21 and unmarried adult children of United States citizens: 30 percent
3   Spouses and unmarried adult children of permanent resident aliens: 20 percent

Any visas not allocated above distributed as follows:

4   Brothers, sisters, and married children of United States citizens and accompanying spouses and children: 50 percent
5   Non-preference applicants: any remaining visas

IMMIGRATION ACT OF 1965

Exempt from preference and numerical requirements: spouses, unmarried minor children, and parents of United States citizens.

1   Unmarried adult children of United States citizens: 20 percent
2   Spouses and unmarried adult children of permanent resident aliens: 20 percent
3   Members of the professions and scientists and artists of exceptional ability [requires Department of Labor certification]: 10 percent
4   Married children of United States citizens: 10 percent
5   Brothers and sisters of United States citizens over age 21: 24 percent
6   Skilled and unskilled workers in occupations for which labor is in short supply [requires Department of Labor certification]: 10 percent
7   Refugees from communist or communist-dominated countries, or the Middle East: 6 percent
8   Non-preference: any remaining visas [since there are more preference applicants than can be accommodated, this has not been used]

Source: Roger Daniels, *Coming to America: A History of Immigration and Ethnicity in American Life* (New York: Harper Collins 1990), 342.

to what degree to change it. The basic thrust of the 1965 law—which technically was not a new law but a series of amendments to the 1952 act—was to replace national quotas and origins with overall hemispheric limits on visas issued: 170,000 for persons from the eastern hemisphere, 120,000 for those from the western hemisphere. No country in the eastern hemisphere was to have more than 20,000 visas in any one year. (In a 1976 statute, hemispheric limits would be abandoned for a global ceiling of 290,000 visas, with the 20,000 per nation caps applying everywhere.) These provisions seemed to establish an annual limit of 290,000 immigrants, a little lower than immigration was actually running in the mid–1960s. Those 290,000 visas were to be distributed according to a system of preferences similar to those of the 1952 act. But, as had been the case during the life of the McCarran-Walter Act, two parallel systems were also adopted. The first, essentially a continuation from the 1924 and 1952 acts, exempted certain close relatives from both preference requirement and numerical limits. The second system added refugees of all kinds and, as it turned out, in unprecedented numbers, even though the 1965 act had set aside only 6 percent of preference visas (17,400 annually) for refugees. The new law also abolished the Asia-Pacific triangle concept. The bill retained most of the barriers that Congress had been erecting to limit entry to the country since the 1880s, most significantly the LPC clause, the requirements for mental and physical health, and the various ideological and moral tests. The new law very much resembled its immediate predecessor but placed a much heavier emphasis on family reunification, as Table 3.3 comparing their preference provisions demonstrates.

Lyndon Johnson signed the bill into law in a ceremony on Liberty Island in New York Harbor with the then still-dilapidated and unused buildings on Ellis Island in the background: "This bill that we sign today is not a revolutionary bill. It does not affect the lives of millions. It will not reshape the structure of our daily lives, or really add importantly to either our wealth or our power."[27] Johnson was not indulging in uncharacteristic understatement. He was saying what his experts had told him. He and they saw the 1965 act as redressing the wrongs of 1924 and 1952, what he called the wrong done to those "from southern and eastern Europe." Members of his administration had testified before Congress that few Asians would enter under the new law, a misperception also held by the leading Asian American organization, the Japanese American Citizens League, which complained that for the foreseeable future Asians would continue to be discriminated against, even though post-1965 discrimination would be de facto rather than de jure.

In practice, the law has worked quite differently than any of its sponsors expected. Looking backward and expecting the future to resemble the past, they ignored the evidence of the data available to them. As we have seen, despite the restrictions of the 1952 act, the incidence of Europeans among immigrants to the United States had dropped steadily even while the volume of total immigration had risen. Yet the experts continued to believe the great fallacy that there were large numbers of European immigrants ready, qualified, and able to come to America. Most seemed to think that 20,000 annual arrivals from many European countries would absorb most of the eastern hemisphere preference visa slots. Had the 1965 act, or something very much like it, been passed in 1952 when Truman recommended a full-scale revision of immigration law, such a result might well have obtained. But by 1965 most of those western Europeans who wished to come were not likely to meet LPC and other restrictions and, of course, eastern Europeans were not then free to come. Growing numbers of Latin Americans and Asians had been coming to the United States since the years of World War II, and once such persons had permanent resident status a whole cohort of relatives became eligible to enter the country as second preference immigrants. And as soon as these immigrants became United States citizens— as unprecedented numbers of them did in the minimum five-year waiting period as Elliott Barkan's studies have shown[28]—more persons became eligible as first, fourth, and fifth preference immigrants, while others could enter exempt from numerical preference. And of course, those brought in could and did start the same procedure. Since the 1965 act went into effect this kind of chain migration, in which related immigrants follow one another as links in a chain, has accounted for a preponderance of all non-refugee migration. Such a

TABLE 3.4 Source of United States immigrants, 1950s and 1980s (%)

	1951–60	*1981–89*
Asia	6	42
Latin America	25	42
Europe	52	11
Africa and other	2	3
Canada	15	11

Source: William P. O'Hare and Judy C. Felt, *Asian Americans: America's Fastest Growing Minority Group* (Washington, DC: 1991), 6.

TABLE 3.5 Asian Immigrants to the United States, by Nation, 1980–89

Nation	*Number*	*% Asian migrants**
Vietnam	679,378	24
Philippines	473,831	17
China†	433,031	15
Korea	338,891	12
Laos‡	256,727	9
India	253,781	9
Cambodia	210,724	7
Other	61,699	2
Thailand	59,638	2
Pakistan	55,900	2
Japan	41,739	1
TOTAL	2,863,339	100

Source: William P. O'Hare and Judy C. Felt, *Asian Americans: America's Fastest Growing Minority Group* (Washington, DC: 1991), 2.

* Includes refugees
† Includes Republic of China (Taiwan), Hong Kong, and Macao. In addition, thousands of immigrants from Southern Asia are ethnically Chinese and so identify themselves in United States censuses.
‡ Includes Hmong.

process is likely to continue as long as the law stays essentially as it is and conditions in most of Asia and Latin America remain as they are.

Although the law speaks of an annual global ceiling of 290,000, that applies *only* to those subject to numerical limitation. Thus legal immigration, which averaged a quarter of a million annually in the 1950s, increased to a third of a million annually in the 1960s, nearly 450,000 annually in the 1970s, and to more than half a million annually in the 1980s. Increasingly, this was immigration from Asia and Latin America, as is clear from the data in Table 3.4, which compares the percentage shares of the immigration that came from various regions in the 1950s with those for the 1980s; and Table 3.5, which shows the Asian nations from which immigrants came in the period 1980–89.

The 1965 law, which remains the basis for immigration into the United States,[29] has not worked out in the way that either its proponents or its opponents expected. Perhaps the most misleading aspect of the law involves the presumed 20,000 cap on entries from any one nation. That cap applies only to those entering subject to "numerical limitation," so that in a given year, for example 1985, there were 48,000 legal entries by Filipinos and 35,000 by Koreans, to cite only the two most numerous Asian groups that year. The cap has been a chimaera.

Although in the congressional debates over the 1965 law there was the usual restrictionist oratory about opening the floodgates, not even the most consistent restrictionist in Congress in 1965 predicted that in the 1980s some six million legal immigrants would enter the United States. Nor did anyone even hint that Latins and Asians would so completely dominate American immigration. By the 1980s more than four-fifths of all legal immigrants came from either Asia or Latin America: if there was a way of accurately including illegal immigrants in the calculations, this figure would undoubtedly exceed nine-tenths. The 1965 act, intended to redress past grievances of European ethnic groups and to give more than token representation to Asians, has, in one sense, turned traditional immigration patterns to the United States on their head.

In another sense, however, the patterns of immigration have remained consistent. People have tended to emigrate to the United States when a clear economic and/or social advantage could be gained from doing so. In the years after 1965, the average Briton or German or Scandinavian could see no such advantage in emigration; neither could the average Japanese. Most of those Europeans who wished to emigrate were in Eastern Europe. However, many Irish, the one western European group that sought entry in large numbers, were disadvantaged in their attempts to enter because there were too few recent legal Irish immigrants to provide the close blood kin to produce an effective chain migration. Many Irish therefore resorted, in fairly large but indeterminate numbers, to illegal immigration.

Under the 1965 law the golden door had swung open much wider, but an entirely different mix of peoples was provided with legal access. The executive and legislative branches of the United States government had not only ended the blatant discrimination against Asians but had also created a new system that could be used by Asians to make themselves the most favored beneficiaries of the new law. The first result was intended, the second totally unintended. Had either branch understood the dynamics of immigration flows, it would have insisted on a different law.

ASIAN AMERICA IN 1993: A SNAPSHOT

A discussion of changes in immigration law affecting Asians would be incomplete without a glance at the kinds of communities the changes have helped to create. To return to the 1990 census, Table 3.6 lists the major components of the Asian American population it reported. It is misleading to speak about Asian Americans as if they were a homogenous group; one only need think of the analogue, European Americans—a phrase that is almost never used—to see how inappropriate such terms really are. This is not to argue that the terms should not be used at all: race—and Asian American is essentially a racial term—

is still relevant in the United States. But those of us who use this term, for whatever reason, must be careful not to give to those it embraces a kind of false homogeneity. Asian Americans are diverse, and their diversities are significant both within and between ethnic groups. In the final analysis, in the years to come, it may well be that class rather than ethnicity will become more important in differentiating among Asian Americans.

We do not yet have detailed socioeconomic data from the 1990 census, but that from the 1980 census showed us sharp disparities in age, gender, residence, education, and income between and within Asian American ethnic groups. Among the longer established groups, internal diversity can most easily be seen in the Chinese American community. While it contains many highly successful individuals, large numbers of Chinese Americans, some of whom are members of families that have been here for generations, live in poverty and deprivation and display the socioeconomic profiles that usually accompany poverty.

Among the newer groups, I will mention only two: Asian Indians and Vietnamese. In purely economic terms, Asian Indians stood at the top of recent Asian immigrant groups, with the highest reported median income, an income that exceeds even that of whites. Asian Indians were the only large Asian American group under-represented in the Far West: only 19.2 percent lived there—fewer than the 34.2 percent in the Northeast, the 23.4 percent in the South, and the 23.1 percent in the North Central states. While in the Northeast many are professionals and business executives—and thus part of the brain and capital drain from Asia—large numbers of other Asian Indians operate small businesses wherever they have settled. They have moved into one special economic niche: owning motels. For example, Asian Indians constitute some 40 percent of motel owners along Interstate 75, which runs between Detroit and Atlanta. Many motels are owned by members of a numerous Gujarati clan named Patel so that a community ethnic joke speaks about "hotel, motel, Patel." Motels require relatively small amounts of capital and large amounts of unskilled labor, the latter often supplied by extended family or clan members. Continuing migration of these family members may well lower average income within the community.

TABLE 3.6 Asian Americans, 1990, by Major Ethnic Group

Group	Number
Chinese	1,643,621
Filipinos	1,403,624
Japanese	850,901
Asian Indians	814,538
Koreans	799,993
Vietnamese	610,904
Laotians (including Hmong)	239,000
Cambodians	210,724

Source: United States, census reports. These figures are taken from listings the Census Bureau provides under the rubric "Asian and Pacific Islander." It includes immigrants from East, Southeast, and South Asia and their descendants, and many Pacific Islanders, but not native Hawaiians. It is not used for Caucasians born in Soviet Asia—of whom there are very few in the United States—or for Iranians and other Asians from the region west of Pakistan generally known as the Middle East, or for most Australians and New Zealanders. As recently as 1970, Japanese and Chinese made up the lion's share—more than 70 percent—of Asian Americans. In 1990 they were only just over a third. There are now very large Filipino, Southeast Asian, Korean, and Asian Indian ethnic groups in the United States, almost all of whom are the result of post-1965 immigration.

Unlike most of the other middle-class Asian Americans, few Asian Indians have adopted Christianity. Hindu temples have sprung up throughout America. Asian Indian family structure has remained highly traditional: in 1980, 92.7 percent of all Asian Indian children under eighteen lived in two-parent families. Asian Indians, despite (because of?) their middle-class status, have suffered increasing instances of anti-Asian racial violence. The worst examples were in Jersey City, where a group of working-class white youths, calling themselves 'dot busters,' for the *bindi*, the small cosmetic dot that married Hindu women traditionally wear on their foreheads, assaulted a number of Indians on the streets, eventually killing one young man, a junior executive with Citicorp.

By contrast, Vietnamese and other Southeast Asian refugees and their children were, as a group, at the very bottom of the socioeconomic indices in 1980. But, as is often true with refugee populations, the community's socioeconomic range was tremendous. Many of the élite of the Republic of Vietnam eventually fled to the West. Former Air Marshal Nguyen Cao Ky, for example, is the proprietor of an upscale liquor store near Washington, DC. At the other end of the spectrum were Vietnamese fisherfolk and the Hmong, whose social and economic organization was essentially premodern.

Most Vietnamese have not been economically successful. More than a quarter (28.1 percent) of all Vietnamese households received public assistance in 1979. While the media delight in reporting the success story—"Vietnamese Girl Wins Spelling Bee"—the reality is that a very large proportion of the Vietnamese American population has joined the under class. Despite determined attempts by refugee resettlement groups to distribute Vietnamese refugees throughout the country, by 1980 significant clustering had already occurred in California where a third of them then lived. That percentage is undoubtedly much higher now. Within California the major concentration point is Orange County south of Los Angeles. Outside California, the major concentration point is Texas, where a tenth lived in 1980. Vietnamese were one of the few contemporary immigrant groups with no sizeable concentration in New York, which had, in 1980, only 2.5 percent of them. Wherever most of them have gone in the United States they have faced a double disadvantage: not only are they foreigners from Asia, but most of them came without capital or the skills necessary to make it in late twentieth-century America.

Thus the conglomerate image of "Asian Americans" is an illusion. Hmong and Japanese are no more alike than Albanians and Scots. Yet because Asian Americans are not Caucasians, the media, the Census Bureau, and almost everyone else will continue to speak of them as if they were one people. The category will almost certainly continue to grow, by immigration and natural increase, both absolutely and relatively. One educated estimate, made in 1985, predicted almost 10 million Asian Americans by 2000. If this prediction is correct—if I had to hazard a guess it would be that it will prove to be too low—Asian Americans will be about 4 percent of the American population, or one person in twenty-five. As recently as 1980 they represented 1.5 percent of the population, or one person in seventy-five, and in 1940 they had represented slightly less than two-tenths of one percent, or one person in five hundred. Whatever the numbers, Asian Americans will surely play an increasingly important role in American life, but a varied one. A substantial percentage of the latest immigrants and their children will join the large number of Asian Americans who have already entered the middle and upper middle classes as their current presence in our élite institutions predicts. Others will, almost certainly, remain mired in poverty. No pan-ethnic appellation or set of attributes can possibly describe them all.[30]

STUDY QUESTIONS

1. What is the significance of the McCarren-Walter Act?

2. How was the "Asia-Pacific triangle" concept a racial as well as national quota?

3. How do Asian Indians and Vietnamese immigrants represent different sectors of the Asian community?

NOTES

1. The Aristotelian nature of the American census requires that there be a race or ethnicity—and only one race or ethnicity for every person enumerated. Persons of mixed ancestry must choose—or have the census choose for them—one of the appropriate categories. If a respondent gives more than one "race," the bureau will count only the one written first. Until 1989 the National Center for Health Statistics always assigned babies of mixed "white" and "non-white" ancestry to the non-white race; since that time all babies are to be assigned to the race of the mother.

2. Data for other regions in the latter period are as follows: Latin America, 42 percent; Europe, 11 percent; Africa and other, 3 percent; and Canada, a percent. These and other relevant statistics may be most conveniently found in two studies from the Population Reference Bureau: William P. O'Hare and Judy C. Felt, *Asian Americans: America's Fastest Growing Minority Group* (Washington, DC: 1991); and Robert W. Gardner, Bryant Robey, and Peter C. Smith, *Asian Americans: Growth, Change and Diversity* (Washington, DC: 1985). For an interpretation, see Harry H.L. Kitano and Roger Daniels, *Asian Americans: Emerging Minorities* (Englewood Cliffs, NJ: Prentice-Hall, 1988); a revised edition is in progress.

3. At their point of highest incidence in the census—1880—there 105,000 Chinese and 2,000 Japanese in a total population of almost 63,000,000.

4. The 1809 ban on the slave trade was the first legislative inhibition of immigration and the prehaps 50,000 slaves illegally brought to the United States after that can be considered as the first illegal immigrants. Apart from that, the only other pre-1882 restriction was an 1875 act barring the entry of "women for the purposes of prostitution" and criminals "whose sentence has been remitted on the condition of emigration."

5. The most comprehensive account of the statutes is E. P. Hutchinson, *Legislative History of American Immigration Policy, 1798–1965* (Philadelphia: University of Pennsylvania Press, 1981). Quotation at page 167.

6. Section 14 of the Chinese Exclusion Act. It should be noted that while other provisions of the act affected only "Chinese laborers," the bar to naturalization covered all Chinese.

7. *Ozawa v. United States*, 260 U.S. 189 (1988) and *United States v. Thind*. 261 u.s. 204 (1922). In the initial case, which involved a Japanese, the court said that "white" in the 1870 statute meant "Caucasian." The second case involved an Asian Indian who, although dark, was ethnologically

"Caucasian." The court, whose composition had not changed, unblinkingly now said that "white" meant white "in the understanding of the common man." Both decisions were unanimous.

8. The American head tax, which started at fifty cents and rose to eight dollars by the time of World War I, was essentially a user fee as opposed to the much larger Canadian head taxes levied on Chinese as a deterrent.

9. The literacy test of 1917 had very little effect. Unlike its predecessors in South Africa and Australia, it recognized literacy in any language or dialect, including specifically Hebrew and Yiddish, and exempted females and other family members under sixteen if the head of the household was literate.

10. The premier account of the heyday of American nativism (first published in 1955) remains John Higham's *Strangers in the Land: Patterns of American Nativism, 1860–1925* (New Brunswick, NJ): Rutgers University Press, 1988).

11. *American Historical Review* 32 (1927), 500.18. It may be conveniently consulted in Marcus Lee Hansen, *The Immigrant in American History* (Cambridge, MA: Harvard University Press, 1940).

12. Higham, Strangers in the Land, 330.

13. The original 1882 language was: "if . . . there shall be found . . . any convict, lunatic, idiot, or any person unable to take care of himself or herself without becoming a public charge . . . such persons shall not be permitted to land." 22 *Stat.* 214. For a detailed analysis, see Patricia R. Evans, " 'Likely to Become a Public Charge': Immigration in the Backwaters of Administrative Law, 1882–1933," doctoral dissertation, George Washington University, 1987.

14. For details, see Roger Daniels, *History of Indian Immigration to the United States: An Interpretive Essay* (New York: Asia Society, 1989); and Premdatta Varma, "The Asian Indian Community's Struggle for Legal Equality in the United States, 1900–1946," doctoral dissertation, University of Cincinnati, 1989.

15. The 1950 census, taken after most of these women had immigrated, still showed Chinese males outnumbering Chinese females 76,000 to 40,000. The imbalance among adults alone was even higher.

16. Authority for this was obliquely authorized in section 202, 64 *stat.* 198 (1950). See also Kitano and Daniels, *Asian Americans*, 303–304.

17. Veto text in *Department of State Bulletin* 27 (14 July 1952), 78–82.

18. This had repercussions outside the New World. As the premier historian of immigration to Britain has written: "Before 1952 a convenient safety-valve for Jamaicans, among whom there was a particularly long tradition of work-migration, had been available in the United States. However, entry into the U.S. was severely curtailed by the 1952 McCarran-Walter Act which limited the number of immigrants from the British West Indies to 800 per year, of whom only 100 could be Jamaicans. This restrictive legislation encouraged Jamaicans to turn towards Britain." Colin Holmes, *John Bull's Island: Immigration and British Society, 1871–1971* (London: Macmillan Education, 1988), 221.

19. These quotations from United States Congress, *Joint Hearings before the Sub-committees of the Committees on the Judiciary* (Washington, DC: U.S. Government Printing Office, 1951).

20. In the years 1951–60, 150, 106 Asian immigrants were enumerated in a total of 2,515,479, an incidence of 6 per cent: in 1961–65, 107,000 were enumerated in a total of 1,450,312, an incidence of 7–4 percent.

21. For a wide variety of reasons, including the admission of family members without numerical limitation, special refugee programs, and the practice of "quota mortgaging," immigration under the 1952 act ran much higher that the theoretical limit. In the last five years of the law, an average of 290,000 persons was admitted annually, more than 188 percent of the supposed

annual cap. For the Truman proposal, see: President's Commission on Immigration and Naturalization, *Whom We Shall Welcome* (Washington, DC: U.S. Government Printing Office, 1953). The title comes from a pro-immigration presidential statement by George Washington.

22. Further power was given to the executive branch under subsection (e) of the same section, which authorized the president to suspend, by proclamation, "for such period as he shall deem necessary . . . the entry of all aliens or any class of aliens . . . or impose on the entry of aliens any restrictions he may deem to be appropriate." Although never used, this is one of the most sweeping grants of presidential power on the statute books.

23. Although few in the conservative Congress would have realized it, the parole authority they were thus using stemmed from Franklin Roosevelt's one-time use of such power to let in fewer than a thousand European refugees in 1944. See Sharon R. Lowenstein, *Token Refuge: The Story of the Jewish Refugee Shelter at Oswego, 1944–1946* (Bloomington: Indiana University Press, 1986).

24. Refugee Relief Act of 1953. 67 *Stat.* 400. For a brief summary of United States refugee policy, see Roger Daniels, "American refugee policy in historical perspective," in J. C. Jackman and C. M. Borden, eds., *The Muses Flee Hitler: Cultural Transfer and Adaptation, 1930–1945* (Washington, DC: Smithsonian Institution Press, 1983), 61–78.

25. Party planks on immigration may be found in Hutchinson, *Legislative History*, 621–43. In 1960 the Republican platform called for keeping the quota system but using the most recent census instead of that of 1920. John F. Kennedy, *A Nation of Immigrants* (New York: 1958).

26. David M. Reimers, *Still the Golden Door: The Third World Comes to America* (2nd ed; New York: Columbia University Press, 1992), has a good account: see chapter 3, "A cautious reform: the Immigration Act of 1965," 61–91.

27. *Department of State Bulletin* 53(25 October 1965), 661.

28. Elliott R. Barkan, "Whom shall we integrate?: a comparative analysis of the immigration and naturalization trends of Asians before and after the 1965 Immigration Act (1951–1978)," *Journal of American Ethnic History* 3 (1983), 29–57.

29. Although there have been several major immigration laws enacted since 1965—chiefly the Refugee Act of 1980, the Immigration Reform and Control Act of 1986, and the Immigration Act of 1990—the 1965 act remains basic. Of the three above, only the Refugee Act of 1980 had an appreciable impact on legal Asian immigration. The 1986 act, which was supposed to halt illegal immigration, has proved to be almost totally ineffective, as most serious students of immigration expected.

30. For a contrasting view, see Yen Le Espiritu, *Asian American Panethnicity: Bridging Institutions and Identities* (Philadelphia: Temple University Press, 1992).

Chapter 4

Nora Hamilton and
Norma Stoltz Chinchilla

Central American Migration
A Framework for Analysis

The subject of Central American migration encompasses a broad range of experiences that challenge traditional approaches to migration studies. Past interpretations of migration have tended to be based on mutually exclusive typologies or to focus on certain dimensions of migration while excluding others. Thus migration could be internal or international; cyclical, temporary, or permanent; voluntary or involuntar; economically or politically motivated (the latter issue often treated in a separate literature on refugees and exiles); motivated by "push" factors in the country of origin or "pull" factors in the receiving country, or the result of individual decisions or underlying structural conditions.

Recent studies of specific migration experiences, however, including those of Central Americans, reveal that the lines of demarcation between the dimensions are rarely clear-cut, and this complexity is now being recognized in theoretical analysis. Economic difficulties or crises may be political generated or aggravated, and economic underde-velopment is often accompanied by political repression (Zolberg 1981, 20; Richmond 1986). Central Americans have migrated for both economic and political reasons, and pre-liminary research on Central Americans who have come to the United States in recent years suggests that in many cases it is difficult to seperate the two (Schoultz 1987, 11–13). Generally, some combination of "push" and "pull" factors influence the decision to migrate, and individual decisions occur within a framework of internal and international structures that condition individual needs and the choices available (Papademetriou

From "Central American Migration: A Framework for Analysis" in *Latin American Research Review,* Vol. 26, No. 1, 1991.

1983, 472–78; Portes and Bach 1985; Zolberg, Suhrke, and Aguayo 1986; Cohen 1987). Temporary moves may become permanent if reasons for leaving continue or are aggravated or the rationale for remaining is increased, as happens when families of labor migrants join them in the host country (Zolberg 1983, 36). Even cyclical migration may establish patterns and networks that become the basis for long-term or permanent migration (Portes 1983, 74–75; Kearney 1986, 353).

Indeed, current migration patterns often have a historical dimension. Although the recent escalation of Central American migration (within the region and to the United States) is in many respects a new phenomenon (Schoultz 1987, 9–10; Ayguayo 1985, 21), the long historical tradition of migration within and between the countries of the region has undoubtedly affected current patterns of migration.

The purpose of this article is to develop a framework for analyzing Central American migration that takes into account historical and contemporary dimensions, economic and political motivations, and domestic and international structures. We will begin by briefly discussing some factors already identified in the theoretical literature on characteristics and causes of migration, focusing on structural approaches as a basis for establishing a framework for examining Central American migration. The subsequent section draws on existing studies and statistical data to discuss the historical and contemporary patterns of Central American migration in the context of this framework. In the conclusion, we analyze the appropriateness of the framework for explaining Central American migration through a series of propositions that can serve as the basis for future studies.

THEORETICAL ISSUES

Many proponents of a structural approach identify migration as resulting from the logic of capitalist development, its penetration into peripheral areas (those at a precapitalist or relatively low level of capitalist development), and the incorporation of these areas into the world economy. One major outcome of capital penetration is the direct recruitment of labor from the peripheral area, whether coerced (as in importing seven and a half million Africans to work as slaves in Europe and its colonies from the fifteenth through the eighteenth centuries) or contracted (as in contracting Eastern European peasants to work in U.S. manufacturing industries in the nineteenth century). The latter process has continued in various forms well into the twentieth century (Portes 1983; Cohen 1987; Zolberg 1983).

Exporting capital from core countries (those having a dominant position within the world economy) to peripheral regions may also produce economic distortions and dislocations that result in emigration by uprooted groups who can no longer find work in their own countries. To the extent that these groups emigrate to the relevant core areas, capital penetration becomes an element in indirect labor recruitment (Cheng and Bonacich 1984; Cornelius 1980). These processes have been accentuated as peripheral areas, and countries become incorporated into an increasingly integrated but highly asymmetrical world economic system. These areas become even more vulnerable to external economic conditions ranging from fluctuations in commodity prices to global recession, again leading to emigration to core areas by uprooted populations.

Exporting capital from core countries has often been accompanied and supported by political penetration and control by the government of the advanced capitalist country, which reinforces the bilateral dominant-dependent relationship between the core country and the peripheral society. This relationship helps to explain the direction of international migration flows (such as Algerians migrating to France and Mexicans to the United States). Once established, patterns of migration continue to operate, partly because of transnational social networks (Bach 1985, 28; Kearney 1986),[1] even when efforts are made to close off opportunities for migration into the dominant country. A prominent example of the persistence of such patterns is demonstrated by the ineffectiveness of U.S. refugee and asylum policies and related efforts to block immigration via more restrictive laws and sanctions (Cheng and Bonacich 1984; Cornelius 1980, 71–72; 1988; Cue and Bach 1980, 257–59; Portes and Bach 1985).[2]

The penetration of capital into peripheral economies occurs on national as well as international levels, with comparable implications for political or economic dislocation, labor recruitment, and other inducements to migrate. At the same time, the peripheral state may play a pivotal role in facilitating conditions for foreign or national capital or both and in managing contradictions that arise from capitalist development. It may directly or indirectly affect emigration if its development policies de-emphasize satisfying internal demands, particularly in a context where cultural penetration creates attraction to actual or perceived opportunities for a higher standard of living in the core (Bach 1985, 25; Portes 1983, 79–81).

While refugee movements tend to be generated by political conflicts that can include political repression, revolutionary movements, and international war, such conflicts result in many cases from economic contradictions—indeed, the same dislocations that lead some to migrate may lead others to revolt. Here the role of the domestic state is again important, because state efforts to control such conflicts often lead to political repression. In short, the dislocations produced by foreign (or domestic) capital penetration and changes in the world economy are not only a direct economic cause of migration but may also be an indirect political cause when they result in revolution or other forms of political conflict. This effect becomes direct when external states intervene politically or militarily and thus share responsibility for generating refugee flows resulting from these conflicts and for determining their course (Zolberg, Suhrke, and Aguayo 1986, 151–52, 156–58).

Finally, foreign states intervene in migration and refugee flows in their "gate-keeping" function, that is, in their immigration and refugee policies. Immigration policy in receiving countries is related to larger domestic and foreign policy concerns, and changes in policy reflect conflicts between domestic groups who benefit from migration flows (in the form of cheap labor, for example) and those who do not (Bach 1985, iii, 24). Refugee policy in prospective receiving countries may also help determine refugee immigration and is often tied to foreign policy, as is evident in the U.S. policy of accepting and even encouraging refugees from communist countries while denying refugee status to individuals fleeing countries friendly to the United States (Zolberg, Surke, and Aguayo 1986, 154–56; see also Teitlebaum 1984; Schoultz 1987, 67–69). As noted above, however, the effectiveness of these laws may be partly neutralized by strong migratory networks.

To summarize, migration can be explained as the effect—or one effect—of contradictions, dislocations, and opportunities resulting from the penetration of capitalism (domestic or foreign) into nations or regions at a lower level of development.[3] These processes affect and are affected by the pre-existing productive structures and the state's role in maintaining those structures, which requires managing the contradictions resulting from class divisions and from the articulation of different structures of production. In concrete terms, this role ranges from promoting specific development models to repressing groups or forces that oppose the dominant economic structure. Penetration by foreign capital is often accompanied and facilitated by political penetration by the external (core) capitalist state, which takes various forms ranging from diplomatic influence to military intervention in political conflicts. The core state also performs a gate-keeping function through its immigration and refugee policy, which in turn reflects foreign and domestic policy concerns.

The above discussion suggests a framework for our analysis of Central American migration in the following section. We shall be specifically concerned with five issues: first, the relationship between capitalist penetration into less-developed or precapitalist areas and migration (how such penetration affects or is a factor in migration); second, the ways and extent to which developed capitalist or "core" economies (and regions) function as "poles of attraction" for immigration directly through labor recruitment or indirectly through cultural, economic, and social influences; third, the implications for migration of state policies on economic development and the role of the state in mitigating, managing, or aggravating contradictions and conflicts emanating from these policies or from the process of development itself; fourth, the ways and extent to which developed capitalist or core states directly or indirectly encourage or discourage migration through political or military intervention as well as through immigration and asylum policy; and finally, the role of migratory networks in reinforcing preestablished patterns of migration even when the initial conditions accounting for them have been modified or no longer exist.

The following analysis of Central American migration patterns relies on existing studies and statistical data on Central American migration. It includes an extensive study undertaken by CSUCA (the Consejo Superior Universitaria Centroamericana) in the 1970s based on census information from the 1950s, 1960s, and 1970s as well as our preliminary findings on Central American migration to the United States. Although migration within the Central American region predates the colonial period, our analysis will begin with the nineteenth century, the first important period of capitalist development in Central America, and will emphasize the postwar period, one of rapid development of capitalist markets and relations of production. El Salvador was chosen for in-depth examination because it typifies the more general patterns of capitalist development and displacement and also because it is the source of the largest Central American immigrant population in the United States.

MIGRATION PATTERNS IN CENTRAL AMERICA

Historical Patterns from the Nineteenth Century through World War II

Capitalism's penetration of Central America incorporated the region into the world economy definitively when coffee production was expanded for export in the nineteenth century.[4] Coffee production for export had an immediate impact on migration, although different patterns emerged in each country. In Costa Rica, which had abundant land and limited labor, coffee production expanded into frontier zones and capitalist structures developed immediately: coffee estates hiring wage labor coexisted with family farms that shifted at least partially to coffee production for export. The national population, initially centered in the province of Cartago, gradually extended westward on the central mesa following the expansion of coffee production (CSUCA 1978a, 39–41.) In El Salvador and Guatemala, where precapitalists forms of production and labor prevailed in the indigenous communities and on the agricultural estates, capitalist elements of production were mixed with precapitalist forms of labor appropriation. Both countries passed liberal legislation to bring land into the market by reducing or eliminating *ejidos* and other forms of communal land and by expropriating church properties (Bulmer-Thomas 1987, 20–21; Woodward 1985, 168–69). In El Salvador, peasants expelled from their communities in the central and western highlands were forced to continue subsistence farming as squatters on unused lands on the estates or by migrating to other, generally poorer land in different regions of the country (Browning 1971, 219–20).

Labor for coffee production, however, was initially nonwage and often coerced (in forms of peonage or tenancy), shifting only gradually to wage labor. The estates continued to depend on the subsistence (precapitalist) sector for labor during the harvest through seasonal migration from subsistence farms in other areas of El Salvador (a pattern later replicated in Nicaragua) and in Guatemala through forced recruitment of Indians from the highland communities to work on the coffee estates in the sparsely populated coastal areas or lowlands of San Marcos, Santa Rosa, Quetzaltenango, and Sololá (Santana Cardoso 1975, 16–30; CSUCA 1978a, 77–78; Deere and Marchetti 1981, 43–44). Thus incorporation of the Central American countries into the world economy as coffee producers and exporters was a factor in the cyclical migration patterns still found in these countries as well as in the expulsion of subsistence farmers onto marginal lands.[5]

When banana enclaves were established in the early twentieth century in Costa Rica, Honduras, and Guatemala, and later in Nicaragua, the pattern was repeated of a permanent labor force (based on wage labor in this case) being supplemented by seasonal harvest workers who also depended on small plots that they owned or rented in other parts of the country. Where the banana companies opened up new lands for cultivation (as in the Honduran departments of Cortés, Atlántida, Yoro, and Colón on the northern Atlantic coast), these areas attracted migrants from other parts of the country to either work on the new plantations or establish small farms (CSUCA 1978a, 38).

Growing U.S. economic and strategic involvement in Mexico, Central America, and the Caribbean from the late nineteenth century onward resulted in new patterns of international migration.[6] In Central America, the banana enclaves and particularly the construction of the Panama Canal reinforced existing patterns of international migration, such as immigration by workers from Jamaica and other Caribbean islands to Panama and the Caribbean coasts of Central America, which had begun several decades earlier when the Panama railroad was built. These factors also introduced new migration patterns, such as the emigration of Hondurans to New Orleans.

Legally documented Central American migration to the United States increased in the first two decades of this century from five hundred individuals entering between 1890 and 1900 to eight thousand between 1900 and 1910 and to seventeen thousand between 1910 and 1920. But the number of Central Americans seeking entry to the United States continued to be limited compared with those from other areas, and it fell sharply to less than six thousand in the 1930s, presumably due to quotas restricting the flow of immigrants from the Western Hemisphere during the 1920s (see U.S. INS 1978, t. 13).

By the early twentieth century, patterns of internal migration (and international migration, to a lesser extent) had emerged that would continue for the rest of the century. These patterns can be directly related to capitalism's penetration into precapitalist regions. One notable characteristic of this relationship is that the new zones of capitalist production were areas of expulsion of peasant labor and recruitment zones for seasonal estate labor. When new commercial crops were introduced in the 1940s, this pattern would be intensified.

Migration in the Postwar Period

The period beginning in the 1940s brought dramatic socioeconomic changes resulting from agricultural modernization and industrialization. This period also revealed the inability of traditional economic and political structures to accommodate the changes resulting from modernization, resulting in political conflict and crisis in Nicaragua, El Salvador, and Guatemala.

The 1940s witnessed the fall of dictators who had come to power in the early 1930s in El Salvador, Guatemala, and Honduras, as well as the initiation of reform-oriented governments in several countries determined to end their traditional economic dependence on exporting one or two primary products (coffee, bananas, or both). In Costa Rica and Guatemala, economic reform was accompanied by social and political reform—the establishment of the welfare state and the 1948 revolution in Costa Rica, and a short-lived democratic revolution culminating in a far-reaching but ultimately aborted agrarian reform in Guatemala. Economic changes included introducing new export products (especially cotton and sugar), making technological improvements in agriculture, and expanding roads, ports, and other infrastructure.

Introducing cotton particularly disrupted the peasant economy in the Pacific coastal zones, where cotton production displaced major centers of corn production. In Nicaragua, the cotton estates' expansion in the Pacific states of Chinandega and León forced peasants onto marginal lands in the northern mountainous regions or to the east, where many were then recruited for seasonal labor on the cotton estates. In El Salvador, where the Pacific coastal plain had already been taken over by large estates, tenant farmers who had constituted a resident labor force were driven off the land as cotton production became increasingly modernized, making a large permanent labor force in the cotton regions unnecessary. Lack of access to land forced many former peasants into the cash economy, because money was now needed to buy corn that they had previously grown. Labor for the harvest season was recruited in the slums of the major cities and the most impoverished peasant areas (Williams 1986, 54–65).[7]

According to the CSUCA study, by 1960 each country could be geographically divided into capitalist zones (the modern agricultural export sector and major urban areas) and zones of production for use (subsistence areas). In departments or provinces where production of export crops predominated, land was usually concentrated in large estates or plantations, tenancy or other forms of nonwage labor were replaced by wage workers, and chemical and technological inputs were used more intensively to varying degrees. Usufruct or subsistence areas were generally characterized by proliferating small holdings (*minifundia*) or, particularly in the highlands of Guatemala, community holdings devoted to producing basic grains (corn, beans, and rice) for consumption or domestic sales.

As the above overview indicates, no consistent correlation exists between the capitalist or subsistence nature of agriculture and migration patterns during this period. In El Salvador, Nicaragua, and Costa Rica, departments and provinces with the most dynamic capitalist development generally experienced net emigration, as small producers were pushed off the land by expanding estates. In El Salvador, migration flowed from the western coffee departments of Ahuchapán, Sonsonate, and Santa Ana and from the southern Pacific cotton region of La Paz toward the poorer subsistence departments in the north and east. One exception was Usulután, an important coffee- and cotton-growing region, which experienced net immigration. In Nicaragua, the expansion of coffee and later cotton production in the Pacific and central departments pushed peasants to the north central provinces of Jinotega and Nueva Segovia and to the frontier regions of San Juan and Zelaya. Other departments with net immigration were Managua, including the capital city (a strong pole of attraction) and Chinandega, a growing area of capitalist agriculture that was also a frontier area. In Costa Rica, the expansion of coffee production in the central mesa pushed subsistence agriculture into the peripheral lowland regions. Once again, this flow of migration from capitalist to subsistence zones has been accompanied by a reverse cyclical migration as *minifundistas* migrate temporarily to coffee, cotton, or banana zones for the harvest.

In Honduras, in contrast, the expansion of coffee, tobacco, sugarcane, and grain production, especially in the fertile northern region (also a center of banana production), attracted migrants who had been pushed from more densely populated areas where expansion of export-oriented production resulted in the land being monopolized. Thus the northern zone's attraction was as much the availability of land as the growth of capitalist production, and as a result, the expansion of capitalist estates worked by wage labor was accompanied by the extension of small and medium holdings in this region (CSUCA 1978a, 85, 311–13).

In Guatemala, only six departments registered population increases between 1950 and 1964 (Escuintla, Izabal, Guatemala, Retalhuleu, Suchitepequez, and Petén), while sixteen others registered declines, including all of those with a high proportion of Indians. The major zones of attraction fell into three categories: the newly industrializing urban centers, especially Guatemala City in the department of Guatemala; capitalist departments of the southern coast (Escuintla, Retalhuleu, and Suchitepequez) and Izabal in the northeast, a center for banana production; and zones of new colonization like Petén and Izabal (CSUCA 1978a, 83–114, 311–12). Internal migration within Guatemala was reinforced after the reversal of the short-lived agrarian reform of the early 1950s and expansion of export agriculture (including increased cotton production in the southern zone) throughout the 1950s and 1960s. Migration of rural workers from subsistence farming to large, export-oriented plantation areas increased notably on both seasonal and permanent bases, and migration from rural to urban areas accelerated despite relatively little expansion in formal employment.

The inconsistent relationship between the introduction of cotton production and migration can be partly explained by two factors. In some cases, peasants moved to forested areas along the Pacific coast that were being cleared for cultivation. After they had cleared the area and planted corn for two or three seasons, however, peasant cultivators were expelled to make room for cotton plantations. At the same time, in the first years of cotton production, much of the work was labor intensive and required permanent as well as seasonal labor, with growers giving peasants access to small plots of land in return for labor. This arrangement changed as cotton production became increasingly mechanized. While large numbers of seasonal workers were still wanted for the harvest, the need for permanent labor declined, resulting in workers being expelled from the estates (Williams 1986, 52–60).[8]

Seasonal migration of rural workers also extended across borders. Salvadorans migrated seasonally not only to the cotton-growing areas of their own country but also to Guatemala (where they constituted 10 percent of the seasonal labor force for cotton), to Nicaragua, and, prior to the soccer war, to Honduras (Williams 1986, 63). Guatemalan Indian workers migrated to harvest coffee in Chiapas in southern Mexico. According to one source (Monteforte Toledo 1959, 61), Guatemalan Indian braceros have crossed the Mexican border to work in coffee harvests since at least the 1920s, attracted by the wages, a low cost of living, and the possibility of bringing back contraband to sell at a profit. Some ten to fifteen thousand men and women reportedly crossed the border periodically for this reason in the late 1950s; in the next twenty years, the number grew to an estimated sixty thousand (Clay 1984, 46–49). Some Guatemalans inevitably ended up settling in Chiapas as a result of these migrations, with some blending into the local society and passing for Mexican. Others continued to preserve their distinct indigenous culture. Small-scale trade across the border followed the flow of labor, with both movements falling outside the realm of official regulation.

Migration across borders was also affected by political factors. The massacre of peasants following the 1932 uprising in the western states of El Salvador encouraged emigration to Honduras and other parts of the country (see below). Political upheaval or repression has also led to a periodic exodus of Guatemalans to other countries, as occurred following the ouster of the dictator Jorge Ubico in 1944 and the overthrow of the 1944–1954 revolution in 1954, a change that ushered in strong repression in subsequent decades.

Central American migration to the United States remained limited but continued to grow nonetheless. After declining to less than six thousand in the 1930s, it jumped to more than twenty-one thousand in the following decade (possibly reflecting U.S. recruitment of labor during the war years) and doubled again between 1951 and 1960 (U.S. INS 1978, t. 13).[9] The small number of Central American migrants, however, and the lack of data on country, age, and sex make it difficult to analyze these trends more specifically.

The Case of El Salvador

The dynamics of migration processes can be better understood by examining in greater detail historical developments in one country. As the smallest and most densely populated country in the region and source of the largest number of Central American immigrants to the United States, El Salvador exemplifies how capitalist penetration has resulted in extensive population movement within a limited space.[10]

In the second half of the nineteenth century, coffee displaced indigo as El Salvador's chief export, and elements of capitalist production began to displace subsistence production and previous production relations. Indigo production, hampered by the lack of roads and other infrastructure and by the mercantilist restrictions imposed by Spain on trade with Europe, had expanded only gradually over the centuries of colonial rule. But coffee production expanded rapidly in response to increasing prices for coffee on the world market, facilitated by the construction of roads, ports, and railroads. Although indigo production had coexisted with subsistence production, expanding coffee production involved dispossessing small subsistence producers, particularly communities in the western highlands of Santa Ana, Sonsonate, and Ahuachapán.

These processes were expedited by control of the state by the emerging coffee oligarchy. It enacted a series of liberal measures that eliminated flexible conditions of land tenure and usage, including communal forms of production, and instituted individual ownership of private property as the dominant form of tenure. Where legislation failed to dislodge the communities, force was used. The state role in establishing capitalism in El Salvador thus included constructing infrastructure to facilitate commercialization, passing legislation reinforcing private property in the means of production, eliminating communal property, and repressing those who resisted this restructuring (Browning 1971, 155ff.).

Although the shift to capitalist forms of property ownership was rapid, elements of precapitalist relations of production remained in El Salvador. To insure a permanent labor force, the coffee landowners often established nucleated villages for workers, who also received food in partial payment for their labor. But the landowners continued to depend on the subsistence sector for seasonal labor, provided by migrants from other regions of the country.

As noted above, at least two patterns of population movement resulted from the expansion of coffee production. First, the expulsion of subsistence peasants from their communal lands in the western departments forced many to migrate to other parts of the country, often to marginal rural areas for subsistence farming. Many went to the northern departments of Chalatenango, Cabañas, and Morazán, areas that were to become strongholds of guerrilla activity in the 1970s and 1980s. Second, a pattern of cyclical migration was reinforced as subsistence peasants from other parts of the country (including the northern departments) migrated temporarily to the coffee regions during the harvest season. Also reinforced was the pattern whereby migratory peasant families formed squatter settlements wherever they found unused land—on the fringes of private estates, on government land, along the roads and highways, and eventually even in the riverbeds that intersect the capital city of San Salvador. Partly a result of population pressures, squatting also constitutes a form of resistance to the concept of private ownership of land, an idea alien to the traditional concept of possession based on living on and working the land (Browning 1971, 219–21, 259–64; Pearce 1986, 45–46).

A drop in world coffee prices in the 1920s pushed many of the smaller coffee producers off the land when they defaulted on loans, leading to further concentration. This outcome was followed by a more dramatic drop in coffee exports in 1931 during the world depression, which led to massive unemployment of rural workers in the western zones of the country. This development proved to be central to the peasant uprising in this region in 1932, which was brutally repressed by the military government of General Maximiliano Hernández Martínez. Land concentration in the 1920s, unemployment resulting from the depression in the early 1930s, and particularly the 1932 massacre (in which an estimated thirty thousand peasants were killed) caused a major migratory flow from the western and central region of El Salvador toward the eastern provinces, especially Usulután, San Miguel, Morazán, and La Unión. Migrants also went to neighboring countries, especially Honduras, where they provided labor for banana plantations on the Caribbean coast (Durham 1979, 431; CSUCA 1978a, 141).

In the period following World War II, expanding production of cotton (particularly in the southeastern coastal zones of La Paz, Usulután, and San Miguel) and sugar (chiefly in the central and southwestern departments of San Salvador, Cuscatlán, San Vicente, La Libertad, and Sonsonate) increased land pressures and migration internally and to Honduras. According to the CSUCA study, by 1950 zones of capitalist penetration had encompassed the agro-export departments of the west (Santa Ana, Ahuachapán, and Sonsonate), the more urbanized west-central areas (especially San Salvador) and La Libertad, and the southern coastal departments (especially La Paz). The northern, central, and eastern states (Chalatenango, Cuscutlán Cabañas, San Vicente, Morazán, and La Unión) made up a subsistence region devoted chiefly to grain production with relatively low productivity. San Miguel had elements of both (CSUCA 1978a, 144–45). Prior to 1950, the subsistence areas were the main zones of in-migration (particularly Cabañas, Chalatenango, Morazán, and La Unión), which may be explained by the expulsion of rural workers and peasants from the western regions as a result of unemployment and repression in the 1930s combined with the expulsion of tenant farmers and smallholders from La Paz and other cotton-growing areas in the postwar period.

Beginning in 1950, industrial modernization was also stimulated under the governments of Colonels Oscar Osorio (1950–1956) and José María Lemus (1956–1960). Taking advantage of high world prices for coffee, the government began building infrastructure: completing the Pan American and coastal highways, starting construction of the Acajulta port (in Sonsonate), expanding hydroelectric plants, and extending housing construction. With infrastructure expanding and new legislation promoting industry (including the tariff-free import of capital goods and raw materials as well as tax exemptions), profits from coffee and cotton exports that had been deposited abroad began to be invested in industry. Foreign investment in manufacturing also grew rapidly, and when world coffee prices dropped at the end of the 1950s, foreign loans began to displace export earnings as a major source of financing (CSUCA 1978a, 147–50).

The 1950s brought a marked change in the pattern of migration flows in El Salvador. Subsistence regions of the north and east, including the provinces adjacent to Honduras, lost population, while San Salvador and La Libertad and to a lesser extent Ahuachapán and Sonsonate in the west began to attract migrants. In San Salvador, La Libertad, and the eastern department of San Miguel, migrants largely moved to urban areas, while migrants to Sonsonate and Ahuachapán chose rural areas (also true of La Paz). But in the southern coastal area (including the department of La Paz and southern parts of San Vicente, Usulatán, and San Miguel), cotton estates continued to expand into grain-producing areas, a major factor in continued migration to Honduras (CSUCA 1978b, 72–75, 327–28). As for internal migration, 36 percent of net negative migration flows came from the poorer subsistence provinces of Cabañas, Chalatenango, and Morazán. Thus the flow of migration from the west to the north and east, typical of the pre-1950 period, had been reversed, with population flows from the north and east moving toward the center and west.

One explanation for this shift in migration patterns is that it was primarily a rural-urban flow, particularly to San Salvador, which grew by more than fifty-five thousand inhabitants. Between 1950 and 1961, 73 percent of all migrants moved to the cities, and 41 percent to the department of San Salvador. Other departments with major urban centers (Santa Ana, San Miguel, and La Libertad) recorded net urban migration gains ranging from three to six thousand (CSUCA 1978b, 73–85). Because the economy was expanding in the 1950s, one may surmise that the growth of industry and urban services enhanced the attractiveness of urban areas of these departments. At the same time, net rural gains occurred in the western coffee-producing departments of Ahuachapán and Sonsonate and the southern cotton department of La Paz. In the coffee regions, limited possibilities for expanding into new areas suitable for growing coffee resulted in intensive use of labor and technology to increase output and thus take advantage of the coffee boom. Finally, the decline in productivity in basic grains suggests that the poorer lands of the northern and eastern zones were becoming less productive, another possible explanation for out-migration from these areas.

Emigration to Honduras continued to increase, with Salvadorans finding work on banana plantations in the northern coastal area of Honduras or establishing their own farms closer to the Salvadoran-Honduran border. Estimates of Salvadorans in Honduras increased from twenty-five to thirty thousand in the late 1930s, to one hundred thousand in 1949, to three hundred and fifty thousand by the 1960s (Durham 1979, 59, 124–25). As Durham points out, striking parallels between internal migration and migration to Honduras suggest similar causation (see Durham 1979, t. 2.6, p. 61).

Finally, increased labor demands during the harvest resulted in large seasonal migrations to work in the coffee, sugar, and cotton harvests between October and April, particularly in November and December. During the rest of the year, migrants returned to their homes to survive on savings, farm subsistence plots, or work in the urban informal sector. Based on estimates of the economically active rural population and the labor needs at the peak of the harvest season in each state, one study posited two major seasonal flows: from San Salvador, Sonsonate, and Cuscatlán to the coffee harvests of Ahuachapán and Santa Ana; and from Morazán, Cabanas, and La Paz to Usulután and San Miguel (CSUCA 1978b, 352–54). By 1970 an estimated five hundred thousand temporary workers were making this annual pilgrimage (Achaerandio 1983, 4).

Thus in El Salvador, internal migration, international migration, and seasonal migration represent three responses to capitalist penetration and its consequences for subsistence production and government initiatives to insure conditions for production, whether through repression, legislation, or incentives to investment. The shift from subsistence to commercial agriculture for export meant expanding commercial estates at the expense of smallholdings and driving small peasant producers to more remote areas of the country, to Honduras, and to new squatter settlements on the fringes of private agricultural estates or on unused rural or urban land. Labor-saving technological innovations resulted in rural workers being expelled into subsistence rural areas or urban centers, which became poles of attraction due to expanding industry and urban services. Finally, declining productivity in subsistence areas in the north and east turned these regions into zones of permanent emigration to urban areas of El Salvador or to Honduras. They also provided seasonal migrants to work on coffee, sugar, and cotton estates.

Migration in the 1960s and 1970s

Quantitative and qualitive changes in Central American migration flows beginning in the 1970s, particularly in international migration, can be explained largely by events of the 1960s and 1970s. These decades were characterized by contradictions built into rapid modernization based on foreign investment in a context where traditional socioeconomic structures remained intact, as in Nicaragua, Guatemala, and El Salvador. Demands for change resulting from modernization and its effects were resisted by traditional political structures, which responded with increased repression that intensified opposition.

As indicated, the period following World War II brought agricultural modernization based on expanding export agricultural into cotton and sugar production and, in El Salvador and Guatemala, on limited industrialization. By the end of the 1950s, however, economists, business groups, and government officials in these societies had recognized the limitations of depending on commodity exports and were seeking to promote import-substitution industrialization by creating a regional market (reducing or eliminating tariffs between the Central American countries) and by attracting foreign investment. Regional integration succeeded in obtaining foreign investment (primarily from the United States and later from Western Europe and Japan), chiefly in processing and assembly industries and in nontraditional export crops. Creation of the Central American Common Market and consequent foreign investment fostered impressive rates of growth, which averaged 7.7 percent in the region as a whole during the 1960s. But like previous modernization projects, this one led to numerous dislocations that affected rural and urban areas.

Modernization's impact on the rural areas where most Central Americans lived and worked varied according to country and situation. In some cases, it meant the takeover of peasant lands or Indian communities when members of the landowning oligarchy expanded their estates or government officials seized control of areas where new industrial projects had raised land values (as in the northern Transversal strip of Guatemala). In other cases, modernization caused a shift from subsistence farming to growing cash crops destined for U.S. supermarkets (like cauliflower and snow peas). In still other cases, it meant a reduction in the work force due to mechanized agriculture and the shift in production from agriculture to livestock in response to the market for beef created by rapid growth in hamburger and fast-food chains in the United States. Thus several patterns emerged: the proleterianization or semiproletarianization of the peasantry, a shift from subsistence to market-oriented production, and, in some cases, reduced availability of agricultural jobs (Chinchilla and Hamilton 1984b, 240–42).

In El Salvador, agricultural modernization caused a dramatic shift in land tenure. In 1961, 11.8 percent of rural households were landless; by 1971, 29.1 percent owned no land, and by 1975, 40.9 percent. In addition, the percentage of farms having less than one hectare increased from 40.4 to 49 percent between 1950 and 1971 (Deere and Diskin 1984, 18).

The precarious economic conditions in which many Central Americans lived were aggravated by increasing inflation in the 1970s, due largely to the increased prices of imports (particularly petroleum), which in turn affected prices of agricultural and manufactured products. Prices of imported inputs for manufacturing industry increased by 11.4 percent annually between 1970 and 1978, and the overall inflation rate increased by 12.8 percent annually between 1970 and 1977 (Weeks 1985, 68–71, 148–49). As a result of changes in the previous two decades, substantial sectors of the population that had previously depended wholly or partly on subsistence farming now depended on cash income and were therefore hit hard by price increases. Even in the sectors that benefited from minimum-wage laws and wage adjustments, wage increases could not keep up with price increases.

In addition to the economic dislocations accompanying modernization, the 1960s and 1970s witnessed an increased U.S. presence in El Salvador, particularly in the form of multinational corporations investing in manufacturing. In contrast to Guatemala, Honduras, and Costa Rica, where U.S. banana companies had operated for decades, and Nicaragua, which had a long history of U.S. military, political, and financial intervention, direct U.S. penetration in El Salvador was relatively new. In all five countries, however, increased contact with U.S. manufacturing, commercial, and financial interests undoubtedly expanded information about the United States, including work and educational opportunities. Employment in U.S. companies may also have made migration to the United States more accessible: a worker in a Texas Instruments plant in San Salvador could, at least hypothetically, transfer his or her skills to an electronics assembly plant in the United States. Or a domestic servant working for an American family in Nicaragua could work for a similar family (or, in some cases, the same family) in the United States. The growth of a low-wage, semi-informal economy in the United States during the 1970s, based on services or subcontracting, took advantage of an increasing undocumented labor force and provided work for immigrants from Central America and other areas.

Additional factors led to dislocations in specific countries. The 1969 war between El Salvador and Honduras abruptly ended Salvadoran migration to Honduras and caused the rapid repatriation of an estimated two hundred thousand Salvadorans. This return migration drastically aggravated already serious pressures on the land and undoubtedly increased the number and proportion of landless rural workers in El Salvador between 1961 and 1971. In Guatemala too, economic dislocations were aggravated by other factors.

During the 1960s and 1970s, a succession of military presidents and their colleagues exploited political positions to amass personal wealth. In the mid-1970s, for example, they engaged in rapacious speculation in the northern Transversal strip crossing several states in the highland region, which became the construction site for a road and an oil pipeline to the coast (Black, Jamail, and Chinchilla 1984). During this time, entire Indian communities were displaced into other regions of the country or across the border into Mexico.

Finally, a factor generally discussed in studies of refugee populations, rather than in migration studies, was increasing governmental and extragovernmental repression, which targeted groups seeking to organize around issues and problems resulting from economic dislocations: peasant organizations set up to contest land takeovers, labor unions demanding increased wages and improved working conditions, protests by Indian communities who had lost their land in Guatemala, and demonstrations against increases in food prices and bus fares in the major cities. Death squads made up of members of the landowning oligarchy and security and military forces in Guatemala and El Salvador targeted peasant leaders, union militants, and political activists. In El Salvador in 1969, the military formed a paramilitary organization among peasants known as ORDEN (short for the Organización Democrática Nacionalista) to carry out surveillance and even assassinations of selected leaders and militants (Black, Jamail, and Chinchilla 1984, 83–97; Montgomery 1982, 88–89).

All these factors significantly affected migration during the 1960s and 1970s. Migration flows increased substantially, and new patterns emerged. For the period from 1950 to 1973, the CSUCA study of Central American migration suggests three trends. First, mobility increased in these years: the number of internal migrants doubled in Guatemala, tripled in Nicaragua, and quintupled in Honduras (comparable figures for El Salvador were not available). Second, regions with agricultural modernization tended to expel population except in areas that also contained frontier or new colonization zones (such as Izabal in Guatemala). Third, new subsistence areas and urban centers became zones of attraction (CSUCA 1978a, 322–27).

In Costa Rica, the dominant migration trend from the 1920s (net emigration from the central mesa where coffee production predominated) was reversed in the early 1960s due to new economic circumstances. Beginning in the 1920s, labor surpluses had emerged in the central mesa and the wages of coffee workers declined, causing an exodus to the surrounding lowlands, which became the new frontier for subsistence farmers. Gradually, large landowners also amassed vast holdings in these regions. In the 1960s and 1970s, U.S. and multinational lending agencies as well as the Costa Rican government began to promote livestock production for beef export, which expanded these estates further and shifted production from agriculture to livestock. For example, in the Pacific north province of Guanacaste, cattle estates expanded at the expense of small farms, and the shift of agricultural estates to livestock production required much less labor and caused increasing unemployment. This trend led to a shift in migration patterns, with migrants leaving the cattle-producing areas of the lowlands for other peripheral areas or urban centers, particularly the capital city of San José. But despite growth in industrial production (7.1 percent annually between 1965 and 1973), the capital-intensive nature of production meant that new employment in industry was limited, increasing from 11.7

percent to only 12.9 percent between 1963 and 1973 (Taylor 1980). As Edward Taylor summarized the situation, "The Costa Rican peasant—once small landholder in the meseta, displaced, then small landholder in the periphery, again displaced—is left with no alternative but to set out on a trek which will almost invariably take him to the urban center. Yet the system which strips the peasant of his livelihood in the countryside denies him a livelihood in the city. For most migrants, there will be no jobs available wherever their migrations take them" (Taylor 1980, 89).

A similar dynamic appears to have affected migration trends in El Salvador, where the centralization and urban attraction evident in the previous decade became even more pronounced between 1961 and 1971.[11] San Salvador attracted by far the largest number of migrants (40.8 percent of the total), followed by La Libertad and Sonsonate. The remaining departments reported net emigration. These figures, however, tend to hide the intensity of migration flows because many department have experienced levels of emigration and immigration (often in the form of exchange with adjacent departments), possibly reflecting the high population density (CSUCA 1978b, 82–83, 85). This kind of exchange has occurred in the two largest urban centers after San Salvador: Santa Ana, with thirty-two thousand immigrants and almost fifty-seven thousand emigrants, and San Miguel, with thirty-one thousand immigrants and fifty-one thousand emigrants (CSUCA 1978b, 83–89). The poorest rural areas, in the mountainous northern departments of Chalatenango, Cabañas, and Morazán, have experienced high levels of net emigration. In fact, it appears that both capitalist and subsistence rural areas have become areas of net emigration, presumably reflecting the fact that no "new" subsistence areas exist in El Salvador.

Deteriorating conditions in the countryside, as indicated by increasing numbers of landless rural families, and the attraction of the urban centers as a result of industrialization (especially San Salvador) undoubtedly contributed to migration trends in this period. But as noted, the growth of industry and related services were able to absorb only part of the growing work force because of the capital-intensive nature of new industry. While the manufacturing sector grew by 24 percent between 1961 and 1971, employees in industry increased by only 6 percent. Growth in urban and industry-related services could not absorb the difference between the numbers of rural-urban migrants and jobs available in manufacturing. By the early 1970s, 40 percent of the nonagricultural labor force was working in the informal sector, and unemployment in San Salvador had reached 10 percent (Armstrong and Shenk 1982, 47; Deere and Diskin 1984, 32).

As indicated above, the number of Guatemalans migrating to southern Mexico increased from an annual average of ten to fifteen thousand in the 1950s to an estimated sixty thousand per year in the 1970s. The expulsion of Salvadorans from Honduras during the 1969 war also augmented Salvadoran migration to Guatemala, which has been estimated between 1973 and 1984 at seventy thousand, most going to the frontier and central-south departments or to Mexico (Torres Rivas 1985, 28).

This period also saw dramatic changes in patterns of migration to the United States. As noted, prior to the mid-1960s, a small but growing number of immigrants migrated from Central America. During the following decade, the number of legally admitted Central American immigrants more than doubled, from forty-five thousand between 1951 and 1960 to more than one hundred thousand between 1961 and 1970, and exceeded one hundred and thirty-four thousand during the 1970s (U.S. INS 1978, tt. 13, 14; U.S. INS 1984, t. IMMI.2). The number of illegal immigrants increased even more dramatically, as indicated by the number deported, most of them for having "entered without inspection or with false documents." Moreover, the U.S. Immigration and Nationalization Service (INS) estimates that for every undocumented person apprehended, another three to five remain in the United States undetected. Between 1969 and 1978, the number of Guatemalans deported increased from one hundred to twelve hundred and the number of Salvadorans from one hundred to thirty-four hundred (U.S. INS 1978, t. 27).

Growth in the number of Central Americans coming to the United States in the 1970s has been documented in a study of Central Americans and Mexicans in California based primarily on the 1980 census. This count found that 40 percent of Central American immigrants living in California in 1980 had entered during the previous five years and that 63 percent of these lived in Los Angeles. More than half of the Central American immigrants were women, 45 percent of those over twenty-five had completed high school, about 25 percent had attended college, and some 30 percent had worked in white-collar occupations. Thus in California, at least, Central American immigrants came disproportionately from the upper educational and occupational segments of the population in a region where only one-eighth of the economically active population had completed more than six years of school (Wallace 1986, 659–64). Most Central American migrants who arrived in the United States before 1975 presumably came for economic reasons, but by the second half of the 1970s, many were escaping violence, repression, or persecution at home, which began to accelerate in the mid-1970s.

This immigration coincided with a period of economic restructuring in the United States that involved a decline in traditional manufacturing industries accompanied by growth in high-technology industries and high- and low-skilled services (Sassen 1988). Once in the United States, many of the Central Americans were employed in low-paying jobs in the rapidly growing service sectors, in manufacturing sectors that rely on low-cost foreign labor (like the garment industry), or in agriculture.

Thus the dramatic increase in internal migration, intraregional migration, and the number of Salvadorans and Guatemalans coming to the United States during the 1970s can be correlated with deteriorating economic conditions, increased repression in their own countries in the late 1970s, and perceived opportunities and "indirect" labor recruitment in the United States. Conditions in Central America worsened further in the late 1970s and the 1980s, when the economic situation deteriorated into a regionwide crisis while political polarization and conflict deepened in Guatemala, El Salvador, and Nicaragua.

Population Movements since the Late 1970s

In the last fifteen years or so, war and political upheaval in Nicaragua, El Salvador, and Guatemala compounded by rapidly deteriorating economic conditions have resulted in massive dislocations in all three countries. In Nicaragua, the Somoza regime countered the Sandinista campaign with massive repression, including extensive bombing of rural areas and finally the major cities, prior to the Sandinista victory in July 1979. In El Salvador, revolutionary movements that had developed throughout the 1970s coordinated forces and began a military offensive in the early 1980s. During the same period in Guatemala, a revolutionary movement emerged incorporating Indian and non-Indian (*ladino*) populations.

These revolutionary offensives resulted in escalating violence by military and security forces as well as by death squads. In Guatemala, government-instigated terrorism against opposition leaders in urban areas combined with a brutal counterinsurgency campaign against the Indian population that killed thousands and displaced hundreds of thousands. Nicaragua had not yet recovered from the effects of the revolution against Somoza when the new Sandinista government was confronted by counterrevolution, organized and financed by the U.S. Central Intelligence Agency. In El Salvador, the war against the guerrilla forces often involved attacks against civilian populations in rural areas, including the massacre of the entire population of villages believed to be sympathetic to the guerrillas. Beginning in 1979, the United States became more and more enmeshed in these conflicts, resulting in an exponential increase in the militarization of the region as well as in the technological level of conflict, particularly in El Salvador (Leach, Miller, and Hatfield 1985).

Political repression and war have also aggravated the region's economic stagnation, an additional factor in displacement and migration. In El Salvador, national production declined 33 percent between 1978 and 1983, and by the mid-1980s, gross national product per capita had fallen to the level of the 1950s. The causes include massive capital flight and economic distortions resulting from U.S. financing of balance of payments, which has sustained the commercial sector while production declined (Weeks 1985, 191). Salvadoran unemployment is estimated at 33 percent, and estimates of combined unemployment and underemployment range from 50 to 75 percent (*Coyuntura Económica* 1989).[12]

The combined effects of political crisis, war, and the economic crisis aggravated by political conditions have transformed a normal migration flow into massive displacement and exodus. In terms of internal displacement, it has been estimated that by 1987 up to a million Central Americans (including a quarter-million Nicaraguans, one hundred thousand to a quarter-million Guatemalans, and half a million Salvadorans) had been displaced within their own countries (Fagen 1988, 75).

In El Salvador, the first wave displaced by the war were peasants from rural areas in the northern province of Chalatenango and the northeastern province of Morazán. During 1980 these first major guerrilla strongholds came under heavy government attacks that included massacres of civilian populations (U.S. Committee for Refugees 1984, 9). Initially, most of the displaced persons remained in their departments, moving only from the rural areas to cities and towns, presumably hoping to return to their homes soon (CONADES 1983, 2). But new waves of refugees followed the first as the war intensified and expanded to other zones of El Salvador, and the movement from rural areas to municipalities was accompanied by displacement to the larger cities, especially San Salvador. Between 1980 and 1982, the military and security forces' campaign against the organized opposition and peasants suspected of sympathizing with the guerrillas reached massive levels in the cities as well as the countryside, accounting for the huge increase in Salvadorans dislocated to other countries. In 1984 the military launched a drive to eliminate the civilian population from guerrilla-controlled or -contested zones, including massive bombing and strafing of designated areas followed by the destruction of homes and crops. In 1985 the guerrilla forces expanded their operations to all departments of El Salvador, including the little-affected western region, which led to increased military operations in these regions. The new initiatives exacerbated the continuing displacement of Salvadorans (Montes Mozo et al. 1985, 35–40, 80–83).

Various studies of the displaced population in El Salvador indicate that it consists of the most destitute sectors of the Salvadoran population, whose situation has been made even more desperate as a result of their circumstances. Of the displaced, the vast majority (80 to 90 percent) come from rural areas, more than half are under fifteen years of age, and half are illiterate. The mortality rate is high (24.4 per thousand, according to one study, 67 percent of the deaths claiming children under five). Already low levels of employment have decreased as a result of displacement: unemployment increased from 58 to 74 percent of the economically active population after forced migration, according to one study (Alens 1984).[13]

In Guatemala, military attacks against the indigenous populations in the northern departments caused massive displacements, with those who could fleeing to Mexico or the United States. Some of those displaced within Guatemala were subsequently obliged by force or hunger to return to areas controlled by the military and to join civil patrols to help the counterinsurgency campaign of the armed forces.

In Nicaragua, those displaced directly or indirectly by the Contra war include the indigenous population near the Honduran border, who were resettled in the interior, and small peasant families in the north central departments of Nicaragua. Some indigenous families later returned to the border areas.

Overall, emigration to other countries also increased substantially. Between 1971 and 1978, the annual rate of Salvadoran emigration was 5.1 per thousand inhabitants; by 1978–1980, it rose to 16.2 per thousand (Torres Rivas and Jiménez 1985, 28). Refugees seemed to follow patterns established during previous migration: Nicaraguans went to Honduras, to Costa Rica, and more recently to the United States; Salvadorans went to refugee camps in Honduras and in smaller numbers to Nicaragua and Costa Rica as well as to Guatemala, Mexico, and the United States; Guatemalans usually went to Mexico and the United States and sometimes to other Central American countries. Much migration within Central America consisted of rural populations moving to border regions: Nicaraguans into Costa Rica and Honduras, Salvadorans into Honduras, and Guatemalans into southern Mexico.

Nearly all the estimated two hundred thousand Nicaraguans who had fled between April 1978 and April 1979 (most of them to Costa Rica and Honduras) returned to Nicaragua when the Sandinistas won in 1979. A new exodus began in the 1980s, however, partly in opposition to the Sandinista government and partly aggravated by the U.S.-financed Contra war. This wave included Miskito Indians and other indigenous populations of the Atlantic coast region. By 1987, twenty-two to one hundred thousand Nicaraguans were living in Costa Rica, forty-three thousand in Honduras, and up to twenty thousand in Guatemala (Fagen 1988, 75–76). Following agreements between the Sandinista government and the Atlantic coast indigenous groups, several thousand members of these groups returned to Nicaragua.[14]

By 1987, some 85 percent of the Central Americans who had left their countries were living in Mexico and the United States. Most of them passed through the Soconusco zone of Mexico, a narrow fertile plane along the Pacific coast that has become the traditional entering point for Central American emigrants. Although many Guatemalans and most Salvadorans continue on to Mexico City and in some cases to the United States, the Mexican states near the Guatemalan border, especially Chiapas, have become major centers for Central Americans. Nearly all of these migrants belong to indigenous populations from the northern and western highland states of Guatemala. Being of Mayan descent, they have a heritage similar to the population of Chiapas, to which they are also linked by trade and by social and kinship ties.

The indigenous Guatemalan population that has fled to Chiapas consists of two major groups. The first is made up of Guatemalan heads of household who have traditionally migrated to Chiapas from the western states on a seasonal basis to work on the coffee plantations in the Soconusco region. After 1979, as the Guatemalan government's counterinsurgency program targeted indigenous communities in these areas, the number of migrants in Chiapas grew as new groups arrived, sometimes with their families, and seasonal migrants stayed on rather than return to Guatemala as in the past. A second group consists of families from the northern states, particularly the regions of Quiché, Alta Verapaz, Izabal, and El Petén, which had been affected by the Franja Transversal project in the 1970s. In the early 1980s, indigenous communities in these areas were also subjected to brutal government persecution. The survivors fled first to the mountains and then en masse to Mexico, where they lived in refugee camps along the frontier in Chiapas. Some were subsequently moved to camps in Campeche and Quintana Roo. Since 1986, some three thousand have returned to their homes in Guatemala, but most remain discouraged by continued military control of the countryside (Aguayo and Fagen 1988, 1–7; Aguayo 1985, 29–38; Manz 1988, 145–55; Salvadó 1988).[15]

Central Americans who have traveled on to Mexico City and other parts of Mexico are much more difficult to analyze than those in Chiapas. In the first place, they are scattered, having traveled individually or in families rather than as entire communities. Most are undocumented, and many attempt to pass as Mexicans. Studies of Central Americans in Mexico City have found that unlike the migrants in Chiapas, they are younger, urban, middle- or lower-middle-class, and relatively well-educated. Thus they are in a much better position than the indigenous migrants in Chiapas to take advantage of informal migration networks established by family members or friends who have previously migrated to the United States (Aguayo 1985, 42–45, 160).[16]

Finally, the number of Salvadorans and Guatemalans coming to the United States since 1979 has continued to grow. Since 1988 the number of Nicaraguans has also increased rapidly, motivated by opposition to the Sandinista government or disintegrating economic conditions. Because most of these migrants are undocumented, exact figures are not available. Salvadorans continue to represent the second-largest number of nonlegal immigrants apprehended by the INS (after Mexicans). The number of undocumented Salvadorans apprehended doubled between 1977 and 1981 from eight to sixteen thousand and reached seventeen thousand in 1985 (data from the INS). Most observers, noting the increased number of Salvadorans and Guatemalans in Los Angeles and other major U.S. cities, believe that the rate of increase has actually been much greater. One recent study estimates that three-quarters of a million to 1.3 million Central American migrants are living in the United States, two-thirds of them Salvadorans, and up to one-fifth Guatemalans (Ruggles and Fix 1985, 45–47). The U.S. General Accounting Office estimates the number of undocumented Salvadorans in the United States at six to eight hundred thousand (U.S. GAO 1989).

The majority of Central Americans (up to a half million) live in Los Angeles, with substantial numbers in San Francisco, Texas (especially Houston), Washington, New York, Chicago, New Orleans, and Miami. Many have been able to take advantage of existing migration networks through Mexico, and some have obtained help from family, friends, or even communities already established in the United States (Rodríguez 1987; Ruggles and Fix 1985; Schoultz 1987, 30–33; Montes Mozo and García Vázquez 1988, 28–29). Those lacking such networks have tended to come to areas with established Latino populations that have cultural and sometimes political affinities (like the Mexicans in Los Angeles or Cubans in Miami). While Salvadorans constitute the majority of Central Americans in most cities (followed by Guatemalans), Nicaraguans predominate in Miami and Hondurans in New Orleans (Ruggles, Manson, Trutko, and Thomas 1985; Ruggles, Fix, and Thomas 1985).

The large number of undocumented Salvadorans and Guatemalans coming to the United States in the 1970s and 1980s indicates that U.S. immigration restrictions have had little impact on the number of Central Americans arriving, although they undeniably affect the process of migration (for example, in forcing migrants to depend on expensive and often unreliable coyotes as "guides"). They also affect the experience of immigrants once they arrive. Similarly, while U.S. refugee and asylum policies tend to reflect foreign policy concerns and thus have tended to discriminate against Central Americans with the partial exception of Nicaraguans, little evidence suggests that they have deterred immigrants from coming or from returning if deported. It is still early to evaluate the consequences of the Immigration Reform and Control Act (IRCA), which grants amnesty to undocumented immigrants who can prove they arrived prior to 1982 but penalizes employers for hiring workers who cannot prove they are here legally. Most preliminary studies indicate, however, that IRCA has had little effect in deterring immigrants from coming to the United States, although the law has made it more difficult for them to obtain employment (Espenshade et al. 1988).[17]

To what extent does the influx of Central Americans since 1979 represent a continuation of previous immigration patterns rather than a qualitatively new phenomenon? Because of the recent arrival and undocumented status of most Central Americans in the United States, information on this population is fragmentary and even contradictory. Compared with the Salvadorans displaced within El Salvador or in refugee camps in Honduras or with Guatemalans in Mexican refugee camps, the majority coming to the United States appear to have higher levels of education and income, similar to those in Mexico City (Ruggles and Fix 1985; Montes Mozo and García Vázquez 1988, 14–24). But Salvadorans' educational and income levels are undoubtedly lower on average than those of earlier migrants to the United States, and a larger proportion come from rural areas.

It would thus be a mistake to assume that Central Americans migrating to Mexico and the United States during the 1980s represent a simple continuation of previous migration flows. Aside from the greater numbers and socioeconomic differences, many of those coming after 1979 have directly experienced violence or repression, including the assassination of family members, or have themselves been targets of detention, interrogation, and even torture. Many Central Americans living in Mexico and the United States assert that survival and personal safety are their primary motivations for emigrating. Although rural communities in Guatemàla and El Salvador have been the major victims of military violence, persons targeted for repression by death squads and security forces tend to be urban dwellers who are relatively well-educated, including labor and party leaders, students, and professionals (Aguayo and Fagen 1988, 30; Chinchilla and Hamilton 1984a, 11–17; Montes Mozo and García Vázquez 1988, 13; Aguayo 1985, 43, 146, 154). Some young men from El Salvador flee recruitment by the armed forces or the guerrillas (Montes Mozo and García Vázquez 1988, 31). In short, those immigrating since 1979 appear to represent a broader socioeconomic spectrum than past immigrants to the United States, and a large proportion are coming for reasons related to the war.

Many who have not been affected directly by violence and conflict have been affected indirectly, like the factory workers who have lost their jobs because the conflict has prevented production from continuing (Rodriguez 1987, 22). Thus the situation is complex, because individuals and families often immigrate to another country for a combination of economic, social, and political reasons and also because the economic difficulties of the Central American countries have been prolonged and aggravated by political conflict (Stanley 1987, 146).

Current migration flows exhibit elements of both continuity and change. War, increased levels of violence, and conditions of economic crisis generated or aggravated by the political situation have become key factors in migration to the United States, to other Central American countries, and to Mexico. At the same time, like regional migrants, recent migrants to the United States for whatever reasons are taking advantage of previously established patterns of migration and networks of family, friends, or other Latino communities already in the country.

SUMMARY AND CONCLUSIONS

The foregoing analysis confirms that national and international capital penetration, resulting structural changes, and foreign intervention are central to explaining Central American migration. This review of the Central American migration experience also demonstrates that causal processes are complex and that careful analysis of each situation is necessary to determine precisely how they will affect migration.

Effects of Capitalist Penetration on Migration

Capitalist expansion in its various forms has resulted in migration between capitalist and precapitalist sectors in each country, while constantly reducing the size of precapitalist sectors and the capacity of capitalist sectors tó absorb new workers. But while our earlier discussion suggests that capitalist penetration results in migration from less-developed to more-developed areas, the Central American experience indicates that the direction and patterns of migration vary according to conditions and structures within the peripheral economy or region.

Virtually all major instances of capitalist penetration have led to internal or international migration: the introduction and expansion of the coffee export economy in the nineteenth century; the creation of U.S. banana enclaves at the turn of the century; agricultural modernization by introducing technological innovations in existing crops and introducing or expanding estates that produce new export crops (especially cotton and sugar) in the postwar period; and industrial modernization in the 1960s and 1970s via creation of the Central American Common Market and increased foreign investment.

In addition to the direct effects of capital penetration, the changing dynamic of world capitalism has affected Central American economies in at least two respects. First, it has directly or indirectly affected penetration of foreign capital in the region. Thus the expansion of U.S. capitalism at the turn of the century was manifested in its growing economic and political hegemony in the Caribbean region, evidenced in Central America in the expansion of United Fruit (and later Standard Fruit) and in U.S. political, military, and financial intervention in Nicaragua. Second, economic cycles, booms, and depressions directly affect economies tied into the world market, whether through depressed (or increased) commodity prices, the opening of new export markets or closing of existing ones, or the transfer of inflated costs through the import of raw materials, machinery, or other agricultural and industrial inputs.

One response to changes and dislocations resulting from these global trends has been migration. Massive unemployment among Salvadoran coffee workers caused by depression-generated production cutbacks in the 1930s was one factor (along with the *matanza* of 1932) in the migration from the western coffee regions to central and eastern sectors of the country and into Honduras. Inflation produced by the oil crisis of the 1970s was passed along to consumers in Central America through higher costs of imported consumer goods or inputs to production and contributed to the dislocations of the 1970s that led many Central Americans to emigrate north. Currently, cotton workers in El Salvador are being driven from the southeastern regions of the country by production cutbacks, while world cotton prices remain well below the costs of production.

Although a relationship can be established between capital penetration and migration in Central America, the extent and direction of this migration vary according to a number of factors. If the affected region is sparsely populated or relatively uninhabited, then little or no migration may result, or the region may even become a zone of attraction, as occurred with the development of banana enclaves along the northern coast of Honduras in the early twentieth century and the agricultural expansion following World War II. In some cases, migration to these areas may be reversed, as occurred with the opening of certain areas for cotton cultivation in the postwar period. In such cases, peasants are drawn to clear forested areas, then expelled as cotton plantations take over areas they have cleared and planted in corn; or a labor force attracted to the region to work on cotton plantations in return for small plots of land is subsequently expelled as cotton becomes increasingly mechanized.

In more densely populated areas, where precapitalist structures of production exist, peasants are pushed from their land when it is taken over for capitalist production. In some instances, they may migrate to more developed urban centers, but in other cases, they migrate to more marginal areas to reestablish a subsistence economy. This pattern has recurred in several Central American countries: in El Salvador and parts of Guatemala with the introduction of coffee production in the nineteenth century; in El Salvador and Nicaragua with the expansion of cotton production in the postwar period; in Costa Rica with the transfer of agricultural land to livestock production in the 1960s and 1970s; and in Guatemala with the shift from subsistence to cash-crop production in the highlands and more dramatically with the expulsion of the indigenous population from communal lands during the development of the northern Franja Transversal in the 1970s. As opportunities for subsistence agriculture contract, migration takes the form of emigration to neighboring countries, as exemplified by Salvadorans moving to Honduras.

Capitalist penetration has also resulted in migration to the core economy itself, once a relationship is established between the core and peripheral economies. Thus factors determining the direction of migratory flows of uprooted populations include the existence of unincorporated areas in the home or neighboring countries where peasant agriculture can be resumed (an increasingly limited option in Central America), the existence and nature of opportunities in the capitalist sector of the economy, and the existence of structural and institutional ties between the peripheral economy and that of the core.

Capitalist or Core Economies as "Poles of Attraction" for Labor through Economic, Social, and Cultural Influences

The same process of capital penetration that pushes peasant cultivators off the land often results in cyclical migration due to seasonal labor recruitment as peasants migrate to work in coffee, cotton, and sugar harvests—a process evident in virtually every country in Central America. Also, areas of capitalist penetration may become poles of attraction with the opening of new lands for settlement (as in Honduras) or in response to actual or perceived opportunities for jobs, education, and other services resulting from urbanization and industrializaton. Such opportunity has been at least one factor in rural-urban migration during the postwar industrialization in several countries. The fact that in many cases these opportunities did not materialize is evidenced by the large percentages of urban populations found in the informal sector (particularly in El Salvador), even before the political conflicts and economic crisis of the 1980s. The cultural and economic penetration accompanying the expansion of foreign investment during the 1960s and 1970s undoubtedly became a factor of attraction operating in conjunction with factors of expulsion (the dislocations accompanying modernization) to account for increase migration to the United States during this period. Immigration to the United States also followed a pattern of "indirect" labor recruitment as new Central American immigrants were absorbed into low-paying jobs in agriculture, industry, and the rapidly expanding service sectors in the 1970s and early 1980s.

The Role of the Peripheral State in the Development Process and in Managing Resulting Contradictions

The role of the state in capital accumulation has affected migration significantly. One example is the legislation enacted by liberal governments to insure land and labor for coffee production during the nineteenth century. It eliminated forms of communal property and forced smallholders off their land in El Salvador and forced indigenous communities in the Guatemalan highlands to supply labor during the harvest seasons. Another example is the creation of development poles by providing infrastructure and incentives to encourage investment. Other state policies have also affected migration, such as military recruitment in El Salvador and Nicaragua, which has led to an exodus of young men of draft age to neighboring countries, Mexico, and the United States.

Efforts to manage contradictions arising from the development process or resulting dislocations have been most successful in Costa Rica. In general, however, and particularly in Guatemala, El Salvador, and Nicaragua, the state has leaned heavily, if not exclusively, toward repression, which has led to politically motivated emigration. Examples are numerous: the matanza in El Salvador in 1932, which drove Salvadoran peasants from the western departments eastward and into Honduras; the destruction of indigenous villages in Guatemala and repression in other parts of the country in the early 1980s, which has driven hundreds of thousands of Guatemalans into Mexico and the United States; and the combination of persecution and war that has led to the exodus of a substantial proportion of the Salvadoran population. It can be argued that the failure or inability of these states in the past to successfully manage the contradictions resulting from capitalist production and its articulation with precapitalist modes accounts for the current political crises in these countries.

Foreign Intervention and Migration

Intervention by foreign states in internal conflicts may intensify or prolong these conflicts, in turn aggravating conditions that lead to displacement or emigration, but no clear relationship exists between migration and policies on immigration, asylum, and refugees. Foreign (particularly U.S.) intervention has been a factor in intensifying and prolonging the current conflict in El Salvador and in resulting population dislocations. The bombing and strafing of rural areas utilizing bombers, helicopters, and other equipment supplied by the United States since 1984 has directly caused population flight from these areas.[18] Moreover, the Reagan administration's emphasis on a military solution was an important factor in prolonging the war, aggravating the economic crisis, and stimulating the continued flow of migration from El Salvador to other countries. U.S. financing of the Contra war was directly and indirectly responsible for population dislocations and economic crisis in Nicaragua and the flow of refugees and migrants into neighboring countries and to the United States. In Guatemala, where U.S. intervention is less obvious today, a long history exists of foreign military and political intervention, including the U.S.-directed counterinsurgency programs of the 1960s, foreign training of military personnel, and assistance by foreign advisors in the antiguerrilla campaign of the early 1980s.

Overall, U.S. foreign policy appears to have been more effective in generating refugees than U.S. immigration and refugee policies have been in preventing their entry. The latter policies have primarily made migration and the sojourn in the United States more difficult. This situation has been aggravated by IRCA (for all but those eligible for amnesty), although it is too soon to evaluate the effectiveness of the new law in stemming the flow of migrants.

The Role of Migratory Patterns and Networks

Patterns of migration established in earlier periods may continue to operate even when the original conditions for migration no longer exist or when new causes of migration are introduced, due in part to networking among families or community members at the points of immigration and emigration. This tendency has been particularly evident in the movement of migrants and refugees across borders during the past decade, which appears to follow previous patterns of migration where possible (Nicaraguans into Honduras and Costa Rica, Salvadorans into Honduras and Guatemala, Guatemalans into southern Mexico). In some cases, such migration takes advantage of relationships established in the receiving country through prior migration. Some Central Americans entering the United States have followed migratory networks established by earlier Latino immigrants to communities with cultural and perhaps political similarities. By the mid-1980s, however, a large proportion of the Central American migrants had relatives or friends in the United States, many of them in major urban centers where entire networks from the sending communities may have been established. These social networks reinforce the structural and institutional ties between core and periphery in determining the direction of migratory and refugee flows.

In conclusion, while Central American migration in the 1980s is a quantitatively and qualitatively new phenomenon, the factors identified in our analytical framework help to explain it. What distinguishes the massive population movements in Central America today from those of the past is the conjuncture of several factors: an economic crisis, a consequence of the changes in the capitalist world economy and their specific forms in each Central American country, combined with political conflict arising from the growing contradictions between capitalist modernization and the backward socioeconomic structures maintained over time by the repressive state apparatus. U.S. involvement in these conflicts has prolonged and intensified them without resolving the structural contradictions from which they emerged. Prolonging the conflicts has in turn aggravated the economic crisis, which cannot be expected to disappear once the conflicts end. Thus one effect that can be anticipated is the continued dislocation, displacement, and migration of substantial sectors of the Central American populations.

STUDY QUESTIONS

1. In what ways did structural changes in Central America make individuals susceptible to push and pull factors that encouraged migration?

2. In what ways did Costa Rica minimize the effects of capital penetration?

3. What factors produced the unique migration patterns in El Salvador?

NOTES

The authors would like to thank the reviewers and editors of *LARR* for their very helpful comments and suggestions.

1. Kearney develops the concept of an articulatory migrant network linking the sending communities with daughter communities in the receiving country or region (1986, 353–55).
2. Wayne A. Cornelius, "Migrants from Mexico Still Coming and Staying," *Los Angeles Times*, 3 July 1988, Metro section.
3. We are not contending that capitalist penetration necessarily leads to migration or that migration necessarily results from capitalist penetration. The relationship between the two depends on the nature of capitalist penetration and the characterics of the peripheral area, among other factors. But capitalism is a major factor in historical and contemporary patterns of migration, including many cases where this relationship is not immediately obvious.
4. Incorporation of Central America into the world economy actually began in the colonial period with mineral exploitation and the creation of landed estates producing cacao, indigo, and other dye products for export. These activities functioned via the *repartamiento* (a system of forced recruitment of labor for a specified task or period of time), debt peonage, and other forms of coerced labor. Incorporation into the world economic system was sporadic, however, with landed estates shifting from export production to production for subsistence and local markets when export potential contracted (Woodward 1985, 41–47). When the coffee economy developed in the nineteenth century, the affected Central American economies became fully integrated into the world market (Santana Cardoso 1975, 54).
5. Immigration (chiefly from Europe) also played a role in expanding coffee production, particularly in Guatemala, where German planters emerged as an important segment of the landowning class. In El Salvador, families of European immigrants also figured prominently in establishing coffee plantations (Browning 1971, 146–47). Coffee technology was imported by German and French immigrants as well as by Colombians in Costa Rica.
6. For a thorough, well-documented discussion of Caribbean migration, see Chaney (1985).
7. Williams notes that cotton production led to modernizing production of other crops as well (such as coffee), further reducing the need for a permanent labor force on the agricultural estates. He views cotton production as a major force in destroying the peasant family, because elimination of access to land meant that women were forced to find work in the urban areas to supplement the seasonal agricultural work of male members of the family (Williams 1986, 70–71).
8. In El Salvador, legislation mandating a minimum wage for rural workers in 1965 became an additional reason to minimize the use of permanent labor. The extension of social security coverage to rural workers in Guatemala had a similar effect (Williams 1986, 59).
9. Chaney notes similar patterns for Jamaicans coming to the United States (1985, 113–14).
10. Although it might be expected that population-density pressures would exacerbate dislocations resulting from structural rigidities and capitalist penetration, comparison of internal migration in Guatemala and El Salvador during the 1960s shows that the rate of migration (the porportion of migrants to the total population) is roughly the same in both countries (approximately 15 percent). This finding suggests that El Salvador's greater population density has not affected rates of migration (CSUCA 1978b, 83). Durham points out that while geographic population density in El Salvador is seven times greater than in Honduras, the difference in arable density (agriculturally active population divided by land in cultivation) is less that 1.5 times that in Honduras (Durham 1979, 109–10). Thus population density alone cannot be taken as explaining Salvadoran migration, although it is undoubtedly a contributing factor.

11. Migration statistics for the two periods are not directly comparable because the census did not include categories for migration until 1971. Figures for 1961 consist of estimates based on comparing the population in each department according to the 1961 census with projected population changes since 1950.

12. See also "Informal Economy Cushions Unemployment," *Central America Report* (27 May 1988): 159–60.

13. Since 1986 some efforts have been made to repopulate rural areas, including the Salvadoran government program United to Reconstruct and efforts by the affected population themselves, aided by church or other nongovernmental organizations. Conditions in repopulated zones continue to be insecure, however, and many in the repopulated communities confront the danger of military attack as well as the difficulties of reconstruction (Americas Watch 1987, 155ff).

14. "New Attention to Refugee Crisis," *Central America Report* (29 July 1988): 225–27.

15. Ibid.

16. For the reasons noted above, the results of these studies are limited and cannot be generalized. One poll (incorporating a large number of students) found that most Central Americans were employed with good incomes, while another (of Central Americans receiving refugee assistance) found 70 percent unemployed and only 10 percent with jobs commensurate with their previous work experience (Aguayo 1985, 46). In short, the studies suggest the varieties of Central American experience in Mexico but cannot be taken as representative of the entire Central American population.

17. Although the INS has reported a decline in the number of arrests of undocumented migrants attempting to cross the U.S.-Mexican border since 1986, this decline may be partly attributed to a reduction of INS agents in the San Diego area. See Patrick McConnell, "Too Few for So Many," *Los Angeles Times*, 5 Nov. 1989, pp. A3, A48. By the beginning of 1990, however, it was widely agreed that the number of undocumented migrants had increased dramatically, and INS arrests in the period from October 1989 through March 1990 were up 50 percent from the same period in the previous year. See Patrick McConnell, "Illegal Border Crossings Rise after Three-Year Fall," *Los Angeles Times*, 22 Apr. 1990, pp. A1, A34–35. Refugee associations in Los Angeles reported an increase in the number of Salvadorans coming to the area following the November 1989 FMLN offensive. The growth in the number of undocumented immigrants is also apparent in the growing number of street vendors and in the increase in day laborers congregating at street corners in the Los Angeles area. See Cornelius, "Migrants from Mexico Still Coming," *Los Angeles Times*, 3 July 1988, Metro section.

18. As this example demonstrates, when analyzing the role of the state, it is difficult to separate the role of domestic regimes from that of the U.S. government, partly because the influence of the latter is often overwhelming and partly because they are generally aligned. Two notable exceptions to alignment are the Arbenz government in Guatemala (1950–1954), whose program for developing national capitalism in Guatemala conflicted with the interests of U.S. capital as epitomized by the United Fruit Company, and the Sandinistas in Nicaragua, whose efforts to extricate themselves from dependence on the United States clashed with the drive for continued hegemony in the region by the U.S. government or the factions that currently control it. More often, differences arise over means rather than goals, such as the occasional disagreements between the U.S. government and the Salvadoran military regarding the internationally permissible level of repression.

REFERENCES

Achaerandio, Luis 1983 "Introducción al problema de los desplazados en El Salvador (1980–1983)." *Boletín de Psicología (San Salvador)* 2 (July–September).

Aguayo, Sergio 1985 *El éxodo centroamericano: consecuencias de un conflicto.* Mexico City: Secretaría de Educación Púlica.

Aguayo, Sergio, and Patricia Weiss Fagen 1988 *Central Americans in Mexico and the United States.* Washington, D.C.: Hemispheric Migration Project, CIPRA, Georgetown University.

Alens, Alex 1984 *Socio-Demographic and Economic Characteristics of Displaced Persons in El Salvador.* Washington, D.C.: Intergovernmental Committee for Migration, Hemispheric Migration Project.

Americas Watch 1987 *The Civilian Toll, 1986–1987: Ninth Supplement to the Report on Human Rights in El Salvador.* New York: Americas Watch.

Armstrong, Robert, and Janet Shenk 1982 *El Salvador: The Face of Revolution.* Boston: South End Press.

Bach, Robert L. 1985 *Western Hemispheric Immigration to the United States: A Review of Selected Research Trends.* Washington, D.C.: Center for Immigration Policy and Refugee Assistance, Georgetown University.

Black, George, Milton Jamail, and Norma Stoltz Chinchilla 1984 *Garrison Guatemala.* New York: Monthly Review Press.

Browning, David 1971 *El Salvador: Landscape and Society.* Oxford: Clarendon Press.

Bulmer-Thomas, Victor 1987 *The Political Economy of Central America since 1920.* Cambridge: Cambridge University Press.

Castillo Rivas, Donald 1980 *Acumulación de capital y empresas transnacionales en Centroamérica.* Mexico City: Siglo Veintiuno.

Chaney, Elsa M. 1985 *Migration from the Caribbean Region: Determinants and Effects of Current Movements.* Hemisphere Migration Project Occasional Paper Series. Washington, D.C.: Center for Immigration Policy and Refugee Assistance, Georgetown University.

Cheng, Lucie, and Edna Bonacich, Eds. 1984 *Labor Immigration under Capitalism: Asian Workers in the United States before World War II.* Berkeley and Los Angeles: University of California Press.

Chinchilla, Norma Stoltz, and Norma Hamilton 1984a "Characteristics of Central American Migration to Southern California." Paper presented at the Illinois Conference of Latin Americanists, University of Illinois, Chicago, 15–17 November.

———. 1984b "Prelude to Revolution: U.S. Investment in Central America." *In the Politics of Intervention,* edited by Roger Burbach and Patricia Flynn, New York: Monthly Review.

Clay, Jason W. 1984 "Guatemalan Refugees in Mexico: An Introduction." *Cultural Survival Quarterly* 8, no.3 (Fall): 46–49.

Cohen, Robin 1987 *The New Helots: Migrants in the International Division of Labor.* Brookfield, Vt.: Gower.

CONADES (Comision Nacional de Asistencia a la Poblacion Desplazada) 1983 *Detalle por municipio de la población desplazada hasta el 31 de octubre de 1983.* CONADES mimeo, San Salvador.

Cornelius, Wayne A. 1980 "Mexican Immigration: Causes and Consequences for Mexico." In *Sourcebook on the New Immigration: Implications for the United States and the International Community,* edited by Roy Simon Bryce-Laporte. New Brunswick, N.J.: Transaction.

———. 1988 "Los migrantes de la crisis: The Changing Profile of Mexican Labor Migration to California in the 1980s." Paper presented at the conference "Population and Work in Regional Settings," El Colegio de Michoacán, Zamora, 28–30 November.

Coyuntura Economica 1989 "Condiciones de vida y fuerzas sociales." *Coyuntura Económica* 4, no. 24 (Mar.–Apr.): 34–38. Published by the Instituto de Investigaciones Económicas, Universidad de El Salvador.

CSUCA (Consejo Superior Universitaria Centroamericana) 1978a *Estructura agraria, dinámica de población y desarrollo capitalista en Centroamérica.* San José: Editorial Universitaria Centroamericana.

―――. 1978b *Estructura demográfica y migraciones internas en Centroamérica*. San José: Editorial Universitaria Centroamericana.

Cue, Reynaldo A., and Robert L. Bach 1980 "The Return of the Clandestine Worker and the End of the Golden Exile: Recent Mexican and Cuban Immigrants in the United States." In *Sourcebook on the New Immigration: Implications for the United States and the International Community*, edited by Roy Simon Bryce-Laporte. New Brunswick, N.J.: Transaction.

Deere, Carmen Diana, and Martin Diskin 1984 *Rural Poverty in El Salvador: Dimensions, Trends, and Causes*. Geneva: International Labour Office, World Employment Programme Research.

Deere, Carmen Diana, and Peter Marchetti 1981 "The Worker-Peasant Alliance in the First Year of the Nicaraguan Agrarian Reform." *Latin American Perspectives* 8, no. 2 (Spring): 40–73.

Durham, William H. 1979 *Scarcity and Survival in Central America: Ecological Origins of the Soccer War*. Stanford, Calif.: Stanford University Press.

ECLAC (Economic Commission for Latin America and the Caribbean) 1986 *The Economic Crisis: Policies for Adjustment, Stabilization, and Growth*. Santiago: Cuadernos de la CEPAL.

Espenshade, Thomas J., Frank D. Bean, Tracy Ann Goodis, and Michael J. White 1988 *Immigration Policy in the United States: Future Prospects for the Immigration Reform and Control Act of 1986*. Washington, D.C.: Urban Institute.

Espenshade, Thomas J., and Tracy Ann Goodis 1985 *Recent Immigrants to Los Angeles: Characteristics and Labor Market Impacts*. Washington, D.C.: Urban Institute.

Fagen, Patricia Weiss 1988 "Central American Refugees and U.S. Policy." In *Crisis in Central America: Regional Dynamics and U.S. Policy in the 1980s*, edited by Nora Hamilton, Jeffry A. Frieden, Linda Fuller, and Manuel Pastor, Jr. Boulder, Colo.: Westview.

Kearney, Michael 1986 "From the Invisible Hand to Visible Feet: Anthropological Studies of Migration and Development." *American Review of Anthropology* 15:331–61.

Kritz, Mary M., Ed. 1983 *U.S. Immigration and Refugee Policy*. Lexington, Ky.: Lexington Books.

Leach, Jim, George Miller, and Mark O. Hatfield 1985 *U.S. Aid to El Salvador: An Evaluation of the Past, A Proposal for the Future*. Report to the Arms Control and Foreign Policy Caucus, U.S. Congress. Washington, D.C.

Manz, Beatriz 1988 *Refugees of a Hidden War: The Aftermath of Counterinsurgency in Guatemala*. Albany State University of New York.

Monteporte Toledo, Mario 1959 *Guatemala: monografía sociológica*. Mexico City: Instituto de Investigacions Sociales de UNAM.

Montes Mozo, Segundo, et al. 1985 *Desplazados y refugiados salvadoreños*. Preliminary report. San Salvador: Universidad Centroamericana *José Simeón Cañas*.

Montes Mozo, Segundo, and Juan Jose Garcia Vasquez 1988 *Salvadoran Migration to the United States: An Exploratory Study*. Washington, D.C.: Hemispheric Migration Project, Center for Immigration Policy and Refugees Assistance, Georgetown University.

Montgomery, Tommie Sue 1982 *Revolution in El Salvador*. Boulder, Colo.: Westview.

Papademetriou, Demetrios G. 1983 "Rethinking International Migration: A Review and a Critique." *Comparative Political Studies* 15, no.4 (Jan.):469–98.

Pearce, Jenny 1986 *Promised Land: Peasant Rebellion in Chalatenango, El Salvador*, London: Latin American Bureau.

Portes, Alejandro 1983 "International Labor Migration and National Development." In Kritz 1983.

Portes, Alejandro, and Robert L. Bach 1985 *Latin Journey: Cuban and Mexican Immigrants in the United States*. Berkeley and Los Angeles: University of California Press.

Richmond, Anthony H. 1986 "Sociological Theories of International Migration: The Case of Refugees." *Current Sociology* 36, no. 2 (Summer): 7–25.

Rodriguez, Nestor P. 1987 "Undocumented Central Americans in Houston: Diverse Populations." *International Migration Review* 21, no.1 (Spring): 4–26.

Ruggles, Patricia, and Michael Fix 1985 "Impacts and Potential Impacts of Central American Migrants on HHS and Related Programs of Assistance: Final Report." Washington, D.C.: Urban Institute.

Ruggles, Patricia, Michael Fix, and Kathleen M. Thomas 1985 "Profile of the Central American Population in the United States." Washington, D.C.: Urban Institute.

Ruggles, Patricia, Donald Manson, John Trutko, and Kathleen M. Thomas 1985 "Refugees and Displaced Persons of the Central American Region." Washington, D.C.: Urban Institute.

Salvado, Luis Raul 1988 *The Other Refugees: A Study of Non-Recognized Guatemalan Refugees in Chiapas, Mexico*. Washington, D.C.: Hemispheric Migration Project, Center for Immigration Policy and Refugee Assistance, Georgetown University.

Santana Cardoso, and Ciro Flamarion 1975 "Historia económica del café en Centroamérica (siglo xix): estudio comparativo." *Estudios Sociales Centroamericanos* 4, no. 10.

Sassen, Saskia 1988 *The Mobility of Labor and Capital: A Study in International Investment and Labor Flow*. Cambridge: Cambridge University Press.

Schuooltz, Lars 1987 "Central America." Manuscript prepared for New York University Research Project, Immigration Policy and U.S. Foreign Relations with Latin America.

Stanley, William Deane 1987 "Economic Migrants or Refugees from Violence? A Time-Series Analysis of Salvadoran Migration to the United States." LARR 22, no.1:132–54.

Taylor, J. Edward 1980 "Peripheral Capitalism and Rural-Urban Migration: A Study of Population Movements in Costa Rica." *Latin American Perspectives* 7, nos. 25.26 Spring–Summer): 75–90.

Teitlebaum, Michael S. 1984 "Immigration, Refugees, and Foreign Policy." *International Organization* 38, no. 3 (Summer).

Torres Rivas, Edelberto 1985 *Report on the Condition of Central American Refugees and Migrants*. Hemisphere Migration Project Occasional Paper Series. Washington, D.C.: Center for Migration Policy and Refugee Assistance, Georgetown University.

Torres Rivas, Edelberto, and Dina Jimenez 1985 "Informe sobre el estado de las migraciones en Centroamérica." *Anuario de Estudios Centroamericanos* 11, no. 2: 25–66.

U.S. Committee for Refugees 1984 *Aiding the Desplazados of El Salvador: The Complexity of Humanitarian Assistance*. Washington, D.C.: U.S. Committee for Refugees.

U.S. GAO (General Accounting Office) 1989 *Central America: Conditions of Refugees and Displaced Person*. Washington, D.C.: GPO.

U.S. INS (Immigration and Naturalization Service) 1978 *Annual Report*. Washington, D.C.: U.S. GPO.
———.1984 *Statistical Yearbook of the Immigration and Naturalization Service*. Washington, D.C.: U.S. GPO.

Wallace, Steven P. 1986 "Central American and Mexican Immigrant Characteristics and Economic Incorporation in California." *International Migration Review* 20, no. 3 (Fall): 657–71.

Weeks, John 1985 *The Economies of Central America*. New York: Holmes and Meier.

Williams, Robert G. 1986 *Export Agriculture and the Crisis in Central America*. Chapel Hill: University of North Carolina Press.

Woodward, Ralph Lee 1985 *Central America: A Nation Divided*. 2d ed. New York: Oxford University Press.

Zolberg, Aristide R. 1981 "International Migration in Political Perspective." In *Global Trends in Migration Theory and Research on International Population Movements*, edited by Mary M. Kritz, Charles B. Keely, and Silvano M. Tomassi. Staten Island, N.Y.: Center for Migration Studies.
———. 1983 "Contemporary Transnational Migration in Historical Perspective: Patterns and Dilemmas." In Kritz 1983.

Zolberg, Aristide R., Astri Suhrke, and Sergio Aguayo 1986 "International Factors in the Formation of Refugee Movements." *International Migration Review* 20, no. 2 (Summer): 151–69.

Immigrants in a
Changing Economy

Introduction

The critical pieces in this section give emphasis to the crucial dimensions of gender and social class in the study of Asian and Latino immigration. The distinctive role of immigrant women is the focus of two articles represented in this collection, emphasizing the centrality of gender as an analytical concept used in gaining a more complete understanding of contemporary capitalism.

The diverse class composition of the new immigration stands in stark contrast to that of an earlier era when there was a higher degree of uniformity, reflecting the shift into an information-based economy that requires highly trained intellectual labor in addition to those who assume the menial tasks traditionally associated with immigrant groups.

The essays offer insights into the development of such metropolitan centers as Los Angeles, New York, Chicago, and Miami as destination points for Asian and Latino immigrants. Issues of family life, community development, access to political power, and labor organization within the respective Asian and Latino immigrant groups are placed within the context of the social turbulence created by the vagaries of a rapidly changing political-economic system that is now global in its farflung reach.

Chapter 5

Maura I. Toro-Morn

Gender, Class, Family, and Migration
Puerto Rican Women in Chicago

Recently, there has been a surge of scholarly interest about immigrant women (Diner 1983; Ewen 1983; Glenn 1986; Hondagneu-Sotelo 1992; Lamphere 1987; Simon and Brettell 1986; Weinberg 1988). Although women have always participated in population movements (Tyree and Donato 1986), suddenly newspaper reports are calling women the "new immigrants." Initial attempts at making immigrant women visible owe much to the efforts of feminist researchers of the 1960s and 1970s (Morokvasic 1983). The first wave of research on immigrant women helped to fill in the gaps by calling attention to the presence of women in migratory movements and by providing the much needed descriptive detail on the employment status and family situations of particular groups, but, according to Morokvasic (1983), this early research did not break with the traditional individualist approach so pervasive in immigration research. It continued to analyze women as if their decisions to migrate were determined by their individual motives and desires; consequently, important questions were left unanswered: How do we account for women's migration, and should the migration of women be treated in the same conceptual framework as male migrants or do they require separate analysis? Recently, a new wave of research has begun to correct some of the problems unresolved by the earlier research. Scholars have begun to move beyond the additive approach to articulate how gender affects and shapes the migration process (Hondagneu-Sotelo 1992; Kibria 1990). This new research shows that immigrant women's relationship to market and nonmarket conditions is unique. The place of immigrant women in the labor market is shaped by

From *Gender & Society*, Vol. 9, No. 6, December 1995. Reprinted by permission of Sage Publications, Inc.

class and their statuses as immigrants and racial/ethnic minorities; this intersection creates a particular and distinct experience (Glenn 1986).

Much empirical research has been done linking the entrance of women into labor migrations because of the emergence of export-led manufacturing zones in the Caribbean, Mexico, and Asia (Fernandez-Kelly 1983; Sassen-Koob 1984). In addition, studies have examined the incorporation of immigrant women into the labor force (Garcia-Castro 1985; Prieto 1986) and the consequent labor market outcomes in terms of occupational distribution and income differences from native populations (Boyd 1986; Simon and Deley 1986; Sullivan 1984; Tienda, Jensen, and Bach 1984). Still, much empirical work remains to be done to explain how these processes differ by race and ethnicity.

This article examines how working-class and better-educated middle-class Puerto Rican women enter the migration process, how gender relations shape their move, and how women adapt to their new homes in the United States. Specifically, I focus on the experiences of married working-class and middle-class women. My interviews suggest that while both groups migrated to the United States as part of what sociologists have called a "family stage migration," there are important differences between them that challenge our understanding of women's migration.

In the first part of this article, I explore how working-class and middle-class Puerto Rican women moved to the United States. I pay particular attention to the language women used to describe this process. While middle-class women talked about their migration as motivated by professional goals, working-class Puerto Rican women talked about how they came to take care of their children, husbands, and families. When confronted with these answers, I found that the experiences of married working-class women did not fit the traditional explanations found in the migration literature. Here, I draw on the feminist construct of productive and reproductive work, to argue that our current definition of "labor migration" is too narrow. Not all labor migrations need to relate to productive activities (i.e., the entrance of immigrant women in the labor market). One very important aspect of labor migrations should include the work of women who migrate and do not necessarily join the labor force, but stay and do the reproductive work that supports families and immigrant communities. Within this category, there are women who migrate as wives, as grandmothers, or as relatives, and whose major responsibility is to help with the reproductive tasks—be they housework or child care—of their own families and/or their extended families.

The second part of this article explores how, once in the United States, both working-class and middle-class Puerto Rican women had to confront the duality of being responsible for the reproductive work that takes place at home and the productive work outside the home. The interviews indicate that both working-class and middle-class Puerto Rican women tried to provide as much continuity in the process of forming and re-creating family life. Again, important class differences emerged when comparing married working-class and middle-class migrants. The interviews suggest that working-class husbands may have accommodated to their wives temporary employment, but that did not change the traditional division of labor within the household. Instead, working-class women had to develop strategies to accommodate their roles as working wives. Middle-class women developed strategies both as family members and as individuals in the process of adjusting to life in Chicago. The strategies they devised, however, reflected their class position. When juggling family and work responsibilities, educated and professional women have career goals equal standing alongside family obligations.

METHODOLOGY

From March 1989 to July 1990, I interviewed women in the Puerto Rican community of Chicago, which covers the areas of West Town, Humboldt Park, and Logan Square. I participated in community activities and attended cultural events. These activities allowed me to meet the women of the community and, through informal snowball sampling techniques, to select interviewees. The interviews took place in the homes of the informants and lasted between one and three hours; interviews were conducted in Spanish. The interview questions were organized around a series of themes, ranging from their migration history to family, work, and community experiences.

The sample of married women consisted of seventeen informants. Eleven were mostly working class, with little education, who came to Chicago in the early 1950s and 1960s. Generally, at the time of migration, they were married—or were soon to be married—and most had children. The six professional and educated women in the sample had all migrated in the late 1960s and had over fourteen years of education at the time of their move. Most educated informants described themselves as predominantly middle class and from urban backgrounds in Puerto Rico. At the time of the interview, two informants had earned doctorate degrees. Ten respondents were in their sixties; seven were in their forties and fifties. Different respondents will be identified by pseudonyms.

Being Puerto Rican and bilingual, I was able to establish a rapport with informants. Most of the older migrant women spoke little English, and conducting the interviews in Spanish facilitated the exchange. By the same token, being fluent in English allowed women to use the language with which they felt most comfortable; sometimes the interview started in Spanish and ended in English. On other occasions, women switched back and forth.

GENDER, CLASS, AND MIGRATION

The most significant movement of Puerto Ricans to the United States took place at the end of World War II (Dietz 1986; Falcon 1990; History Task Force 1979; Pantojas-Garcia 1990). In the late 1940s, the impact of U.S. investment and modernization of the economy transformed Puerto Rico from a predominantly agricultural to an industrial economy. Operation Bootstrap, as the development model became popularly known in Puerto Rico, attracted labor-intensive light manufacturing industries such as textiles and apparel to Puerto Rico by offering tax incentives, cheap labor, and easy access to U.S. markets (Dietz 1986; Pantojas-Garcias 1990). These changes in Puerto Rico's economy had profound consequences for Puerto Rican families. The development model was unable to create enough jobs, and working-class Puerto Ricans began to leave the island, heading for familiar places like New York City and new places like Chicago. News about jobs spread quickly throughout the island, as informal networks of family members, friends, and relatives told people of opportunities and helped families migrate.

My interviews suggest that working-class women and their families used migration as a strategy for dealing with economic problems. Married working-class women, in particular, talked about migration as a family project. For them, migration took place in stages. Husbands moved first, secured employment and housing arrangements, and then sent for the rest of the family. Even single men frequently left their future brides in Puerto Rico, returning to the island to get married as their employment and economic resources permitted. Some women came as brides-to-be, as they joined their future husbands in Chicago. For example, Rosie's mother came to Indiana in order to join her husband working in the steel mills. He had been recruited earlier, along with other workers in Puerto Rico. Once at the mills in Indiana, these men often found better jobs and moved on. They went back to Puerto Rico, got married, and returned to Indiana. Others arranged for the future brides to join them in Chicago. Alicia's explanation indicates how these decisions took place within the family context.

> My husband and I were neighbors in San Lorenzo. Before he left to come to Chicago, he had demonstrated an interest in me. Initially, I did not accept him, because I did not want to get married so young. We started corresponding and I agreed to the relationship. . . . In one letter, he asked me to marry him and come to live with him in Chicago. I told him that he needed to ask my father's permission. . . . He wrote to my father but my father did not agree . . . it took some convincing by my cousins who were coming to Chicago so that he would let me come and get married. My cousin took it upon himself to be responsible for me and that's how I came. Within two weeks of getting here, we got married.

Alicia's experience suggests that even within the constraints of a patriarchal society, single women were active in negotiating their moves to Chicago.

Married working-class women left the island to be with their husbands and families, even though some reported to have been working before leaving. Lucy and Luz were working in apparel factories in Puerto Rico when their unemployed husbands decided to move. Economic opportunities seemed better for their husbands in the United States and they both quit their jobs to move. For others, like Teresa and Agnes, both husband and wife were looking for work when news about job opportunities came via relatives visiting the island. Similarly, Agnes also came with her husband in the 1970s after a cousin who was visiting from Chicago convinced them that there were better job opportunities for both of them.

Working-class women also talked about the struggles over the decision to move. Fear of the unknown bothered Lucy. In addition, with a baby in her arms and pregnant with a second child, Lucy did not have anyone to help her in Chicago, but accompanied by her sister and her youngest child, Lucy followed her husband. Shortly after her migration, Lucy's mother and her sister-in-law arrived to care for the children while Lucy worked. Asuncion's husband could not find work in Puerto Rico either, so he migrated to Chicago with his relatives. Asuncion took a vacation from work and came to visit. Her family

> started talking about how they were recruiting case workers in the welfare office that could speak Spanish. They all had connections there and could very easily help me get a job. In fact, I went just to try it.

Asuncion gave in to the pressure and started working while still holding her job in Puerto Rico:

> I worked for six months, but I had so many problems. I wanted to go back. Life here [in Chicago] is really different when compared to the Island's. I was really confused. I cried a lot. I had left my children behind and I missed them a lot.

In fact, Asuncion went back to Puerto Rico because she missed her daughters; she was uncertain about what would happen to her marriage. She remembered how she felt when her husband took her to the airport:

> I really did not know whether I was going to see him again. He wanted to stay here and start a new life. I really did not care about what would happen to us and our relationship; I thought about my daughters. I owe it to my mother that my marriage was saved. After I returned to Puerto Rico, she sat me down and told me that my place was to be with my husband. That he was a good man and that my place was next to him. That I had to think about my children growing up without a father, so I returned again.

As Asuncion's case illustrates, she struggled between her husband's needs in Chicago and those of her children on the Island. Ultimately, moving to Chicago meant maintaining the family and saving her marriage.

Victoria's story is somewhat similar. She was living in her hometown of Ponce when she fell in love with the son of a family visiting from Chicago. She became pregnant and, in keeping with Puerto Rican culture, was forced to marry him. Without consulting with Victoria, the young man's parents sent him a ticket so that he could return to Illinois. Once in Chicago, he expected she would follow.

> I did not want to come. . . . One day he sent me a ticket for me and my baby girl. I sent it back because I did not want to come. But he sent it back again. So I had to come. . . . I had no idea where I was going, I had lived all my life in Ponce and had never left Ponce. I was so scared.

In 1966, she followed her husband to Chicago against her will. The emotional and cultural shock was very strong:

> I cried my eyes out. In Puerto Rico, you are always outside and carefree. Here, we lived in small apartments, we could not go outside. We could not open the windows. We did not know the language.

When her second child was to be born, Victoria was so intimidated with the city that she asked her mother to send a plane ticket so that she might give birth in Puerto Rico. Within less than a year, she had returned to Puerto Rico. Eventually her husband joined her also, but he was not happy. Soon he began to disappear and neglect his responsibilities as a father. In one of his escapades, he went back to Chicago. Once again, he sent for her. This time, however, Victoria began to analyze the situation in different ways.

> In Puerto Rico, I did not have any money to pay rent, electricity, and other bills or even feed my babies. I recognized it was a difficult situation, but I thought to myself

that if I stayed I had less opportunities to do something with my life. So, I thought that if I returned and brought my other brother with me they could help me and eventually even my mother could come and I could get myself a job. I had noticed that there were factories close to where we lived and my sister-in-law had offered to help as well. My brother who had moved with me the first time had gotten married and brought his wife with him.

Victoria had changed; as a married woman who followed her husband to Chicago, she began to develop her own agenda and use migration as a way for its realization.

Of the women who followed their husbands to Chicago, only two (Luz and Rita) complained that their husbands failed to fulfill their end of the bargain, forcing them to use migration as a way to assert their claims as wives. Lucy's husband had just returned from the military when he began talking about migrating to Chicago. Initially he went to Indiana where some relatives helped him find a job. When he was laid off, he learned through other friends that there were job opportunities in Illinois. He then moved to Chicago, promising to send for the family once he secured employment. But, according to Luz, he had been working for quite a while and had not sent for her and the children. Also, he was not sending any money to support the family. Instead, her husband kept putting off sending for her, and she was forced to confront him. Finally, Lucy left Arecibo in 1951 to join her husband and save her marriage. Rita was also forced to confront her husband by letter, reminding him of his promise to bring the rest of the family to Chicago. Even though it was over 20 years ago, Rita stated with emotion that she

> had to write him a letter. Because it had been over a year and he didn't send for me. I had three babies and I was alone. When he left, he said that he was going to send for me shortly and it had been a year and I was still waiting.

He replied that he did not want her to come, because living in Chicago was hard and she and the children would not be able to get used to the weather. She replied, "Either you send the ticket or send me the divorce papers." Apparently, this was a typical problem for Puerto Rican women when their husbands preceded them in migration. Juarbe (1988) reported that Puerto Rican women migrants in New York experienced similar problems. Juarbe's (1988) informant, Anastacia, stated that after her husband had migrated, he did not want her to come. He had been living and working for over three months. He wrote occasionally but did not send any money. Apparently, she had some money saved and was able to buy the ticket without his knowledge. Anastacia wrote him a letter announcing her arrival.

Middle-Class Migrants

The migration of educated and professional middle-class Puerto Ricans to Chicago remains an unanswered empirical question. Sanchez-Korrol's (1986) study of migration to New York City hints at the possibility that middle-class Puerto Ricans had been involved in the migration process; furthermore, surveys by the Planning Office in Puerto Rico between 1957 and 1962 found higher literacy levels and English proficiency among migrants than among the population as a whole (Rodriguez 1989). Pantojas-Garcia (1990) comes closest to analyzing the changing political economy in Puerto Rico and its impact on middle-class and educated workers. He points out that skilled and professional workers have increasingly joined semiskilled and unskilled workers in the migration process. As Pedraza (1991) points out, despite the growing importance of the "brain drain" as a type of migration, from a gender perspective, it remains the least understood.

In contrast to working-class migrants, moving was a joint family project for married middle-class women. In addition, the language this group used to describe the move differs from that of the working-class married woman. Middle-class women came with their husbands and had an agenda of their own. Aurea met her husband while attending the University of Puerto Rico. Initially, the couple moved from San Juan to Boston to enable her husband to take a university position. In 1971, a new job opportunity brought them to Chicago. In fact, Aurea talked about moving as a mutual arrangement between her and her husband. She saw the move to Chicago as an opportunity to join community and political struggles. Shortly after arriving in the city, they bought a house—something that took years for working-class families to accomplish.

Brunilda had just completed her bachelor's degree and was working as a field researcher for the University of Puerto Rico when she was asked to work with a group of American scholars who came to Puerto Rico to conduct research in the 1970s. The researchers were very pleased with her work and offered her a position if she would relocate to Chicago. They promised they would help her to make the transition. She had just been married when the job offer came, and she felt that was a big problem:

> My husband did not want to come, he said that he did not know English. He just did not want to come. I told him that there were no doubts in my mind as to what that job meant for me. It was a great opportunity, and I was not going to let it go. If he did not want to come, then I guess that was it, I knew I was coming with him or without him.

In this case the roles changed. It was the husband who was asked to follow his wife; initially he resisted, but the job meant so much to Brunilda that she was willing to sacrifice her marriage. Brunilda, therefore, moved within a professional rather than a family network. In addition, she did not live close to other Puerto Ricans in Chicago because the research team found her a place to stay closer to the university. After completing her work with the university researchers, Brunilda started graduate studies at a local university. She went to school full-time for a year and in 1971 started working as a community organizer in the south side of Chicago.

Vilma had moved from San Juan to Wisconsin to go to graduate school. While in Madison, she met her future husband and they moved in together. They had completed their degrees when he was offered a job in Chicago. In 1986, they both relocated to Chicago. Vilma described her move

> as very traditional in terms that I had just finished my master's and was looking for a job when my "compañero" (living-in boyfriend) got a job offer in Chicago. I followed him to Chicago, but I came not only for him, but also knowing that in Madison there was no professional future for me.

Comparing the migration of married working-class and middle-class Puerto Rican women offers some insights into how gender and class shapes the migration process. As my interviews suggest, both working-class and middle-class Puerto Rican women found themselves migrating as part of a family migration. Married working-class women came to support their husbands and be with their families. In other words, their roles as mothers and wives compelled them to migrate. The narratives suggest that some women struggled over the decision to move. In contrast, educated married middle-class women were less encumbered by such relations of authority. They shared in the decision making and were less dependent on other family members to make the move. As Vilma's and Brunilda's stories indicate, these middle-class migrants clearly had professional agendas of their own. How does each confront the problem of balancing family and work responsibilities?

GENDER, FAMILY, AND WORK

In Puerto Rican culture, there is a gender-specific division of labor consisting of men's work (*trabajo de hombre*) as the providers and women's work (*trabajo de mujer*) as the caretakers of the home and children. Underlying this gender division of labor is a patriarchal ideology, machismo, emphasizing men's sexual freedom, virility, and aggressiveness, and women's sexual repression and submission (Acosta-Belen 1986). Machismo represents the male ideal and plays an important role in maintaining sexual restrictions and the subordination of women. This ideology rationalizes a double standard where a woman can be seen as *una mujer buena o una mujer de la casa* (a good woman or a good homemaker) or as *una mujer mala o una mujer de la calle* (a bad woman or a woman of the street). A man has to show that *él lleva los pantalones en la casa* (he is the one who wears the pants in the family) and that he is free to *echar una canita al aire* (literally meaning, blow a gray hair to the wind; culturally; it means to have an affair).

The counterpart of machismo is *marianismo* in which the Virgin Mary is seen as the role model for women (Sanchez-Ayendez 1986, 628). Within this context a woman's sexual purity and virginity is a cultural imperative. Motherhood, in Puerto Rican culture, lies at the center of such ideology. A woman is viewed in light of her relationship to her children and, as Carmen, one of my informants, put it, in her ability "*dar buenos ejemplos*" (to provide a good role model).

Among working-class Puerto Ricans, gender roles are very rigid (Safi 1984). Although industrialization and the entrance of women in the labor force completely contradicts this ideal of *la mujer es de la casa* (women belong to the home), in Puerto Rico the domestic role of working class women remains intact. Working mothers are primarily responsible for the care of the home and the children.

In Chicago, in keeping with this ideology surrounding family values, some working-class husbands resisted their wives working. The men would take a double shift so that wives could stay home, take care of the children, and do housework. Carmen stayed home to care for her children and was very proud of her accomplishments as a mother, but economic necessity obliged other husbands to conform to women's work outside the home. Like Lucy said, "I did not come here to work, but I had to." Alicia elaborates, "In those days one paycheck was like nothing. We put together both paychecks and there were times that he had very little next to nothing left. By that time there were other relatives living with us and there were lots of mouths to feed."

The same network of family and friends that helped in the process of migration helped working wives find employment in Chicago factories. Josefa, Lucy, Luz, Rita, and Teresa all reported working in factories. Chicago's political economy in the 1950s allowed these women to find factory jobs with relative ease; however, most working-class married women viewed employment as a temporary necessity. The way women talked about their work experiences reflected this attitude. Josefa and her husband worked not only to meet the family needs but also to take care of the medical expenses of their child; when her daughter started going to school, she stopped working. Alicia worked in a factory prior to getting pregnant; after having the baby, she stopped working. When the family wanted to buy a house, Alicia went back to work for two years. After her second child, she stopped working altogether. Brunilda started working in a factory immediately upon arriving from Puerto Rico, but when she became pregnant, she stopped. Lucy was the only married respondent who stayed in the factory for a prolonged period of time. Eventually, she stopped working when she got sick.

Although most working-class married women gave in to their husbands' wishes for them to stay home, Rita illustrates how a woman resisted those traditional roles and even sought to change them. Rita's husband did not want her to work. According to Rita:

> After I got to Chicago, my husband didn't want me to work. But I wanted to work. I wanted to work because you can meet people, learn new things, and one can also leave the house for a while. I saw all the women in the family, his sisters and cousins, working and earning some money, and I wanted to work too. They used to tell me that I should be working. But I had four children, and who was going to take care of them?

Rita succumbed to the pressure and started working secretly for about three months. When asked how she managed to work without her husband knowing about it, Rita replied that

> since he left to work very early, I found someone to take care of my smallest child, and the others went to school. My work hours were from 9:00 to 3:30, so by the time my husband got home, I had everything done. I had the house clean, the children were cleaned and had eaten, and I was all put together. My husband did not like when I was not put together.

Rita eventually told her husband about her work escapades because she did not like doing things *a la escondida* (in hiding); however, her husband's traditionalism prevailed, and Rita was forced to give up working. To relent was a blow, because the money she had earned had gone to clothe the children and to purchase a sewing machine. Note the tone of pride:

> With the money I earned I was able to buy my sewing machine and I felt so proud of myself that I was to buy it with my own money. We saved a lot of money afterwards. I sew for the family; I felt so proud.

Although she gave in to her husband's traditionalism, Rita found a source of pride and accomplishment even within the confines of the house. She may have stopped working, but her contributions to the household continued as she was able to sew the children's clothing and other items for the house and the family.

Others reported that they stopped working for wages but continued to contribute to the family's income by working in their husbands' neighborhood stores. They used the word "helped," but, in reality, they actually ran the stores while their husbands worked elsewhere.

Puerto Rican men may have accommodated to the wife's employment, but the traditional division of labor within the family did not change. Lucy best articulated the working woman's problem:

> It was very hard work because I had to take care of the house, the children, and the store. Since my husband never learned how to drive, I had to learn to drive. I had to go to the warehouse, do the bookkeeping, everything. In the store, I used to do everything. My husband helped, but I was practically in charge of everything.

Puerto Rican working mothers, regardless of whether they worked outside the home or with their husbands in the family business, were still responsible for the care of the children and housework. Child care first became a problem at the time of migration, since families could not afford to travel all at once. A strategy women used to deal with this problem was to leave the children in Puerto Rico in the care of grandparents. This arrangement was a widespread practice in the Island for many years.

Once the family was in Chicago, women developed short-term arrangements to deal with the daily problems of child care. Shift work represented one strategy that couples used to allow these women to stay home with the children. The husband could work the day shift, and the wife worked at night. Haydee's father worked the day shift in a factory, while her mother worked the evening shift as a cook in a hotel. Josefa worked the night shift in a candy store; her husband worked the day shift. I asked Josefa if they ever switched, where he worked nights and she worked days. She replied that working at night allowed her to take care of her daughter during the day.

When children were school age, both husband and wife might be able to work during the day. For wives, however, there was always the added responsibility of returning home to care for the children and do the household chores. Here, girls were introduced to the household responsibilities very early and were left to care for younger brothers and sisters. When Claudia reached nine years, she acquired household responsibilities. She was given keys to the apartment, and after school she was expected to clean the kitchen, pick up around the house, and start dinner. This was also a way mothers trained their daughters in the traditional gender roles.

Given the ease of migration, other working-class women brought over relatives with them to help care for the children, suggesting that women can get involved in the migration process to do the reproductive work, allowing other women to do work outside the home. Lucy and Daniela brought their mothers, and Teresa brought a younger sister to Chicago to help take care of the children. Teresa's sister stayed home and took care of her children until she met a fellow and got married. That was when Teresa then turned to a woman in her building who took care of them for a small fee. Teresa gave her $12.00 weekly for the two girls and provided their food.

Sanchez-Korrol (1983, 98) found the same kind of informal child-care practices in the early "colonias" in New York City in which "childcare tasks previously undertaken by relatives defaulted to friends and acquaintances outside the kinship network who provided the services in exchange for a prearranged fee." This grassroots system served both employed women and women who had to stay at home. The arrangement usually consisted of bringing the child, food, and additional clothing to the "mother-substitute" and collecting the child after work. This system provided a practical way to increase family earnings and was an extralegal system with advantages not found in established child-care institutions. These informal child-care arrangements allowed children to be cared for in a familiar environment, where there was mutual trust, agreement between the adults involved, and flexibility. Children were cared for in a family setting where the language, customs, and Puerto Rican traditions were reinforced.

When Teresa stopped working, she became a child-care provider for the women in her building. Now, she no longer cares for other people's children, but instead cares for her own grandchildren. Teresa's history represents an example of the cycle of care that women provided. Such a cycle may begin when a woman places her children with a neighbor while she works. Then she may care for other neighbors' children while they work and, finally, care for her own children's children.

Middle-Class Migrants

Middle-class women placed their career goals equally alongside their family responsibilities. Rosa talked about how she had managed to work full-time in Puerto Rico and go to school to acquire an associate's degree because her extended family helped take care of the children and the household chores. In Chicago, since they did not have their extended family, they had to adjust differently. Shortly after arriving in the city, Rosa had given birth to her youngest child and opted to stay home with her children until they were of school age. Rosa recognized that she wanted to be with her children, but she also wanted to stay active.

> When I arrived, I saw a lot of possibilities, but I chose to stay home with my baby because I wanted to be with my children. When the baby was three years old, I started thinking what can I do to keep myself busy? In Puerto Rico, I had always worked. and I was not used to a full-time mom. I was very independent. I was very active. So I started helping the church. I started just because I wanted to get out of the house.

Eventually it became a full-time job. Then, when she started working full-time, her husband took on more household responsibilities:

> Here he has learned all kinds of domestic chores. At times I get home from work and he has everything ready, I don't have to do a thing in the house. Other times, we decide to go out for dinner.

Brunilda could not have made it without her husband, who helped her take care of the children as she pursued both her educational goals and, later, her political activism:

> My husband was very understanding of my goals and political interest. We shared many of the household responsibilities. . . . I have to admit that I spent a lot of time outside of the house during my children's childhood; for that I am a little bit sorry.

Later on she elaborated on her struggles and how she resolved them:

> When you are a professional, you face what Americans call "conflicting priorities." It's like I want to be everywhere at the same time. For me, community work has always interested me, whereas being a housewife has always been secondary. I feel more gratification in my role as a professional.

At the time of the interview, Brunilda worked as a professor in a local university. Aurea too placed her community activism (which was her professional orientation) alongside her family responsibilities:

> For me, both are part of the same process. I define my family network beyond the nuclear family, or better yet, beyond the traditional American concept of the nuclear family. My family is part of my social activism.

I asked whether this brought about any conflicts. She replied:

> Without doubt, my husband is part of this sexist society and obviously expects privileges that this society accords men, but we have worked and negotiated these roles quite successfully; moreover, we both made a political pact. It worked rather well because he shares the same vision of the world and social change as I do.

CONCLUSION

Evidence from this research has only begun to show how, in the context of a changing political economy, migration emerged as a strategy for families across class backgrounds. Initially, migration was a strategy working-class families used to deal with shrinking economic opportunities for the men in the family, but eventually middle-class, better-educated men and women joined working-class Puerto Ricans in the migration process.

The political economy that rendered working-class husbands unemployable forced women to migrate to Chicago as part of a family strategy. Gender relations within the family were a major factor shaping the migration of married working-class women to Chicago. Some married women went willingly, thinking that the move would improve their families' financial situation. Others resisted, but ultimately their roles as mothers and wives compelled them to follow their husbands to Chicago.

Whether working class or middle class, Puerto Rican women—like other immigrant women—confront a basic duality in family and work. Families provide economic and emotional support. They see the family as the only area where people are free to be themselves, and where people come for affection and love, but the family is also an institution that has historically oppressed women (Glenn 1986). When individuals and families confront economic deprivation, legal discrimination, and other threats to their survival, conflict within the context of the family is muted by the pressure of the family to unite against assaults from the outside. The focus on the family as a site of resistance often underestimates how certain family arrangements can be oppressive to women. Often misunderstood by scholars is the reproductive work of women on behalf of the family and the benefits such work brings to the men (Glenn 1987, 192).

Working-class women saw themselves in keeping with Puerto Rican culture as primarily *mujeres de la casa*, but many found themselves working, albeit temporarily, given the family's economic situation. Here, families accommodated to the wives' temporary employment, but in ways that did not challenge the traditional patriarchal structure in the family. Wives were still responsible for cooking, cleaning, and child care. Given this situation, working-class married women developed strategies to accommodate their roles as working wives.

The area of child care best reflects the resourcefulness of working-class Puerto Rican women migrants in developing accommodating strategies. Some women left their children behind in Puerto Rico, others brought relatives from Puerto Rico to help them. Still others turned to older daughters as helpers. Some became involved in a cycle of child care similar to the one developed by Puerto Rican women migrants in New York City.

Married working-class Puerto Rican women adapted to life in Chicago in ways that did not disturb traditional family arrangements. They also developed strategies to resist some arrangements. Some sought to change their husbands' view about work outside the home and created networks to help accomplish their goals. Others stopped working for wages, but continued contributing as mothers, giving them influence and power within the family. In addition, some women remained active in income-generating activities, such as working in the family business. When husbands neglected their responsibilities as fathers, women took charge of the household, providing for their children and family.

Although middle-class women felt differently about work and family obligations, they also struggled over their roles as mothers and wives. They rejected traditional ideologies about women's roles and saw no conflict in doing both. Some husbands supported them, but when husbands resisted, they also negotiated the work and family responsibilities. Their class position afforded them options, such as staying home until they were ready to return to work, hiring help, postponing having children, and organizing their schedule around their children's schooling. This study has only begun to explore a very small slice of the Puerto Rican experience in Chicago, namely that of married working-class and middle-class women. Much empirical work needs to be done to fully understand how gender shapes the migration process for other groups of Puerto Rican women in different family arrangements and across class backgrounds.

STUDY QUESTIONS

1. What is the duality of labor that women face?

2. Do middle-class women face this duality?

3. Does Puerto Rican migration to Chicago reflect a "family strategy" of migration?

REFERENCES

Acosta Belen, Edna. 1986. *The Puerto Rican woman: Perspectives on culture, history, and society*. New York: Praeger.

Boyd, Monica. 1986. Immigrant women in Canada. In *International migration: The female experience*, edited by R. Simon and C. Brettell. Totowa, NJ: Rowman and Allanheld.

Dietz, James L. 1986. *Economic history of Puerto Rico: Institutional change and capitalist development*. Princeton, NJ: Princeton University Press.

Diner, Hasia R. 1983. *Erin's daughters in America: Irish immigrant women in the nineteenth century*. Baltimore: Johns Hopkins University Press.

Ewen, Elizabeth. 1983. *Immigrant women in the land of dollars: Life and culture on the lower east side 1890–1925*. New York: Monthly Review Press.

Falcon, Luis M. 1990. Migration and development: The case of Puerto Rico. In *Determinants of emigration from Mexico, Central America, and the Caribbean*, edited by S. Diaz-Briquets and S. Weintraub. Boulder, CO: Westview.

Fernandez-Kelly, Maria. 1983. *For we are sold, I and my people: Women and industry in Mexico's frontier*. Albany: State University of New York Press.

Garcia-Castro, Mary. 1985. Women versus life: Colombian women in New York. In *Women and change in Latin America*, edited by J. Nash and H. Safa. South Hadley, MA: Bergin and Garvey.

Glenn, Evelyn N. 1986. *Issei, Nisei, War Bride: Three generations of Japanese women in domestic service*. Philadelphia: Temple University Press.

Glenn, Evelyn N. 1987. Women, labor migration and household work: Japanese American women in the pre-War period. In *Ingredients for women's employment policy*, edited by C. Bose and G. Spitae. Albany: State University of New York Press.

History Task Force. 1979. *Labor migration under capitalism: The Puerto Rican experience*. New York: Monthly Review Press.

Hondagnea-Sotelo, Pierrette. 1992. Overcoming patriarchal constraints: The reconstruction of gender relations among Mexican immigrant women and men. *Gender & Society* 6:391–415.

Juarbe, Ana. 1988. Anastasia's story: A window into the past, a bridge to the future. *Oral history Review* 16:15–22.

Kibria, N. 1990. Power, patriarchy, and gender conflict in the Vietnamese immigrant community. *Gender & Society* 4: 9–24.

Lamphere, Louise. 1987. *From working daughters to working mothers: Immigrant women in a New England industrial community*. Ithaca, NY: Cornell University Press.

Morokvasic, M. 1983. Women in migration: Beyond the reductionist outlook. In *One way molet. Migration and female labor*, edited by A. Phizacklea. London: Routledge and Kegan Paul.

Pantojas-Garcia, Emilio. 1990. *Development strategies as ideology: Puerto Rico's export led industrialization experience*. Boulder, CO: Lynne Rienner.

Pedraza, Sylvia. 1991. Women and migration: The social consequences of gender. *Annual Review of Sociology* 17:303–25.

Prieto, Yolanda. 1986. Cuban women and work in the United States: A New Jersey case study. In *International migration: The female experience*, edited by R. Simon and C. Brettell. Totowa, NJ: Rowman and Allanheld.

Rodriguez, Clara. 1989. *Puerto Ricans: Born in the U.S.A*. Boston: Unwin Hyman.

Safa, Helen. 1984. Female employment and the social reproduction of the Puerto Rican working class. *International Migration Review* 18: 1168–87.

Sanchez-Ayendez, Melba. 1986. Puerto Rican elderly women: Shared meanings and informal supportive networks. In *All-American women: Lines that divide, ties that bind*, edited by Johanetta Cole. New York: Free Press.

Sanchez-Korrol, Virginia. 1983. *From colonia to community: The history of Puerto Ricans in New York City, 1917–1948*. Westport, CT: Greenwood.

———. 1986. The forgotten migrant: Educated Puerto Rican women in New York City, 1920–1940. In *The Puerto Rican woman: Perspectives on culture, history and society*, edited by E. Acosta Belen. New York: Praeger.

Sassen-Koob, S. 1984. Notes on the incorporation of Third World women into wage-labor through immigration and off-shore. *International Migration Review* 18:1144–67.

Simon, Rita, and Caroline Brettell. 1986. *International migration: The female experience*. Totowa, NJ: Rowman and Allenheld.

Simon, Rita, and Margo Corona Deley. 1986. Undocumented Mexican women: Their work and personal experiences. In *International migration: The female experience*, edited by R. Simon and C. Brettell. Totowa, NJ: Rowman and Allanheld.

Sullivan, Teresa. 1984. The occupational prestige of women immigrants: A comparison of Cubans and Mexicans. *International Migration Review* 18:1045–62.

Tienda, Marta, Leif Jensen, and Robert L. Bach. 1984. Immigration, gender, and the process of occupational change in the United States, 1970–80. *International Migration Review* 18:1021–43.

Tyree, Andrea, and Katharine Donato. 1986. A demographic overview of the international migration of women. In *International migration: The female experience*, edited by R. Simon and C. Brettell. Totowa, NJ: Rowman and Allanheld.

Weinberg. Sydney Stahl. 1988. *The world of our mothers: The lives of Jewish immigrant women*. New York: Schocken Books.

Chapter 6

Marifeli Pérez-Stable and
Miren Uriarte

Cubans and the Changing
Economy of Miami

In memory of Mauricio Gastón,

> *who forged the way in analyzing Cubans in a changing Miami.*

The experience of Cubans in Miami appears to stand apart from the Latino inequalities elsewhere in the U.S. economy. However mythical the "golden exile" (Portes, 1969) might have been, the perception of the successful Cuban is deeply ingrained among Cubans, other Latinos, and the general population. In important ways, the data back up these perceptions. Cubans earn higher incomes, have higher educational levels, and register lower poverty rates than other Latinos. Most Cubans in the United States, moreover, arrived as political exiles after the revolution of 1959. Thus, their migration differed markedly from that of Mexicans and Puerto Ricans.

Nonetheless, the "success story" has been "dysfunctional" for the characterization of Cuban communities, especially for those among them who do not quite live up to the prevailing image.[1] The other side of the Cuban story, particularly in South Florida where most Cubans in the United States live, has clearly not received adequate attention. In this chapter we do not dismiss the predominant view of Cubans in U.S. society, but an analysis of their labor market participation in Miami over four decades delineates their profile in ways that allow for more meaningful comparisons with other groups.

The incorporation of Latino groups in the U.S. economy has elicited two sorts of explanations. The first focuses on human capital. Latinos—whether immigrants or long-time residents—are seen as having educational levels and work experience that do not easily fit the labor markets of the urban areas where they live and are therefore at

From *Latinos in a Changing Economy.* Edited by Rebecca Morales and Frank Bonilla. Reprinted by permission of Sage Publications, Inc. (1993).

a disadvantage in relation to other groups. Higher educational levels and labor market participation seem to place Cubans in a more advantageous position.

The second explanation emphasizes the centrality of economic structures from several different perspectives. One highlights the tendency of the labor market to segregate workers of different characteristics (i.e., race, ethnicity, and gender) into distinct economic sectors. Drawing upon structural theories of labor market segmentation, Portes and his colleagues have elaborated the primary paradigm for analyzing the Cuban economic experience in South Florida (Portes and Bach, 1985; Portes and Manning, 1986; K. L. Wilson and Portes, 1980). The Cuban enclave in Miami has provided a path of incorporation comparable to the primary sector and more beneficial to Cubans than the secondary labor market.

Other structural arguments underscore the overall transformation of the U.S. economy, marked by a sharp decline in production jobs and the rise of a service economy. Focusing on the role of U.S. cities in the international economy, Sassen (1991) notes the development of "global cities" (New York and Los Angeles) has expanded a segmented service sector where growing numbers of low-wage jobs are available for immigrants and minorities. Kasarda (1989) argues a "skills mismatch" greatly affects minorities, that is, their skills are best suited for the displaced industries and not appropriate for the ascending sectors. Waldinger (1986) contends an "ethnic queue" of minorities and immigrants has formed for the jobs vacated by whites; foreign-born workers are decidedly at the end (Waldinger, 1986). Regardless of their specific focus, these authors agree economic transformation has eliminated many manufacturing jobs, created low-wage employment, reinforced poverty, and resulted in growing income inequalities.

In this chapter we use the 1950, 1970, and 1980 U.S. Census Public Use Micro Data Sample and the 1988 Current Population Survey for the Miami SMSA to describe the effect of economic transformation on the insertion of Cubans into the economy of Miami.[2] We start, however, by looking at Miami and Havana during the 1950s, with an eye for their emergent, though truncated, complementarity. Our purpose is to establish the structural context into which Cubans brought their human and other capital. The initial "skills match" was an important component of the relative ease with which the Miami economy incorporated the exiles. We next examine the extent of economic transformation in Miami in light of industrial and occupational changes between 1950 and 1988. We then analyze the differential effect of these changes on the major racial/ethnic groups, paying particular attention to Cubans. Finally, we conclude with some suggestive notes on our findings and their implications for the paradigms used to understand the Cuban experience.

MIAMI AND HAVANA: DEVELOPMENT TRENDS BEFORE 1959

An often-ignored aspect of the Cuban experience in Miami is the complementarity in the patterns of development between the sending and receiving economies of the immigrants: those of Havana and Miami during the 1950s. These patterns and their aborted prospects constitute an important structural context for the entrance of Cubans into Miami after 1959. In Miami, Cubans, especially *habaneros*, stepped into familiar terrain. Their human capital and their know-how tapped the potential in the socioeconomic context of Miami, and consequently their skills found their market match. These links and trends of the 1950s are an important, if so far overlooked, element in analyses of the formation of the Cuban enclave in Miami and the emergence of the region as the gateway to Latin America.

One of the consequences of the social revolution of 1959 was the migration of more than one-half million Cubans during the 1960s. The earliest exiles were especially unrepresentative of the Cuban population during the 1950s. They came from the wealthier, predominantly white, better educated, more urban, higher status occupational sectors of prerevolutionary society. Some arrived with little except a few personal belongings. Many managed to transfer some assets to the United States. A few had investments outside of Cuba well before the revolution. All came with substantial human capital and, just as important, with the insight that belonging to the Cuban middle class gave them into U.S. culture. During the 1950s, Cuba, particularly Havana, experienced substantial U.S. influence. At the time, no other group of Latin Americans could have entered the United States as prepared to succeed as middle-class Cubans were during the early 1960s. That Miami and Havana had been undergoing transformations that augured complementarity and competition, moreover, allowed the exiles to step into familiar territory.

Since the 1920s, tourism, real estate, construction, trade, and financial services had brought considerable expansion to Miami. The trade sectors were the most important employer, accounting for 31% of total employment in 1950. Services, especially the unskilled type supportive of tourism, were the second leading source of employment. Construction and transportation each accounted for about 7%–10% of Miami earners (Ballinger, 1936; Muir, 1953). Although manufacturing represented less than 10% of total employment, the city nonetheless had one of the fastest rates of industrial growth in the United States during the 1940s and 1950s.[3] Largely because of tourism, links to the Caribbean were growing. Miami was often the first stop before traveling farther south. But these expanding ties were also rooted in the developing importance of Miami as a financial center for foreign trade, particularly to Latin America. New Orleans, however, still retained preeminence as the U.S. gateway to the South. Some observers underscored the (then) 20 million potential customers in the Caribbean Basin as an incentive for South Florida manufacturing (Wolff, 1945, p. 66). The recession of the late 1950s hit Miami earlier and harder, and lasted longer than in the rest of the country (Center for Advanced International Studies, 1967). Thus, the profile of Miami when the Cuban exiles first arrived has been somewhat distorted. On the surface, Miami might have seemed not much more than a hard-pressed resort town. Underneath, however, longer term trends pointed to emerging transformations that the early influx of mostly upper- and middle-class Cubans undoubtedly encouraged.

During the 1950s, Havana was more decisively experiencing rapid changes. The capital was the motor behind the incipient transformation of dependent Cuban capitalism. With about 25% of the total population, Havana had nearly 31% of the economically active population. More disproportionate was its share of the more educated sectors of the labor force: 54% of all professionals, 40% of all managers, nearly 60% of all office workers, about 40% of all skilled workers, and 54% of all service workers (*Oficina Nacional de los Censos Demográfico y Electoral*, 1955, pp. 1, 183, 196). Havana was the principal site for the expanding industrialization then taking place in Cuba. Eight of the 14 industrial enterprises employing 500 or more workers were in its vicinity (U.S. Department of Commerce, 1955, pp. 73–74). Construction and tourism were also flourishing. During the 1950s, total wages in Havana province increased about 22%, even as those of all other provinces, especially Camagüey and Oriente, declined (R.C. Bonilla, 1983, pp. 416–417; Banco Nacional de Cuba, 1960, pp. 151–153).[4] Consumer culture was rapidly making inroads in the capital. Imports of consumer durables were growing significantly, and most were destined for the *habanero* public (Banco Nacional de Cuba, 1960, p. 190). Moreover, *habaneros* were increasingly using credit to maintain their life style.

In 1958, Havana certainly overshadowed Miami. Manufacturing, banking, construction, and tourism (as well as gambling and other underworld operations) were proliferating. All of these endeavors had actual or potential counterparts in Miami. During the 1960s, U.S. investments in Latin America increased rapidly and significantly contributed to the internationalization of the larger economies in the region (Cardoso & Faletto, 1979). We will never know how Cuba might have developed without the revolution. Given the special relationship with the United States, Cuba—and especially Havana—might have occupied a central space in the internationalization process of the 1960s and 1970s. The geographic proximity between Havana and Miami might also have meant that South Florida might have become the U.S. gateway to Latin America. Without the revolution, Havana and Miami would have likely shared that portal. Thus, even without the exiles, the days of Miami as just a tourist town might well have been numbered.

THE MIAMI ECONOMY, 1950–1988

Between 1950 and 1988, Miami underwent profound economic and demographic transformations. The restructuring process in the Miami SMSA entailed prodigious growth in the service sector, particularly in the high-end services, and the stagnation of the small manufacturing sector. In an industrial taxonomy of 94 metropolitan areas in the United States, Bluestone, Stevenson, and Tilly (1992) categorized them according to changes in aggregate employment levels and industrial structure. Between 1973 and 1987, Miami experienced trends similar to those of Boston and Los Angeles: significant expansion in nonagricultural sectors and much smaller changes in total manufacturing employment. Until the 1970s, these trends, however, were not well established.

Between 1950 and 1988, total employment increased from just over 150,000 to more than 850,000. Miami experienced expansion and then decline in manufacturing, a steady decline in construction, and the rapid growth of the service sector (Figure 6.1). Manufacturing increased its share of workers through the 1950s and 1960s and started to decline during the 1970s. By 1988, the share of workers in manufacturing appeared to have returned to 1950 levels. In contrast, construction had undergone sharp and steady declines over the four decades. By 1988 the share of earners in this sector was 40% of what it had been in 1950.

Trade and services have always been significant in the Miami economy, accounting for about half of all Miami workers through the four decades. During the 1960s, important changes in composition first became apparent. By 1970, the high-end services overtook the

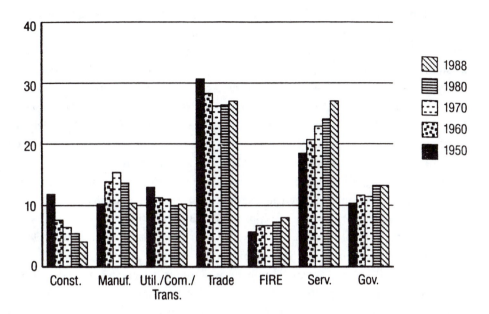

FIGURE 6.1 Industrial Distribution of Employment, Miami Metropolitan Area, 1950–1988 (in percent)

Source: Florida Department of Labor and Employment Security.

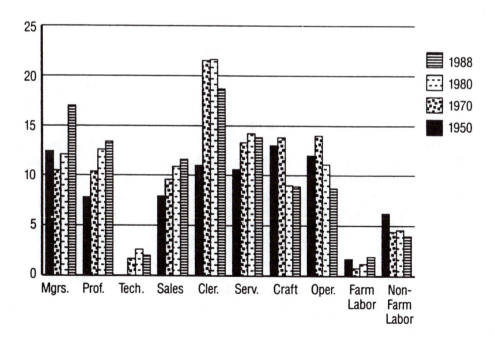

FIGURE 6.2 Occupational Distribution of Earners, Miami Metropolitan Area, 1950–1988 (in percent)

Sources: U.S. Census PUMS 1950–1980; CPS 1988.

low-skilled jobs in personal services and the tourist industry. The restructuring process continued in favor of financial and other professional services until 1988, when there appears to have been a slight reversal in the relationship between the two service sectors. Just as significant, high-end services displaced retail trade as the major employment sector. Although retail trade had recovered slightly from the decline occurring between 1970 and 1980, it remained well below the levels of 1950. During the 1980s, as Miami consolidated its place in the structure of international finance, the high-end service sector employed somewhat under a third of earners. The days of the tourist town were long gone.

Two major trends mark the changes in the occupational structure of Miami during these four decades (Figure 6.2). First, there has been a marked increase in the managerial and professional occupations at the expense of those occupations requiring lesser skills. Miami's share of workers in more highly skilled occupations has increased steadily from 20% in 1950 to 31% in 1988. By comparison, the share of earners in clerical and other low-end services appears to have stabilized after rising sharply during the 1960s. Craft, operative, and laborer occupations have undergone a significant relative decline. Second, the occupational opportunities for low-skilled workers have narrowed. By 1988, the Miami profile appears to have consolidated: Clerical occupations still account for the largest number of workers, with the sum of managers and professionals/technical personnel representing one third of earners in Dade County. Crafters, operatives, and laborers continued to decline.

Demographic changes, especially in racial/ethnic makeup, are even more significant (Figure 6.3). Between 1950 and 1990, the population of Miami nearly quadrupled from 495,084 to 1,937,094. In 1950, 83% of the population was non-Hispanic white, 13% black, and 4% Latino.[5] By 1970, blacks and Latinos had increased their share of total population to, respectively, 15% and 23%. In contrast, the share of non-Hispanic whites had decreased by 21 percentage points.[6] After 1970, non-Hispanic whites continued to decline, representing only 32% of the Miami SMSA population in 1990, while blacks increased their share to 19%. By 1990, Latinos had become the largest group, accounting for 49% of the population.[7] During the late 1980s, Latinos were 40% of the working-age population; Cubans represented about 20% of Miami's workers. Diversification of the Latino population also characterizes the period (Figure 6.4). During the 1960s and 1970s, Cubans constituted about 70% of the Latino population. The remaining 30% were Central/South Americans and Dominicans (20%), Puerto Ricans (8%), and others (2%). By 1990, however, the Cuban share of the Latino population had decreased to 59% and that of Central/South Americans and Dominicans had increased to 31%. Puerto Ricans remained at 8%.

With the change in population came a transformation in the region's labor force. As the Latinization of Miami went forward, the proportion of non-Hispanic white earners across industrial sectors and occupations declined dramatically, while that of Latinos increased. Latino gains were particularly salient in manufacturing and high- and low-end services, all ascending sectors of the economy during the 1970s and, excepting manufacturing, during the 1980s as well. The black share of earners across sectors has largely remained constant. The composition of the labor force in different occupations adds another dimension to growing diversity. A clear racial/ethnic order emerged where

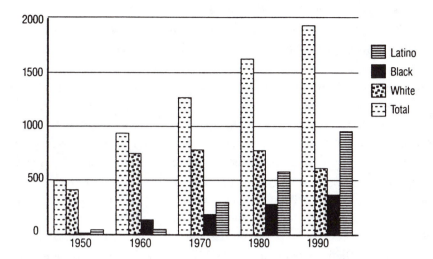

FIGURE 6.3 Population of Dade County, Florida, 1950–1990 (in thousands)
Source: Research Division, Metropolitan Dade County Planning Department.

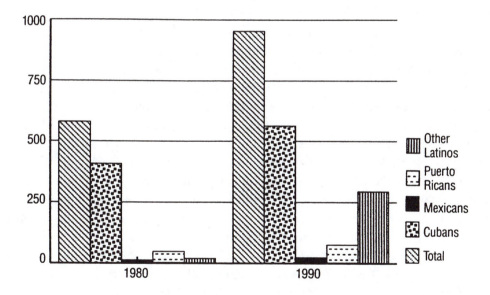

FIGURE 6.4 Latino Population of Dade County, Florida, 1980–1990 (in thousands)
Source: U.S. Census.

non-Hispanic whites dominated the higher salaried and more prestigious occupations, with Latinos beginning to make modest inroads. But both Latinos and blacks were more likely to be employed in occupations of lower socioeconomic status. During the 1970s and 1980s, these trends consolidated. By 1988, non-Hispanic whites were solidly ensconced in the expanding high-level management and professional/technical occupations. Blacks and Latinos, although increasing their share of earners in these sectors, continued to be underrepresented.

THE DIFFERENTIAL EFFECT OF ECONOMIC TRANSFORMATION:
NON-HISPANIC WHITES, BLACKS, AND CUBANS IN MIAMI

How the three main racial/ethnic groups have fared in the restructuring of the regional economy is an important aspect of the recent history of Miami. According to industrial and occupational distributions by racial/ethnic groups, as well as data on income and poverty, non-Hispanic white earners have fared the best. Between 1950 and 1980, they steadily increased their participation in the ascending economic sectors and in the highest status occupations in the new industries of South Florida (Tables 6.1 and 6.2). Non-Hispanic white workers have successfully made the occupational shifts concomitant to the new economic conditions. By 1988, 41% were employed as managers, technicians, and professionals; 43% labored as low-status white-collar workers in service, sales, and clerical occupations. Only 6% were still employed as operatives and laborers.

Rising incomes and declining poverty rates among non-Hispanic whites have resulted from the increase of their participation in the higher status occupations and the expanding sectors of the economy. Between 1950 and 1980, non-Hispanic whites experienced steady growth in their mean total income, although the rise was particularly dramatic among the men (Figure 6.5). During the 1980s, non-Hispanic white male income stagnated although that of females continued to rise. Non-Hispanic white poverty rates— low to begin with—declined slightly (Table 6.3). Poverty rates among non-Hispanic white earners, however, rose from 4.5% in 1970 to 5.3% in 1988, a local manifestation of national trends of growing numbers of working poor.

In contrast, blacks have fared much worse. Although increasing numbers of blacks have penetrated the ascending sectors of the economy, they have done so primarily in the lower status occupations. Black earners have particularly suffered, because sectors where they were once strong and occupations they once dominated have declined. Construction, for example, employed 21% of black workers in 1950 and only 6.2% in 1980. Similarly, 32% of black workers were laborers in 1950 and only 8.6% in 1980. The percentage of black workers in the low- and high-end services has increased rather sharply. In fact, the highest percentage increase among black earners has come among those in the high-end service sector. In 1950, 5% of black earners were employed in high-end services; by 1980, 28% were so employed.

The changing economy of Miami has brought significant changes for black occupational opportunities. Black managers, technicians, and professionals increased sharply: More than one out of five black earners was employed in these occupations in 1988. Changes in occupational structures have, however, limited the jobs available to low-skilled workers, where blacks are disproportionately represented, and may thus have led significant numbers to abandon the labor force. Between 1950 and 1980, black operatives and laborers declined from 50% to 24%, and those in clerical, sales, and service jobs increased from 20% to 52%.

This reversal may partially explain the decline of 15 percentage points in the labor force participation of black males and the rise by 21 percentage points in that of black women.

Black gains in the high-status occupations have not translated into a higher mean income relative to non-Hispanic white and Cuban males. Rising steadily between 1950 and 1980, mean income for black men has consistently remained below that of their

TABLE 6.1 Selected Industries of White, Black, and Cuban Earners, Miami Metro Area, 1950–1988

	1950			1970			1980			1988		
	W	B	C	W	B	C	W	B	C	W	B	C
Agri	2.8	4.1	*	1.0	5.7	0.8	1.2	3.5	1.2	1.4	—	2.0
Constr	7.7	21.0	*	6.9	10.0	5.3	6.2	6.2	6.7	8.0	8.8	6.8
Trad Mfg	7.7	1.4	*	10.1	6.7	32.9	8.2	7.4	24.0	7.6	7.3	13.7
Trans	8.7	7.4	*	7.9	5.9	4.1	7.5	7.3	5.6	4.1	5.8	9.9
Commun	1.3	0.1	*	2.1	1.3	0.8	2.2	1.8	1.3	2.2	*	3.1
Wh Trade	6.9	6.3	*	5.5	4.1	4.7	5.2	3.7	6.9	4.9	*	5.8
Re Trade	21.2	14.4	*	19.5	13.3	17.8	19.8	15.8	16.9	20.0	14.6	16.4
Hi Serv	10.2	4.9	*	22.3	19.3	13.1	31.2	28.3	22.0	27.2	27.0	23.6
Lo Serv	11.9	20.7	*	16.4	27.6	16.8	10.0	15.3	10.2	9.8	18.2	13.0
Pub Adm	4.6	*	*	4.4	2.6	0.8	4.8	6.3	2.5	3.3	3.6	2.7
Hi Mfg	—	—	—	0.7	*	1.7	1.0	0.9	1.6	1.4	*	1.4
Utilities	1.5	3.3	*	1.0	0.5	*	1.3	2.4	0.6	1.0	*	1.4

Sources: U.S. Bureau of the Census, PUMS (1950, 1970, 1980), CPS (1988).

Note: (*) cell count too small; (—) data not available. Columns do not add up to 100% because of missing or not available data and because we did not include Mining and Defense. Moreover, the PUMS column totals are well below 100%.

TABLE 6.2 Selected Occupations of White, Black, and Cuban Earners, Miami Metro Area, 1950–1988

	1950			1970			1980			1988		
	W	B	C	W	B	C	W	B	C	W	B	C
Managers	13.3	3.0	*	13.0	1.5	6.1	15.4	5.3	9.9	22.4	6.9	17.5
Profession	8.9	1.4	*	12.4	5.8	5.2	15.3	9.2	8.3	16.4	12.2	11.6
Technician	—	—	—	1.6	*	2.6	3.1	2.3	2.1	2.5	2.3	2.1
Sales	9.7	1.4	*	11.6	2.7	6.5	12.8	5.9	9.6	12.3	6.1	11.6
Clerical	12.5	1.9	*	24.0	13.9	17.3	23.7	19.2	22.2	20.2	14.5	19.9
Service	8.3	16.3	*	10.5	32.4	10.3	11.9	26.6	11.4	11.2	23.7	9.6
Crafts	15.5	1.4	*	14.7	7.5	15.1	8.0	6.9	10.8	8.3	9.9	8.9
Operatives	11.5	12.5	*	9.0	18.7	32.7	5.8	13.0	19.3	3.8	11.5	14.4
Farm Labor	1.3	4.1	*	0.3	3.9	*	0.7	3.1	0.9	*	5.3	*
N-farm Labor	1.2	31.6	*	2.9	13.1	4.0	3.2	8.6	5.5	2.2	7.6	3.8

Sources: U.S. Bureau of the Census, PUMS (1950, 1970, 1980), CPS (1988).
Note: 1950 U.S. Census aggregated professionals and technicians;(*) cell count too small; (—) data not available. Columns do not add up to 100% because of missing or not available data and because we did not include Mining and Defense. Moreover, the 1950 PUMS column totals are well below 100%.

TABLE 6.3 Rates of Poverty in the Working-Age Population and Among Earners, Miami Metro Area, 1970–1988

	1970	1980	1988
White population	10.7	8.9	8.7
Black population	29.4	25.7	27.6
Cuban population	13.4	15.2	17.2
White earners	4.5	4.6	5.3
Black earners	20.1	15.3	16.1
Cuban earners	8.2	5.8	6.6

Note: 100% Federal Poverty Standard.
Sources: U.S. Bureau of the Census, PUMS (1970, 1980), CPS (1988).

counterparts in the other two main groups. In 1988, moreover, mean black male income was lower than that of non-Hispanic white females. Black female income also rose steadily throughout the period. Interestingly, the mean income of black women was lower than that of non-Hispanic white females and higher than that of Cuban females. During the 1980s, black women appear to have suffered significant losses in mean income, and by 1988, Cuban women surpassed them (Figure 6.5).

Not surprising, betweeen 1970 and 1980, poverty rates for working-age blacks remained high. Although declining slightly during the 1970s, poverty rates were rising again during the 1980s. In 1988, black women had the highest poverty rates for working-age blacks: Nearly three quarters of all black poor were women and one-third of all black women were poor. Poverty was also concentrated among the younger and oldest age cohorts: in 1988, 36% of blacks 16–24 and 46% over 60 were poor, compared to 21% of those 25–59. The relative absence of jobs available to young blacks and the availability of low-paying jobs for black women seem to be contributing factors to the profile of black poverty in Miami. Black poverty rates have been about three times those of non-Hispanic whites. In contrast to non-Hispanic whites, however, poverty among black earners decreased from 20% in 1970 to 16% in 1988. This relative decrease notwithstanding, black earners suffer poverty rates three to four times greater than those of non-Hispanic whites.

The Cuban experience lies somewhere between that of blacks and non-Hispanic whites. Cubans have generally been successful in entering the ascending sectors of the economy, particularly during the 1980s. In the 1960s, as manufacturing rose in importance in the Miami economy, it employed one-third of all Cubans. During the 1970s, as the sector declined, so did the percentage of Cubans. By 1988, 14% of Cuban earners worked in manufacturing. During the 1970s, Cubans rapidly entered the high-end service sectors. By 1988, high-end services employed more Cubans than any other sector, 23.6%. In many ways, the sectoral experience of Cubans resembles that of non-Hispanic whites.

Occupationally, however, Cubans have had a different experience. Although Cubans have made substantial inroads in the high-status occupations, a large percentage of Cubans are still in the lower paying jobs. Between 1970 and 1988, Cuban earners in the high SES occupations registered the largest relative gains among the three groups: 14%

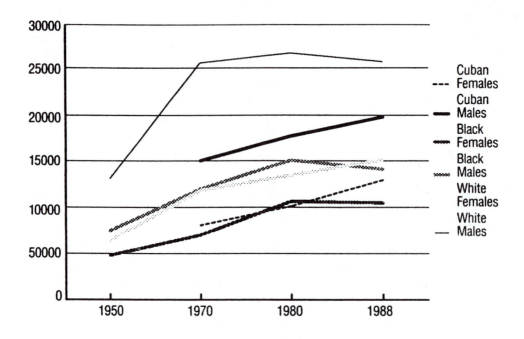

FIGURE 6.5 Mean Total Income of Earners, by Race and Ethnicity, Miami Metropolitan Area, 1950–1988 (in 1982–1984 dollars)

Note: All figures refer to income in year prior to survey.
Sources: U.S. Census PUMS 1950–1980; CPS 1988.

to 31.2%. Nevertheless, a large percentage of Cubans still work in the lower paying occupations. In 1970, 71% of Cuban workers worked in sales or as clerks, service workers, operatives, and laborers. By 1988, 59% continued to do so, whereas 49% of non-Hispanic whites and 62% of blacks did.

In many ways, Cubans have also had to make occupational shifts similar to those of blacks: from operatives and laborers to white- and pink-collar employment. In 1970, Cuban earners were about equally employed in low-paying white-collar and service sectors (33.6%) as in operative and laborer occupations (36.7%). By 1988, only 18% remained in the declining operative and laborer occupations, whereas 41% now had jobs in the low-paying service occupations. The shift is more rapid than that experienced by blacks and cushioned by a significant representation in the ascending occupational sectors. The labor force participation of Cuban men declined during the 1970s and subsequently stabilized; that of Cuban women remained stable and high throughout the period.

A closer look at the distribution of Cuban earners across the industries and occupations where they are most prevalent provides an illustration of their sectoral and occupational shifts (Table 6.4).[8] First, those industries and occupations historically representing the bulk of Cuban earners (80% in 1980) accounted for about 70% in 1988. Cubans appear to be moving into new sectors, primarily communications and transportation. Second, Cuban earners in 1988 manifest a sharp decline in the percent employed in

TABLE 6.4 Cuban Incomes by Industry and Occupation, Miami Metro Area, 1980 and 1988 (actual dollars)

Industry	Occupation	Distribution of Earners		% Sector's Earners		Mean Income	
		1980	1988	1980	1988	1980	1988
Manufacturing	Man/Prof/Tech	2.0	0.7	8.5	5	15,398	33,000
	Sal/Cler/Serv	4.4	2.1	18.2	15	9,395	15,900
	Oper/Lab	17.6	9.9	62.9	72.5	6,820	8,833
	Craft	2.5	1	10.2	7.5	8,861	18,333
Hi Services	Man/Prof/Tech	8.4	11	38.3	46.3	15,925	33,811
	Sal/Cler/Serv	13	11.6	57.2	49.2	8,377	12,163
Retail Trade	Man/Prof/Tech	2.8	4.1	16.7	25	14,057	28,226
	Sal/Cler/Serv	10.2	9.3	60.3	56.6	6,688	8,199
Lo Services	Man/Prof/Tech	1.6	3.1	15.4	23.7	13,007	16,504
	Sal/Cler/Serv	6.4	6.9	59.6	52.6	6,750	10,598
WH Trade	Man/Prof/Tech	1.5	2.1	21.2	35.3	18,469	23,416
	Sal/Cler/Serv	4.4	2.4	49.7	41.1	10,585	14,642
Construction	Man/Prof/Tech	1.2	2.1	17.9	30	17,340	40,308
	Oper/Lab	1.7	1	25.6	15	9,597	11,793
	Craft	3.2	3.1	46.9	45	11,207	14,957

Sources: U.S. Census PUMS 1980, CPS 1988.

manufacturing across all occupations. The trends in other sectors point to increases among the higher status occupations and declines among the lower paying ones. The only exception were the low-end services, where Cuban earners increased their share among both high- and low-paying occupations. Third, distribution within each sector reveals a similar pattern of transition from the lower to the higher paying occupations. Manufacturing is the only exception where the remaining Cuban earners are concentrated in the lowest status occupations.

Finally, the distribution shows that only about 20% of Cubans conformed to the profile of success: managers and professionals in manufacturing, construction, the high-end services, and wholesale and retail trade. Most Cuban earners had a rather different experience: they worked as operatives and laborers in manufacturing and as office clerks, service workers, and salespeople in the service sectors and wholesale and retail trades. Although varying by sector, the difference in earnings between the high- and low-paying occupations is substantial. The 1988 Current Population Survey data appear to underscore widening income differentials between these two types of occupation.

Income and poverty trends support the indications of growing polarization. Between 1970 and 1988, earnings for Cuban workers as well as the rate of poverty among the working-age population and among earners increased. While incomes of non-Hispanic whites stagnated and those of blacks declined, those of Cuban males rose sharply. The mean income of Cuban females similarly rose, surpassing that of black women in 1988 but remaining well below that of non-Hispanic white females. Paralleling rising incomes were increases in poverty among the working-age population. In 1970, 13% lived in a poor household; by 1988, that rate was 17%. As among blacks, poverty among Cuban earners decreased during the 1970s and increased during the 1980s. Poverty among working-age Cubans appears to be concentrated among women and those over 60. Sixty-eight percent of all Cuban poor were women and 52% elderly. Women constituted 58% of low-wage earners: They made up 70% in the service and clerical occupations in the low- and high-end services and 54% of the operatives in manufacturing.

Explaining the Experience of Cubans in Miami

The incorporation of Cubans into the Miami economy has been generally successful. Rising poverty levels and growing earnings polarization notwithstanding, the economic experience of Cubans differs radically from that of other Latinos in their cities of major concentration as well as from that of other minorities in Miami itself. Cubans have entered the ascending sectors of the regional economy at both higher and lower levels. Although there is a continued concentration of substantial numbers in the manufacturing sector and in low-level occupations, there is also evidence Cuban earners are making a steady transition to higher paying occupations throughout the economy.

Human capital explanations are the most prevalent. Educational attainment—higher for Cubans that for other Latinos—is often mentioned to explain their labor market success. However, in the context of Miami, the higher education levels do not appear to be as important as the earnings Cubans obtain at different levels of education in comparison with others in Miami. Between 1970 and 1988, the levels of educational attainment of Cuban earners have been closer to those of blacks than those of non-Hispanic whites (Table 6.5). In 1988, an equal percentage (67%) of black and Cuban earners had at least a high school degree; the rate for non-Hispanic whites was 88%. Cubans have a slightly higher percentage of college graduates (17%) than blacks (14%). The rate for non-Hispanic whites is 26%.

TABLE 6.5 Educational Attainment of Earners by Race, Miami Metro Area, 1970 to 1988

	White			Black			Cuban		
	1970	*1980*	*1988*	*1970*	*1980*	*1988*	*1970*	*1980*	*1988*
6 yrs or less	4.5	2.4	*	17.6	8.1	*	20.2	16.2	11.1
7 yrs to H.S.	27.1	16.3	11.3	44.2	31.4	26.3	33.6	24.3	22.0
H.S. Graduate	35.1	33.4	38.4	25.0	32.4	36.5	23.7	27.6	28.9
Some College	19.2	24.3	24.1	7.2	18.6	17.5	12.5	17.8	20.6
College Graduate	14.1	23.6	25.8	2.7	8.6	13.9	9.7	13.4	17.4

Sources: U.S. Census PUMS 1970 and 1980, CPS 1988.
Note: (*) cell count too small.

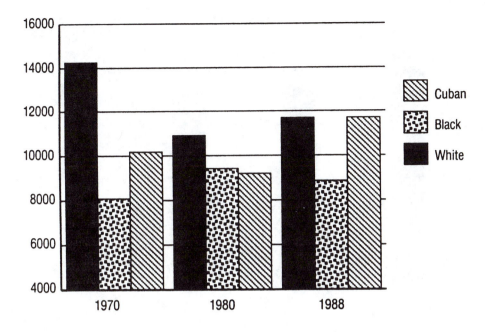

FIGURE 6.6 Earnings of Persons With Some High School Education in Wage and Self-Employment, Miami Metropolitan Area, 1970–1988 (in 1982–1984 dollars)

Sources: U.S. Census PUMS 1970, 1980; CPS 1988.

But, without doubt, Cuban earners are able to maximize the income potential of their educational attainment relative to other minorities. Across different educational levels, Cuban earnings are closer to those of non-Hispanic whites. For example, among earners with less than a high school education, Cuban earnings were more likely to approximate those of non-Hispanic whites, whereas those of blacks tended to lag considerably (Figure 6.6). The gains are even more marked for those with a college education. In 1988, Cuban college graduates earned incomes slightly below non-Hispanic whites and substantially higher than black college graduates (Figure 6.7).

Human capital explanations also focus on the "business know-how" of Cubans as a factor in their higher rates of self-employment. Cubans have, in fact, higher rates of self-employment than other groups in Miami (Figure 6.8). In 1988, rates of self-employment among Cubans (8.5%) surpassed those of non-Hispanic whites (7.4%) and were well above those of blacks (2.9%) in 1988.[9] Similarly, the mean self-employment earnings of Cubans relative to non-Hispanic whites has increased steadily. More important, among Cubans and non-Hispanic whites, mean earnings from self-employment are higher than income from wage and salaries, whereas for blacks the reverse is the case.

The enclave economy appears to have enhanced the effect of education and work experience for Cubans in the Miami labor market. Although the data used in this paper do not allow the measurement of the effect of ethnic-owned enterprises on the incorporation of Cubans into the Miami economy, they do suggest the strength of the enclave. The

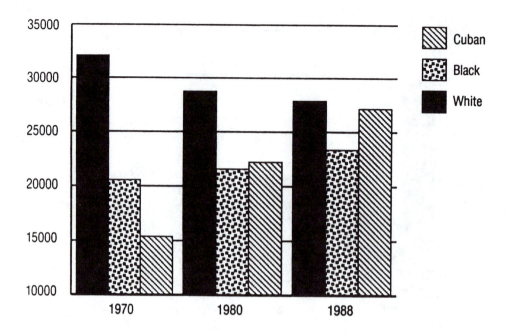

FIGURE 6.7 Earnings of College Graduates in Wages and Self-Employment, Miami Metropolitan Area, 1970–1988 (in 1982–1984 dollars)

Sources: U.S. Census PUMS 1970, 1980; CPS 1988.

occupational shifts that all Miamians have undergone appear to have been buffered for Cubans as a result of the opportunities available to them, but not to others within the enclave. Although enclave earnings are lower than in the mainstream economy, the class diversity of the enclave has allowed Cubans across the occupational spectrum to exercise their human capital in a more protected environment. The enclave has thus facilitated the transition of Cubans into the mainstream sectors. During the 1980s, this transition appears to have accelerated and most likely explains the sustained increases in Cuban earnings.

Perhaps the most critical value of the enclave is the opportunity it affords for a mode of insertion that does not subject newcomers to the same degree of exploitation and discrimination as the primary and secondary labor markets. Enclave participation, even if exploitative, furnishes the immigrants with the opportunity to connect into a myriad of social networks and consequently gain more rapid social mobility. The high rates of self-employment for Cubans who left the island during the 1970s and the Mariel boat lift in 1980 point to the preeminence of structural factors. Although largely lacking the endowed human capital of earlier immigrants, the more recent entrants have nonetheless had better economic outcomes than Latino immigrants with comparable qualifications in other areas of the country (Portes and Bach, 1985, pp. 205–216; Portes and Jensen, 1989).

Although the Portes paradigm is quite powerful, one of its relative weaknesses lies in the explanation for the origins of the enclave. This is no small matter. Understanding how Cuban exiles founded the businesses and established the networks that produced the

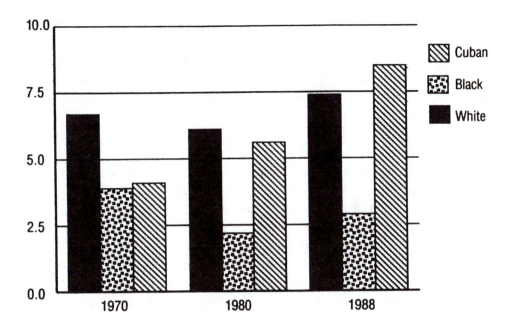

FIGURE 6.8 Self-Employment Rates, by Race and Ethnicity of Earners, Miami Metropolitan Area, 1970–1988

Sources: U.S. Census PUMS 1970, 1980; CPS 1988.

enclave is a central question. Answering it allows the model to transcend the notion of "Cuban exceptionality." Where the original capital that formed the enclave came from is perhaps its most crucial starting point. Portes gives us several answers. First, and perhaps most evident, the Cuban migration included many persons who already had investments and savings in the United States or brought substantial capital that allowed them to become rentiers or start new endeavors. Moreover, many Cuban exiles, because of their pre-1959 dealings with U.S. companies, had useful business connections that served them well when applying for credit and establishing new enterprises. Next, Portes mentions a South American bank in Miami that, when the first exiles arrived, employed Cuban bankers. These bankers proceeded to issue loans to their conationals on the basis of prior knowledge about the applicants' record and experience in Cuba. In the same vein, Portes points to wealthy South Americans who invested their capital in Miami because of political upheavals in their native countries. Primarily in commerce and construction, this venture capital allowed small Cuban distributors and contractors the opportunity to grow beyond the enclave. Its extent and weight are understandably difficult to determine, but drug-related capital accumulation is mentioned. Finally, he underscores the role of individual savings in the smaller, more ethnic-oriented enterprises characteristic of the later entrants who lacked previous business experience and capital from Cuba (Portes, 1987).

These are all eminently convincing components of a structural explanation for the origins of the enclave. Nonetheless, a more complete framework needs to include at least two additional factors. In the first place, as outlined above, the patterns of Cuban development—particularly those of Havana—are crucial aspects of the context in which the initial migration occurred after 1959. Portes and Bach (1985) are quite right to insist on the "relational dynamics" within the international economy as the foundation for migrations. Following their lead, we are arguing for the importance of the specific regional context in establishing the structural framework for the development of the Cuban enclave in Miami after 1960.

The complementary development of Havana and Miami during the 1940s and 1950s allowed Cubans, especially the *habaneros*, to step into familiar territory. Manufacturing firms—not unlike the ones they had left behind in the industrial belt around Havana—came quickly to be controlled by Cubans at the top, and at the same time offered a safe place for lower skilled Cubans to enter the labor market. The enclave also developed a service sector in which experienced entrepreneurs transplanted their business acumen from Havana to *la calle ocho* and provided entry-level jobs for their compatriots.

The second set of considerations is the host of political and ideological factors that, although not exclusively determinant in the origins of the enclave, should be included in the analysis. Silvia Pedraza-Bailey (1985) rightfully focused on the role of the federal government. The United States invested nearly $1 billion in assisting the Cubans because they were fleeing communism. In many ways, it was a multifaceted community development strategy. In its 12 years of existence, federal assistance to Cuban refugees encompassed direct cash assistance, food subsidies, and guaranteed health care for needy individuals as well as college loans for Cuban students, training and retooling programs for professionals, and English-language instruction and financial assistance for those establishing small businesses. State intervention reinforced the advantages of the Cubans, and in turn enhanced the ability of the exiles to contribute to the transformation of the South Florida economy. No other Latino group or community has had the benefit of similar levels of targeted investment and state intervention sustained over a significant period of time.

More recently, Carlos Forment (1989) has argued for the role of ideology within a political and structural context in the emergence of the enclave during the 1960s. The geopolitics of the Caribbean after the Cuban revolution and the interplay of the U.S. state and exile counter-revolutionary movements articulated a political discourse that significantly contributed to the development of a Cuban collective identity. Forment contends political convictions and activities are as important in community formation as the market forces and state intervention that Portes et al. and Pedraza-Bailey, respectively, emphasize. The role of the Central Intelligence Agency in providing some exiles with capital and business experience through the establishment of proprietary fronts should, for example, be mentioned, even if the full range of evidence is difficult to obtain (Argüelles, 1982; Forment, 1989). The downfall of Eastern European socialism, the disintegration of the Soviet Union, and current uncertainties about the future of Cuba itself, moreover, have reinforced the weight of ideological concerns in Cuban ethnic identity.

Two important questions in relationship to the future of the Cuban enclave are, first, the role of second-generation Cubans in the enclave economy, and second, the effect on the enclave on the growing diversity of the Latino population in Miami. There are indications from the data analyzed here that the retail enterprises in the enclave may serve as an entry point into the labor market for younger Cubans, particularly the retail trade sector. The question of whether they will fuel a second generation of the Cuban enclave or, as in other ethnic groups, the younger generation will immediately transcend it has not yet been answered. Similarly, there is evidence that "Other Hispanics" have very quickly attained even higher levels of self-employment than Cubans. Just a cursory observation of the main establishments of the enclave reveals that Central Americans are easily penetrating it both as owners and as workers. Nicaraguans are the main national group involved, which underscores the weight of the political and ideological factors framing the development and maintenance of the enclave.

CONCLUSIONS

In this chapter we bring out new facets of the images of Cubans in Miami. Although still impressive, the Cuban experience is considerably more complex than the success story would indicate. Miami developed very differently from the pattern anticipated during the 1930s and 1940s. As the U.S. gateway to Latin America was emerging, revolution convulsed Havana—Miami's Latin American counterpart. Consequently, many of the Cubans who were fueling the transformation of Havana during the 1950s made their way to Miami. Their presence in turn provided an added impetus to the development of Miami. During the 1960s, Miami and the exiles became an almost perfect match. Cubans thus look less like superachievers and more like a group intelligently transferring their skills to a propitious environment.

Our perspective allows us to underscore some general lessons. First, the Cuban experience exemplifies successful state and private sector strategies on the adjustment and incorporation of immigrants. Encouraging the development of the enclave allowed Cubans the resources to control their own community. Far from the "social welfare" approach so characteristic of public and private sector policies toward other Latinos, which so diminish and disempower individuals and communities, Cubans had the opportunity to exercise control over their community. Community development and community control, important pillars in the struggles of most Latino communities, have been critical factors in the attainments of Cubans in Miami. The fear of permanent separation from the mainstream that the independent development of Latino and immigrant communities often raises, as well as the concern that strong ethnic identity retards economic advancement, did not materialize in the Cuban case.

A second important lesson is the breadth of the Cuban Refugee Program and other federal initiatives to support the adaptation of Cubans. The range of programs offered tops any Latino community's wish list: educational opportunities; retraining programs; English-language instruction; small business loans; college loans independent of need; and nonstigmatized direct cash benefits, health care, and food for those in need. Although these programs are not solely responsible for the Cuban success, they did provide a buffer against the initial, often traumatic experience of immigrants. No other Latino group has enjoyed similar favors. In this sense, the Cuban experience is indeed unique and needs to be underscored when comparing Cubans to other Latinos.

A growing concern is the state of race relations in Miami, and our study likewise points to some insights. Three concurrent economic processes underlie relations among the three main groups. The first is the overwhelming success of non-Hispanic white workers who, after all, constitute the most important success story. Far from the sense of loss embodied in the slogan—" Will the last American to leave Miami, please bring the flag?"—non-Hispanic whites have been the principal beneficiaries of the economic transformations of the past four decades. Nevertheless, the Latinization of Miami has not been welcomed, the success of English-only legislation being but one example of undoubtedly white dissatisfaction. Cuban attainments in Miami have undoubtedly most closely challenged the hegemony of non-Hispanic whites. Moreover, the ever-closer economic ties between Miami and Latin America underscore the importance of the Cuban success beyond the enclave. The prospects of continued Cuban advancement amid non-Hispanic white relative stagnation frame a most important backdrop to ethnic relations in Miami.

The second economic process underlying race relations is the marginalization of the black community. Blacks have not fared well in the processes of economic change in Miami. That change, set in motion well before the Cubans first arrived in the city, never took blacks' best interests into consideration. The advantages that some blacks have derived from their insertion in the ascending sectors of the economy are dwarfed by the severe disadvantages endured by the bulk of the black community. Although Cubans seem all-powerful from the perspective of blacks, Cubans are in fact less privileged than blacks think them to be. Up to the 1980s, the socioeconomic profiles of the two groups were more alike than different, especially when compared to non-Hispanic whites. However, as Cuban economic outcomes improved and those of blacks declined, and particularly as Cubans have attained more political power, the social separation and distrust between the two groups have become exacerbated.

The third process in understanding race relations in Miami is the changes within the Latino community itself. During the 1980s, the increase in the Latino population has been quite significant. Other Latinos, the principal contributors to that growth, appear to be taking advantage of the enclave. Not all, however, are doing so. Tensions between Cubans and Puerto Ricans may stem from the latter's lesser access to the protection of the enclave. For Cubans, now in titular control of the political structures, managing the demographic transition taking place in Miami is proving to be a more difficult task than achieving economic success. The future of group relations, indeed, depends on the economic and social development of the black and other Latino communities in Miami. Policies need to favor community-based economic development and employment and educational opportunities—policies similar to those that supported the successful incorporation of Cubans into the Miami economy.

STUDY QUESTIONS

1. Did the class position of Cuban immigrants before 1959 ease assimilation?

2. If we accept the contention that "in 1958, Havana certainly overshadowed Miami," does this represent a unique migration to and from "evenly" developed areas?

3. How did Miami's economy and demographics change following increased Cuban immigration?

NOTES

Author's Note: Research funded through the Inter-University Program for Latino Research and a 1989 Faculty Development Grant from the Research Foundation of the State University of New York to Pérez-Stable. Françoise Carre and Michael Stoll of the Gastón Institute at the University of Massachusetts provided invaluable help in analyzing the data. We thank Guillermo Grenier, Edwin Meléndez, Yolanda Preito, and Andrés Torres for their comments. We are, of course, solely responsible for the analysis.

1. Prohías and Casal (1973) first pointed out the "dysfunctional" consequences of the "success story."

2. The 1950 PUMS is a 1/100 composite sample for Miami State Economic Area, Code 70 (sample size: 3,894). The 1970 PUMS is a 1% sample for the Miami SMSA, Code 3302 (sample size: 9,347). The 1980 PUMS is a 5% "A" sample of the Miami Metro Area (Dade County) Code 043–052 (sample size: 58,884). The PUMS data sets used in the study employed the Miami Metropolitan Area defined in the 1980 PUMS for the extraction of the samples for 1950 and 1970. The 1988 March CPS is for the Miami SMSA (sample size: 1698). The 1960 PUMS is not used because data were reported statewide. The 1960 data reported were drawn from the sources noted.

3. *Psychosocial Dynamics in Miami* (Coral Gables, FL: University of Miami, January 1969, p. xxxvi). The report notes Miami led the United States in rates of increase in new manufacturing plants, new manufacturing payrolls, and new manufacturing value added.

4. The total wage bill excluded the salaries of sugar agricultural workers and only partially included other agricultural wages. See Pérez-Stable (1993) for a fuller analysis of Cuban development during the 1950s.

5. In 1950, there was no Latino identifier in the U.S. Census. The identification of Latino ethnicity in the 1950 PUMS was based on surname of the respondent or on Hispanic country of birth for respondent. Cubans are not identifiable as a distinct group in the 1950 PUMS.

6. The 1970 PUMS identifies Latinos by the birthplace of the parents.

7. Beginning in 1980, the U.S. Census contained a Latino identifier that asked respondents to identify their Lation background as well as the specific national group.

8. Because of the reduced cases in the cells, the figures for 1988 only provide an indication of trends and should be cautiously read.

9. Self-employment among Central Americans in Miami (8.7%) surpasses the high rates of Cubans.

REFERENCES

Argüelles, L. (1982, Summer). *Cuban Miami: The roots, development and everyday life of an emigre enclave in the U.S. national security state. Contemporary marxism,* 5, 27–43.

Ballinger, K. (1936). *Miami millions: The Dance of the Dollars in the Great Florida Land Boom of 1925.* Miami, FL: Franklin Press.

Banco Nacional de Cuba. (1960). *Memoria 1958–1959.* Havana: Editorial Lex.

Bluestone, B., Stevenson, M.H.,Tilly, C. (1992). *An Assessment of the Impact of "Deindustrialization" and the Special Mismatch on the Labor Market Outcomes of Young White, Black, and Latino Men and Women Who Have Limited Schooling.* The John McCormack Institute of Public Affairs, University of Massachusetts, Boston.

Bonilla, R. C. (1983). *Escritos Económicos.* Havana. Editorial de Ciencias Sociales.

Cardoso, F.H., & Faletto, E. (1979). *Dependency and Development in Latin America.* Berkeley: University of California Press.

Center for Advanced International Studies. (1967). *The Cuban Immigration, 1959-1966, and its impact on Miami-Dade County, Florida* (A study conducted for the Department of Health Education and Welfare, HEW WA 66 05). Coral Gables: University of Miami, Research Institute for Cuba and the Caribbean.

Forment, C.A. (1989, January). *Political Practice and the Rise of an Ethnic Enclave: The Cuban-American Case, 1959-1979. Theory and Society,* 18, 47–81.

Kasarda, J.D. (1989). *Urban Industrial Transition and the Underclass. Annuals of the American Academy of Political and Social Science,* 501, 26–47.

Muir, H. (1953). *Miami, U.S.A.* Coconut Grove, FL: Hurricane House.

Oficina Nacional de los Censos Demografico y Electoral. (1955). *Censos de población, viviendas y electoral: Informe general.* La Habana: P. Fernandez y Ciá, S. en C.

Pedraza-Bailey, S. (1985). *Political and Economic Migrants in America: Cubans and Mexicans.* Austin: University of Texas Press.

Portes, A. (1987, October). *The social origins of the Cuban enclave economy in Miami. Sociological Perspectives,* 30, 340–372.

Portes, A. & Bach, R.L. (1985) *Latin journey: Cuban and Mexican immigrants in the United States.* Berkeley: University of California Press.

Portes, A., & Jensen. L. (1989, December). *The enclave and the entrants: Patterns of ethnic enterprise in Miami before and after Mariel. American Sociological Review,* 54, 929–949.

Portes, A., & Manning, R.D. (1986). The immigrant enclave: Theory and *empirical examples.* In S. Olzak & J. Nagel (Eds.), *Comparative ethnic relations.* Orlando, FL: Academic Press.

Sassen, S. (1991). *The global city: NewYork, London, Tokyo.* Princeton, NJ: Princeton University Press.

U.S. Department of Commerce. (1955). *Investment in Cuba.* Washington, D.C.

Waldinger, R. (1986). *Through the eye of the needle: Immigrants and enterprise in New York's garment trade.* New York: New York University Press.

Wolff, R.P. (1945). *Miami: Economic Pattern of a Resort Area.* Coral Gables, FL: University of Miami.

Wilson, K., & Portes, A. (1980). *Immigrant Enclaves: A Comparision of the Cuban and Black Economies of Miami. American Journal of Sociology,* 86(2), 295–319

Chapter 7

Paul Ong and Evelyn Blumenberg

Scientists and Engineers

From Silicon Valley to Route 128, from laboratories in major research universities to private think-tanks, Asian Pacific American scientists and engineers have made enormous contributions to the U.S. economy. A few have risen to the pinnacles of their professions as Nobel Prize winners, presidents of universities, and executives of "high-tech" corporations. Far more important are the hundreds of thousands who receive less public recognition but nonetheless perform invaluable services. While this infusion of Asian Pacific Americans has brought immeasurable benefits to this nation, their presence has raised numerous issues that must be resolved to maximize individual potential and the national interest.[1]

To understand the importance of this group of professionals, we start by first summarizing the role of technology and of scientists and engineers (S&Es) in the U.S. economy. Despite a sizable expansion of the S&E labor force over the last two decades, the United States has failed to produce sufficient numbers during a time when technology has come to play a more important role in determining the competitiveness of nations in the global economy. The next section examines the phenomenal growth and characteristics of the Asian Pacific S&E labor force. Asian Pacific scientists and engineers have very high levels of educational attainment, are concentrated in research and development, and are overwhelmingly comprised of the foreign-born but U.S.-educated. The third section focuses on the supply of immigrants, which is governed by a complex process involving the "Westernization/Americanization" of higher education on a global scale and by

From *The State of Asian Pacific America: Economic Diversity, Issues & Policies*, edited by Paul Ong. LEAP Asian Pacific American Policy Institute and UCLA Asian American Studies Center (1994).

immigration regulation. Together, these two factors have created an extremely educated labor pool of Asian Pacific S&Es who fill critical positions in the U.S. economy. The final section examines how well these professionals are faring. The analysis indicates earnings parity, although immigrants are likely to earn less than non-immigrants. The major issue confronting Asian Pacific Americans in these fields is the "glass ceiling," specifically the barriers to upper management positions.

SCIENTISTS AND ENGINEERS

The economic well-being of the United States depends on its technological capacities (Porter, 1990; Grossman and Helpman, 1991; Nelson and Wright, 1992; Dollar and Wolff, 1993). Since World War II, investments in higher education and research and development (R&D) and the expansion of a highly educated labor force have contributed to increasing productivity and a rising standard of living. More recently, technology has taken on importance in terms of international trade. One indication is the fact that America's exporting industries are more technologically intensive than America's manufacturing base as a whole; exporting industries employ a higher proportion of highly-educated workers than the rest of the economy (Abowd and Freeman, 1991, pp. 17–18). The industries where we have an advantage over other nations are those where we have a technological edge.

Scientists and engineers are crucial in determining this nation's technological capacity through their role in the creation of basic knowledge, the transformation of it to practical applications, and designing and operation of complex and sophisticated equipment. Scientists and engineers are central to the innovation of products and production processes. They are the critical personnel for complex projects such as the Information Superhighway, the Joint International Space Station, the Human Genome Project, and SEMATECH, the joint public-private R&D venture in semi-conductors. Their contributions are not limited to these high-profile endeavors. S&Es apply their talents to improving everyday electronic and mechanical equipment, drugs and chemical-based products, and thousands of other goods. As a group, S&Es comprise a significant part of the labor force in what Robert Reich calls the symbolic-analytic services (1992), which constitute the key sector of advanced economies.

While this nation's high-technology labor force has expanded, the growth is less than one might expect given the increasing importance of technology, both domestically and internationally. Between 1970 and 1990, the number of S&Es climbed from 1.8 million to 2.9 million, according to the U.S. Census.[2] Despite this increase, the growth of the S&E labor force (65 percent) only slightly outpaced the growth of the total labor force (51 percent). In other words, S&Es as a percentage of the total work force increased only marginally (from 2.2 to 2.4 percent). Moreover, changes in the educational levels do not indicate an unambiguous upgrading. On the positive side is a decline in the proportion of S&Es with less than four years of college education, which decreased from 41 percent 1970 to 30 percent in 1990. On the other hand, the proportion with some graduate training has not increased. In 1970, 25 percent had five or more years of college education, while in 1990, 23 percent had post-bachelor's degrees. Other data reveal that the problem is particularly severe at the doctorate level. Total Ph.D. production in S&E increased rapidly after 1960, peaked in 1972, and then declined until the late 1970s; only in the 1980s has the number of science and engineering Ph.D.s increased, but much of this is tied to an increase in the number of foreign students (Atkinson, 1990).

The difficulty this nation faces in producing an adequate supply of S&Es at the right time and in the right place is rooted in the very nature of the labor market for these workers. This country has suffered from niche and cyclical shortages due to changes in public expenditures and rapid expansions or contractions of industries associated with product cycles and business cycles. For example, defense spending, long the single largest source of public expenditure on R&D and the production of high-technology goods, first built up the aerospace industry and then later decimated it, dislocating thousands of aerospace engineers (Ong and Lawerence, 1993). In contrast, the rapid growth in high-technology sectors in micro-electronics has heightened the demand for highly educated scientific workers, even while this nation has lost production to off-shore and foreign operations (Ong and Mar, 1992).

The sudden fluctuation in demand throws the market into disequilibrium. In the short term, the supply of S&Es is unable to adjust quickly. This is caused in part by a limitation on the transferability of skills across fields; consequently, a shortage in one industry cannot be easily relieved by recruiting individuals working in other industries. Moreover, the number of new entrants cannot be rapidly expanded. The effective number of new entrants is determined by the number of students who entered higher education years earlier, when the relative attractiveness of the field could have been very different. In other words, response to changes in demand takes years, by which time the need could have reversed or shifted to other sectors.[3]

Producing S&Es with advanced training suffers from not only fluctuations in demand but also from a more basic market imperfection. Research and development, as a public good, generates social benefits that may not be captured as profits by private industry. One consequence is that investments in R&D can be lower than optimal from a societal perspective. This flaw has been the basis for government incentives to R&D, but despite these efforts R&D expenditures as a percentage of GND declined throughout much of the 1970s and 1980s.[4] The inability of private enterprise to completely internalize the benefits of R&D translates into lower salaries for highly trained workers and dampens the demand for graduate degrees in technology fields. Northrup and Malin (1985) find that since the mid-1960s the starting salaries of Ph.D., master's, and bachelor graduates with engineering and technology degrees have converged; between 1966 and 1982, the relative difference between the monthly starting salary of a Ph.D. and master's and between master's and baccalaureate declined by more than one-half.

An analysis of 1990 census data show that the returns to advanced degrees may not be sufficiently high to attract individuals to pursue graduate studies.[5] For both scientists and engineers, earning a master's degree increases hourly wages by 14 to 15 percent, which is considerably higher than working two additional years, generating a 3 to 4 percent increase annually.[6] These estimates are likely to be biased upward because the admissions process creams the most talented, so some of the increase should be attributed to the screening and not just to the education. There appears to be sufficient incentives despite the trends in starting salaries of S&Es with master's versus those with bachelor's. For those who continue with their education, completing a doctorate would increase wages by about another 9 percent for scientists and 15 percent for engineers relative to those with a master's degree. Nonetheless, difficulties in completing the required course of study and uncertainty over employment opportunities make the venture risky and lead to a lower expected rate of return (Ehrenberg, 1992). It takes at least another four years after completion of a master's degree to complete a doctorate, time that can be used to acquire on-the-job experience that also increases wages. The adjusted net returns to a doctorate, then, do not appear to offer enough financial incentives for many to continue. Of course, factors other than financial reward contribute to the decisions of those who do pursue advanced studies, but at the aggregate level they do not completely offset the shortcomings inherent in the labor market.

CHARACTERISTICS OF ASIAN PACIFIC ENGINEERS AND SCIENTISTS

No other minority group has contributed more to the technological capacity of this nation than Asian Pacific Americans. Although the S&E labor force is still largely non-Hispanic white, Asian Pacific Americans have become an increasing presence. They accounted for less than 2 percent in 1970 but nearly 7 percent by 1990. This increase has been driven by an incredible growth of the Asian Pacific S&E labor force. During the two decades, the number jumped from about 21,000 to 150,000, an increase of 603 percent. Extrapolating from recent trends, it is likely that there are now over a quarter-million Asian Pacific scientists and engineers. Like the larger Asian Pacific population, the S&Es come from ethnically diverse groups. Chinese comprise the largest ethnic group (34 percent), followed by Asian Indians (23 percent), Japanese (12 percent), and Filipinos (10 percent).

The presence of Asian Pacific Americans varies considerably by field and level of education, as well as by place of employment and activity. Table 7.1 summarizes estimates from the 1980 and 1990 Censuses.[7] While Asian Pacific Americans are under-represented among those without a bachelor's degree, they are extremely over-represented among those with graduate degrees.[8] They comprise one-sixth of those with either a master's or professional degree. Their greatest presence is among engineers with a doctorate degree, comprising over one-fifth of this group. Moreover, Asian Pacific S&Es are highly concentrated at the centers of high technology. For example, in Silicon Valley, America's premier site for the production of semi-conductors and other related electronics products, they comprise one-quarter of all scientists and engineers and over one-third of those with advanced degrees.[9]

Along with higher levels of education, Asian Pacific Americans are more likely to participate in research and development. Table 7.2 summarizes the primary activities of white and Asian Pacific S&Es with at least a bachelor's degree.[10] One distinctive difference is that Asian Pacific Americans have a lower probability of being in management positions; this phenomenon will be discussed later. The other important racial difference is the relatively high numbers whose primary activity is R&D, 34 percent compared to 24 percent for whites. This is not unexpected given the educational characteristics of

TABLE 7.1 Racial Distribution of Engineering and Scientific Labor Force, 1980 and 1990

	NH-White	Asian Pacific	Others
1980, All			
Total	90%	4%	6%
Less than BA	90%	2%	8%
BA	91%	4%	5%
MA/Prof.	87%	8%	5%
Ph.D.	83%	14%	3%
1990, All			
Total	85%	7%	8%
Less than BA	87%	3%	10%
BA	87%	6%	7%
MA/Prof.	81%	12%	7%
Ph.D.	81%	15%	4%
1990, Engineers			
Total	86%	7%	7%
Less than BA	89%	2%	8%
BA	87%	7%	6%
MA/Prof.	80%	14%	7%
Ph.D.	73%	22%	6%
1990, Scientists			
Total	85%	7%	9%
Less than BA	84%	3%	13%
BA	86%	6%	8%
MA/Prof.	83%	11%	6%
Ph.D.	84%	13%	4%

Estimated from U.S. Bureau of the Census, 1990 1% Public Use Microdata Sample.
The total may not equal 100 percent because of rounding.

Asian Pacific Americans. Having an advanced degree increases the odds of participation in R&D (for all S&Es, the figures are 18 percent for those with a bachelor's, 27 percent for those with a master's or professional degree, and 41 percent for those with a doctorate). Variations in educational composition, however, account for only about one-third of the racial difference.[11] Within degree categories, Asian Pacific Americans exhibit a higher probability of doing research and development, and the greatest difference is among those with a doctorate degree, 14 percentage points.

Another unique characteristic of the Asian Pacific S&E labor force is the prominence of immigrants. While 92 percent of non-Asian Pacific S&Es in 1990 were born in the U.S., only 17 percent of Asian Pacific S&Es were. Nearly half of the foreign-born (47 percent) arrived during the 1980s. The composition by nativity varies by degree level, with the percentage of U.S.-born falling with higher educational attainment. While 27 percent of those without a bachelor's degree were U.S.-born, only 6 percent of those with a doctorate were U.S.-born. Being an immigrant, however, does not imply being foreign-educated.

TABLE 7.2 Primary Activity of Those Employed as Scientists and Engineers

	R&D	R&D Management	Other Management	Other
1982, All				
White	24%	6%	13%	57%
Asian Pacific	34%	5%	8%	54%
1982, Bachelor's				
White	18%	5%	15%	61%
Asian Pacific	21%	3%	10%	66%
1982, Master/Prof.				
White	27%	8%	12%	53%
Asian Pacific	33%	6%	9%	52%
1982, Ph.D.				
White	40%	7%	4%	49%
Asian Pacific	54%	6%	1%	39%
1989, Ph.D.				
White	36%	8%	9%	47%
Asian Pacific	52%	8%	3%	37%

Sources: U.S. Department of Commerce, Survey of Natural and Social Scientists and Engineers, 1989; National Science Foundation (1991a).

In fact, the vast majority are educated in the United States, as documented by Table 7.3.[12] This is particularly true for those with advanced degrees.

THE SUPPLY OF IMMIGRANT S&Es

Given the dominance of immigrants among Asian Pacific S&Es, it is important to examine this particular supply more closely. INS (Immigration and Naturalization Service) data reveal the magnitude of the flows. Between 1972 and 1985, over 50,000 S&Es from the major Asian Pacific sending sources (India, South Korea, the Philippines, Taiwan, Hong Kong, and China) became permanent immigrants (Ong, Cheng, and Evans, 1992, p. 545). More recent data show that another 17,000 became permanent immigrants between 1989 and 1991. Several factors contribute to the influx of Asian Pacific immigrant S&Es. A necessary condition is the "Westernization" of higher education in the technical fields, which creates an international labor pool, and the United States has played the key role in this process in recent decades (Ong, Cheng, and Evans, 1992). This is manifested in the adoption of Western and American curriculum in the technical fields by universities throughout Asia and other parts of the Third World. Frequently, the courses are taught by professors trained in the U.S.[13] This process has created an international class of workers receiving roughly the same basic education in the sciences and engineering. However, given the limitations of higher education in Asia, this applies primarily to undergraduate education.

TABLE 7.3 Scientists and Engineers in 1982 by Nativity and Place of Education

	U.S.-Born	Foreign-Born U.S.-Educated	Foreign-Born Foreign-Educated
NH-White	94%	4%	2%
Asian Pacific	21%	63%	16%
Others	75%	19%	5%
Asian Pacific American by Education			
Bachelor's	36%	31%	33%
Master/prof.	16%	78%	6%
Ph.D.	8%	83%	9%

Source: U.S. Department of Commerce, Survey of Natural and Social Scientists and Engineers, 1989.

The "Americanization" process works in another and even more important way. Given this country's preeminence in technology during much of the post–World War II period, the U.S. emerged as the most desirable place to study for students from developing nations.[14] Between the academic years of 1954–55 and 1990–91, the foreign-student population in the U.S. grew from 34,232 to 407,529. There are more foreign students studying in this country than the total for the next three leading host countries. Over one-half of the foreign students in the U.S. are from Asia, and another fifth are from other Third World nations. In engineering and science, the number of foreign students increased from 18,545 in 1959–60 to 145,740 in 1990–91, with the vast majority coming from the Third World.

Foreign students are particularly noticeable in graduate programs. For example, while foreign students comprised less than one-tenth of the engineering undergraduates in 1985, they made up over one-quarter of those in master's programs and over two-fifths in doctorate programs (Falk, 1988, p. 58). Although the figures in the sciences are less dramatic, foreign students nevertheless comprise a significant number of the graduate students in these fields as well. In the two fields taken together, the percentage of non-U.S. citizens receiving doctorates from U.S. universities more than doubled from 16 percent in 1960 to 34 percent in 1990. By 1990, 7,444 foreign-born earned doctorate degrees in science and engineering, up from only 3,295 in 1970 (National Science Foundation, 1991a). The increase has continued despite both the fluctuations in the total number of science and engineering doctorates granted during the 1970s and the improvement of educational institutions in developing countries.

Asians make up the largest contingent of foreign students studying in the U.S. The total number from Asia grew from less than 10,000 in the mid-1950s to 130,000 by 1989–90 (Zikopoulos, 1991, p. 14). For the latter year, nearly one-half were in engineering and scientific fields (46 percent), and among the Asians in these fields, over two-thirds were graduate students. With this heavy concentration, it is not surprising that Asians comprised a large majority of all foreign students in science and engineering—63 percent of all foreign students and 74 percent of those in graduate studies.[15]

Almost one-quarter (23 percent) of all science and engineering Ph.D.s conferred in 1990 were awarded to Asian-born students (National Science Foundation, 1991a).

The countries of origin among foreign-born Asian science and engineering doctorates have shifted over the years. In 1960, over half of the doctorates awarded to foreign-born Asian students went to individuals born in China and India (59 percent). Among the remaining Asian countries, Korea and Japan were the countries of origin for roughly 8 percent each. By 1990, an increasing number of students entered from Taiwan and Korea. Seventy-one percent of foreign-born Asian Pacific scientists and engineers in 1990 were from four countries — the People's Republic of China (20 percent), Taiwan (20 percent), Korea (19 percent), and India (14 percent).

While most came under the assumption that they would return and contribute to the development of their home country, many, perhaps a majority, stayed in this country after completing their education. This is particularly true for those with advanced degrees. A little more than one-third (35 percent) of all non-U.S. citizens receiving doctorates in 1990 planned to seek employment or further training outside of the U.S.; the majority intended to remain in the U.S., perhaps largely in hopes of gaining permanent immigrant status (National Science Foundation, 1991a). Data on Taiwanese students indicates how extreme this no-return phenomenon can be. Between 1961 and 1981, only 15 percent of the 86,000 persons who went abroad to study returned, and the large majority of these emigrated to the United States (Liao and Hsieh, n.d.). Even among those who do return to their native countries, many eventually come back to the United States. The stayers, along with the returnees who re-migrate and emigrants trained in their native country, constitute the total supply of Asian Pacific immigrant S&Es.

Several factors contribute to the flow of highly educated Asian Pacific Americans. The first is that the sending countries are less attractive places for these students to pursue their career. These countries have not achieved a level of economic development that would generate the necessary demand for these types of workers, lack the technological infrastructure needed to support sophisticated research and development, and generally offer low salaries. Although these disadvantages slowly wane as development proceeds, the United States still offers far superior employment and career opportunities. Because the frame of reference that influenced educational and career choices is international, the low rate of return for advanced degrees within the U.S. labor market, which was discussed at the beginning of this chapter, is not a disincentive for Asian foreign students. Indeed, receiving such a degree can offer a high rate of return because it increases the probability of working in the U.S. for these individuals.

The odds of becoming a permanent resident are shaped by immigration regulations. After the enactment of the 1965 Immigration Law, Asian Pacific Americans have qualified for occupation-based visas, which have been made available to those who can fill positions where there is a labor shortage.[16] Given the shortages of the S&E labor market, the immigration law has created a major avenue for migration of those with college and university degrees in science and engineering, especially those with advanced degrees. Although the regulations were tightened in the mid-1970s, there are still nonetheless large flows of Asian S&Es.

TABLE 7.4 Immigrant Scientists and Engineers, 1989-91

	Engineers	Math/ Computer Science	Scientists	Total
Total Asian Pacific	13,063	2,504	1,433	17,000
% of All Immigrants	46%	52%	38%	46%
Country of Birth				
India	32%	26%	41%	32%
Taiwan	16%	31%	14%	18%
China	14%	14%	18%	15%
Hong Kong	6%	9%	4%	6%
Mode of Entry				
Adjusters, occup.	34%	61%	50%	40%
Non-adjusters, occup.	13%	12%	13%	12%
Other adjusters	8%	12%	13%	9%
Settlement by State				
California	37%	28%	21%	34%
New York	10%	16%	17%	11%
New Jersey	8%	20%	9%	10%
Illinois	6%	6%	5%	6%
Texas	5%	5%	7%	5%

Estimates from U.S. Immigration and Naturalization Service, Immigrant Public Use Tapes, 1989 to 1991 Fiscal Years.

This can be seen in Table 7.4. Adjusters, those who had entered the country on temporary visas, comprised nearly half of all immigrants, and most received permanent residency through one of the occupational categories. Among the adjusters, 44 percent held F1 visas (student), and another 39 percent held H1 visas (temporary worker). The presence of so many H1s indicate that many students underwent an intermediate step in becoming a permanent resident. The data also indicate that one-quarter of the non-adjusters entered through the occupational categories. Thus, over half of these new immigrants entered to fill positions in areas of labor shortages.

The flow of Asian Pacific immigrants has helped meet the demand for S&E workers in the U.S. Moreover, regulations help screen workers so that immigrants tend to help fill niches within shortage areas. These immigrants are not necessarily first in the hiring queue. U.S. employers prefer hiring permanent residents or citizens. The literature cites a number of reasons for this preference. First, the labor certification process, the process in which employers document that they have made a good-faith effort to hire U.S. citizens before hiring immigrants, may impose additional costs on employers in the form of tedious paperwork and delays, costs that could be avoided if employers hire permanent residents or U.S. citizens (Finn, 1988; Cannon, 1988). Second, many foreign graduates from U.S. universities have difficulties obtaining security clearances and may, therefore, be unsuitable candidates for employment in defense-related industries (National Research Council, 1988). And finally, a preference for U.S.-born workers may ultimately rest on racial or ethnic prejudices.

Despite the above factors, about half of U.S. firms that use S&Es hire foreign-born employees (National Science Foundation, 1986). Frequently, this hiring occurs when there are few or no other applicants in the labor queue for a position. This is particularly true when the opening is for those with graduate training. It is this latter factor that helps explain why the educational levels of Asian Pacific S&Es tend to be very high.

In some cases, the matching of jobs and immigrants can alleviate shortages at the aggregate level. Fields in which employers most frequently report shortages to the National Science Foundation tend to be the fields with high inflows of foreign nationals (Finn, 1988). For example, in 1980–81 employers reported few shortages of recently graduated Ph.D. students in the life and social sciences; consequently, the percentage of foreign nationals in these two fields was small, 8 percent and 6 percent respectively. However, within engineering, the relationship between immigration and areas of relative aggregate shortage is not so apparent, because foreign nationals constituted between one-third and one-half of all new Ph.D.s entering the U.S. work force regardless of the relative degree of shortage in a particular sub-field of engineering. In these areas, the matches are defined at the level of individual positions.[17]

EARNINGS AND GLASS CEILINGS

How well Asian Pacific scientists and engineers fare can be measured by their earnings and their representation in management positions. Aggregate measures of earnings indicate a convergence of earnings between Asian Pacific Americans and (non-Hispanic) whites. For example, the median annual salary for Asian Pacific doctoral S&Es as a percentage of the median for whites grew from about 93 percent in the early 1970s to 100 percent in the later 1980s (National Science Foundation, 1991). The latter figure is consistent with an analysis of 1990 census data, which yield an earnings ratio of 99 percent between Asian Pacific Americans and NH whites. For scientists and engineers at all educational levels, the ratio is 97 percent. There is also rough parity when the data are analyzed by broad occupational categories (see Table 7.5).

The above comparisons, however, do not reveal if Asian Pacific Americans earn the same as NH whites after accounting for factors such as education, occupation, and immigrant status that should influence wages. Data indicate that the two populations are not comparable because Asian Pacific Americans are more likely to hold advanced degrees, to work as engineers, and to be immigrants. When the 1990 data is disaggregated by degree and broad occupational groupings, the results show that Asian Pacific Americans generally earn less than their NH white counterparts, in some cases about one-tenth less. Several factors, such as type of activity, age and years of professional experience, gender, nativity, place of education, and place of employment can account for observed differences. Moreover, discrimination also affects earnings.[18]

TABLE 7.5 Median Annual Earnings, 1989 (x 1,000)

	Engineers		Scientists	
	Non-Hispanic Whites	Asian Pacific	Non-Hispanic Whites	Asian Pacific
All Ed. Level	$40.5	$40.8	$35.0	$34.6
Less Than Bachelor's	$36.5	$36.0	$30.6	$26.0
Bachelor's	$40.8	$37.0	$34.9	$32.0
Master's/Prof.	$49.6	$45.0	$40.0	$40.0
Ph.D.	$57.2	$54.0	$48.0	$44.0

Estimates from U.S. Bureau of Census, 1990 1% Public Use Microdata Sample.

Analyzing "pure" racial difference is best done by examining U.S.-born scientists and engineers, because any discrepancy in pay for immigrants may be due to cultural and linguistic factors rather than racial differences. Our analysis indicates that U.S.-born Asian Pacific scientists earned more than their NH white counterparts after controlling for observable factors, but finds no inter-group difference among engineers.[19] The higher earnings of Asian Pacific scientists may be due to differences in the quality of education, since they are more likely to have attended elite universities. In other words, there may be some bias against this group that is not detected due to our inability to control for quality of education. Although we do not know of any study of engineering that controls for this factor, one study of recent college graduates in all fields that controls for the quality of education finds lower earnings for Asians, *ceritis paribus* (Weinberger, 1993).

Among Asian Pacific Americans, there are significant differences of wages by nativity, time of entry into this country, and place of education. An analysis of 1990 data indicates that recent Asian Pacific immigrants (in the country for five years or less) in the sciences earn about one-fifth to one-quarter less in hourly wages than their U.S.-born counterparts, and that recent immigrants in engineering earn about one-third less than their U.S.-born counterparts.[20] The gap declines with additional time in the U.S., and disappears after 20 to 25 years. The wage differences are even greater in terms of annual earnings, indicating recent immigrants not only receive a lower wage but also work fewer hours. Moreover, wage differences may be due to the increase in the number of Asian Pacific scientists and engineers who enter the U.S. without an American education; thus, the lower earnings of recent immigrants may reflect unobserved differences in the quality and type of education among immigrant cohorts. An analysis of the 1989 Survey of Natural and Social Scientists and Engineers, which contains information on place of education, indicates that those with a foreign education earn about 10 percent less than those with a U.S. education, and that there are no differences in the wages between the U.S.-born and foreign-born employees with a U.S. education after controlling for other factors.[21]

Immigration regulations may contribute to the low wages of new immigrants. In order to hire an alien, employers must prove that no U.S. worker is qualified and available for that position and that the job offer meets prevailing wages. The positions that are least likely to be filled are those where the offering wage fails to attract domestic applicants.[22]

Foreign scientists and engineers may be willing to accept lower salaries in order to obtain full-time employment in the U.S., a prerequisite for permanent residency (Gruenwald and Gordon, 1984).[23] For example, Asian Pacific doctoral scientists and engineers who are temporary residents earn only 82 percent of the median annual salaries of those with permanent residency (National Science Foundation, 1991). However, the low salaries can only be a short-run phenomenon because when residency is established, the worker is no longer bound to their first place of employment. As they operate more freely in the labor market, their wages would begin to converge with their U.S.-born counterparts.

Despite the improvement in earnings of immigrants with length of residence in the U.S., Asian Pacific Americans continue to confront a "glass ceiling" that denies them entry into top managerial positions. The statistics in Table 7.2 clearly show that they have a substantially lower probability of being in management; and this finding remains true within degree levels. When they do enter management positions, they do so within the area of Research and Development. Few rise to executive positions in this area of employment. For example, in 1992 there was not a single Asian Pacific executive in the large computer and semi-conductor firms in Silicon Valley, despite the fact that Asian Pacific Americans comprised the largest minority group in the high-technology industries of that region (Pollack, 1992). The glass ceiling also exists within academia. According to a 1985 survey by the National Research Council, less than 9 percent of Asian Pacific American faculty at four-year institutions listed administration as their primary work activity, compared with 17 percent of the entire faculty (Miller, 1992). Asian Pacific Americans have been noticeably absent, at least until very recently, from leadership positions as deans, institute heads, and advisory board members.

This lack of upward mobility is not due to a lack of economic incentives or interest. In both the sciences and engineering, S&Es whose primary activity is managerial earn about one-fifth more than S&Es with other duties.[24] Moreover, a majority of Asian Pacific S&Es express a desire to move up to administrative positions (Wong and Nagasawa, 1991). Even those who state that they do not want administrative positions may be discouraged by the poor prospects facing Asian Pacific Americans; thus they have adjusted their expectations accordingly. If the explanation is based on neither economic nor individual motivation, then what is the cause?

One clue comes from our analysis of the 1989 Survey of Natural and Social Scientists and Engineers, which indicates that the difference in composition by nativity plays a major role in the racial gap. The first column in Table 7.6 reports the unadjusted Asian Pacific-to-NH white odds ratios of being in management. The value of .67 means that Asian Pacific Americans are only two-thirds as likely to be in a management position as NH whites. Given the earlier discussion, it is not surprising that the odds are better for R&D management but worse for other managerial positions. The second column reports the odds ratios after adjusting for a number of independent factors, including immigrant status and whether one is educated in the U.S.[25] With these controls, the odds ratios increase significantly, and when past managerial experience is included, the ratios indicate parity. The results reveal that immigrants were considerably less likely to hold non-R&D management positions. Compared to U.S.-born, immigrants with U.S. educations

TABLE 7.6 Asian Pacific-to-NH-White Odds Ratios of Being in Management

	Unadjusted	Adjusted by current characteristics	Adjustment including prior management experience
Management	.67	.91	1.00
R&D Management	.84	.96	1.09
Other Management	.58	.90	.97

See text for explanation of estimates.
Source: 1989 Survey of Natural and Social Scientists and Engineers.

are one-fifth less likely to hold R&D management positions, and immigrants with foreign education are one-half less likely to hold these positions. Since Asian Pacific Americans are more likely to be immigrants, this has contributed to their lower representation in management positions.

One interpretation for why immigrants face poorer prospects centers on cultural and language differences (Miller, 1992; Hoy, 1993). Despite a functional command of English, many may lack key verbal and communication skills. Moreover, many may lack assertiveness skills that are deemed necessary for leadership positions. Whether or not they actually lack these attributes, the characterizations are widely held by employers and senior executives. In one survey of industry leaders, "language difficulties were repeatedly mentioned as factors" in lowering the prospects of foreign engineers moving into upper management (Cannon, 1988, p. 110). However, foreign engineers have an excellent chance of gaining access to management positions in R&D organizations, where access to technical management is based on professional criteria (Cannon, 1988, p. 113). In other words, Asian Pacific Americans are viewed as good technicians but not managers (Park, 1992).

It is not clear how much cultural and language differences really adversely affect managerial ability and how much the perception is used to rationalize decisions based on other biases.[26] Moreover, there is a danger that these perceptions form the basis for racial stereotypes that create "statistical" discrimination, a form of discrimination where individual Asian Pacific Americans are judged on the basis of the "group mean" rather than on their own merits. Such racial stereotypes can potentially harm not just immigrants but also U.S.-born.

The glass ceiling has two consequences. One, it forces some Asian Pacific Americans to pursue the entrepreneurial path. This has been true in several cases in Silcon Valley (Park, 1992). While this may be a factor in some individual cases, it is not clear that the glass ceiling has had a significant impact on entrepreneurial activity at the aggregate level.[27] Data from the 1989 Survey of Natural and Social Scientists and Engineers show that the self-employment rates of Asian Pacific Americans and NH whites are both 6 percent. Of course, the Asian Pacific rate might have been lower in the absence of the glass ceiling, but nonetheless, actual entrepreneurship is not a major phenomenon among Asian Pacific scientists and engineers.

The second consequence of the glass ceiling is reverse migration.[28] Ong and Hee (1993) argue the following:

> Several factors contribute to the reverse migration. The newly industrialized economies now have the resources to pay globally competitive salaries, and have the scientific and technical infrastructure that allows the highly educated to continue their career. At the same time, there is a sense that the United States is not the land of the unlimited opportunity. Certainly the existence of the glass ceiling is causing some Asian Pacific Americans to reconsider the pursuit of their career goals in the U.S. (p. 150).

While reverse migration is still a minor flow and its role in the transfer of technology across international boundaries is limited, the phenomenon is indicative of the potential and far-reaching consequences of the unequal opportunities facing Asian Pacific American scientists and engineers.

CONCLUDING REMARKS

The evidence clearly shows that Asian Pacific scientists and engineers, particularly those with advanced degrees, have helped this nation fill a crucial labor need. Without the growth of Asian Pacific S&Es, particularly the immigrant component, the shortages of highly educated labor in the technical fields, and the corresponding losses to the economy, would have been enormous. Future developments will create a need for an even larger Asian Pacific S&E labor force.

As other nations have developed their technological infrastructure, increased their R&D expenditure, and benefited from the international flow of knowledge, we have entered into an era of worldwide technological competition. During the last two decades we have seen that capturing or maintaining technological leadership is a pivotal factor in defining a nation's comparative advantage and the competitiveness of firms. In the new global economic order, trade is increasingly based on nations specializing in selective technology-based industries. Although the United States still holds or shares the lead in several fields, it is no longer preeminent in all areas.

In order to remain competitive, this nation must accelerate the growth in its technological work force and improve the quality of this work force as well. Those with highly specialized graduate training are essential for research and development, which is in turn necessary to expand the frontiers of technology. The advantage that this nation had enjoyed in this area has waned. Compared to several industrialized nations (Japan, Germany, and France), this nation in the 1960s had a substantially higher ratio of scientists and engineers in R&D to the total labor force, and although the U.S. has maintained this ratio over time, the other countries have been closing the gap (Nelson and Wright, 1992). Whether this nation can stop or even reverse this relative decline will depend on its ability to produce a larger supply of S&E workers and to upgrade their education and training.

Unfortunately, the growth patterns described in the beginning of this chapter do not portend a sanguine future. Ensuring a new supply of highly educated S&Es will be more problematic in the near future. The supply of scientists and engineers at the baccalaureate level will decline over the coming decade due to a drop in the college-age population

(Atkinson, 1990). The size of the 22-year-old cohort in the U.S. peaked at about 4.3 million in 1991 and will decline to approximately 3.2 million by 1996. The one hope is that the decline in the college-age population could be offset by an increase in the proportion of students receiving bachelor's degrees in science and engineering.

Asian Pacific Americans have the potential of being a major source to fill this critical need. The supply based on those who are either U.S.-born or U.S.-raised will increase dramatically because their numbers have grown with the overall Asian Pacific population, because they are more likely to attend college, and because they are more likely to major in the sciences and engineering. However, this future "domestic" supply is smaller than the supply of S&E immigrants that prevailed in the 1970s and 1980s.

Unfortunately, there is no guarantee that the flow of S&Es from Asia will remain high. The increased number of slots for occupational immigrants under the 1990 Immigration Act will make it possible for Asian S&E immigrants to migrate. At the same time, other forces are working against this. With increased economic development, Asian countries will become better able to educate their students at home, to create professional opportunities for their graduates, and to pay internationally competitive salaries. The impact can already be seen, for example, in the increase during the 1980s in the rate of return of Asian students who studied in the United States. Several countries are making the transition from being "exporters" of S&E talent to being "re-importers" of highly educated and highly experienced personnel. They have established programs that actively recruit Asian Pacific scientists and engineers with work experience, and this bilateral internationalization of the S&E labor market will undoubtedly increase the size of reverse migration. While developments in the sending countries will be important, they by themselves are not likely to decrease the flow of immigrants significantly.

A potentially far more important force that threatens the supply of Asian Pacific S&Es is the current anti-immigrant sentiment. The central but unanswered question is whether this xenophobic political movement will produce new restrictions on immigration from the Third World, which will affect not only scientists and engineers, but all Asian Pacific Americans.

STUDY QUESTIONS

1. What role do technology, scientists, and engineers (S&Es) play in the U.S. Economy?

2. Discuss the growth and characteristics of the Asian Pacific S&E labor force. Discuss the significance of Asian Pacific American scientists and engineers in the U.S. economy.

3. How does a glass ceiling limit upward mobility in the technical fields? Is the problem only a cultural and language issue?

NOTES

1. The wording of this sentence is borrowed from a report by the National Research Council entitled *Foreign and Foreign-Born Engineers in the United States—Infusing Talent, Raising Issues* (1988).

2. The 1970 statistics are calculated from Bureau of the Census, 1973. The 1990 statistics are estimated from the 1% Public Use Microdata Sample. There are differences in the definition of educational attainment. The 1970 data are reported by the number of years of education completed for the experienced civilian labor force, while 1990 data are reported by degree received for the total experienced work force.

3. The fluctuations in demand generate disequilibrium between supply and demand, and a "cobweb" effect (Freeman, 1971). Given that the short-run supply is inelastic, increased demand translates into higher wages. The initial shortage can lead to a surplus in the future because the current generation of new students respond to the increases in wages by majoring in the field where there is a shortage. If this cohort graduates at a time when the demand for their services has waned, the influx of students can eventually flood the market, inducing yet another cycle of falling wages and reduced enrollments.

4. The decline in R&D expenditures is, in part, due to the fact that the problem of public goods is internationalized in a global economy.

5. This is based on standard wage regressions where the log of annual earnings and the log of estimated hourly wages are the dependent variables. The sample was drawn from the 1990 1% Public Use Microdata Sample and contained only U.S.-born respondents in a scientific or engineering occupation who had earned at least $1,000 in 1989. To reduce the ambiguity of what a professional degree means, the sample was restricted to those with either a bachelor's, master's, or doctorate degree. Our model includes independent variables for gender, race, years of experience, educational degree, geographic region, and consolidated metropolitan areas. Separate regressions were estimated for scientists and for engineers.

6. The effects are roughly the same in terms of annual earnings.

7. The estimates are based on those who were in the labor force (employed, or unemployed but looking for work) and were classified in a S&E occupation or taught in a S&E field at the college/university level. The 1990 census provides educational information by degree, but the 1980 census does not. We assumed that those with four or five years of college had a bachelor's degree, while those with eight or more years of college, the top reported category, had a doctorate. Those with more than five years but less than eight years of college were classified as having master's or professional degrees. We tested the sensitivity of our definition of those with a bachelor's degree. Using only four years of college led to an unrealistically high estimate of the number with a master's or professional degree. The limitation of the 1980 data probably led to the inclusion of persons without a Ph.D. in the doctorate category.

8. In 1990, 33 percent of the Asian Pacific S&Es had a master's or professional degree, and another 12 percent had a doctorate degree. For all other S&Es, the respective statistics are 17 percent and 5 percent.

9. These estimates are based on the 1990 5% PUMS. Asian Pacific Americans are also overrepresented among production workers (Park, 1992).

10. The 1982 estimates are based on respondents who worked in a scientific or engineer occupation. We use whites rather than non-Hispanic whites in this analysis because the published 1989 report does not provide statistics for the latter group. Because an overwhelming majority of white S&Es are not Hispanic, there is very little difference in the 1982 statistics for NH whites and whites.

11. This is based on calculating the proportion of Asian Pacific S&Es that would be in R&D if they experienced the white participation rate by each of three degree levels—those with a bachelor's degree, those with a master's or professional degree, and those with a doctorate times the proportion of Asian Pacific Americans with a doctorate degree. This hypothetical

rate is 27 percent, which is 3 percentage points higher than that for all white S&Es but still 7 percentage points lower than the observed rates for all Asian Pacific S&Es.

12. The statistics are based on respondents with at least a bachelor's degree and who classified themselves as a scientist or engineer by profession (education and experience).

13. For example, in 1988 over two-thirds of the S&E faculty at Seoul National University South Korea's premier institution, had a foreign doctorate, and nearly three-quarters of this group received their training in the United States (Seoul National University, 1988).

14. The statistics on foreign students come from Zikopoulos, 1991b.

15. The concentration of Asians is not new, but the data show that their relative share has increased over the last few decades. Students from Asian countries received 42 percent of all non-U.S. science and engineering doctorates awarded in 1960–64 and 68 percent in 1990 (NSF, 1991).

16. Prior to 1965, U.S. laws favored highly skilled individuals; but racial bias in the immigration law prevented large numbers of Asians from taking advantage of these quotas.

17. The immigrant supply also helps address cyclical shortage due to periodic fluctuations in the demand for scientists and engineers.

18. See Harberfeld and Shenhav (1990) for an analysis of salary discrimination of women and black scientists.

19. This is based on the regression outlined in note 2. The results indicate that annual earnings and hourly wages of Asian Pacific scientists were 10 percent higher than for NH whites. The estimated parameters were significant at only the $p<.10$ level, but this may be due to the small number of U.S.-born Asian Pacific Americans in the sample. The results indicate no statistically significant differences between Asian Pacific and NH white engineers. The results also show that women and blacks earned less than men and NH whites, which is consistent with the literature.

20. This is based on standard wage regressions, where the log of annual earnings and the log of estimated hourly wages are the dependent variables. The sample was drawn from the 1990 1% Public Use Microdata Sample and contained Asian Pacific respondents in a scientific or engineering occupation who had earned at least $1,000 in 1989. To reduce the ambiguity of what a professional degree means, the sample was restricted to those with either a bachelor's, master's, or doctorate degree. Our model includes independent variables for gender, race, years of experience, educational degree, geographic region, consolidated metropolitan areas, year of entry, and English-language ability. Separate regressions were estimated for scientists and for engineers.

21. The earnings regressions include as independent variables gender, race, years of professional experience, age, educational degree, geographical region, year of entry, managerial activity, part-time work, and place of education. Although there is no control for English language ability, the analysis of the 1990 census data for Asian Pacific scientists and engineers indicate that excluding this variable does not bias the included variable. This is not surprising since Asian Pacific Americans in these fields tend to have at least a fair command of English; thus the estimated parameter for this variable is often insignificant. The sample includes respondents working in a S&E occupation who had at least $1,000 in earnings. Separate regressions are estimated for scientists and for engineers. The sample for scientists is small (n=337) and did not produce robust estimates. The results discussed in the text are based on the analysis of engineers.

22. This individual aspect of the wage-induced shortage of S&Es with advanced degrees is discussed earlier, where there is an adverse effect on the decision to pursue advanced studies.

23. This explanation, however, cannot account for the fact that in 1989 U.S.-born Asian Pacific doctoral scientists and engineers earned only 92 percent of that of white doctoral scientists and engineers (NSF, 1991).

24. This is based on an analysis of the 1989 Survey of Natural and Social Scientists and Engineers. The annual earnings regressions includes as independent variables gender, race, years of professional experience, age, educational degree, the sector of employment, geographic region, year of entry, managerial activity, and part-time work. The sample included U.S.-born respondents working in a S&E occupation and had at least $1,000 in earnings.

25. The estimates are based on a sample of only paid workers with income in the U.S., between the ages of 30 and 64, and excludes those working in hospitals, the military, and international agencies. Scientists and engineers are defined by experience and education, which includes individuals who were working outside a scientific or engineering occupation. The analysis uses logit regression, and the list of independent variables also includes gender, degree, marital status, presence of children, age, years of experience in the profession, geographic region of employment, type of employment organization (public, etc.), and occupational categories.

26. Certainly, the economic advancement made by Asian countries based on different leadership styles would suggest that behaviors rooted in Asian Pacific culture are not inherently bad for effective management. Partial acceptance of this has come as American corporations adopt some Japanese practices. Of course, managerial styles cannot be completely transplanted given differences rooted in history and larger institutions.

27. Because high-tech industries have been rapidly expanding and changing, they offer Asian Pacific Americans, and others, the opportunity to "get in at the ground level" and build a fortune. Many of the largest Asian Pacific companies are in this sector, including Wang Laboratories, Computer Associates, AST Research, Everex Systems, and Advanced Logic Research (Pollack, 1992).

28. The fascination with "returning" as a solution to the frustration felt by Asian Pacific Americans who are blocked from moving up was captured by the 1986 movie *The Great Wall*, directed by Peter Wang. The movie begins with the protagonist, a Chinese American engineer, being passed over for a management position that he believed he should have received. His response was to return to China for a visit, with a possibility of staying. In the end, however, he realizes that he and his family belong in the U.S.

References

Abowd, J. and Freeman, R. (1991). *Immigration, Trade, and the Labor Market*. Chicago: University of Chicago Press.

Atkinson, R. (1990). "Supply and Demand for Scientists and Engineers: A National Crisis in the Making." *Science*, 248, 49–54.

Cannon, P. (1988). "Foreign Engineers in U. S. Industry: An Exploratory Assessment." In *Foreign and Foreign-Born Engineers in the United States, Infusing Talent, Raising Issues* (pp. 105–123). National Research Council, Committee on International Exchange and Movement of Engineers. Washington, D.C.: National Academy Press.

Dollar, D., and Wolff, E. (1993). *Competitiveness, Convergence, and International Specialization*. Cambridge, Massachusetts: The MIT Press.

Ehrenberg, R. (1992). "The Flow of New Doctorates." *Journal of Economic Literature*, 30(2), 830–875.

Falk, C.E. (1988). "Foreign Engineers and Engineering Students in the United States." In *Foreign and Foreign-Born Engineers in the United States, Infusing Talent, Raising Issues* (pp. 31–78). National Research Council, Committee on International Exchange and Movement of Engineers. Washington, D.C.: National Academy Press.

Finn, M. (1988). "Foreign Engineers in the U.S. Labor Force." In *Foreign and Foreign-Born Engineers in the United States. Infusing Talent, Raising Issues*. National Research Council, Committee on the International Exchange and Movement of Engineers. Washington, D.C.: National Academy Press.

Grossman, G., and Helpman, E. (1991). *Innovation and Growth in the Global Economy*. Cambridge, Massachusetts: MIT Press.

Gruenwald, A. and Gordon, C. (1984) *Foreign Engineers in the United States: Immigration or Important?* Manpower Committee, United States Activities Board. New York: Institute of Electrical and Electronic Engineers Inc.

Hoy, R. (1993). "A 'Model Minority' Speaks Out on Cultural Shyness." *Science, 262*, 1117–1118.

Liao, C. and Hsieh, H. (nd.) *A Review of the Current International Migration Policies in Taiwan, the Republic of China*. Unpublished manuscript, Center for Pacific Rim Studies, University of California, Los Angeles.

Miller, S. (1992, November 13). "Asian-Americans Bump Against Glass Ceilings." *Science, 258*, 1224–1228.

National Council. (1988). *Foreign and Foreign-Born Engineers in the United States: Infusing Talent, Raising Issues*. Committee on the International Exchange and Movement of Engineers. National Research Council. Washington, D.C.: National Academy Press.

National Science Foundation. (1986). "Survey of 300 U.S. Firms Finds One-half Employ Foreign Scientists and Engineers." *Highlights*.

National Science Foundation (1991a). *Characteristics of Doctoral Scientists and Engineers in the United States: 1989*. Detailed Statistical Tables. Washington, D.C.: U.S. GPO.

National Science Foundation. (1991b). *Science and Engineering Doctorates: 1960–1990*. Surveys of Science Resources Series. Washington, D.C.: U.S. GPO.

Nelson, R. and Wright G. (1992). "The Rise and Fall of American Technological Leadership: The Postwar Era in Historical Perspective." *Journal of Economic Literature, 30* (4), 1921–1964.

Northrup, H. and Malin, M. (1985). *Personnel Policies for Engineers and Scientists*. Philadelphia: Industrial Research Units, The Wharton School, University of Pennsylvania.

Ong, P., Cheng, L., and Evans, L. (1992). "Migration of Highly Educated Asian and Global Dynamics." *Asian and Pacific Migration Journal, 1*, 3–4.

Ong, P. and Hee, S. (1933a). "The Growth of the Asian Pacific American Population: Twenty Million in 2020." In *The State of Asian Pacific America: Policy Issues to the Year 2020*. Los Angeles: LEAP and UCLA Asian American Studies Center.

Ong, P. and Mar, D. (1992). "Post-Layoff Earnings Among Semiconductor Workers." *Industrial and Labor Relations Review, 45*(2), 366–379.

Park, E. (1992). "Asian American in Silicon Valley: Race and Ethnicity in the Postindustrial Economy." Ph.D. dissertation, Ethnic Studies, University of California, Berkeley.

Pollack, A. (1992, January 14). "It's Asians' Turn in Silicon Valley." *New York Times*, pp. D1 and D5.

Porter, M. (1990). *The Competitive Advantage of Nations*. New York: The Free Press.

Reich, R. (1992). *The Work of Nations*. New York: Vintage Books.

Warner, J. and Bass, S. (1972). *The Urban Wilderness: A History of the American City*. New York: Harper & Row.

Wong, P. and Nagasawa, R. (1991). "Asian American Scientist and Engineers: Is There a Glass Ceiling for Career Advancement?" *Chinese American Forum, 6*(3), 3–6.

Zikopoulos, M. (Ed.). (1991a). "Open Doors, 1990–1991." In *Report on International Education Exchange*. New York: Institute of International Education

Chinese Staff and Workers' Association
A Model for Organizing in the Changing Economy?

"We left our homeland and our relatives behind trying just to make a meager living in this country. We work very hard for less than $3.00 an hour, yet our bosses refuse to pay us." Lee, a mild-mannered, bespectacled, middle-aged woman in her Sunday best spoke emotionally in Cantonese dialect to a crowd of onlookers at the corner of Canal and Baxter, the busiest intersection in New York City's Chinatown. At this noonday rally in 1991, Lee stood on top of a makeshift platform with eight fellow workers—six Chinese seamstresses, one Latina seamstress, and one male steam presser—appealing for community support. They chanted, "We want justice! We are no slaves! Pay our wages now!" The owners of Wai Chang Fashions, Inc., owed Lee $3,000, another woman $6,000 (one year's back pay), $10,000 total to a couple who worked there together, and $1,900 to a 70-year-old man.

The problem at Wai Chang started in July 1990. The owners stopped weekly wage payments, claiming a "minor" cash-flow problem. Later, they alleged that the manufacturers had not paid them, although everyone knew the finished goods had been delivered and the factory was working on new orders for the same manufacturers. Then the owners maintained they could not pay because their partners had full control of the money.

As the workers' demands for wage payments grew more insistent, the owners threatened to report their undocumented status to the Immigration and Naturalization Service. The bosses even invoked the names of Chinatown underworld figures to intimidate the workers.

From *Social Policy,* Winter 1994. © 1994 by Social Policy Corporation.

After six months of nonpayment, Wai Chang workers—who spoke no English and had no knowledge of their rights—approached the Chinese Staff and Workers' Association for assistance. The association helped them to file a complaint with the New York State Labor Department. However, the department halted the investigation when its investigators "could not locate the owners." It also refused the workers' request to contact manufacturers who subcontracted to Wai Chang to withhold their payments until the back wages were paid.

The workers filed criminal charges against the owners with the New York State Attorney General's office. Four months later, the owners, Wai Chee Tong and Stanley Chang, were charged with 41 criminal misdemeanor counts for failing to pay wages and keep accurate payroll records. They had owed over $80,000 in unpaid wages, the largest case ever brought to court in the garment industry.

But the prosecution could not move forward because the two owners "disappeared." Wai Chang workers had to apply for a warrant for their arrest. They spent weeks assisting the Attorney General's office to track down the owners. On December 17, 1991, they found Stanley Chang and had the police arrest him. Still, Chang was able to walk back on the streets after bail. The Wai Chang workers' case, which took three years to be heard in Brooklyn Criminal Court, is still unresolved; although the court ruled in their favor, they have been unable to collect the court-ordered back pay.

A TURNING POINT

In spite of their failure to get their money, the Wai Chang workers inspired others by showing they were not afraid to stand up and fight, even though many of them were undocumented. They won a major psychological victory—a turning point in Chinese immigrant women workers' struggles.

Soon after hearing of Stanley Chang's arrest, workers at Judy's Place Fashion, a unionized shop (Local 23-35 of the International Ladies' Garment Workers' Union) in Chinatown, also went to the Chinese Staff and Workers' Association for help. The owner of Judy's Place owed workers over $20,000. The association nudged the New York State Labor Department and the ILGWU local to get on with the case. Both started investigations slowly, and went no further when they "could not find the owner."

The workers quickly realized they had to rely on their own efforts. Several took time out from their jobs and tailed the owner from his home to another garment factory he managed in Queens, and confronted him. The owner fled. The workers quickly called a press conference to publicize the situation and to press the union and the Labor Department to take immediate action. The workers stepped up the pressure by holding public information rallies and setting up tables in Chinatown to solicit residents' signatures demanding official action. After five months of struggle, the owner, Jimmy Tse, finally paid the workers their wages.

Under the present casualized labor conditions, a community-based organization like the Chinese Staff and Workers' Association, with bilingual skills and community ties, is better able to deal with this kind of situation than a traditional bureaucratized union. Traditional unions and labor departments began at a time when they were dealing with big industries and big businesses. Today, conditions are different; with industry fragmented and capital highly mobile, a different kind of organizing model is often needed.

For the Chinese Staff and Workers' Association, winning even this most basic victory was not easy. Garment workers had to take time away from work, which they could ill afford. "We were afraid of losing our present jobs, since we had to take days off to talk with the union and the Department of Labor, and to look for the owner," Mrs. Luk, a Judy's Place worker explained. "We gave up time with our families to attend meetings. My husband once asked me not to commit too much time. But I knew that I was not only fighting for the money, but also for our dignity." She concluded by saying: "No one will help you if you don't stand up for yourself."

Nonpayment of back wages is a common problem throughout New York City. According to the state's Department of Labor, in 1989 there were 2,342 complaints of withheld wages it was acting on against 1,723 establishments. And that figure is just the tip of the iceberg—many other victims have not reported violations for fear of retaliation.

Owners are not afraid of breaking the law, knowing the indifference of the labor departments and the unions, and the leniency of punishment for the crime. And owners know that most violations will never be reported because of workers' fear of retaliation and, among undocumented residents, of trouble with the INS.

Besides, the owners have learned numerous tricks to evade legal accountability. Withholding wages at both unionized and non-unionized Chinese garment factories has developed to epidemic proportions. Seamstresses tell each other, "If your wages have never been withheld, you are lucky. Bosses are withholding wages as a 'normal' accounting practice nowadays."

WE'RE NOT ASKING MUCH. . .

Getting paid for one's labor is the most basic right of a worker. The garment workers are not asking for much—they're not asking to be paid more than minimum wage, not asking for a 40-hour work week, overtime pay, a clean working environment, or job security. They know they will not get these. All they want is what they were hired for. As one Wai Chang worker put it, "We are not asking much . . . we just want payment for the work we have done."

Few outsiders know the extent of deprivation in Chinese-owned garment factories. On June 29, 1993, the Chinese Staff and Workers' Association organized a townhall meeting at PS 124 in Chinatown to give the garment workers an opportunity to speak out. Administrators from federal and state labor departments, representatives from the offices of members of Congress, and the New York City Council were invited. They, along with some 300 Chinatown residents, sat jammed into the elementary school's auditorium, listening to emotional testimonies from dozens of workers listing a litany of abuses at their work places. The workers testified that work days in excess of 12 hours are increasingly common, that wages have dropped for many to only $2.00 an hour, and that owners have been using youth gangs to threaten them. And the most strident and consistent complaint was still the issue of withholding wages.

Several speakers urged more effective action on the part of the authorities. One ex-Wai Chang worker criticized the law for classifying the crime of nonpayment as a misdemeanor. She urged the lawmakers to pass legislation making nonpayment a felony, subject to extended prison terms and heavy fines.

Impervious to the gravity of the situation in Chinatown, some of the government representatives at the meeting focused on the problem purely from the point of view of current laws. A state labor official rejoined the subject at hand by insisting that for owners not to pay the minimum wage of $4.25 an hour constituted a violation of the law. Such owners should be reported to the authorities, he insisted. Another state official lectured the workers that they had to press "official charges" before her office could take action against the owners—in effect, blaming the workers' "docility" for their troubles. One could hear gasps of amazement from the workers, realizing how out of touch the authorities were the realities in Chinatown.

BACK TO THE BASICS

New York's Chinatown is not alone; around the country, especially in communities with a high density of recent immigrants, are pockets where flagrant violation of labor laws and primitive intimidation of workers are the norm. The reasons are manifold—lack of law enforcement, inadequate regulation, a changing global economy, to name a few. Once, the obvious place for workers to turn would have been labor unions. In the 1930s, for example, unions were able to make significant gains. The well-organized workers were able to force government to recognize their right to organize, to legalize collective bargaining, to form the National Labor Relations Board to mediate management-labor disputes, to set up labor departments to maintain labor standards, and to pass legislation to guarantee minimum wage and social security benefits.

Today, however, labor officials and unions have lost touch with rank-and-file workers. Having made these gains and established labor peace, unions and labor authorities became institutionalized. Workers' rights are now expected to be protected by labor bureaucrats and union officials without the workers' participation.

But without the rank-and-file power behind unions and labor bureaucrats, management has been able to gain the upper hand, particularly since the 1970s. With the restructuring of the U.S. economy and the free flow of international capital, the ability of unions and government to protect workers has declined.

The ILGWU, for example, was once one of the largest and most powerful unions in America. By the end of World War, II, its members were among the highest paid workers in the country. The union adopted a policy of cooperation with management, even assisting the industry's efforts to streamline production and increase efficiency.

This strategy of "organizing from the top" worked for as long as the manufacturing process was concentrated and labor supply was stable. However, management, in search of lower labor costs, proceeded to decentralize into smaller subcontracting systems and to export production overseas. The ILGWU had tied its own survival to an industry whose structure it could no longer control. When the sweatshops reappeared in different decentralized immigrant communities such as Chinatown, the union was powerless to stop the process.

In the 1990s, the union's sole interest is to fight for its own survival by holding on to its dues-paying membership. It is unwilling to assert the rights of workers too forcefully in fear of causing the contractors to shut down or to move away. No wonder it closes one eye to the violation of the employers. The present ILGWU's organizing program is limited to its members' demonstrations in "Buy American" rallies in order to induce Congress to pass restrictive import legislation. This is hardly a problem specific to the ILGWU—it is widely shared by the mainstream labor movement—but the ILGWU is the union with the most direct impact on the Chinese immigrant community. It is an ironic twist for the union's Chinese members here to be picketing against their fellow workers in China and Hong Kong, where the wage level currently stands at around $3.50 an hour—almost comparable to sweatshop rates in the U.S. By all accounts, Hong Kong has better health care, public housing, and public transportation systems. It also has stricter government regulations of factory conditions, and the machines in garment factories are newer than those in the U.S.

The institutionalization of the labor movement has robbed workers of their strength to fight back. Workers have become alienated and isolated; they are not expected to be competent enough to do anything for themselves. Wing Lam, the executive director of the Chinese Staff and Workers' Association, describes this as the "dehumanizing process"; the only way to turn the situation around, he says, is for the workers to get back to the basics, once again building grassroots workers' organizations from the bottom up.

A DIFFERENT KIND OF WORKERS' ASSOCIATION

One model of what such an association might look like is found in the Chinese Staff and Workers' Association and its Women's Committee. The association was originally formed around restaurant workers who were mainly male. Most of the restaurant workers' wives, however, worked in the garment industry, and it soon became clear that issues concerning the two industries were related. The association eventually established a Women's Committee to concentrate on the problems of the garment workers.

The association and the committee see themselves as different from other social-service organizations or agencies. When a worker with a problem approaches the association, the first thing he or she is told is: "We'll help you, if you are willing to take on the fight yourself." The number of paid employees at the association has been kept intentionally small so that, as Wing Lam explains, "the workers would not think that someone else will do everything for them. If that were the case," he continues, "we would not be able to release the full energy of the workers."

It is difficult for workers to learn to do things for themselves, and perhaps even more difficult for Chinese working women. Rohda Lin, formerly the women's organizer, points out that "the first and most difficult task of working with the Chinese women is to raise their level of self-confidence. They tend not to believe that they could do things, or that they could make a difference." Immigrant Chinese women, coming from a male-dominated culture, tend to be reticent, subordinating themselves to men. In the U.S., they feel even more vulnerable without the knowledge of English, burdened with child care and housework, and working at stressful, mindless jobs at garment factories to "supplement" their family income. They feel physically and psychologically tied down and not able to do anything for themselves. All of this contributes to their low self-esteem.

The Women's Committee tries to alter that self-perception by exposing the larger external factors that are affecting women's conditions. Every Sunday afternoon, the committee holds a discussion session attended by women from different factories. They use this opportunity to air their concerns, giving participants a chance to see that others have the same problems, which are not their own fault or due to incompetence.

The committee tries to strengthen the women's confidence by encouraging them to help others. By setting up information tables on the streets of Chinatown, the women explain the issues to the public while at the same time educating themselves to better understand their own relationship to others facing similar problems.

There is a growing number of participants in the women's committee's Sunday afternoon discussion sessions, due in large part to these efforts to build consciousness. The information tables have helped women see that by helping themselves they are also helping others, and that the solution to their problems has to be a collective one.

Of course, there have been drop-outs from the committee. Some could not afford the time, some were afraid of retaliation, others dropped out because of their husbands' objections, others just moved on or became frustrated with the slow pace of change and the obstacles they faced. On the other hand, JoAnne Lum, program director of the association, observes, "We have also had cases where our members were able to persuade their husbands of the importance of their participation, and even recruited their husbands to come around to our activities."

A Question of Strategy

The problems workers face today are clearly different from those that gave rise to modern industrial unions in the earlier part of this century. Service jobs, contingency work, decentralized workplaces, globalized capital, and a government unsympathetic to unions are all part of the economic landscape for increasing numbers of workers in the U.S.

Knowing where to turn for an answer is not easy. Unions currently represent only a small fraction of the U.S. work force, and have not come up with a convincing plan to deal with these larger issues. Government—whether Republican or Democratic—seems intent on equating economic health with increases in the stock market, whatever happens to jobs, wages, or working conditions.

In this context, small, flexible organizations such as the Chinese Staff and Workers' Association that are close to the people, culturally sensitive, and internationally connected may present one model for building a revitalized labor movement in the U.S. Other alternatives are also possible. Some—such as the Teamsters—are working to reform and democratize traditional unions, rebuilding from the bottom up. Others are forming new, independent unions more closely responsive to the new economic situations their members encounter. Still others are addressing the downward pressure globalization puts on wages by building connections between unions in the U.S. and organizations of the workers they are pitted against in developing countries.

Finding a way for workers to deal effectively with a rapidly changing economy is a crucial need. None of these strategies is universally applicable in addressing that issue; none represents the single answer. But we urgently need to look further into all of them—for the problem they are all grappling with is central to our economic well-being for many years to come.

STUDY QUESTIONS

1. How do the vulnerabilities felt by Chinese women immigrants with the language barrier serve to isolate these women?

2. What has been the impact of economic restructuring on unions?

3. How does the Chinese Staff and Worker's association differ from traditional sources of worker empowerment?

Borders and Beyond
Racialized Relations, Ethnicity, and
Social Identity

Introduction

In the changing conditions of the 1990s, racialized social relations and inequalities, as well as racialized ethnic identities, continue to be of immense significance. At the level of the individual, the immigration process shapes social identity and imposes a regime based upon a shared notion of peoplehood or ethnicity. Traditional social theory representing the ideological spectrum once assumed that ethnic social identity was largely epiphenomenal and subordinate to the more compelling forces of liberal pluralism, assimilationism, or class conflict. It can no longer be assumed that the conceptual language of traditional social theory and ethnic relations can provide the analytical clarity necessary to understand the rapidly changing social formations. The new Asian and Latino immigration has forced a theoretical reappraisal of such assumptions, given that a multitude of peoples now living within U.S. borders share no common tradition that is identifiably "American."

That ethnicity and identity are products of material social conditions is seen in the manner by which the concept has been used for purposes of maintaining groups' solidarity in the linked areas of culture, economy, and politics. Asian Americans, for example, have created a composite ethnic identity in the U.S. that has minimized the substantive differences between the many groups with the intention of forming a political bloc to challenge institutional and legal barriers erected to contain people of Asian descent.

As the essays in this section aver, a shared ethnic identity is central to the social and cultural adaptation of the new immigrants from Asian and Latin America, shielding them from the often harsh effects of assimilation into a system of structured social inequality organized along racial lines. The social construction of ethnicity and social identity is in a continual process of formation, dictated by changing historical circumstances and varying political fortunes.

Chapter 9

David Lopez and Yen Espiritu

Panethnicity in the United States
A Theoretical Framework

Though little studied,[1] panethnicity—the development of bridging organizations and solidarities among subgroups of ethnic collectivities that are often seen as homogeneous by outsiders—is an essential part of ethnic change. Indeed, in the United States today it may well be supplanting both assimilation and ethnic particularism as the direction of change for racial/ethnic minorities. In this article we first present a theoretical framework that specifies factors that facilitate and inhibit panethnicity. Within this framework, we review panethnicity among four sets of ethnic subgroups in the United States: Asian Americans, Native Americans, Indo Americans, and Latinos.[2] We conclude with a discussion of the relative importance of structural and cultural factors for understanding panethnicity.

None of the founding fathers of sociology foresaw a prominent role for race and ethnicity in industrial societies.[3] However, subsequent developments have demonstrated that racial and ethnic divisions continue to define lines of social order (and disorder) throughout the world. Exploitation, oppression, and even genocide on the basis of race and ethnicity have been sadly characteristic of the twentieth century. Ethnic cohesion and competition have been correspondingly vigorous and play at least as strong a role in political and social processes today as they did at the beginning of the century. In recent decades the painful process of decolonization called attention to the complexities of race and ethnicity in the Third World and how these complexities rebound back on the center of industrial capitalism (Rex 1983; Horowitz 1985). For example, the migration of non-whites to Australia, Europe, and the United States has increasingly transformed ethnic questions into racial issues.

From *Ethnic and Racial Studies*, Vol. 13, No. 2, April 1990.

Some two decades ago, the black Civil Rights Movement reawakened U.S. sociologists and others to the continuing significance of race in America, and led to increased political awareness among other racial/ethnic groups seeking redress for past and present wrongs. An emphasis on change had been at the center of research on race and ethnicity in the United States since at least the time of Park. But the earlier emphasis had been on establishing determinate models of transformation such as "ethnic succession" and, later, "assimilation". The general idea was that all newly arriving groups to this nation of immigrants went through fundamentally the same stages of cultural, economic, and social incorporation (Gordon 1964). In contrast, one new school of thought (Blauner 1972) made a sharp distinction between the experiences of European and non-white groups in the United States, arguing that the latter were kept in a state of "internal colonialism." Another line of revisionism argued that ethnic consciousness, rather than gradually disappearing, actually developed and increased as part of the American experience (Yancey, Ericksen, and Juliani 1976).

A variety of theories have sought to account for this persistence. Ultimately, the same question underlies them all: the relative importance of external constraints and economic interests as opposed to internal, cultural factors in determining the meaning and development of ethnic and racial categories, hostilities and solidarities. Those scholars who stress the latter emphasize that ethnic bonds are an extension of family feeling, and perhaps even of genetic processes (Schermerhorn 1970; van den Berghe 1981; Horowitz 1985). Culture is seen as a representation of collective consciousness and solidarity. Structuralists, in contrast, emphasize the dependence of ethnic and racial categories on such factors as capitalist expansion, class, and immigration patterns. Ethnicity is inherently mutable, subject to a combination of broad political and economic patterns (Bonacich and Modell 1980; Rex 1983; Geschwender 1988). Rational choice theorists focus on individual responses to these forces and how individual rationality affects ethnic borders (Banton 1983).

In the context of this debate, panethnicity merits greater attention for two reasons. First, as a process, it focuses attention on ethnic change, and thus touches on many of the central theoretical questions in the sociology of ethnicity. Most contemporary researchers, whatever their theoretical perspectives, view ethnicity as a dynamic rather than static social phenomenon. But there is considerable disagreement over the forces behind the dynamics. When ethnic categories are, or appear to be, essentially stable, it is difficult to choose from among the various approaches to ethnicity. But the ebb and flow of panethnic tendencies oblige one to attend to the forces behind these changes.

Second, panethnicity may well be emerging as a significant empirical alternative to either assimilation or ethnic particularism, at least in the United States. Several authors have argued that panethnic generalization is essentially part of a more general assimilation process (Sarna 1978; Vecoli 1983). For earlier European ethnic groups this may well have been the case. Nelli (1970), for example, has shown how immigrants from different parts of Italy fused their regional distinctiveness into a general Italian-American identity, as a step towards assimilation. But on both organizational and interpersonal levels panethnicity may well be providing a third way for the four "peoples of colour" considered here. As often happens in the social sciences, our model of panethnicity may amount to little more than the recognition of an emerging social fact.

The central question to ask of panethnic developments is the degree to which they represent genuine generalization of ethnic solidarity and identity, as opposed to alliances of convenience. Our data relate primarily to organizations, but we believe that they allow us to determine which panethnic political developments involve ethnic generalization at the level of individuals, and which are no more than alliances of convenience, devoid of any ethnic solidarity. We shall argue that the most effective panethnic developments have in fact involved elements of both, with the panethnic cooperation and identity serving as a complement to continuing ethnic particularism. We return to the interrelations of organizational and individual panethnicity at the conclusion of this article.

FACTORS AFFECTING PANETHNICITY

The analysis of social change requires some theory of causation, and the ebbs and flows of panethnicity allow us to test competing theories against the evidence. To that end, we have grouped factors that would seem to affect panethnicity into two broad categories: cultural and structural.[4] Each factor is considered with respect to its variation across subgroups, and the general argument is that the greater the degree of variation from subgroup to subgroup, the less potential for panethnicity. We assess each panethnic group on these factors in two ways: structurally, according to our best reading of how much they vary across subgroups; and historically, by assessing the apparent relative importance of these factors in incidents of panethnic organization and activity.

Cultural Variables: Language and Religion

Volumes have been written about the links between ethnicity and culture, and for many social scientists the two mean pretty much the same thing. Cultural differences are inherently relative and situational, and not easily summarized under broad categories. Nevertheless, we believe that the two clearest components of *ethnic* culture are language and religion. Whatever is meant by "ethnic culture," it cannot include qualities that are the direct consequences of structural conditions. Many of the apparent cultural contrasts between subethnic groups in the United States, for example Mexicans and Cubans or Japanese and Cambodians, are in fact attributable, at least in part, to class background and generational differences. And while the actual content of immigrant cultures can diverge profoundly from their national origins, they remain as fundamental symbolic links to those origins. Language, including symbolic commitment to a waning mother tongue, is at the center of ethnic identity and ethnic conflict worldwide. Subnational groups demand that their language be given official status and used in schools instead of the language of the politically dominant ethnic group. Clearly, if subgroups shared a common language, they would be more likely to join together. The obverse is also true: linguistic dissimilarity among subgroups should be a powerful force for ethnic particularism.

Of our four groups, only Latinos share a common language. Latinos refer to themselves, and are referred to by others, as "Spanish-speaking." They have become the largest official "language minority" in the United States, in spite of persistent evidence that most shift to English nearly as rapidly as other immigrant stocks (Lopez 1982). Native-born Latinos speak English more than Spanish, and lose their facility with Spanish by the third or fourth generation. But the large immigrant and second-generation population, combined with a strong symbolic commitment among subsequent generations, make Spanish and the Hispanic culture that it implies a potentially powerful basis for unity among Latinos.

Among the other three groups, language defines the boundaries of ethnic particularism. Although native-born Asian Americans progressively lose command of their ethnic language at least as rapidly as the children of European immigrants did in the past (Lopez 1982; Veltman 1983), they remain strongly committed to passing at least appreciation for their mother tongue on to their children. Recent Asian immigrants live largely in communities defined in linguistic terms (Conklin and Lourie 1983, pp. 47–52). The overwhelmingly immigrant Indo-American population brings with it the fierce commitment to regional languages that has been at the center of political conflict in India since Independence (Fisher 1980). For Native Americans their tribal language has a religious quality, which they revere even if they speak it little (Snipp 1986, p. 246).

The second discernible aspect of ethnic culture is religion. Today, as in the past, "religion is one of the crucial defining characteristics in ethnic identity and one of the rallying points in ethnic conflict" (Yinger 1985, p. 168). In the United States ethnic churches continue to play an important part in the lives of immigrants and, to a lesser extent, subsequent generations. The tie that binds would seem to be strongest when subethnic groups share a distinctive religion that virtually defines their identity, as in the case of Jewish subgroups. But sharing a religion that is not distinctively their own can also be a powerful cultural bond, even if it is also a potential force for assimilation. On the other hand, when subgroups have distinctive beliefs, then religion can be a force for disunity. Certainly, the absence of any common religion means one less cultural resource for ethnic solidarity.

Again, of our four groups, only Latinos share a common religion.[5] Catholicism binds Latino groups, particularly at local levels where different groups attend the same parish churches, and where services are in Spanish. However, because Catholic parishes are geographically based, subethnic separateness would be reflected in the churches. Catholicism could also be a force for assimilation for those Latinos who move out of ethnic neighborhoods.

In contrast, for American Indians, tribe and ethnicity are sacred, and each has its own religious beliefs and practices. Adherence to the "old beliefs" varies considerably within Native Americans nations, and many have accepted the Western religions brought by missionaries. Various movements have attempted to unite all Indians on a religious/spiritual level by emphasizing the sacredness of the land and the reverence for ancestors (Thomas 1968). However, in general, tribal religions tend to emphasize distinctiveness, not bonds with other groups.

Indo Americans are as diverse and divided religiously as they are linguistically. The majority are Hindus, but regional and caste divisions in Hinduism make it as much a force for division as for unity. Important components of the population are Muslim and Sikh, and religious conflicts between them and Hindus on the Subcontinent often reverberate in the United States. High-status religious sects (e.g., Jains) are also well represented and, like most other Indo Americans, continue to adhere to strict practices of endogamy based on region, religion, caste, and clan (Lopez 1987).

Similarly, there is no overarching religion to bind all Asians, though in this case religion is not a strong force for subethnic parochialism. Asian-American subgroups adhere to various traditions of Western and Eastern religions, as well as a combination of both, or neither. For Filipinos Catholicism provides some basis for subgroup solidarity. And a substantial proportion of Koreans are Presbyterian. For most other subgroups, religious practices are either too diverse or too weak to provide a basis for ethnic solidarity at any level (Melendy 1977, p. 28; Kitano 1981).

Structural variables: Race, Class, Generation, and Geography

It is a commonplace that ethnic groups defined in terms of race[6] tend to be more enduring than groups based on linguistic or other more mutable criteria.[7] Certainly, this has been the case in the United States, where the harsh and uncomprising black/white model has set the tone for all other race relations. Our descent rule allocates anyone with identifiable African origins to the stigmatized "black" category (Harris 1964, p. 56). North Americans try to apply the same dichotomy to other non-Europeans, with varying degrees of success and stigmatization. Generally, when subgroups "look alike" from the perspective of the outsider, they experience a powerful force for panethnic solidarity. When this is not the case, especially when subgroups have distinct "Somatic Norm Images,"[8] recognized both within the group and by outsiders, then race is a barrier to panethnicity.

Racial lumping is an effective force for unity among Asian Americans, American Indians, and Indo Americans. For Asian Americans, racial lumping was brought out most forcefully in the 1982 killing of Vincent Chin, a Chinese American who was beaten to death in Detroit by two white men who mistook him for a Japanese. Among themselves, Asian Americans perceive minor racial differences among Asian subgroups, but boundaries are often blurred and particular individuals are often difficult to categorize. Certainly, most of these fine points are not noticeable to outsiders. Indo Americans have also suffered violent attacks recently. The Indo-American press has characterized these attacks as "racially motivated" and as evidence that all Indians need to unite. Individual color variation is perceived among South Asians, and color is broadly correlated with status in some parts of the Subcontinent (Ghurye 1932; Beteille 1968). But, with a few exceptions, Indo-American subgroups are not clearly distinguishable by color, especially from the perspective of outsiders. Racial lumping and stigmatizing are also a powerful force for unity among American Indians. Like African Americans, Native Americans have received strong infusions of white blood. The degree of racial mixture figures in government definitions of who is Indian, and is certainly a recognized dimension of individual variation within Indian nations. But whites rarely make distinctions of any sort between different Indian groups, especially in urban areas, and when distinctions are made they are on the basis of tribe, not race (Cornell 1988, pp. 132–38).

Racial variation is greatest among and across Latino subgroups in the United States. Throughout Latin America, race and class are broadly correlated, with whites at the top, blacks and Indians at the bottom, and mixed bloods in between. The racial composition of Latino subgroups in the United States, then, tends to reflect the class background of immigrants at least as much as regional variation. Many Puerto Rican migrants are "black" by mainland definition and have experienced direct racism approaching that suffered by non-Latino African Americans (Rodriguez 1980). In contrast, most Cubans and South Americans, reflecting their middle-class backgrounds, look European and can blend into white America. Although Mexican Americans are racially diverse, the average Mexican (or Central American) immigrant is at least part Indian, and the North American Somatic Norm Image (see note 8) of a Mexican is certainly mestizo. Among Latinos there is greater sensitivity to the class-color link and to individual variation, but they too generally recognize these three distinct somatic norms (white, black/mulatto, Indian/mestizo) and associate them with different Latino subgroups. Race and color, in sum, tend to divide Latino subgroups.

The four groups considered here vary substantially in their average class positions. When subethnic groups have distinct average class positions, we expect less potential for panethnic alliance, and even less for any sentimental solidarity. Of course, there is more to material interests than the similarity of one's relation to the means of production. Groups that are quite close in their objective class position can be in competition and bear more animosity towards one another than those farther apart on the class spectrum. Overall, however, we believe that subethnic groups sharing a similar class status are more likely to have a basis for cooperation than for conflict.

Reflecting their diverse origins and experiences of incorporation into the U.S. class structure, Latino subgroups have the most diverse average class positions. The principal wave of Cuban immigrants arrived as middle-class political refugees, and were able to parlay their physical and human capital into a highly successful enclave in Southern Florida. In contrast, the socioeconomic center for Puerto Rican, Mexican, and Central American populations is located somewhere between the secure and the distinctly insecure working class. Of the three major Latino groups, Puerto Ricans have the lowest labor-force-participation rates, the highest unemployment levels, the highest incidence of poverty, and the lowest levels of education. By their numbers, Mexicans and Central Americans look somewhat better off, though the average class status of these groups is constantly diluted by massive continuing immigration (Moore and Pachon 1985; Portes and Bach 1985; Bean and Tienda 1987). Overall, the persistence of socioeconomic differentials among Latino subgroups should limit the potential for panethnic organization, at least between Cubans and others.

In contrast, Indo Americans, Asian Americans, and American Indians are each much more homogeneous socioeconomically. Indo Americans are probably the most homogeneous, and certainly the most prosperous. They come to the United States with the highest level of human, if not material, capital of any immigrant population. Two-thirds of the recent immigrants have four years of college or more, twice the rate for the highly educated Korean immigrants, and six times the Cuban rate. Over half have professional or managerial occupations (the two most common occupations being engineering and medicine), again far outdistancing other immigrant groups (U.S. Bureau of the Census 1983; Xenos et al. 1987) There is some occupational variation across subgroups, but it is more horizontal than vertical.[9]

Like Indo Americans, Asian Americans share relatively equal average status. According to the 1980 census, major Asian American groups had roughly the same median family income, ranging from $20,000 to $27,000 for the four largest groups (Gardner, Bryant, and

Smith 1985). True, great disparities exist within the Asian American grouping, particularly between recently arrived refugees from Indochina and native-born Japanese Americans. However, overall, the major Asian American groups share relatively high status: they earn more than the general U.S. population (Gardner, Bryant and Smith 1985). Indeed, much to their dismay, Asian Americans have been dubbed the "model minority" by outsiders.

American-Indian subgroups are also relatively homogeneous socio-economically, though at the other end of the spectrum. Except for a few rich "oil Indians," Native Americans are the most deprived group in the United States on every available indicator: poverty, illness, life expectancy, and educational attainment (Murray 1982, p. 5). However, this homogeneity does not automatically trigger cooperation: competition for federal money divides tribal and urban Indians. In the eyes of many reservation Indians, urban Indians represent a potential drain on scarce reservation-dedicated resources, despite the fact that they are better off economically (Nagel 1988). Different tribes on contiguous reservations have also experienced conflicts over land and water rights.

Continuing immigration rejuvenates ethnic cultures, reinforces national allegiance, and reminds ethnic members of how little they have in common with other national groups. Therefore, continuing inflows of immigrants can impede the development of panethnicity. However, it is not just continuing immigration *per se*, but rather variation on this dimension across subgroups that affects panethnic development. Subgroups that have been in the United States for the same length of time are more likely to share similar concerns. In contrast, groups differing markedly in generational composition lack a basis for cooperation. Moreover, old-timers may feel intense competition from the newcomers and newcomers may feel excluded by the old-timers.

For three of our four broad ethnic groupings, immigration is a continuing phenomenon, with from half to the vast majority of all adults having been born abroad. But there are significant subgroup variations among two of the groups. Among Asian Americans, only Japanese are overwhelmingly second and third generation, while the vast majority of Vietnamese (90 percent), Koreans (82 percent), Filipinos (66 percent), and Chinese (63 percent) are foreign-born. All but the Japanese subgroup have to contend with continuing large-scale immigration. The contrasts are equally great among Latino subgroups,[10] but, more importantly, each has its own distinctive pattern of immigration that foreign-born percentages only partly convey. Cuban immigration came in two distinct waves; the large flow of middle-class refugees in the 1960s, and the smaller working-class and lumpen Marielito migration in 1980. The great wave of movement from Puerto Rico to the Northeast of the mainland came between 1945 and 1960 (Moore and Pachon 1985, p. 33). Permanent migration from Puerto Rico since then has been modest, allowing the community to stabilize. Mexicans have been in the Southwest since long before Anglos arrived, but the majority trace their origins to immigration early in the twentieth century, and massive immigration from Mexico and Central America continues today.

Over two-thirds of all Indo Americans are foreign-born, and most have arrived in the past two decades via student visas, occupational preferences, and family unification provisions of immigration law. All Indo-American subgroups share a great concern for laws that will allow immigration from India to flourish, and fear restrictions on foreign-trained physicians and engineers. It is for all, quite literally, a family matter. Indo Americans also maintain extremely strong ties with their communities of origin in India, with frequent visits to obtain spouses, to see the family, or to do business (Lopez 1987).

In contrast to the other three groups, Native Americans have no generational (birthplace) split as such, though the emerging urban/reservation distinction does provide a roughly equivalent basis of cleavage. When Indians talk about generation, however, they are usually referring to differences between more traditional older people (especially the old-style leaders) and younger Indians, who were active in the more assertive political movements of the 1960s and 1970s (Stanley and Thomas 1978, pp. 116–17). Given the massive and oppressive nature of Native American social problems, and the degree to which Indians have been pummeled by the twentieth century, it may well be that such generational differences are more significant for them than for other well-established ethnic groups. However these generational conflicts are shared by all tribes, and thus do not impede panethnicity.

Since interests, competition, and conflict in the United States tend to be strongly regionalized, it follows that cooperation is more likely when subethnic groups are concentrated in the same area. This should be especially true when the groups have similar material statuses and interests and are neither in direct competition with each other nor in a relation of exploitation. In particular, smaller groups profit from combining to speak with one voice to local and state governments. In general, we expect that panethnic organization and solidarity are facilitated by geographical overlap and concentration.

Asian Americans are far more concentrated geographically than the general U.S. population. The 1980 census found 56 percent of Asian Americans living in the West, with 49 percent residing in California or Hawaii. Only in these states do Asian Americans comprise a significant portion of the population. Asian-American organization at the national level means essentially an extension of the California base. Additionally, the major Asian-American groups are roughly equal in size, with Chinese comprising 21 percent of the total in 1985, Filipinos 20 percent, Japanese 15 percent, and Vietnamese and Koreans 12 and 11 percent respectively, (Gardner, Bryant, and Smith 1985). Their relatively small numbers make cooperation necessary; their spatial concentration and rough numerical equity make it possible.

In contrast, the three major Latino groups occupy three distinct spaces, and are numerically quite unequal. Mexican Americans constitute over 60 percent of the total, and are concentrated in California and the Southwest, though their numbers are growing across the country. Puerto Ricans are still found primarily in New York and New Jersey, and Cubans continue to concentrate in South Florida (U.S. Bureau of the Census 1981). The overall preponderance of Mexican Americans, as well as the high concentration of each major group in one state or region, makes regional/state alliances meaningless and national ones difficult. A Puerto Rican in New York City and the *hispano* in rural New Mexico may share a language, a religion, and a heritage of exploitation, but they still have little common ground on which to cooperate.

American Indians are divided between reservation and urban dwellers. In 1980 one-third of all American Indians lived on reservations and in the historic area of Oklahoma (excluding urbanized areas); approximately half lived in urban areas (U.S. Bureau of the Census 1988). Indian communities have developed in many major cities, with the largest numbers going to Los Angeles, San Francisco, Chicago, Dallas, Denver, and Minneapolis-St. Paul (Murray 1982, p. 21). Most American Indians lived west of the Mississippi River. In 1980, more than one-half of the population lived in just five states: California, Oklahoma, Arizona, New Mexico, and North Carolina (U.S. Bureau of the Census 1988). Reservation and other rural Indians share many of the same problems, but since their relation to the government is through geographically based reservations they often find themselves in competition with each other as well as with urban Indians.

Asian Indians are spread throughout the United States, with one-third in the Northeast and, in 1980, the smallest segment (one-fifth) in the West. Ninety-two percent reside in urban areas, with New York–New Jersey having by far the largest concentration, and thriving communities in Los Angeles, San Francisco, and Chicago (U.S. Bureau of the Census 1983). However, the prosperity and close-knit nature of Indian subethnic groups means that this geographical dispersion does not lead to the loss of contact that it might among less well-off and less organized ethnic groups.

TABLE 9.1 Factors Affecting Panethnicity: How They Vary Among Major Subgroups of Each Broad Ethnic Group

	Asian Americans	Latinos	Native Americans	Indo Americans
Cultural factors				
Language	different	same	different	different
Religion	different	same	different	different
Structural factors				
Class	same	different	same	same
Race	same	different	same	same
Generation	different	different	same	same
Geographical dispersion	same/ concentrated	different	different	same/ dispersed

Table 9.1 summarizes the factors affecting panethnicity as they apply to our four case studies. Ethnic groups whose components are similar economically, racially, religiously, linguistically, generationally, and are also geographically concentrated, should have considerable panethnic potential. But this is a laundry list, not a theory. In the next section we assess which of these factors have been more important in facilitating or hindering panethnic developments. In particular, we are interested in the relative significance of cultural and structural factors.

PANETHNIC ACTIVISM AND ORGANIZATION

Panethnic activism was prompted by the social struggles that swept across America in the 1960s. These movements—civil rights, antiwar, women, student, and minority group—fought against racism, poverty, war, and exploitation. These social struggles led minority groups to recognize that their interests could be advanced only by forming coalitions. In particular, the civil rights movement had a profound impact on the racial ideology of minority groups, sensitizing them to racial issues. The Black Power Movement instilled pride in one's racial and cultural heritages and set into motion the struggles for Yellow Power, Red Power, and Brown Power (Uyematsu 1971; Cornell 1984, p. 46; Barrera 1988). International events also contributed to ethnic and panethnic activism. The visibility and success of anticolonial nationalist movements in Asia, Africa, and Latin America stirred racial and cultural pride and provided a context for ethnic movements. Student and other progressive forces within the minority populations began to conceive of themselves as part of the Third World struggle, and referred to linkages among U.S. minorities as a "Third World" coalition.

A result of the 1960s movements was the institutionalization of ethnicity. Radicalism gave way to electoral politics and the politics of government funding for social programs. Because ethnic membership could lead to entitlements, minorities, as well as new immigrant communities, have continued to use ethnic political power to improve their economic and social conditions. Whatever the balance of sentiment, most of the subethnic groups within each broad group concur that political alliances at the panethnic level are important, even essential, for protection and advancement. In these new or previously marginalized populations, political power is heavily dependent on the ability of the subgroups to speak with one voice. This is true not only because there is strength in numbers, but also because outsiders (including other minorities) are rarely willing to listen to a myriad of voices representing particular subethnic groups.

But these apparent practical advantages have not led to a total transformation from particularistic to panethnic levels of organization and sentiment. Since numbers count in the American political structure, Asian Americans, Indo Americans, Native Americans, and Latinos have all had to organize to some degree at the panethnic level. However, these four groups have had varying degrees of success in their panethnic efforts. To understand this variability, we need to examine the effect of the structural and cultural factors discussed above on the development and maintenance of panethnicity.

Asian Americans

Asian American subgroups are culturally diverse, both in terms of language and religion. However, outsiders have had little understanding or appreciation of these distinctions. Asian Americans, largely on the basis of race, have often been lumped together and treated as if they were the same (U.S. Commission on Civil Rights 1986). Because the public could not distinguish among Asian groups, racism and deteriorating public attiudes towards Asians affect all members and require organization at the pan-Asian level. Moreover, government agencies use "Asian American" as a unit in economic allocation and political representations. For example, the Census Bureau attempted (unsuccessfully) to collapse all Asian racial codes into one summary Asian-American category for the 1990 census. In addition to this continuing external pressure to be seen as one "racial" minority, Asian Americans share two other important structural similarities: similar average class positions; and geographical and geopolitical concentration in California. During the heyday of the Asian-American movement in the 1960s, most Asian Americans were native-born, though subsequent immigration has had a differential impact on subgroups and has brought new groups into the Asian-American fold.

Pan-Asian identity emerged in the 1960s and became strong both organizationally and sentimentally (Liu 1976). Since the 1960s movement, the term Asian American has been used extensively, especially by professional groups (Jo 1980, p. 106). In large cities and in all regions of the United States, Asian Americans have established pan-Asian organizations to lobby for the welfare, health, and business interest of the entire Asian community (Liu 1976, pp. 6–7; Kuo 1979, pp. 283–84). Pan-Asian media such as *Amerasia Journal, Asian Week* newspaper, and *AsiAm* magazine have also been established. Moreover, single ethnic organizations such as the Japanese American Citizens League and the Organization of Chinese Americans began to take up issues that affect all Asians. Along the same line, single ethnic newspapers such as *East/West News*, a Chinese American newspaper, expanded its coverage to include other Asian-American communities.

The new Asian immigration since 1965 has made it difficult to maintain pan-Asian unity. The newcomers reinforce cultural differences and increase the generational gap among Asian subgroups. The increasingly variegated character of Asian Americans makes it difficult to speak of a shared experience, common sensibility, or unified political outlook (Omi and Winant 1986, p. 143). Furthermore, the new immigration has added to the numerical strength of previously smaller groups such as Filipino American; they are no longer the minority groups. With their numerical dominance, these Asian groups are challenging the established power structure of the Asian American community. Some members have contended that they no longer need to coalesce with other Asian groups.

However, the new immigration has also given Asian Americans an incentive to organize at the panethnic level. In the arena of electoral politics, immigration has boosted the political clout of Asian Americans, particularly in California. By the turn of the century, California's Asians are expected to reach three million, then double by the year 2030 to comprise nearly 16 percent of the state (Bouvier and Martin 1985). With such numbers, Asians can expect to become a political power if they vote and lobby as an Asian bloc. The new immigration has also contributed to the upsurge of violence against Asian Americans (U.S. Commission on Civil rights 1986). Because the public cannot distinguish between Asian groups, Asians have no choice but to concern themselves with a hostility that implicates them all. Regardless of one's ethnic preference, anti-Asian violence requires response at the pan-Asian level.

Two examples highlight the enforced nature of Asian-American panethnicity: one, the reaction to an indiscriminate murder and the other, a reaction to federal attempts to lump all Asians together. In 1982 a Chinese American, Vincent Chin, was clubbed to death by two unemployed auto workers who mistook him for a Japanese. After pleading guilty to manslaughter, both men were fined a mere $3,000 and released. Outraged by these light sentences, Asian Americans across the country rallied and raised funds to continue the legal batle. In publicizing the case, leaders emphasized that all persons of Asian descent are potential victims because of their race. A federal jury ultimately acquitted Chin's killers of civil rights charges, but the Chin case has continued to be an effective symbol of anti-Asian violence, reminding Asians of their racial ties (Takaki 1983; Zia 1984; Fukuzawa 1989).

The second example is somewhat ironic: for the 1980 census, Asian American groups had lobbied successfully for a detailed enumeration of Asians, with separate categories for nine subgroups. The logic behind this was that individual groups needed more recognition, and also that separate counts would result in more accurate (i.e., larger) counts. For the 1990 census, the Census Bureau attempted to collapse all Asian racial codes into one summary Asian American. Asian-American groups united to fight, with eventual success, the Bureau's proposal, claiming that individual group data are needed to target service delivery, and also produced more accurate overall results. To those involved in this struggle there was no contradiction between a concerted pan-Asian effort and the goal of separate counts (Pian 1976; Matsui 1988).

Continuing immigration reinforces cultural differences among Asians, but linguistic and other cultural differences recede into the background with succeeding generations. There seems to be a correlation between panethnic orientation and generation in the United States, in the sense that more established groups (e.g., Japanese and Chinese Americans) lead the panethnic efforts, with smaller recent immigrant groups generally following. The clearest example of a group that resists panethnic organization are the Filipinos, who are not only (by their count) the largest subgroup but are also among the most socioeconomically distinctive. Overall, external pressure and other structural factors best explain the relatively high level of Asian-American panethnic consciousness and organization.

Indo Americans

Indo Americans reflect the regional, linguistic, and religious diversity that make it problematic to consider the Indian subcontinent as one society and that constantly threatens India's political unity. On the other hand, they are bound by several structural commonalities: they are similar economically, racially (at least to outsiders), and generationally; and they are geographically concentrated in major urban centers. These structural similarities would seem to explain why Indo Americans have been comparatively successful in establishing bonds of political if not moral panethnic solidarity.

Indo Americans only came to the United States in large numbers in the 1970s. Utilizing liberalized professional preference and family unification immigration regulations, the half-million or so Indo Americans constitute the best educated immigrant community in the United States today, with physicians and engineers being the two most common occupations (U.S. Bureau of the Census 1983; Xenos, Barringer and Levin 1989, p. 32) Though divided along religious and regional language lines, they do share the second language of the South Asian élites: English. The ties to the homeland for these recent and affluent new Americans are understandably strong (Saran 1985). These ties simultaneously bond Indo Americans together on issues of common interest (e.g., opposition to Pakistan), and divide them, reflecting communal strife in India (e.g., the Punjab).

Indian religious and language communities established particularistic organizations almost immediately upon arrival. Initially these communities were based on broad linguistic and religious lines; as they grew they tended to split along the finer lines of caste and sect. A South Indian Association split into several groups, including one for Tamil Brahmins, one for other Tamils, and the rest for other caste and language-specific groups, as numbers permitted. But at the same time Indo Americans had begun to form new umbrella organizations, both nationally and locally. By the mid-1980s, most metropolitan areas with a significant Indo-American presence had federations composed of most local religious and language region Indian organizations. These federations are often the focus of bitter personal and community rivalries, at times reflecting ongoing conflicts in India. But for the most part, they continue to exist and sponsor genuinely panethic "all-Indian" activities like Independence Day celebrations and conferences on the problems of Indian youth in America. There is also one successful national federation, composed of both national and some active local religious and language region associations. There have been at least two attempts to form national associations composed of individuals rather than organizations but, significantly, both have faded away (Fisher 1980; Lopez 1987).

The national and metropolitan federations of associations bring the diverse Indian communities together on the basis of shared interests: support for India in U.S. foreign policy, immigration policies favorable to Indians, and, increasingly, "racist" attacks against Indo Americans. In this they are strongly supported by the vigorous English-language Indo-American press (*India Abroad, India West*). Leaders have also endeavored to make Indo Americans a certified minority, along with other Asian Americans, in the probably mistaken belief that somehow this will provide material affirmative-action benefits for Indo Americans.[11] In alliance with (East) Asian Americans, they succeed in having Indo Americans included in the list of Asian-American subcategories for the 1980 and 1990 censuses. At state and national levels, they have fought to have Indo Americans included in the list of under-represented minorities eligible for small business loans and government priority contracts. At the last meeting of the national federation, delegates voted to replace "Asian Indian" and "Indo American" with "Indian-American," in explicit parallel with other hyphenated American ethnic groups. To the extent that the dialectical relation between governmental bureaucracies and ethnic groups serves to define group boundaries and identities, such efforts can only reinforce panethnic Indo-American solidarity and identity.

The Indo-American attempts to ally with other Asian Americans are particularly instructive. In Detroit, where the well-established Indo American community has often been the target of violence, they eagerly joined and materially supported the Vincent Chin campaign. Indo-American organizations also involved themselves in the 1980 census effort, and took an equally active role in quashing the recent attempts to return to a single Asian category which, for Indo Americans, would mean no count at all at even the panethnic level.[12] Given their small numbers in most localities and institutions, their exotic character in the eyes of the majority community, and the dangers of being associated with Arabs and Iranians, Indo Americans have good reason to ally with other Asian Americans. But all these attempts to insert Indo Americans into the mainstream of Asian-American communities have brought no genuine increase in social integration.[13]

Most Indo Americans still recognize three distinct levels of ethnicity: the endogamous marriage group defined by subcaste and clan, the language community based on their region of origin in India, and the "all-Indian" level. It is too soon to assess whether or not the successful organizational panethnicity of Indo Americans will translate into social panethnicity, breaking down the strong boundaries of region, religion, and caste.

The single factor that most unites them today, namely, loyalty to their common nation state of origin, will presumably decline in strength among subsequent generations, but it may be replaced by domestic considerations such as discrimination against South Asians in the United States. In the meantime, the three levels of Indo-American ethnicity coexist and, it would seem, complement each other.

Latinos

The Latino label combines colonized natives, legal and illegal immigrants and their offspring, and political refugees under one umbrella. While a common language and religion suggest an underlying cultural commonality, the diverse incorporation experiences of Latino groups have led to significant social and economic differences that hamper the development of panethnic organization and identity. This disunity is compounded by the lack of geographical overlap among the three principal Latino subgroups.

Mutual aid associations and religious brotherhoods are as old as Mexican settlements in California and the Southwest, and several defensive civil rights groups emerged or were reinvigorated in the aftermath of the Second World War. But it was only with the emergence of the Chicano Movement in the 1960s that Mexican-American organizations developed into genuine political organizations oriented to social change. Just knitting together these diverse groups, ranging from Cesar Chavez's farm workers to urban college students, from land hungry New Mexican farmers to the Brown Berets, and combining them with the older civil rights groups like the League of United Latin American Citizens (LULAC), was an exercise in panethnicity. The Chicano movement relied heavily on the ethnic-specific imagery of Mexico and its Indian past, and tended to be most effective at local levels. Puerto Rican militancy originated in the movement for independence for the island, and less radical Puerto Rican politics were enmeshed in the local politics of New York City politics. Cuban-American politics were long oriented to the "liberation" of Cuba, though this has gradually been supplanted as a practical goal by the need to establish a favorable political climate in South Florida for the development and maintenance of Cuban-American prosperity. Obviously these three political impulses have had little to do with each other (Padilla 1985; Moore and Pachon 1985, pp. 169–98).

At the level of national politics, there exists a Hispanic caucus in the House of Representatives, and the National Association of Latino Elected and Appointed Officials (NALEO), which extends to those elected at state and local levels. This is the most significant panethnic Latino organization, and it is essentially a (*de facto* Democratic) congressional alliance between Mexican Americans from the Southwest and Puerto Ricans from the New York City area. It remains to be seen how the newly elected Republican Cuban Congressperson will fit into this alliance. Apart from NALEO, few genuinely panethnic institutions have developed among Latinos. Small circulation magazines, in both English and Spanish, come and go. The most persistent are targeted to special audiences, such as *Replica*, a Spanish-language glossy oriented to conservative and affluent immigrants. Academic leaders and professionals, many of whom come from the student movements of the late sixties and early seventies, have tried to forge links via Hispanic caucuses in academic, political, and professional associations. Many universities have research centers devoted to the study of Latinos but, significantly, most of them continue to be named for and oriented to the locally dominant subgroup, not Latinos generally. The National Association of Chicano Studies accepts research papers on other Latino groups, but the center of concern remains those of Mexican origin. Outside of academe, LULAC has attempted to broaden its membership, but it is still essentially a Texas-based Mexican-American Democratic organization, and expansions of its political and ethnic base (especially to conservative Cubans) have often resulted in turmoil.

Clearly, the regional separation among Latino subethnic groups makes it difficult to assess whether or not they would cooperate more if they did overlap more geographically. Evidence from the one major point of overlap, Chicago, suggests that Mexicans and Puerto Ricans can cooperate, but that this cooperation does not easily lead to social assimilation. Padilla (1985) traced the development of Mexican and Puerto Rican ethnic organizations in Chicago during the 1970s and found a high degree of cooperation in efforts to improve schools and job opportunities. But he concluded that cultural similarities were, if necessary, certainly not sufficient bases for this cooperation: a common sense of economic deprivation and political exclusion and an objectively similar class position were the essential factors. He also noted that the co-operation relied heavily on the activities of a few highly panethnic individuals.

For the past two decades Hispanics have been labeled the sleeping giant among American ethnic groups, about to emerge and exert their strength. Despite indicators that something must happen soon (e.g., the majority of public school students in Los Angeles are now Latino), Hispanics, overall, and most of the subgroups, are still woefully disadvantaged economically and under-represented in most desirable and powerful segments of American society (most notably in politics, where they appear to be losing ground). Many factors contribute to this state of affairs, but surely the complex of forces that work against Latino panethnicity are among the most important. African Americans have much more severe problems of poverty and continuing racism to contend with, but they have also been much more successful politically, due no doubt in large part to the unity that has been imposed upon them from outside.

Native Americans

Linguistically, religiously, and geographically diverse, Native Americans do not generally see themselves as a single people. Like Asian Americans and Indo Americans, Native Americans lack a single cultural heritage to draw upon in the formation of panethnicity. For the most part, Native Americans still maintain their tribal identities. The U.S. government recognizes approximately five hundred tribal entities, over three hundred of which still function as quasi-sovereign nations under treaty status (Murray 1982, p. 5).

The case of Native Americans is unique, because their ethnic organization is largely determined by federal Indian policies. The government appears to pursue a two-pronged strategy. On the one hand, they recognize tribes as geopolitical units and the foci of various government programs and legislation. To avail themselves of the special "privileges" of being Native American, Indians must prove membership with their particular tribe. As such, tribal organizations continue to be essential and inescapable for them. On the other hand, the government insists that Indianness is the relevant ethnic distinction for political policy purposes, thus making pan-Indian organization necessary (Nagel 1982, p. 39).

Unwittingly, some government policies fostered pan-Indianism by facilitating inter-tribal contact and communication. In particular, federal Indian education policies required all Indians to learn English, thus providing the linguistically diverse tribes with a common language for intertribal communication. In addition, the boarding schools established in the early twentieth century provided an opportunity for American Indians to interact with members of different tribes. Many pan-Indian leaders came out of these boarding schools. However, these intertribal links involved primarily individuals, families, or at most, members of religious movements. Formal intertribal alliance for political purposes did not occur until the 1950s when Indians organized against the termination and relocation policy (Lurie 1968, p. 297). This policy sought to assimilate Indians into American society through eliminating reservations and tribal government (Trosper 1981, pp. 284–89). In the past, Indians had organized at the tribal level to protest against undesirable government policies. However, because the termination policy was designed to destroy Indian community life, it affected all Indians and therefore forged pan-Indian cooperation (Lurie 1968, p. 295).

The pan-Indian political movement began with the establishment of the National Congress of American Indians (NCAI) in 1944 (Trosper 1981, p. 248). The NCAI gained more support among American Indians with its successful opposition to the termination and relocation policy. By the 1960s, there was a proliferation of political organizations along both tribal and intertribal lines. Means of communication among Indians improved as mimeographed tribal newsletters and intertribal newspapers appeared (Lurie 1986, p. 295). Influenced by the climate of activism of the late 1960s, pan-Indian political activities turned militant and attracted significant media attention. Led by the American Indian Movement (AIM) and the National Indian Youth Council (NIYC), this Red Power era began with the occupation of Alcatraz Island by "Indians of all Tribes" in November 1969 and continued throughout the 1970s with other attempted and successful takeovers and occupations. In contrast to earlier Indian protests, the Red Power movement organized along supratribal rather than purely tribal lines and the issues and goals of the protest involved all Indians or multiple tribes. The occupation of Alcatraz Island involved Indians of different tribes and its goals were to establish an American Indian studies and cultural center (Nagel 1989). The Red Power movement declined in the 1970s due to increased repression of the movement by law enforcement agencies and the federal government's policy response to the protest action of the early 1970s (Nagel 1988, p. 11).

Because U.S. policies vacillate between recognizing the individuality of specific groups and insisting that they be lumped together for administrative purposes, Native Americans will probably continue to organize at both the tribal and pan-tribal levels. For example, in preparation for the 1990 census, the Census Bureau consulted the national American Indian Census Advisory Committee as well as the regional American Indian tribal governments. The latter focused on enumeration concerns on reservations whereas the Advisory Committee addressed a broader spectrum of issues. There is some evidence that pan-Indianness is growing among the urban Indian population. In 1976 off-reservation Indians founded the National Urban Indian Council to advocate on their behalf for funding. According to the chief executive of the Council, reservation Indians "had a lot of anxiety about the urbans getting organized" for fear that they would divert federal money away from the reservation (Frazier 1980). However, this group has apparently managed to coexist and cooperate with tribally oriented organizations.

The growing urban Indian population plays a special role in Indian panethnicity. Though most maintain links with their tribes, they also face a day-to-day white environment in which their Indianness, not their tribal membership, is their salient ethnic identity. As Indians become increasingly urban we can expect that these external and internal forces for pan-Indianness, combined with the reduced benefits accruing from specific tribal membership in the city, will result in a gradual rise in the importance of the more general American Indian level of identity (Sorkin 1978; Cornell 1988).

DISCUSSION AND CONCLUSION

None of the four sets of ethnic subgroups considered here has completely evolved to a more general level of ethnic identity, but some have gone farther than others. Latinos, the set of subgroups that is culturally the most homogeneous, but which also shares the least in terms of structural characteristics and apparent common interests, are clearly the least panethnic. The other three sets of subgroups are much more diverse culturally. On the other hand, each set shares comparatively common material circumstances, including the dominant society's definition of them as a distinct race apart. And at least two of the three sets—Asian Americans and Indo Americans—have been relatively successful at forging panethnic alliances and at least the kernel of panethnic identities. Their success relative to Native Americans (and Latinos) would seem to be due in part to their comparative affluence and effective intergroup communications, and especially to the absence of major conflicts of interest among subethnic groups.

The question of community affluence merits further comment. It might be argued that the relative effectiveness of Asian-American and especially Indo-American panethnic organization is due not so much to the class and racial homogeneity of these groups, as to the fact that they are so thoroughly middle class and professional in status. Affluence may indeed be a factor, but since it is a structural/material one it does not contradict our general conclusions. Middle-class professionals are joiners, to be sure, but we are concerned not with voluntary formal organization memberships *per se* but rather with the dynamics of panethnic organizations. We suspect, though we lack the data to prove it, that the relative affluence of Indo Americans and Asian Americans broadens organizational participation of all sorts. Affluence, independent of class homogeneity *per se*, is one additional structural factor conducive to panethnicity.

Clearly, structural factors, not cultural commonalities, better explain the emergence and success of panethnicity.[14] This conclusion emerges from examining the incidents that have led to increased panethnic solidarity: all have drawn subgroups together on the basis of some common material concern, not on the basis of common cultural symbols. Asian Americans have been drawn together by the classic "mistaken identity" case of Vincent Chin, and by the need and opportunity to combine and make their "numbers count" in California politics. Indo Americans are brought together by their common political concerns, a perceived rise of attacks against them in the United States, and the hope that being a united certified minority will have its rewards. Native Americans, when they are able to cooperate, come together out of a consciousness of common interest and, above all, by the will of the State. In contrast, Latino subgroups see no compelling material reason to merge their efforts; moreover, they believe that they have cogent reasons to pursue their own paths, developing political and economic power in their regional arenas.

Our evidence for these conclusions has been drawn largely from the level of formal organizations. It can fairly be asked, what is the relation between this and the level of individual behavior and attitudes? Certainly, only a minority of each community is actively involved in panethnic organizations. And our own field work suggests that those individuals who do become active are often marginal to their specific communities. Could it be that we have been looking at nothing more than organizational epiphenomena, devoid of any underpinning in the communities?

We argued above that the organizational level is both intrinsically worthy of examination and that it tells us about the present and future directions of the populations supposedly represented. The cultural and structural factors we discussed are in fact characteristics of the populations, not of organizations, and the organizational developments and responses to events could not exist without at least some popular support. The case of Vincent Chin brought together Asian Americans, not just Asian American organizations, and the lobbying efforts of the National Association of Asian Indian Associations regarding immigration law is supported by, and for the benefit of, Indo-American families, not organizations. Not only do the organizations speak for their constituents; participation in and awareness of panethnic organizations stimulate panethnic consciousness.

We lack the data to draw firm conclusions about the development of panethnic behavior and attitudes among individuals, but we note some suggestive developments that merit further research. Heading the list is that most important of all social facts regarding members of ethnic groups: marriage patterns. Most often used to study rates of assimilation, intermarriage *between* ethnic subgroups is an equally good measure of panethnicity on the level of individuals. Just as intermarriage between major ethnic categories can obliterate boundaries, so intermarriage within these categories (intramarriage) can consolidate subgroups into one panethnic identity. There is evidence that intramarriage is occurring at substantial levels among one of our most panethnic set of subgroups: Asian Americans (Kitano et al. 1984; Shinagaw and Pang 1988; Yu 1983). Panethnic intermarriage, like panethnic organization, is not necessarily just a step towards assimilation.

Finally, we emphasize that in all four of the panethnic groupings considered here the question of race is fundamental. Those three groups that, from an outsider's point of view, are most racially homogeneous are also the groups with the greatest panethnic development. Even the racially variable and often ambiguous Latino population is, in the Anglo view of things, something of a race apart: for example, crime reports regularly use the term "Latin" to refer to someone who appears mestizo. Our conclusions, then, may not be generalizable to sets of panethnic subgroups that are not, to the Anglo American eye, racially distinct. On the other hand, the present and future of ethnicity in the United States is increasingly a question of race. Recent and probably most future immigration will be dominated by non-whites. And those well-established "ethnic" groups that are still most excluded from the American mainstream are racial minorities. For Italians and other whites, panethnicity may indeed have been a step towards assimilation and "Anglo-conformity." But, it is important to emphasize, no non-white ethnic group has ever fully assimilated into American society. Panethnicity among the four racial minorities considered here has been an uneven and slow process. But, given the external pressures and the benefits it promises, panethnicity, in contrast to ethnic particularism or assimilation, may well define the future of ethnicity in the United States.

STUDY QUESTIONS

1. Why do cultural similarities seem less conducive to panethnicity than structural traits?

2. Why might cultural similarities be symbolic rather than material?

3. Why do Latinos "see no compelling material reason to merge their efforts"?

NOTES

The first author acknowledges the support of the Social Sciences Research Council for its support of his research on Indo Americans; the second author acknowledges the support of UCLA's Institute of American Culture and Asian American Studies Center for her research on Asian Americans.

1. Among the few works that deal directly with panethnicity are Trottier (1981); Nagel (1982) and Padilla (1986). The first author of this paper is engaged in a study of panethnicity among Indo Americans; the second is studying Asian American panethnicity.

2. We use the term "ethnicity" to include racial as well as culturally defined groups. "Asian American" is used here in its usual sense of East and Southeast Asian origins, "Indo American" refers to those of south Asian origin, at times including Pakistanis and other national groups, but fundamentally referring to those from contemporary India; "Native American" is used to refer to the first Americans rather than the often preferred "American Indian," simply to minimize confusion with Indo Americans, who increasingly refer to themselves as Indian-Americans; "Latino" encompasses all Hispanics of North, Central, or South American origin.

3. Which is not to say that the traditions emanating from the understandably Eurocentric Marx, Simmel, Durkheim, and Weber are incompatible with attention to ethnicity. Indeed, they represent the four principal sociological approaches to understanding ethnicity in complex societies.

4. We recognize that this is a crude dichotomy, and that greater theoretical impact might result from adherence to some specific school of thought, such as World System Theory or Rational Choice Theory. However, the preliminary nature of this investigation renders such an exercise premature.

5. By most estimates, over 90 percent of U.S. Latinos are at least nominally Catholic (Moore and Pachon 1985, p. 110). As in Latin America, there are important Protestant minorities, usually fundamentalist sects. Most of these hold services in Spanish and are oriented to Spanish-speaking immigrants of all backgrounds.

6. By "race" we mean "social race" in the sense that Wagley and Harris(1958) defined the term over thirty years ago. However, while they used the term with respect to certain racially

defined groups that had little physical basis for the classification, we emphasize the social, and usually external definition of *all* so-called racial minorities. Racial minorities in the United States have, of course, developed cultures that go far beyond simple reactions to domination, and constitute bases for voluntary ethnic solidarity. However, our emphasis here is on the principal forces for social differentiation, and in the U.S. case social definition in terms of race is largely imposed from outside.

7. Frank (1969), Wolf (1982), and others have emphasized that most contemporary socially significant racial categories originated in the uneven division of labor produced by European capitalist expansion. Our views are broadly consistent with theirs, which we view as a starting point in studying the social significance of race, not a conclusion.

8. We adopt Hoetink's (1969) terminology without his accompanying theory of causation. Hoetink's terms are useful because, unlike more common terms such as "stereotype," they relate only to perceived physical average types, without any accompanying "racist" expectations about accompanying social and cultural characteristics. Hoetink emphasizes that, while there are physical bases for Somatic Norms, they are socially derived images, not scientific measurements.

9. For example, Southern Brahmans are more likely to be doctors, and Gujarati Patels are more likely to be in business.

10. The 1980 census indicates the following foreign-born proportions for the population over 18: Mexican American (48 percent), Cuban (97 percent), Puerto Rican (80 percent born on the island), other Hispanic (30 percent). These figures, like those for Asian Americans, are very much out of date, and the pervasiveness of undocumented Latino residents makes even the best estimates only very approximate.

11. In this way they were surely influenced by Indian-style affirmative action, in which specific proportions of university seats and government jobs are set aside for scheduled castes and tribes.

12. Actually, the Census Bureau insisted that its proposed methodology, employing both a summary category and a write-in line to record specific identities, would result in more accurate counts. Indo Americans and other Asian Americans, probably wisely, thought this to be nonsense.

13. Recent interviews in Los Angeles confirm that Indo Americans and East Asians see few similarities with each other, and view any political cooperation as only an alliance of convenience. Interviewees often point to "cultural" differences, but when the considerable cultural differences within each panethnic group are pointed out, they admit that racial differences also play a role. By this they mean both that they see socially significant racial and cultural differences, and also that no Punjabi would ever be mistaken for a Japanese.

14. Some readers may find this theoretical conclusion excessively crude, and we agree that, once cultural factors are taken into account, the question is *which* structural factors and historical sequences. However, this article is devoted to the prior question.

REFERENCES

Banton, Michael. 1983. *Racial and Ethnic Competition*. Cambridge: Cambridge University Press.

Barrera, Mario. 1988. *Beyond Azthlan: Ethnic Autonomy in Comparative Perspective*. New York: Praeger

Bean, Frank and Tienda, Marta. 1987. *The Hispanic Population of the United States*. New York: Russell Sage

Beteille, Andre 1968. "Race and descent as social categories in India." In John Hope Franklin (ed.), *Color and Race*. Boston: Beacon Press, pp. 166–85.

Blauner, Robert 1972 *Racial Oppression in America*, New York: Harper and Row

Bonacich, Edna and Modell, John. 1980. *The Economic Basis of Ethnic Solidarity: A study of Japanese Americans*. Berkeley: University of California Press.

Bouvier, Leon F. and Martin, Philip. 1985. *Population Change and California's Future*. Washington, D. D.: Population Reference Bureau.

Conklin, Nancy Faires and Lourie, Margaret A. 1983. *A Host of Tongues: Language Community in the United States*. New York: The Free Press

Cornell, Stephen. 1984. "Crisis and response in Indian-White relations, 1960–1984." *Social Problems*, vol. 32, pp. 44–59.

————. 1988. *The Return of the Native American Indian Political Resurgence*. New York: Oxford University Press.

Fisher, Maxine P. 1980. *The Indians of New York City*. New Delhi: Heritage Publishers.

Frank, Andre. 1969. *Latin America: Underdevelopment or Revolution*. New York: Monthly Review Press.

Frazier, Gregory. 1980. "Urban Indians enter the political arena." *American Indian Journal* vol. 6. no. 8, pp. 15–18.

Fukuzawa, David. 1989. "The Vincent Chin case and the Detroit Asian American community," *EWGAPA News*, Winter, pp. 1–2.

Gardner, Robert W., Robey, Bryant, and Smith, Peter C. 1985. "Asian Americans: growth, change, and diversity." *Population Bulletin*, vol. 40, no. 4 (monograph series).

Geschwender, James. 1988. "The Portugese and Haoles of Hawaii: implications for the origins of ethnicity." *American Sociological Review*, vol. 53, pp. 515–27.

Ghurye, G.S. 1932. *Caste and Race in India*. London: Kegan Paul.

Gordon, Milton. 1964. *Assimilation in America Life*. New York: Oxford University Press

Jo, Yung-Hwan. 1980. *Political Participation of Asian Americans*. Pacific/Asian American Mental Health Research Center

Harris, Marvin. 1964. *Patterns of Race in the Americas*. New York: W. W. Norton and Company.

Hoetink, Harry. 1969. *Caribbean Race Relations*. New York: Oxford University Press.

Horowitz, Donald L. 1985. *Ethnic Groups in Conflict*. Berkeley: University of California Press.

Kitano, Harry. 1981. "Asian Americans: the Chinese, Japanese, Koreans, Filipinos, and Southeast Asians." *The Annals of the American Academy of Political and Social Sciences*. vol. 454, pp. 125–38.

Kitano, Harry et al. 1984. "Asian-American interracial marriage." *Journal of Marriage and the Family*. vol. 46, no. 1, pp. 179–90

Kuo, Wen H. 1979. "On the study of Asian-Americans: its current state and agenda." *The Sociological Quarterly*, vol. 20, Spring, pp. 279–90.

Liu, William. 1976. "Asian American research: views of a sociologist." *Asian Studies Occasional Report*, vol. 2.

Lopez, David E. 1982. *Language Maintenance and shift in the United States Today: The Basic Patterns and Their Social Implications*. Los Alamitos, CA: National Center for Billingual Research.

————. 1987. "Asian Indians in the United States: a Framework for Research," Working Paper. Department of Sociology, University of California at Los Angeles.

Lurie, Nancy Oestreich. 1968. "An American Indian renaissance?" In Stuart Levine and Nancy Oestrich Lurie (eds). *The American Indian Today*, Baltimore: Penguin Books, pp. 295–327.

Matsui, Robert T. 1988. "Statement of Hon. Robert T. Matsui, a Representative in Congress from CA." In U.S. House (100th Congress), Commettee on Post Office and Civil Service, *Review of 1990 Decennial Census Questionnaire*. Washington, D.C.: Government Printing Office, pp. 45–7.

Melendy, H. Brett. 1977. *Asians in America: Filipinos, Koreans, and East Indians*. Boston: Twayne.

Moore, Joan and Pachon, Harry. 1985. *Hispanics in the United States*, Englewood Cliffs, New Jersey: Prentice Hall.

Murray, David. 1982. *Modern Indians: Native Americans in the Twentieth Century*. Durham: British Association for American Studies.

Nagel, Joane. 1982. "The political mobilization of Native Americans." *The Social Science Journal*, vol. 19, no. 3, pp. 37–45.

———. 1988. "The roots of Red Power: demographic and organizational bases of American Indian activism 1950–1980." Paper presented at the 83rd annual meeting of the American Sociological Association.

———. 1989. "American Indian repertoires of contention." Paper presented at the 84th annual meeting of the American Sociological Association.

Nelli, Humberto. 1970. *Italians in Chicago: 1880–1930*. New York: Oxford University Press.

Omi, Michael, and Winant, Howard. 1986. *Racial Formation in the United States From the 1960s to the 1980s*. New York and London: Routledge.

Padilla, Felix. 1985. *Latino Ethnic Consciousness*. Notre Dame: University of Notre Dame Press.

Pian, Canta. 1976. "Statement of Ms. Canta Pian, Pacific-Asian Coalition." In US House (94th Congress), Committee on Post Office and Civil Service, 1980 *Census Hearing*, Washington, D.C.: Government Printing Office, pp. 32–33.

Portes, Alejandro and Bach, Robert L. 1985. *Latin Journal: and Mexican Immigrants in the United States*. Berkeley: University of California Press.

Rex, John. 1983. *Race Relations in Sociological Theory*. London: Routledge & Kegan Paul.

Rodriguez, Clara et al. (eds). 1980. *The Puerto Rican Struggle*. New York: Puerto Rican Migration Research Consortium.

Saran, Parmatma. 1985. *The Asian Indian Experience in the United States*. Delhi: Vikas Publishing House

Sarna, Jonathan D. 1978. "From Immigrants to ethnics: toward a theory of ethnicization." *Ethnicity*, vol. 5, pp. 370–78.

Schermerhorn, Richard. 1970. *Comparative Ethnic Relations*. New York: Random House.

Shinagawa, Larry Hajime, and Pang, Gin Yong. 1988. "Intraethnic, interethnic, and interracial marriages among Asian Americans in California, 1980." *Berkeley Journal of Sociology*, vol. 33, pp. 95–114.

Snipp, Matthew C. 1986. "Who are American Indians? Some observations about the perils and pitfalls of data for race and ethnicity." *Population Research and Policy Review*, vol. 5, pp. 237–52.

Sorkin, Alan L. 1978. *The Urban American Indian*. Toronto: Lexington Books.

Stanley, Sam and Thomas, Robert K. 1978. "Current demographic and social trends among North American Indians." *The Annals of the Academy of Political and Social Science*, vol. 436, pp. 111–20.

Takaki, Ronald. 1983. "Who really killed Vincent Chin?" *Asian Week*, September 29 p. 7.

Thomas, Robert K. 1968. "Pan-Indianism." In Stuart Levine and Nancy Oestrich Lurie (eds).*The American Indian Today*. Baltimore: Penguin Books, pp. 128–40.

Trosper, Ronald. 1981. "American Indian nationalism and frontier expansion." In Charles Keyes (ed.), *Ethnic Change*. Seattle: University of Washington Press, pp. 247–70.

Trottier, Richard. 1981. "Charters of panethnic identity: indigenous Americans and immigrant Asian Americans." In Charles Keyes (ed.), *Ethnic Change*. Seattle: University of Washington Press, pp. 271–305.

U.S. Bureau of the Census. 1981. *Current Population Advance Report: Persons of Spanish Origin in the United States, March, 1980*. Washington, D.C.: Government Printing Office.

———. 1983. *1980 Census of Population: Detailed Population Characteristics*. Washington, D.C.: U.S. Government Printing Office.

———. 1983. *1980 Census of Population: General Population Characteristics, U.S. Summary*. Washington, D.C.: U.S. Government Printing Office.

———. 1983. *1980. Census of Population: General Social and Economic Characteristics*. Washington, D.C.: U.S. Government Printing Office.

———. 1988. *We, the First Americans*, Washington, D.C.: Government Printing Office.

U.S. Commission on Civil Rights. 1986. *Recent Activities Against Citizens and Residents of Asian Descent*. Washington, D.C.: Government Printing Office.

Uyematsu, Amy. 1971. 'The emergence of Yellow Power in America." In Amy Tachiki, Eddie Wong, and Franklin Odo (eds), *Roots: An Asian American Reader*. Los Angeles: UCLA Asian American Studies Center, pp. 9–13.

Van Den Berghe, Pierre. 1981. *The Ethnic Phenomenon*. New York: Elsevier.

Vecoli, Rudolph J. 1983. 'The formation of Chicago's Little Italics." *Journal of American Ethnic History*, vol. 2, pp. 5–20.

Veltman, Calvin. 1983. *Language Shift in the United States*. Berlin: Mouton Publishers.

Wagley, Charles and Harris, Marvin. 1958. *Minorities in the New World*. New York: Columbia University Press.

Wolf, Eric. 1982. *Europe and the People Without a History*. Berkeley: University of California Press.

Xenos, Peter S., et al. 1987. "Asian Americans: growth, and change in the 1970s." In James T. Fawcett and Benjamin Carino (eds), *Pacific Bridges*. New York: Center for Migration Studies, pp. 249–84.

Xenos, Peter, Barringer, Herbert, and Levin, Michael J. 1989. *Asian Indians in the United States: 1980 Census Profile*. Honolulu: East-West Center.

Yancey, William C., Ericksen, Eugene P. and Juliani, Richard N. 1976. "Emergent ethnicity: a review and reformulation." *American Sociological Review*, vol. 41, pp. 391–403.

Yinger, Milton J. 1985. "Ethnicity." *Annual Review of Sociology*, vol. 11, pp. 151–80.

Yu, Eui-Young. 1983. "Korean communities in America: past, present, and future." *Amerasia Journal*, vol. 10, no. 2, pp. 23–51.

Zia, Helen Y. 1984. "The new violence." *Bridge*, vol. 9, no. 2, pp. 18–23.

Chapter 10

M. *Patricia Fernández-Kelly* and
Richard Schauffler

Divided Fates
Immigrant Children in a Restructured U.S. Economy

Assimilation, perhaps the most enduring theme in the immigration literature, unfolds into descriptive and normative facets. From an empirical standpoint, the concept designates a range of adjustments to receiving environments and points to the manner in which immigrants blend into larger societies. In a normative sense, assimilation is linked to an expectation that foreigners will shed, or at least contain, their natives cultures while embracing the mores and language of the host country. Put succinctly, assimilation has always been more than a convenient word to enumerate the ways in which immigrants survive; it has also been a term disclosing hopes about how immigrants "should" behave.

In this article we revisit the descriptive and normative aspects of assimilation from the perspective of political economy and informed by insights from the field of economic sociology. The first section includes a review of approaches and a discussion of segmented assimilation, a term coined by Portes and Zhou (1993) to denote varying modalities of immigrant incorporation into distinct sectors of American society. The notion is serviceable in that it refines generalizations of the past by pointing to factors that can turn assimilation into an uplifting or a leveling force. At the heart of the discussion is the realization that becoming American encompasses various and sometimes conflicting meanings.

Optimistic accounts of assimilation — captured in the image of the melting pot — coexisted with the early stages of American capitalism when immigrants were the purveyors of labor for an expanding economy. Tales of weary but resolute arrivals at the shores of opportunity became part of collective self-definitions. Assimilation, conceived as the

From *International Migration Review,* Vol. 28 No. 28, 1994.

ideal path towards success, also emerged as the wellspring of national identity. Over the last two decades, economic internationalization has transformed the context in which assimilation takes place. In the Fordist era, workers could envision entry-level jobs as the first step in a journey towards prosperity. At present, when firms often subcontract services and even product assembly, many of the paths toward socioeconomic improvement have been blocked. Will the new immigrants—mostly from Asia and Latin America—replicate earlier patterns of success or face conditions of arrested progress?

Sketched in the second section is a theoretical framework that assigns priority to interpersonal networks and social capital, a process by virtue of which individuals use their membership in a particular group to gain access to valuable resources, including information and jobs. We maintain that, all the more so in a restructed economy, the outcomes of assimilation depend on a series of toponomical—that is, socially and physically situated—factors. Immigrants able to draw upon the knowledge of preexisting groups that control desirable economic assets will share an experience much different from those lacking a social nexus to opportunity and resources of high quality.

Collective identity is itself a significant resource in the process of assimilation. Although the fate of immigrants depends upon macrostructural changes like industrial restructuring, it also varies in congruence with the recasting of collective self-definitions. The immigrant condition forces individuals to observe themselves even as they are being observed by others. As a consequence, immigrants repeatedly engage in purposeful acts to signify their intended character and the way that character differs from, or converges with, that of other groups. A stigmatized identity can turn assimilation into an injurious transition unless immigrants resort to shared repertoires based on national origin, immigrant status, or religious conviction. Some identities protect immigrants; others weaken them by transforming them into disadvantaged ethnic minorities.

There is an ongoing relationship between migration and ethnicity: today's ethnics are the immigrants of the past and vice versa; present immigrants are already forging tomorrow's ethnic identities. New arrivals interact empirically and symbolically with their predecessors. At that juncture the African-American experience has strategic importance for the study of downward assimilation, a process defined by the incorporation of immigrants into impoverished, generally nonwhite, urban groups whose members display adversarial stances toward mainstream behaviors, including the devaluation of education and diminished expectations.

In defining themselves, immigrants of all nationalities hold the image of the urban underclass as a pivotal referent to delineate their own place in the larger society. Most African Americans were never international migrants in the conventional sense of the word. However, as migrants from the rural South during the first half of the twentieth century, they shared commonalities in profile and expectations with migrants from lands afar. In points of destination, blacks faced barriers that resulted in their arrested socioeconomic advancement. Ironically, current analyses focus not primarily on the migrant past of African Americans, but on the distressing behavioral complex surrounding concentrated poverty in the urban ghetto. Yet one way to reframe that phenomenon is as a product of migration under conditions of extreme hostility over extended periods of time. In the third section, we pursue the argument through a comparison of five immigrant groups, Mexicans and Vietnamese in southern California, and Nicaraguans, Cubans, and Haitians in southern Florida. The data to sustain the comparison are drawn from two complementary sources: a national survey of children of immigrants between the ages of twelve and seventeen conducted in 1992 and a series of ethnographic case studies carried out in the latter part of 1993 and early 1994 with a small subset formed by 120 families of immigrant children in the original sample. By combining the strengths of quantitative and qualitative analyses, we draw a profile of diverging adaptations, emerging identities, and segmented assimilation.

The concluding section summarizes findings and reconsiders the central questions in the light of those findings.

ASSIMILATION: OLD AND NEW

By the time the sociologists of the Chicago School turned their attention to immigration in the 1920s, observers of the American experience had been debating its two presumed outcomes—assimilation and phuralism—for almost 150 years. The idea of national integration was captured in essence by Crevecoeur in 1782 when he noted that "here individuals of all nations are melted into a new race of men" (cited in Abramson, 1980:34). In the next century, assimilation in the form of conformity to Anglo-Saxon tradition was expressed as "the tendency of things . . . to mould the whole into one people, whose leading characteristics are English, formed on American soil" (Chickering, 1848, cited in Abramson, 1980:45). Throughout that period, the chronicle of immigration excluded any mention of blacks and indigenous people, focusing primarily on Europeans.

The beginning of the twentieth century witnessed a new phenomenon. for the first time Americans of British origin represented less than half of the country's total population. In the midst of rising demands for immigration restriction, the Carnegie Corporation commissioned the department of sociology at the University of Chicago to produce a series entitled *Studies of Methods of Americanization* (Kivisto, 1990). Prospects for assimilation were good in the United States, the authors reasoned, because, unlike Europe, there were no classes in the new country, and immigrants arrived as individuals, not as groups.

Early theories of assimilation were forged against a distinct socioeconomic background. In the early decades of the twentieth century, the Fordist economy generated millions of jobs, almost a third of which were in manufacturing and most of which required little or no previous skill. The economic expansion that promoted rising wages and mass consumption invested with plausibility the story of the widening mainstream. The expectation was that those still struggling on the river banks would soon be engulfed by the broadening waters of economic progress.

There was a major deviation from that optimistic forecast. As foreigners continued to arrive in the United States, the industrial growth of the North fueled a demand for labor which, at the time of World War I, began to be filled by black migrants from the rural South where cotton agriculture was declining. African Americans appeared in cities like Chicago, New York, Boston, and Philadelphia under conditions that Robert Park (1950) regarded as optimum for assimilation. Yet the process did not bring about the anticipated effects. The experience of black Americans presented a compelling argument against the certain identification of assimilation with economic success. Although Park himself grew increasingly skeptical about assimilation as a beneficial prospect for all racial and ethnic groups, the concept became paradigmatic in the understanding of immigrant adaptation.

Despite efforts by Frazier (1957) and Gordon (1964), the notion of assimilation remained problematic in subsequent years for several reasons. First, it implied that immigrant and American cultures were mutually exclusive and bounded categories. Retaining one's native culture and becoming American were conceived as a zero-sum game; only by giving up ethnic identity could immigrants fully participate in American life.

Second, the question of agency in the process of assimilation remained ambiguous. Was it American society or the immigrant that was doing the absorbing, appropriating, and amalgamating? For the most part, Park and his associates had suggested that the immigrant was the passive object of the host environment. In so doing, society appeared as an unchanging force and the immigrant as the plaint clay of a teleological—and quasi-evolutionary—process that transcended human agency.

Third, what was American took the form of an assumption not a subject for investigation. Since, for the most part, assimilation was not viewed as a reciprocal process, the American condition remained unchanged, stultified. Contestations of the dominant ideology were excluded from discussions about American identity, as were other aspects of the social structure—social class and labor markets in particular.

Finally, the relationship between individual and collective processes was often confused. Park's general description of assimilation and his concept of the marginal man spoke to the plight of the individual. Yet a role was also reserved for communities as mechanisms necessary for individual transitions. This implied relatively autonomous group processes. The paradox entailed in that formulation—how would the last immigrant in a particular group assimilate when the community necessary to facilitate that transition had already disappeared—was not addressed.

In the 1960s and 1970s, the Civil Rights Movement focused attention on the persistent exclusion of African Americans, and new waves of immigrants from Asia, Latin America, and the Caribbean provoked a renewed public debate. Pluralism and assimilation were now challenged by a variety of structural approaches of a neo-Marxist inspiration. Research on immigrant enclaves and middleman minorities turned the original conception of assimilation on its head by describing alternative, and often more effective, modes of incorporation. Self-employment, business formation, and the maintenance of shared cultural understandings outside the American mainstream were shown to enhance and accelerate economic mobility. Those views portrayed assimilation as a deflating pressure threatening immigrants' chances for success in counterposition to earlier, more optimistic, interpretations.

Structural perspectives, as well, acknowledged the importance of personal endowments and shared cultural assets, but they assigned equal priority to patterned arrangements that facilitate or impede economic advancement. Works by Blauner (1972) on internal colonialism, Portes and Bach (1986) on ethnic enclaves, and Bonacich (1980) on middleman minorities, privileged labor market inclusion and exclusion patterns as well as their effect on social mobility. Persistent inequalities were viewed in close relationship to the location of immigrant groups and racial and ethnic minorities within the larger society.

In that context, consensus emerged that the outcome of migration depends on the interaction of three factors: (1) the internal composition of the groups to which immigrants belong, particularly in terms of social class; (2) their degree of concentration in specific locations; and (3) their mode of reception and incorporation into specific labor market strata. The distinction between labor migration, as represented by Mexicans and African Americans, and the immigrant enclave, as illustrated by Cubans, proved to be especially instructive. Cuban success in business formation was partly due to favorable government policies aiding settlement, the presence of a critical mass of entrepreneurs among Cuban exiles, and high levels of concentration in southern Florida. By contrast, the Mexican and African-American migrations were characterized by low levels of internal differentiation, weak or nonexistent resources in the process of adjustment, and high levels of concentration in impoverished neighborhoods. Those differences led, in turn, to varying social profiles and a dissimilar capacity for socioeconomic attainment.

Immigrants have always faced a modicum of discrimination, but their potential for collective progress has depended on a minimal threshold of gradual acceptance. The movement away from the immigrant slum entailed becoming American; almost always, that also meant becoming white. For African Americans, the portal leading to economic improvement was exceedingly narrow. Yet increasing opportunities, especially in manufacturing, enabled even those vulnerable groups to make strides during the first half of the twentieth century. Recent changes operating at the global level raise new questions about the nature of immigrant absorption.

As the economic base shifted from manufacturing to services and information processing, cities suffered a process of deterioration but, paradoxically, they also attracted professionals linked to lucrative sectors of the new economy—international banking and finance, communications, and software design, for example. The presence of a new technocratic class in urban centers invirgorated the demand for labor-intensive products and services—ranging from domestic help to restaurants and customized furniture and apparel—creating interstices for the employment of new waves of immigrants, now from Asia, Latin America, and the Caribbean, many of whom were undocumented. As a result, the global city emerged upon the ruins of the old industrial metropolis as a strategic location for the centralization of coordinating functions vis-à-vis the international economy (Sassen, 1992).

Largely on account of major changes operating at the international level and partly because of regional variations, the options of new immigrants will divide depending on their spatial location, their contact with specific social networks, and their differentiated access to economic and political resources. Those subdivisions are what the notion of segmented assimilation seeks to make comprehensible. The concept builds on structural approaches and applies their insights beyond what has been essentially a discussion of labor market incorporation. The assumption is that amalgamation does take place, but the question is restated to make problematic both the host society and the immigrant population: Assimilation to what? Assimilation by whom? The group which serves as the unique reference point for all immigrants. Before exploring these issues in further detail, we sketch a theoretical framework that assigns priority to social networks.

Social Capital and Immigrant Networks

Network analysis became popular in the 1960s and 1970s partly in reaction to the determinism of structural functionalism and the methodological individualism fostered by multivariate statistical inquiries. Studying the relations between real people and organizations reintroduced human agency into sociological discussions. However, what started as ethnographic work in British social anthropology soon devolved into an exercise in mathematical sociology. The warnings of pioneers—like Boissevain (1979) and Sanjek (1974)—that network analysis might fall prey to technical overelaboration were not heeded. Some current writings on the subject focus on a set of arcane methods, often devoid of sociological meaning, intelligible only to devotees.

Here, we take a different approach by grounding our analysis of social networks in the new economic sociology. A central objective of that field is to elucidate the social underpinnings of economic action. The point bears significantly upon immigration research because, as indicated in the previous section, the character of immigrant assimilation depends largely upon social forces leading to differentiated economic outcomes. Indeed, one way to conceptualize immigration is as a phenomenon of labor mobility sustained by interpersonal networks bridging points of origin and points of destination.

Once an immigrant community emerges in a particular location, it achieves a degree of autonomy from the pressures of the market serving to reduce the cost and risks of migration and allowing for the movement of new immigrants in relatively bounded economic spaces, which Sassen (1995) labels transnational labor markets. The concentration of immigrants within or in the proximity of global cities depends, to some extent, on the changing nature of labor demand, but also on the existence of networks formed by individuals who repeatedly cross borders from specific areas of origin to specific areas of arrival. Many of those immigrants appear less interested in blending into the host society than in acquiring there the means to maintain status and visibility in their home towns. The existence of international networks, facilitated by the same forces that promoted globalization, allows individuals to retain social proximity to their communities despite geographical distance.

Perhaps a social network's most important feature is its internal differentiation in terms of class allowing for what Jeremy Boissevain (1974) calls multiplexity, that is, the presence of miscellaneous links established by persons of a dissimilar status, connected in various forms, who move in several fields of social activity. A plurality of linkages and roles facilitates institutional overlap. The integration of groups of various sizes into the larger society takes place via personal connections. Although kinship and camaraderie are wellsprings of trust and reciprocity, even distant contacts with influential members of their network can work to the advantage of individuals. Mark Granovetter's (1990) discussion of strong and weak social ties speaks to that point. A balanced mixture of strong and weak ties reduces isolation and increases the likelihood that persons and groups will gain access to assets such as entrepreneurial know-how, jobs, and information. The opposite is also true: a network's reduced differentiation in terms of class can translate into low levels of multiplexity and, therefore, its separation from vital resources.

The importance of social networks is exemplified by the functioning of the immigrant enclave. In assembling a remarkable business conglomerate in Miami, Cubans relied on social contacts within and outside their own group. They avoided discrimination from mainstream financial institutions by obtaining loans to capitalize their firms from banks whose owners and personnel were Latin American and, therefore, Spanish speaking. Beyond their strong feeling of membership in the same community, Cubans benefited from their inclusion in a network characterized by high levels of class heterogeneity; that, in turn, enabled its members to establish multiple connections. The opposite is true about Mexicans and African Americans, whose social networks are characterized by low degrees of internal differentiation in terms of class.

Those cases, as well, underscore the importance of social capital and its relationship to quality of resources. Several major writings lead to an understanding of social capital as an incorporeal but vital good accruing to individuals by virtue of their membership in particular communities (Coleman, 1988). Social capital is distinct from human capital in that it does not presuppose formal education or skills acquired through organized instruction. Instead, it originates from shared feelings of social belonging, trust, and reciprocity. The concentration of immigrants of various nationalities in particular niches of the labor market occurs as a result of word-of-mouth recommendations. Those, in turn, are made possible by immigrants' membership in social networks whose members vouch for one another.

A dramatic illustration of the workings of social capital is Kasinitz and Rosenberg's (1994) study of business activity in an empowerment zone located in the notoriously destitute ghetto of Red Hook, Brooklyn. Although many businesses in the zone employ multiethnic work forces, including crews of West Indian security guards, they refuse to hire local blacks. Prejudice plays a role in this curious subdivision, but the causes of exclusion and inclusion are more complex. West Indians are joined to the employment structure through personal contacts and endorsements. Native blacks share the same physical spaces with the businesses in question, but they are socially disconnected and, therefore, bereft of the necessary links to obtain jobs. In that case, the primary reason for ghetto unemployment is not the lack of nearby opportunities but the absence of social networks that provide entry into the labor market.

As important as social capital is the quality of the resources that can be tapped through its deployment. Interpersonal networks are distinguished as much by their ability to generate a sense of cohesion as by the extent to which they can parlay group membership and mutual assistance into worthwhile jobs and knowledge. What distinguishes impoverished from wealthy groups is not their different capacity to deploy social capital—survival of the poor also depends on cooperation—but their varying access to resources of high quality. Those resources are often embedded in physical locations not available to the impoverished. Similarly, what immigrant children learn about becoming American hinges on what they see around them and the types of contacts they are able to establish. The characteristics of living quarters, local businesses, places of leisure and entertainment, and, most decisively, schools have a powerful impact in shaping their prospects (Matute-Bianchi, 1986).

To summarize, social networks are complex formations that channel and filter information, confer a sense of identity, allocate resources, and shape behavior. Individual choices depend not only on the availability of material and intangible assets in the soci-

ety at large, but also on the way in which the members of interpersonal networks interpret information and relate to structures of opportunity. Characteristics such as size and
composition, location and degree of spatial concentration, and the nature of the transactions between their members invest social networks with distinct profiles. Identities
forged within intercept with others imposed by external groups. In the next section, we
compare the experience of several groups swept into the United States by old and new
migrations and provide a framework for the understanding of their options.

THE VARIOUS MEANINGS OF BECOMING AMERICAN

The data for this analysis are drawn from a 1992 survey of 5,263 children of immigrants
and from in-depth interviews conducted with a subsample formed by 120 of those children and their parents. For the original survey, eighth- and ninth-grade students in Dade
County (Miami), Broward County (Fort Lauderdale), and San Diego schools were randomly
selected who met the following definition of second generation: those born in the United
States with at least one foreign-born parent or born abroad but having resided in this
country for at least five years. Questionnaires were administered to these students in
schools selected to include both inner-city and suburban settings and student populations
with varying proportions of whites, minorities, and immigrants. In the Miami sample, two
predominantly Cuban private schools were also included. The sample is evenly divided
between boys and girls; the average age of the youngsters was about fourteen.

The follow-up interviews were conducted with a subset of those originally surveyed.
The national-origin groups were stratified on the basis of sex, nativity (U.S.-born or foreign-born), socioeconomic status based on father's occupation, and family structure
(two-parent families consisting of the biological parents of the child or other equivalent
care providers). In Miami, the Cuban group was also divided between public and private
school students. Names, within the cells thus created, were picked randomly by country
of origin for the largest groups in the original sample —Cubans, Nicaraguans, Haitians,
and West Indians (mostly Jamaicans and Trinidadians) in Dade and Broward Counties;
and Vietnamese, Mexicans, Filipinos, Cambodians and Laotians in San Diego. Our analysis begins with cursory descriptions of five illustrative cases.

AN ETHNOGRAPHIC SAMPLER

Haitian Strivers

Being admitted into the home of Aristide Maillol in Sweetwater, Miami, transports the
visitor into a transfixed space. The location is American but the essence is that of rural
Haiti. Aristide's mother does not speak English. Her eyes drift to the floor when explaining in Creole that her husband is hospitalized and she had to leave her job as a janitor in
a local motel to attend to his needs. There is consternation and reserve in her demeanor.[1]

In the tiny sitting area adjoining the front door, a large bookcase displays the symbols
of family identity in an arrangement suitable for a shrine. Framed by paper flowers at the
top is the painted portrait of Mrs. Maillol and her husband. Crude forms and radiant col-

ors capture the couple's dignity. Below in three separate shelves, several photographs show Aristide's brother and three sisters. The boy smiles confidently in the cap and gown of a high school graduate. "The girls are displayed individually and in clusters, their eye beaming, their hair pulled back, their attires fitting for a celebration. Interspersed with the photographs are the familiar trinkets that adorn most Haitian homes. Striking, however, is the inclusion of several trophies earned by the Maillol children in academic competitions. At seventeen, Aristide's brother had already been recruited by Yale University. Young Aristide, who is fifteen and wants to be a lawyer, speaks eloquently about the future:

> We are immigrants and immigrants must work hard to overcome hardship. You can't let anything stop you. I know there is discrimination, racism . . . but you can't let that bother you. Everyone has problems, things that hold them back, but if you study . . . [and] do what your mother, what your father, tell you, things will get better. . . . God has brought us here and God will lead us farther.

In silence, Mrs. Maillol nods in agreement.

Nicaraguan Sliders

That evening, in little Havana, the Angulo family prepares for dinner in the shabby apartment. Originally from Managua, Nicaragua, Mr. Angulo holds a degree in chemistry and for a time was the manager of a sizable firm in his home country. His wife belongs to a family with connections to the military. They arrived in Miami in 1985 when their son, Ariel, was eight and their daughter, Cristina, was only two years old. Both think of themselves as exiles but are not recognized as such by the authorities. In earnest, Mr. Angulo explains:

> We came with high hopes, escaping the Sandinistas, thinking this was the land of opportunity . . . ready to work and make progress, but we were stopped in our tracks. We haven't been able to legalize our situation. Every so often, we get these notices saying we'll be thrown out of the country; it is nerve-wracking. As a result, we haven't been able to move ahead. Look around; this is the only place we've been able to rent since we came [to Miami]. . . . I work for an hourly wage without benefits, although I perform the duties of a professional for a pharmaceutical company. They know they can abuse my condition because I can't go anywhere; no one will hire me!

Mrs. Angulo, who works as a clerk for a Cuban-owned clinic, worries that Ariel, who is approaching college age, will not be eligible for financial assistance. She does not expect him to go beyond high school, although she and her husband place a premium on education and have typical middle-class aspirations. As it is, Ariel cannot even apply for a legal summer job given his undocumented status. He attends a troubled school, where he mingles primarily with other Central Americans and African Americans. Conflict is rampant and academic standards are low. He complains that other students ridicule Nicaraguans. Ariel feels that his parents are too demanding; they do not understand the pressures at school or give him credit for his effort. Even more distressing is the fact that he cannot speak either English or Spanish fluently. Almost seventeen, he shares with his mother a dim view of the future.

Cuban Gainers

Ariel's experience is in stark contrast with that of fifteen-year-old Fernando Gómez, whose family migrated to Miami in 1980 as part of the Mariel boatlift. Originally from Oriente (Manzanillo), Cuba, Mr. Gómez was employed as a heavy equipment operator and then as a clerk for the same metallurgical firm prior to his migration to the United States. Since his arrival, he has worked as a mechanic for Dade County. His wife, who used to be a teacher in Cuba, now works providing care for the elderly. Although they hold working-class jobs, the couple's tastes evince an upwardly bound thrust. Their home is part of a Cuban-owned residential development that combines pathways bordered by russet tile and luscious vegetation with pale exteriors, wrought-iron gates, and roofs of an Iberian derivation. The family's living room is embellished with new furnishings.

Proudly, Mr. Gómez states that he has never experienced discrimination; he is not the kind of man who would ever feel inferior to anyone. He expects Fernando, an even better student than his older brother, to go far. There is no doubt that he will finish college, perhaps work toward an advanced degree. Although Fernando wants to become a policeman like his brother, Mr. Gómez dismisses that intent as a passing whim; he would like his son to work with computers because "that is where the future of the world is."

Mexican Toilers

More than 3,000 miles away, in south central San Diego, Carlos Mendoza's home stands next to a boarded-up crack house. Prior to the police raid that shut it down, the Mendoza family had covered their own windows with planks to avoid witnessing what went on across the alley. The neighborhood is an assortment of vacant lots, abandoned buildings, and small homes protected by fences and dogs. Fourteen years ago, the family entered the United States illegally in the trunk of a car. Their goal was to earn enough money to buy a house in their hometown in Michoacan, and although they succeeded—and purchased the house in San Diego as well—they laughingly note that somehow they never made it back to Mexico. The family has now achieved legal status under the amnesty program promoted by the 1986 Immigration Reform and Control Act.

For the past ten years, Mr. Mendoza has worked as a busboy in a fancy restaurant that caters to tourists, a position he secured through a Mexican friend. He is a hard-working and modest man who wants his son, Carlos, to study so that he can get a good job: "[I want him] to be better than me, not for my sake but for his sake and that of his own family." Mrs. Mendoza irons clothes at a Chinese-owned laundry, and complains bitterly that her employers are prejudiced toward her and other Mexicans.

Carlos is doing well in school; he was the only boy at Cabrillo Junior High to be elected to the honor society last year. He wants to become an engineer and go back to Mexico. Life in San Diego has been hard on him; the gold chain his parents gave him as a gift was ripped from around his neck by neighborhood toughs; his bicycle remains locked up inside the house, for to ride it would be to lose it to the same local bullies. His younger sister, Amelia, is not doing as well in school and dresses like a *chola* (female gang member), although she insists it is only for the style. Her parents worry but they feel helpless.

Vietnamese Bystanders

Forty blocks to the east, in another working-class neighborhood populated by Mexicans, Vietnamese, and blacks, Mrs. Ly and her daughter Hoa sit in their tiny apartment surrounded by several calendars and clocks, a small South Vietnamese flag, two Buddhist shrines, and four academic achievement plaques. Two of Mrs. Ly's daughters have maintained perfect grades for two years in a row. Hoa, her mother explains, is behind; her grade point average is 3.8 rather than 4.0.

Since their arrival in the United States in 1991, neither Mrs. Ly nor her husband have held jobs; they depend on welfare, although Mrs. Ly is unclear about where exactly the money they receive comes from. Back in Vietnam, she and her husband sold American goods on the black market and supplemented their income by sewing clothes. Leaving their country was filled with trauma; they are still a bit in a daze. In San Diego, the family is isolated; people in the area resent the new arrivals. More than anything else, what keeps the Lys and other Vietnamese families apart is the language barrier: "We can't speak English," says Mrs. Ly, "so the girls don't go out much, they stay home. I raise my children here the same as I raised them in Vietnam: to school and back home."

Hoa's only friend is Vietnamese. Her mother would like her to have more American contacts so that she could learn the language and the culture of their new country. Eventually, she would like her daughter to get an office job or a job in retail sales. Hoa disagrees; she would like to be a doctor.

The cases sketched above provide a glimpse into dissimilar experiences, and the variations are not arbitrary; they are representative of the groups to which the families belong. Nicaraguans expected the treatment afforded to Cubans under what they regarded as similar circumstancs. For many, those expectations were dashed as a result of the poltical complexities surrounding the relationship between the United States and Nicaragua. Bereft of supports in the receiving environment, many of these new immigrants are experiencing a rapid process of downward mobility, although many have middle-class backgrounds. Those of humbler provenance are unable to advance. Especially disturbing is the predicament of children who, confined to immigrant neighborhoods but having spent most of their lives in the United States, cannot speak English or Spanish easily. Unable to regularize their immigrant status and facing acute economic need, many of those youngsters are choosing low-paying jobs over education. With an increasing number of high school dropouts and out-of-wedlock pregnancies, many Nicaraguan youth appear to be recapitulating aspects of the African-American trajectory (Fernández-Kelly, 1994).

Cubans, by contrast, represent an unusual case of immigrant success partly owing to conditions antithetical to those characterizing Nicaraguan migration. The first large cohorts arrived in Miami during the 1960s, prompting the customary response of more established populations: departure to the suburbs. In the beginning, Cubans, too, were perceived as an undesirable minority. Nevertheless, by contrast to other arrivals, they were a highly stratified mass that included professionals as well as an entrepreneurial elite. As a result, many were able to escape the pressures of the labor market through self-employment and business formation (Portes and Rumbaut, 1990). That, a shared and vehement opposition to the Castro regime, and assistance from the U.S. government allowed Cubans to form a cohesive community. They proceeded to reconstitute the social foundations to which they had been accustomed, including the establishment of a private school system for those who could afford it.

In 1980, the Mariel boatlift jolted Miami with new waves of mostly working-class immigrants, many of whom were of Afro-Caribbean descent They, too, were received with a modicum of hostility that included the ambivalent feelings of older Cubans. Nevertheless, continued support on the part of the U.S. government and the preexisting ethnic enclave allowed the newcomers to adjust rapidly. To this day, the tribulations of every *balsero* (rafter) arriving in Miami, in flight from communism, elicit admiration and reignite feelings about a shared historical experience.

Haitians represent a strategic case that contains, alternatively, elements akin to those found in the Cuban experience and others closer to the experience of Nicaraguans. Despite the ordeal of illegal migration and prejudice in the receiving environment, a substantial number of Haitians, like Aristide Maillol and his brother, are doing surprisingly well in the United States. There is evidence that their fledgling success is rooted in deliberate attempts to disassociate themselves from the stigma imposed upon black populations in the United States through an affirmation of their national identity and their religious fervor.

Other Haitians, however, appear to be blending into impoverished black groups living in ghettos such as Miami's Liberty City. A growing number of Haitian youngsters are showing up in alternative schools, detention centers, and penal institutions (Stepick and Dutton-Stepick, 1994). Given their poverty-stricken status and recent arrival, Haitian immigrants were pushed into area where rental properties were abundant and real estate prices were low. As a result Little Haiti, a teetering concentration of Haitian homes and businesses, emerged in close proximity to inner-city neighborhoods, and it is from its dwellers the many Haitians are learning their place in American society.

As in the cases of Vietnamese and Mexicans, when Haitian children speak of discrimination, they are often thinking of the verbal and physical abuses they experience at the hands of native black Americans in their neighborhoods and schools. But by contrast to the first two groups, who attend schools characterized by higher levels of ethnic diversity, Haitians do not have alternative referents in their familiar environments. In those circumstances, the choices are clearly bifurcated: either conscious attempts at self-distinction or yielding to the norm through conformity. Insular and destitute environments can rapidly translate conformity into socioeconomic stagnation or decline. Mexicans represent the longest unbroken migration of major proportions to the United States. Partly as a result of their widespread undocumented status and partly because of geographical proximity, many Mexicans do not see moving to the United States as a long-term decision; instead, they see themselves as sojourners, guided by an economic motive, whose real homes are south of the border. Expectations about the duration if their stay in areas of destination diminish Mexicans' involvement in entrepreneurship and business formation (Roberts, 1995). That attitude, as well, has an impact upon children's prospects because, as Portes (1993:27) puts it: "It is difficult to reach for the future when you are constantly confronting your past." With little differentiation in terms of social class, Mexicans do not hold enough power to resist the embattled conditions in the neighborhoods where they live.

FIGURE 10.1

	Gainers	Bystanders	Strivers	Toilers	Sliders	Survivors
Internal Differentiation by Class	+++	+ -	+ -	-	+ -	-
Type of Reception	+++	++	-	-	-	- - -
Quality of Resources	+++	+ -	-	-	-	- -
Degree of Spacial Concentration	++	+ -	++	++	+ -	+++
Length of Time in Area of Destination	+	- -	- -	++	- -	+++
	1960>	1975>	1980>	1930>	1980>	1630>

The Vietnamese experience is marked by paradox. An early wave of exiles in the 1970s—many of whose members started small businesses in the United States—was followed by larger groups of peasants and unskilled workers who confronted harsher-than-usual journeys. In areas of destination they faced hostility, but their rapid legalization entitled them to public assistance and other benefits—up to 50 percent of Vietnamese in California are on welfare (Kitano and Daniels, 1988). Lack of English fluency and the absence of a larger and cohesive community to depend on have translated into acute degrees of isolation. However, in this case isolation added to a widespread faith in education, discipline, and family unity are producing children who are high achievers. The Vietnamese continue to be in, but not of, the United States.

Figure 10.1 summarizes the nonrandom character of the conditions experienced by the immigrant groups studied. Each group has been assigned a label that captures a distinctive experience (Cubans as Gainers; Vietnamese as Bystanders; Haitians as Strivers; Mexicans as Toilers; and Nicaraguans as Sliders). To complete the comparison, we have added a sixth group (native blacks as Survivors). The purpose of the classification is not to create yet another hypology of migration, but to decouple the characteristics of segmented dissimilation from national and ethnic referents, thus exposing the outcomes of migration as a function of the factors listed in the column on the left: Internal Differentiation by Class; Type of Reception; Quality of Resources; Degree of Spatial Concentration; and Length of Time in Area of Destination. The first four dimensions designate decisive toponomical factors underpinning the aftermath of various kinds of migration.

Although Figure 10.1 condenses the generalized experiences of the various groups, it does not capture their internal diversity, especially in terms of social class. Its sole purpose is to serve as a heuristic device for understanding the patterns of adaptation under discussion. The positions occupied by the types in the figure should be understood as approximate points along a continuum. Thus, Type of Reception ranges from highly positive — as indicated by three plus signs — to extremely hostile — as indicated by three minus signs.

Gainers, characterized by high levels of class differentiation, experienced a relatively hospitable reception, including prompt legalization, government support, and low levels of discrimination. For those reasons, they were able to tap resources of high quality, such as effective schools and adequate, affordable housing. Their spatial concentration worked advantageously, facilitating the use of social capital to gain access to information and other desirable assets. Their experience of socioeconomic mobility markedly diverges from that of Survivors, for whom spatial concentration in antagonistic environments translated into diminished connections to the larger society, resources of low quality, and diminished ability to parlay social capital into economic advantage. While Gainers thrive, Survivors endure. The other groups occupy intermediary positions within those two extremes.

The length of time in areas of destination bears a direct relationship to the consolidation of positive or negative behavioral outcomes. Over extended periods of time, low levels of class heterogeneity added to hostile modes of reception, resources of low quality, and high degrees of spatial concentration inevitably lead to a hardening of negative traits among the children and the grandchildren of internal and international migrants. In the case of African Americans, the time line extends beyond the period covered by The Great Black Migration from the rural South (1910–1970) to include a longer stretch which is part of that group's historical memory.

SURVEY FINDINGS

Survey materials contribute additional insights to the picture made vividly real by the testimonies of immigrant children and their families. Table 10.1 condenses information about school performance, parental human capital, and children's aspirations. Some differences and similarities are worth noting. Not surprisingly, Cuban children in private schools display high grade point averages and the highest standardized test scores, followed by the Vietnamese whose grades are better but whose scores lag due to lower English proficiency. Cuban students in private schools dramatically exceed the performance of those in public institutions, illustrating the critical effect of social class even within that highly intergrated community. Although they are experiencing downward mobility, the scores of Nicaraguan children, many of whom have middle-class backgrounds, are relatively high. Haitians and Mexicans display comparatively low scores, as generally found in predominantly working-class populations.

Even with that in mind, the contrast between Haitians and Mexicans is noteworthy. On the aggregate, the Haitian indicators are consistent with the divided experience sketched earlier, and those of Mexicans confirm their characterization as a highly homogeneous and vulnerable group. Figures on parents' educational achievement, socioeconomic status, and occupational aspirations are compatible with those profiles. And yet, regardless of national origin and social class, most immigrant children voice high educational aspirations, with Haitians second only to Cubans in private schools in their ambition to go beyond college. Again, it comes as no surprise that Mexicans constitute the only group a large proportion of whose members expect never to achieve a college education.

Table 10.2 provides information about the friendship networks of the various populations. Regardless of national origin, most children associate with members of their own group, and a large number of their friends are foreign-born. Within that context, nevertheless, Cubans have the highest degree of contact with members of their own group and

TABLE 10.1 School Performance, Parental Human Capital, and Children's Aspirations[a]

	School Performance				Parental Human Capital				Child's Aspirations			
	GPA[b]	Std Math Test[c]	Std Reading Test[c]	English Index Score[d]	Percent Father College Grad	Percent Mother College Grad	Father Occup SEI[e]	Mother Occup SEI[e]	Occupational Aspirations[f]	Less than College (%)	College (%)	Graduate School (%)
Cuban—private school (N=183)	2.6	80	69	15.3	55	42	50.4	47.3	65.4	3	32	67
Cuban—public school (N=1,044)	2.2	56	45	15.4	24	18	37.5	36.9	62.9	18	37	46
Nicaraguan (N=344)	2.3	55	38	14.8	45	31	39.2	30.5	62.7	21	34	45
Haitian (N=178)	2.3	45	30	15.2	16	15	29.1	29.4	65.6	16	34	50
Mexican (N=757)	2.2	32	27	13.9	9	5	26.3	24.9	58.3	39	32	29
Vietnamese (N=371)	3.0	60	38	13.4	24	14	34.2	32.4	61.8	23	40	37

[a] All column differences between national origin groups significant at the .001 level.
[b] Grade Point Average as reported by school district.
[c] Stanford Achievement Test 8th edition, percentile score.
[d] Self-rated proficiency in reading, writing, speaking and understanding English.
[e] Duncan socioeconomic index score, based respectively on father's/mother's current occupation.
[f] Treiman occupational prestige index score for child's desired occupation.

TABLE 10.2 Friendship Networks[a]

| | Number of Close Friends from Abroad | | | Percentage with Friends Who Are[b] | | | | |
	None (%)	Some (%)	Many or Most(%)	Cuban (%)	Nicaraguan (%)	Haitian (%)	Mexican (%)	Vietnamese (%)
Cuban—private school (N=183)	1.1	5.5	93.4	**98.9**	7.3	0	na	na
Cuban—public school (N=1,044)	2.5	23.2	74.2	**93.8**	29.0	3.3	na	na
Nicaraguan (N=344)	5.1	18.8	76.2	78.1	**79.4**	3.9	na	na
Haitian (N=178)	9.8	43.9	46.2	26.1	4.2	**87.3**	na	na
Mexican (N=757)	6.6	44.6	48.8	na	na	na	**82.9**	4.5
Vietnamese (N=371)	6.5	38.6	54.9	na	na	na	17.2	**83.1**

[a] All column differences between national-origin groups are significant at the .001 level.
[b] Percentage of those who report having close friends abroad (i.e., excludes those with none). Numbers in bold represent the right-to-left axis of conationals. Numbers in *italics* represent the asymmetrtical pairs of nationalities on left-to-right axes.

Divided Fates

TABLE 10.3 Perceptions of Discrimination[a]

	Percent who Experience Discrimination	Percent of Those Discriminated Against Who Attribute It to:			Percent Residing in U.S. 5–9 Years	Percent Born in U.S.
		Whites	Blacks	Cubans		
Cuban—private school (N=183)	31.7	46.4	28.6	1.8	3.3	91.3
Cuban—public school (N=1,044)	39.1	31.6	28.9	3.7	10.1	67.6
Nicaraguan (N=344)	50.6	27.8	22.2	25.0	57.8	7.6
Haitian (N=178)	62.4	35.8	29.4	9.2	28.7	43.3
Mexican (N=757)	64.3	42.2	34.4	na	28.4	60.2
Vietnamese (N=371)	66.3	37.9	40.2	na	42.3	15.6

[a]All column differences between national origin groups are significant at the .001 level.

the lowest proportion of friendships with outsiders. Oddly, Nicaraguans report a higher degree of relations with Cubans than Cubans voice with respect to Nicaraguans. Similar albeit smaller disparities are found in the contrasting testimonies of Haitians with respect to Cubans and of Mexicans with respect to the Vietnamese. Those discrepancies are explained by two tendencies: that of Cubans and Vietnamese to see themselves as enclosed communities and that of Haitians, Mexicans, and Nicaraguans to be more permeable to other groups in their environments. In addition, the relationship among Nicaraguans, Haitians, and Cubans is marked by status differences; often, the latter are reluctant to admit they know Nicaraguans and Haitians. That tendency is mirrored by Nicaraguans' generalized feelings that Cubans discriminate against them. In other words, Cubans and Vietnamese display the least degree of porousness of the groups studied.

Most revealing is the information contained in Table 10.3 on perceptions of discrimination and self-identification. Cuban youth report the least discrimination, a fact that is understandable; it is hard for anyone to feel rebuffed when, as Table 10.2 indicates, the overwhelming majority of his contacts are with members of his own group. Nevertheless, Cuban children in public schools experience higher levels of discrimination from both blacks and whites than do those in private schools. In contrast to private institutions, public schools expose children to a plurality of ethnic and national groups and are, therefore, less able to shield them from friction. With the exception of the Vietnamese, all other groups report higher levels of discrimination from whites than from blacks.

Only Nicaraguans see Cubans as a significant source of discrimination. That may be related to a panethnic effect in Miami where the Hispanic community is internally diversified in terms of national origin, with the Cubans occupying a preeminent position and, therefore, becoming easily identifiable as a source of discrimination, particularly toward other Hispanics. On the other hand, the case of Mexicans in San Diego invites reflection because, despite the existence of a large coethnic community, membership in it does not shield Mexicans from discrimination. That, too, may be an effect of localized factors—a continued climate of hostility against Mexican immigration in California has been recently exacerbated by a severe economic downturn following a fiscal crisis of the state government and deep cuts in military spending. Mexicans have become convenient scapegoats for heightened rates of joblessness. Finally, the recently arrived Vietnamese report the most discrimination, a reflection of the negative public reception that greeted their arrival. In addition, they tend to live in working-class neighborhoods populated by black Americans but without the benefit of a "Little Saigon" that might insulate them from conflict.

The data in Table 10.4 summarize selected characteristics of the schools attended by immigrant children in our sample. The patterns revealed are consistent with the descriptions offered earlier. Taken as a whole, Cuban families show a higher degree of class heterogeneity—as reflected in the proportions of children receiving free or subsidized lunch, a proxy measure for poverty. Mexican children are located in schools that mirror their positions at the lower end of the class hierarchy. Most Haitian children are to be found in predominantly black, inner-city schools given the proximity of Haitian residential settlement in contiguity to ghettos. Table 10.4 underscores the extent to which schools function as segregative forces sorting out children in terms of social class and location.

Ethnic Idenities

Ethnographic chronicles underscore the vital role of collective identities in the process of assimilation. Even under auspicious conditions, migration is an experience that pushes individuals and groups to acquire new knowledge as they negotiate survival and adjustment. Immigrants learn how they fit in the larger society through the contacts they establish in familiar environments. Whether youngsters sink or soar frequently depends on how they see themselves, their families, and their communities. For that reason, the immigrant life is preeminently an examined life. Iterative processes of symbolic and factual association and detachment shape immigrants' self-definitions. Schools play a major role in that respect (Matute-Bianchi, 1986).

At school, children mingle with groups differentiated by their own self-perceptions and the perceptions of external observers. Especially when they equate success with localized power attained through conflict and physical force—as in the case of youth gangs—those groups can exert a strong downward pull upon immigrant children. The paths that lead youngsters toward specific clusters is complex. However, one of the most effective antidotes against downward mobility is a sense of membership in a group with an undamaged collective identity. The Méndez children illustrate that proposition.

But for the fact that they are illegal aliens from Nicaragua, sixteen-year-old Omar Méndez and his younger sister Fátima could not be closer to the American Dream. They have grown up in Miami since they were five and three years old, respectively. They are superb students full of spirit and ambition. They attend a school where discipline is strict and where teachers are able to communicate with parents in Spanish. Most decisively,

TABLE 10.4 Socioeconomic Status of National Origin Groups[a]

	Low SEI[b] (%)	Middle SEI (%)	High SEI (%)	% Attend Majority Black School[c]	% Attend Majority Latin School	% Attend Majority White School	% Attend Central City School[d]	% Attend >2/3 Poor School[e]	% Attend 1/3–2/3 Poor School	% Attend <1/3 Poor School
Cuban—private school (N=183)	7.7	49.2	43.1	0	100	0	0	0	0	100
Cuban—public school (N=1,044)	25.8	60.1	14.1	2.1	84.2	3.9	26.1	31.1	28.8	40.0
Nicaraguan (N=344)	23.8	65.8	10.4	7.3	79.4	1.5	27.6	39.4	16.3	44.3
Haitian (N=178)	31.0	61.9	7.1	66.9	3.4	2.8	83.7	66.9	12.9	20.2
Mexican (N=757)	66.9	30.4	2.7	.4	17.7	.4	57.7	51.3	38.0	10.7
Vietnamese (N=371)	45.3	46.9	7.7	.3	.8	0	50.3	39.2	18.8	41.9

[a] All column differences between national origin groups significant at the .001 level.

[b] Based on score on composite index using father's and mother's occupations, education, and home ownership. Corresponds to working class (e.g., busboys, janitors, laborers), middle class (small business owners, teachers), and upper middle class (lawyers, architects, executives).

[c] Majority in these three columns means greater than 60% of students who attend the school. Note that we cannot distinguish within the Latin group between immigrants and U.S.-born students.

[d] Geographically located within the central city area of Miami and San Diego.

[e] "Poor" here is measured by the proxy variable of the percentage of the student body eligible for federally funded free or subsidized lunch.

they see themselves as immigrants, and that identity protects them from negative stereotypes and incorporation into more popular but less motivated groups in school. In Fátima's words: "We're immigrants! We can't afford to just sit around and blow it like others who've been in this country longer and take everything for granted." To maintain her independence, she withdraws from her peers and endures being called a "nerd." She does not mind because her center of gravitation lies within her family.

Mariá Ceballos, a Cuban mother, agrees with Fátima. She despairs about her daughter's interest in material trinkets and her low levels of academic motivation. "At Melanie's age," she states, "I was very determined; maybe because I was born in a different country. I wanted to prove that I was as good as real Americans. My daughter was born here and [therefore] she doesn't have the same push."

Among vulnerable groups, the ability to shift ethnic identity often provides a defense from stigma and an incentive to defy leveling pressures. How they define themselves depends on the context. Miguel Hernández, an illegal Mexican alien in San Diego since 1980, explains that he and his wife define themselves "[depending on] who we are talking to. If we are talking to American people and they don't know the difference, we say 'Latinos;' that's easier for them and we avoid hassles." Miguel consciously avoids being labeled a Chicano because "it's a slang word for lower-class types who don't know who they are. They don't want to be Mexicans, but they don't want to just be Americans; they don't even speak English but they don't know Spanish either [and they] fight for and about everything."

In answering questions about who they are, immigrants resort to antinomies, defining other groups in terms opposed to the ones they use to define themselves. Others are generally symbolized by the casualties of earlier migrations, especially inner-city blacks. Typically, immigrants see blacks as the victims of their own individual and collective liabilities. Martin López, a Mexican father, explains:

> Blacks in this country . . . don't want to work; [they] feel very American. They know government has to support every child they breed. [As immigrants] we can't afford to slacken the pace; we have to work hard.

Given phenotypical commonalities with black Americans and disadvantages derived from the locations where they live, the issue of identity is paramount among Haitians. Madeleine Serphy, an ambitious girl at fifteen, has strong feelings about African Americans:

> It may be true that whites discriminate, but I have no complaints [about them] because I don't know many [whites]. . . . But blacks, they're trouble; they make fun of the way we [Haitians] speak. . . . They call us stupid and backwards and try to beat us up. I was always scared, so I [tried] to do well in school and that's how I ended [in a magnet school]. There, I don't stand out as much and I can feel good about being Haitian. . . . Haitian is what I am; I don't think about color.

For working-class Cubans, the problem of identity is equally complex, but for different reasons. As members of a successful group, many resent being melded into the broader classification of Hispanic. Such is the case with Doris Delsol, an assertive divorcee who lives on welfare because of a disabling affliction. Although her daughter, Elizabeth, experienced some early setbacks in grade school, Mrs. Delsol doggedly sought paths to uplift her. "We Cubans are not used to failure," she explained. She does not like being called Hispanic because:

> We all speak [Spanish] but there are differences. [Cubans] always had self-respect, a sense of cleanliness and duty towards children, a work ethic. Miami used to be a clean city until the Nicaraguans came and covered everything with graffiti.

About American blacks, Mrs. Delsol thinks they are adversarial to all kinds of people, disruptive, prone to ruin their homes, and lazy. In her view, both Nicaraguans and blacks evince attitudes opposite to those of Cubans.

Ironically, many Nicaraguans think of themselves as Hispanics precisely because they hold perceptions similar to those voiced by Mrs. Delsol. They experience a strong dissociational push away from their own national group. Sixteen-year old Elsie Rivas avoids discrimination by shifting between a Hispanic and a Nicaraguan self-definition at school and at the supermarket where she works. She doesn't like the way Nicaraguans speak:

> They are vulgar, ignorant. . . . When I am with my Cuban friends I can speak to them normally, but some Nicaraguans make me feel ashamed and I am tempted to deny my nationality; they make all of us look bad because of the way they express themselves, with all the bad words and the cussing.

As the majority of immigrant children, Elsie's younger sister, Alicia, does not care for those distinctions. She feels "Nicaraguan-American because my parents came from Nicaragua and I like the food, but I am really American, more American than those born in this country; here is where I grew up and here is where I am going to stay."

The perceptions of immigrants and their children about themselves and other groups are not always accurate. However, what matters is that, as social constructions, those perceptions are an integral part of a process of segmented assimilation that will eventually yield what Bellah (1985) calls "communities of memory." In their journey, the immigrant children of today are already forging tomorrow's ethnic identities. Contact, friction negotiation and their eventual incorporation into distinct sectors of the larger society will depend, in the final analysis, upon the insertion of immigrant children into various niches of the restructured economy. Collective self-definitions will improve or worsen depending upon the structure of opportunity.

CONCLUSIONS

Our purpose in this study has been to unfold the various meanings of assimilation for immigrants arriving into locations distinguished by an assortment of physical, social, and economic characteristics. We have argued that a limited number of toponomical—that is, socially and physically situated—features determines the outcomes of migration. Our analysis was based on survey and ethnographic data about a small number of groups. However, we have noted that each group represents an experience associated not so much with cultural or national features, but with the attributes of its reception in areas of destination, the character of resources available to it, its degree of internal differentiation in terms of class, its degree of spatial concentration, and the length of time the group's coethnics have resided in the United States.

There is no mystery to tales of immigrant success or failure. Economic globalization has fostered major transformations, of transnational markets unlikely to disappear through purely legislative initiatives. The alternative for policy cannot be solely the regulation of immigrant streams to the exclusion of a more important aspect: the implementation of measures that facilitate the adjustment of new arrivals and increases their connection to the institutions of the larger society. The experience of Gainers show that a welcoming reception in areas of destination—including government initiatives to facilitate immigrant adoption—can have long-term benefits. The opposite is also true. Over extended periods of time, hostile receptions have had predictable results: isolation, social dismemberment, and the concentration of behavioral pathologies. For policymakers the lesson is clear—the nightmare of an urban underclass need not be repeated among the protagonists of the new migration if we give attention to the lessons of the past.

Once established, immigrant networks acquire a degree of relative autonomy from market forces reducing the costs and risks of migration and promoting the flow of information. When they are internally stratified in terms of class, the spatial concentration of immigrants can yield advantages for the group to which they belong and for the larger society. This, too, has importance for immigration policy. In the 1960s, when the Cuban exile first began, millions of dollars were spent needlessly to scatter the banished around the United States in the belief that this best contributed to their social incorporation. Instead, Cubans gravitated back to Miami where the strength of numbers, connections and entrepreneurial know-how quickly translated into economic prosperity. Atomization and geographical dispersion could have had very different results.

Finally, we have begun a discussion of the ways in which immigrants shape identities through repeated interaction in empirical and symbolic fields with other ethnic groups. Our point has been to underscore the salience of collective self-definition in the process of segmented assimilation. There is an interactive relationship between the opportunity structure and the way individuals and groups perceive themselves and others. The self-image of the immigrant is, ironically, a hopeful image often bolstered by negative definitions of other groups that have experienced arrested mobility. Whether those hopeful images survive will depend on whether immigrant children succeed or fail in the new economy.

Study Questions

1. What is the "Oppurtunity Structure" and how does it relate to children's self-image?

2. Does the essay suggest that opportunity is the same within ethnic groups?

3. Why do Mexican newcomers appear more homogeneous than Haitian newcomers?

Note

1. The names in these narratives are pseudonyms.

REFERENCES

Abramson, H. 1980 "Assimilation and Pluralism." In *Harvard Encyclopedia of American Ethnic Groups.* Ed. S. Thernstrom. Cambridge, MA: Harvard University Press.

Baker, R. and W. Dodd, eds. 1926 *Public Papers of Woodrow Wilson.* New York: Harper.

Bellah, R. N. et al. 1985 *Habits of the Heart: Individualism and Commitment in American Life.* Berkeley: University of California Press.

Blauner, R. 1972 *Racial Oppression in America.* New York: Harper & Row.

Boissevain, J. 1979 "Network Analysis: A Reappraisal," *Current Anthropology,* 20:392–394.

Bonacich, E. 1980 "Class Approaches to Ethnicity and Race," *Insurgent Sociologist,* 10.

Bourne, R. 1916 *The Radical Will: Selected Writings.* New York: Urizen Books.

Coleman, J. 1988 "Social Capital in the Creation of Human Capital." *American Journal of Sociology (Supplement),* S95–121.

Fernández-Kelly, M.P. 1994 "Towanda's Triumph: Social and Cultural Capital in the Transition to Adulthood in the Urban Ghetto," *International Journal of Urban and Regional Research,* 18(1):89–111.

———.1993 "Labor Force Recomposition and Industrial Restructuring in Electronics: Implications for Free Trade," *Hofstra Labor Law Journal,* 10(2):623–717. Spring.

———. 1990 "International Development and Industrial Restructuring: The Case of Garment and Electronics in Southern California." In *Instability and Change in the World Economy.* New York: Monthly Review Press.

Fernández-Kelly, M. P. and A. M. Garcia 1990 "Power Surrendered, Power Restored: The Politics of Work and Family among Hispanic Garment Workers in California and Florida," In *Women, Change and Politics* Ed. I. Tilly and P. Guerin. New York: Russell Sage Foundation.

Frazier, E. F. 1957 *Race and Culture Contacts in the Modern World.* New York: Knopf.

Gordon, M. 1964 *Assimilation in American Life: The Role of Race, Religion, and National Origins.* New York: Oxford University Press.

Ganovetter, M. 1990 "The Old and New Economic Sociology: A History and an Agenda." In *Beyond the Marketplace.* Ed. R. Friedland and A.F. Robertson. Hawthorne, NY: Aldine de Gruyter.

———.1973 "The Strength of Weak Ties," *American Journal Sociology,* 78:1360–1380.

Grosfogel, R. 1993 "World Cities in the Caribbean City System: Miami and San Juan." Paper presented at the conference World Cities in the World System, Blacksburg Virginia. April.

Harrison, B. and B. Bluestone 1988 *The Great U-Turn: Corporate Restructuring and the Polarizing of America.* New York: Basic Books.

Herzog, L. 1991 "Cross-National Urban Structure in the Era of Global Cities: The U.S.-Mexico Transfrontier Metropolis," *Urban Studies,* 28:519–533.

Kallen, H. 1924 *Culture and Democracy in the United States.* New York: Boni and Liveright.

Kasinitz, P. and J. Rosenberg 1994 "Missing the Connection: Social Isolation and Employment on the Brooklyn Waterfront." Working Paper, Michael Harrington Center for Democratic Values and Social Change. Queens College of the City University of New York.

Kitano, H. and R. Daniels 1988 *Asian Americans: Emerging Minorities.* Englewood Cliffs, NJ: Prentice Hall.

Kivisto, P. 1990 "The Transplanted Then and Now: The Reorientation of Immigration Studies from the Chicago School to the New Social History," *Ethnic and Racial Studies,* 13:455–181.

Lemann, N. 1991 *The Promised Land: The Great Black Migration and How It Changed America.* New York: Vintage Books.

Lieberson, S. 1980 *A Piece of the Pie: Blacks and White Immigrants since 1880.* Berkeley: University of California Press.

Matute-Bianchi, M. G. 1986 "Ethnic Identities and Patterns of School Success and Failure among Mexican-Descent and Japanese-American Students in a California High School," *American Journal of Education*, 95:233–255.

Park, R. 1950 *Race and Culture*. Glencoe, Il; The Free Press.

Park, R. and E. Burgess 1924 *Introduction to the Science of Society*. University of Chicago Press.

Persons, S. 1987 *Ethnic Studies at Chicago 1905-45*. Urbana: University of Illinois Press.

Portes, A. 1995 "Children of Immigrants: Segmented Assimilation and its Determinants." In *The Economic Sociology of Immigration: Essays on Networks, Ethnicity, and Entrepreneurship*. New York: Russell Sage Foundation.

———. 1993 "The Longest Migration," *The New Republic*, 26:38–12. April.

Portes, A. and R. Bach 1986 *Latin Journey: Cuban and Mexican Immigrants in the United States*. Berkeley: University of California Press.

Portes, A. and Rubén Rumbaut 1990 *Immigrant America: A Portrait*. Berkeley: University of California Press.

Portes, A. and M. Zhou 1993 "The New Second Generation: Segmented Assimilation and Its Variants," *Annals of the American Academy of Political and Social Science*, 530:74–96.

Roberts, B. 1995 "The Effect of Socially Expected Durations on Mexican Migration." In *The Economic Sociology of Immigration: Essays on Networks, Ethnicity, and Entrepreneurship*. New York: Russell Sage Foundation.

Sanjek, R. 1974 "What Is Network Analysis and What Is It Good For?" *Reviews in Anthropology*, 1:588–597.

Sassen, S. 1995 "Immigration and Local Labor Markets." In *The Economic Sociology of Immigration: Essays on Networks, Ethnicity, and Entrepreneurship*. New York: Russell Sage Foundation.

———. 1992 *The Global City: New York, London, Tokyo*. Princeton, NJ: Princeton University Press

———. 1988 *The mobility of Capital and Labor*. Cambridge: Cambridge University Press.

Sassen, S. and A. Portes 1993 "Miami: A New Global City," *Contemporary Sociology*, 22:471–177.

Simons, S. 1901 "Social Assimilation," *American Journal of Sociology*, 6:790–822; 7:53–79, 234–248, 386–404, 539–556.

Stepick, A. and C. Dutton-Stepick 1994 "Preliminary Haitian Needs Assessment." Report to the City of Miami, June.

Chapter 11

Aída Hurtado,
Patricia Gurin, and
Timothy Peng

Social Identities—A Framework for Studying the Adaptations of Immigrants and Ethnics
The Adaptations of Mexicans in the United States

Immigration studies have generally been guided by historical and structural models and methodologies (see Bean and Tlenda 1987; Pedraza 1990; and Portes and Rumbaut 1990, for overviews of immigration research with special emphasis on immigration to the United States). Historical and structural approaches have also predominated in studies of the persistence of ethnicity as a critical aspect of social life and politics worldwide (see Connor 1992; Olzak 1983; Smith 1993; and Tiryakian and Rogowski 1985, for overviews of this literature). A limitation of these treatments of immigration and ethnicity (and of the relationship between them) is the tendency to ignore processes by which the effects of history and social structure occur at the individual level.[1] Many scholars call for social psychological analyses that show how history and macro-social features of the environment produce individual modes of adaptation to immigration, including the construction and reconstruction of ethnicity as one of the modes. A social psychological analysis would tie macro-social characteristics to micro-social characteristics of immediate social contexts in which individuals, families, and groups live. Particular economic conditions, state policies and procedures, size and dispersal/concentration of groups across states and regions affect likely modes of adaptation because they heighten or lessen social categorization and salience of group boundaries, and because they increase or decrease opportunities for intragroup and intergroup contact, communication, competition, cooperation, and social comparison.

This paper uses Tajfel's Social Identity Theory (Tajfel 1978, 1981; Tajfel and Turner 1979) as a framework for a social psychological analysis of a limited set of cultural adaptations of persons of Mexican origin living in the United States. Tajfel's conceptualization of social identity, which emphasizes the causal role of social categorization and social comparison, is the most widely used framework in psychology for explaining identity formation, persistence, and change. It should therefore be particularly helpful in understanding how immigrants' social identities change as a result of living in a new country. Tajfel's theory also allows for the study of ethnics — the descendants of former immigrants — because of the multiple group memberships that combine former affiliations with new ones. As a case in point, we examine Mexicans in the United States because they illustrate how social identities can change over time and affect their cultural adaptations.

The process that Mexicans in the United States undergo is similar to that of other immigrant groups. Their social identities are socially constructed from the knowledge individual members have about their group's collective history and from their experiences in various social structures in the United States. Historical and structural influences operate through a variety of social processes, but following Tajfel, we emphasize their effects on social categorization, social comparison, and what is made problematic psychologically as individuals form social identities. These psychological processes affect both the content and structure of social identities. We further argue that social identities then serve as mediators of cultural adaptations.

To capture how social identities may change as a result of the group's social psychological experiences, we examine the social identities for two groups of Mexicans in the United States: first-generation immigrants and longer-term residents who by virtue of birth are U.S. citizens. We argue that first generation Mexican immigrants are primarily affiliated with the social groups from their country of origin and have yet to transfer their identification to groups in the United States. Second and later generations show in their social identities affiliations based on their ethnic group's history as well as their current contact with groups in the United States. The distinction between immigrant generations is unusually important for Mexicans in the United States.

First, the U.S. history of the later generations of Mexican descendants spans an especially long time period. Some Mexicans in the United States come from families who lived in what was Mexico and became U.S. territory following the U.S. Mexican War of 1848. Others come from families who immigrated later in the nineteenth century and in the relatively continuous flows of immigration that have occurred since then, even when flows from other countries were reduced to a trickle or entirely cut between 1924 and 1965 (Schaefer 1984; Portes and Rumbaut 1990). Thus, the long collective history of U.S. citizens of Mexican descent has great meaning in their cultural, political, and psychological adaptations.

Second, Mexico's proximity further exaggerates the distinction between first- and later-generation Mexican descendants. Geographical proximity promotes the case with which first-generation immigrants from Mexico can renew the psychological meaning of Mexico through visits, returning to Mexico to live, reentering the United States but often with the aspiration of a permanent return to Mexico, and maintaining bonds with family members residing in Mexico. This homeward orientation helps explain why Mexican immigrants' naturalization rate is the lowest among the immigrant groups that now form the core of contemporary immigration to the United States (Portes and Rumbaut 1990). Members of the later generations also have ties with Mexico, but fewer than those that typify first-generation immigrants.

Thus, for historical and ecological reasons, first- and later-generations of Mexican descendants live in two different social contexts, different enough that the content and structure of their social identities differ markedly. We test this prediction through exploratory and confirmatory factor analyses. We further expect that their uniquely patterned identities will mediate the cultural adaptations of both groups. We test this prediction by within-group multivariate regressions in which social identities are used as predictors, along with demographic and structural controls, to explain cultural adaptations.

Tajfel's Identity Theory

Social Psychological Processes

A full examination of identity requires distinguishing categorical and group aspects of identity from personal and dispositional aspects. We think of ourselves as part of social categories and groups. We also think of ourselves as having psychological traits and dispositions that give us personal uniqueness. This paper is concerned with social identities—the aspects of an individual's self-concept that derive from one's knowledge of being part of categories and groups, together with the value and emotional significance attached to those memberships (Tajfel 1981).

Tajfel argues that the formation of social identities is the consequence of three social psychological processes. The first is *social categorization*. Nationality, language, race or ethnicity, skin color, or any other social or physical characteristics that are meaningful in particular social contexts can be the basis for social categorization and thus the basis for the creation of social identities. In a series of field studies in many societies and cultures, Tajfel and his colleagues provide evidence of the ubiquitousness of social categorization. In a series of experimental laboratory studies they have also demonstrated that even when individuals are told that they have been categorized on a random basis, the cognitive processes that should result from social categorization generally take place. Because categorization has effects even in such "minimal group conditions" and because categorization occurs in all human societies, it is viewed as the natural and universal basis of identity formation. Psychologists who work within the Tajfel tradition treat social categorization and identity formation almost as "hard wired" aspects of the mental make-up of humankind. Nonetheless, there is also evidence of wide sociocultural variation that defines what characteristics are used to categorize people into groups.

The second process that underlies the construction of social identities is *social comparison*. Psychologically, Tajfel argues that social comparison inevitably follows social categorization. Once individuals are categorized, they naturally tend to compare their group(s) with others. Societal evaluation is also critical in social comparison. According to Tajfel, the characteristics of one's group(s) as a whole (such as a group's status, its richness or poverty, or its ability to reach its aims) achieve significance in relation to perceived differences from other groups and the value connotation of these differences (Tajfel 1978).

The third process involves *psychological work*, both cognitive and emotional work, that is prompted by what Tajfel assumes is a universal motive — to achieve a positive sense of distinctiveness. This motive can be fulfilled through feeling good about the groups into which individuals have been categorized and is activated by the discomfort that follows being categorized into devalued groups. The groups and categories that are most problematic for a sense of positive distinctiveness — ones that are disparaged, memberships that have to be negotiated frequently because they are visible to others, ones that have become politicized by social movements, etc. — are the most likely to become social identities for individuals. Moreover, it is these identities that become especially powerful psychologically. They are easily accessible; individuals think a lot about them; they are apt to be salient across situations; they are likely to function as schemas, frameworks, or social scripts. Unproblematic group memberships — ones that are socially valued or accord privilege, those that are not obvious to others — may not even become social identities. This helps explain the rarity of a white identity or a Yankee identity or an identity as a man. Or when individuals do construct social identities around these kinds of group memberships, the identities are not likely to be salient, easily accessible, or psychologically important across situations. Such identities usually depend on particular social circumstances to be made salient and to be given psychological meaning. Tajfel's theory, therefore, leads the analyst to pay most attention to social categorizations and group memberships that are likely to require the most negotiation and psychological work to gain a positive sense of distinctiveness.

A criticism of the Tajfel framework, however, is that it pays scant attention to historical and structural conditions that might suggest what these social characteristics and group memberships are likely to be. The main structural variable in Tajfel's theory of identity formation is blocked exit. There are many other structural conditions and many historical circumstances that need to be considered, however, in applying the Tajfel framework to identity expressions among immigrants and ethnic communities.

HISTORICAL AND STRUCTURAL INFLUENCES

Historical and structural differences between first and later generations of Mexican descendants should affect the complexity and types of social categorizations and social comparisons they are subjected to, and thus the structure and content of their social identities. We use the Tajfel framework and draw upon marked features of the social contexts of first and later generations to make general predictions and to interpret our results.

Our first prediction is that the *structure of social identities* will be more differentiated among later generations than among first-generation immigrants. This prediction is based on social structural and historical conditions that should affect the number of social categorizations and comparisons the two groups are likely to encounter.

Later generations, because of their greater competence in English, greater geographic dispersal, and greater occupational differentiation are located in more variable and complicated social structures in the United States than are first-generation immigrants. These structural characteristics increase the probability of having contact with multiple groups (ethnic groups, occupational groups, political groups) in U.S. society. These contacts are likely to result in numerous social categorizations that are drawn about these persons of Mexican descent and that they draw about others, as well as the likelihood that they will compare themselves to multiple groups. In contrast, the first-generation immigrants' greater dependence on Spanish, greater likelihood of living in concentrated Mexican ethnic neighborhoods, and greater occupational restrictions to laborer and operative job categories limit their intergroup contact and increase the probability that social categorization and comparison will center on the differentiation between Mexicans and U.S. residents. Living in these more restricted social contexts, their social identities are likely to be less numerous as well.

History also plays a role in the expected greater differentiation of the later generations' social identities. For them, the history that matters is the history of how Mexican origin people came to live in what is now the United States, and how they have been treated as U.S. citizens. It is a history well known and preserved in Mexican-American families, communities, and institutions; it's a history that centers: (1) on conquest of land through the Treaty of Guadalupe Hidalgo which ended the Mexican-American War of 1848; (2) on appropriation in the latter half of the nineteenth century of landholdings of the new U.S. citizens of Mexican origin by Anglo lawyers and corporations, and by a federal law in 1892 according grazing privileges on public grasslands and forests to anyone but Mexicans; and (3) on cycles throughout the twentieth century of recruiting and expelling Mexican labor (Schaefer 1984).[2]

Historical events become part of individual psychology through cultural mechanisms—family stories, communal stories, movies, and songs. The family histories of members of the later generations include stories of relatives or family friends who lived in old Mexico before the Mexican-American War; who lost their personal lands in the period when Mexican-origin persons "became outsiders in their own homeland" (Moquin and Van Doren 1971:251); who were deported despite being U.S. citizens; or who had relatives from Mexico who perhaps came to the United States illegally but eventually settled and reared U.S.-born children, later to be faced with deportation. Of course, there are also positive stories of success and commitment to the United States. Indeed, the sheer complexity of the U.S.-based history is what fuels a sense of a unique *Chicano* self that the first-generation immigrants find difficult to share. The history and politics that are relevant to immigrants' social identities focus more on Mexico than on the experience of Mexicans in the United States.

The complex, collective U.S.-based history has produced multiple constructions of ethnicity that are available for the later generations to use as they construct their own social identities. Alvarez (1973) explicitly ties collective modes of dealing with this history to generational constructions of ethnic identity. Members of the later generations can draw on all of these generational modes. Alvarez delineates four generations: the Creation Generation (1848–1900) who experienced loss of national identity, common language, and cultural ties with country women and men; the Migrant Generation (1900–1942) who fled Mexico's political upheavals and economic problems and who were variously recruited and expelled for labor in the United States; the Mexican-American Generation (1942–1966) whose participation in World War II and in the economic expansion following the war strengthened their sense of loyalty to the United States; and, the Chicano

Generation (1966 to present) who, as the most economically stable, affluent, and educated group of Mexican descendants, nonetheless developed a critique of their parents' loyalty to the United States and formed a new sense of self that was neither oriented to Mexico nor an assimilated American. From a social identity framework, a Chicano sense of self is based on a social comparison with the U.S. mainstream, the "new" reference group, which results in higher expectations of what U.S. society should allow Mexicans in this country to accomplish. Indeed, from Tajfel's framework, the development of a Chicano social identity stems largely from blocked opportunity. This is how Alvarez describes the most recent mode, a uniquely Chicano construction of identity.

> So you are a loyal "American". . . . If you are such an American, how come your coun-
> try gives you less education even than other disadvantaged minorities, permits you
> only low status occupations, allows you to become a disproportionately large part of
> casualties in war, and socially rejects you from the most prestigious circles? As for
> me, I am a Chicano, I am rooted in this land, I am the creation of a unique psycho-his-
> torical experience. I trace part of my identity to the Mexican culture and part to the
> United States culture, but most importantly my identity is tied up with those con-
> tested lands called Aztlan. I have a unique psycho-historical experience that I have a
> right to know about and to cultivate as part of my distinctive cultural
> heritage.(Alvarez 1973:25)

First-generation immigrants, Alvarez contends, are very similar to the Creation Generation (1848–1990), whose reference group was Mexican citizens in Mexico and who felt the restricted opportunities in the United States were still better than what they could hope to accomplish in Mexico:

> The price the Mexican(s) . . . had to pay in exchange for higher wages received for stoop
> labor in the fields and for lower work status in the cities was a pervasive, universal sub-
> jugation into a lower caste that came about silently and engulfed him, long before he
> became aware of it. . . . He had learned to enjoy a higher wage than he would have had
> in Mexico and to accept a degrading lower caste position. His lower socio-economic
> position in the United States was never sallent in his mind. (Alvarez 1973:931)

Alvarez emphasizes that each generation succeeds one another, providing the potential for new manifestations of ethnic identification built upon the psycho-historical experiences of their predecessors.

How might these generational modes of dealing with the U.S.-based collective history of Mexican descendants affect the structure of the social identities of the later generations? These culturally defined and generationally-specific modes provide *multiple* models that members of the later generations can use in thinking about their own identities. Across time, persons of Mexican descent developed many ways of dealing with ethnicity. While particular generations developed prototypic conceptions of what it means to be an American of Mexican descent, the new identities did not replace older ones. New ways of thinking about the self and about ethnicity were added as older ways were refined and retained as well. Each generation had a richer cultural repertoire of identity constructions to draw upon. Multiplicity is the cultural, historical legacy of the later generations, a legacy that the first-generation immigrants lack. The structure of social identities of the later generations should show the effect of this historical, cultural heritage through greater multiplicity of identities.

We also predict that the *content of social identities* of first and later generations would differ. Birth in Mexico, and status as a sojourner in the United States, should produce a Mexican and/or Latin American construction of social class and political identities for the first generation. Since class consciousness and its significance in national politics are greater in Latin America than in the United States, we expect to see its impact in how the first generation conceptualizes identities around worker and political symbols. Moreover, the statuses of immigrant and manual worker invoke many negative stereotypes that first-generation immigrants have to negotiate in a U.S. political climate that has become increasingly hostile to immigration. These problematic statuses should produce identities constructed specifically around immigrant and manual workers. We also expect that United States/American symbols and labels would be especially problematic for the first generation, who have not yet settled their eventual citizenship and residency decisions.

The U.S. nativity of the later generations is expected to shape the content of their social identities in distinctively American ways. We expect to see evidence of a politicized identity constructed from the symbols given political meaning by the Chicano political movement of the 1970s. The interpretations of history and transformation of the very term, Chicano, from a once invidious one to a term of pride and defiance reflect what Tajfel means by a social change strategy. We expect to find at least one identity that would represent this mode. We also expect to find a merger of ethnicity and/or nationality with social class among the later generations who have been affected by a political culture in which class is rarely as powerful as ethnicity or race. And finally, the tendency in many official documents, in the rhetoric of political leaders, and in state policies defining protected minorities of lumping all Mexican-origin persons together, and often lumping all persons of Latin American origin or of Spanish linguistic backgrounds together, should make the term Mexican and being a Spanish speaker especially problematic for later generations. They are aware of shared history and of shared treatment; but they are also aware of great internal variations among people who are treated "as if their internal similarities and external differences from the majority were real" (Portes and Rumbaut 1990:138).

Finally, we predict that the identities that emerge around problematic statuses (immigrant, manual worker, U.S. citizen for the first generation; Mexican, Spanish speaker for the later generations), and those that reflect a political, collective construction of selfhood (a Chicano self for the later generations, a working-class construction for first generation) would be the most psychologically implicated in the cultural adaptations of the two groups.

Research Methods

The Sample

The analyses reported here are based on the benchmark survey conducted in 1979 of persons of Mexican descent under the auspices of the Institute for Social Research of the University of Michigan. The survey was based on the first probability sample of Mexican-ancestry households in the Southwestern United States (California, New Mexico, Arizona, Texas, and Colorado) and in the Chicago metropolitan area. It was the first study whose sample was representative of almost 90 percent of the total U.S. population of Mexican ancestry identified in the 1970 U.S. Census (Santos 1985). In addition to its representativeness, the significance of the Chicano Survey also lies in the comprehensiveness of the topics covered: labor force participation, language issues, cultural preferences, social identity, family related issues, and mental health. No other survey based on such a broad spectrum of this population has included such in-depth coverage of U.S. Mexicans' attitudes and views on such diverse topics. The main limitation of these rich data, however, is the lack of a comparison with other ethnic groups, which in turn restrict the type of analyses that can be conducted. Although we could not transcend this limitation, we bypassed it by creating two subgroups within the same sample: *Chicanos* and *Mexicanos*.

The two subsets of the sample respondents used in the analyses are *Mexicanos* who are individuals born in Mexico—first-generation immigrants. *Chicanos* are individuals who were born in the United States but had a parent(s) or grandparent(s) born in Mexico—second or later generations.

An additional structural control was introduced by using the respondents' language preferences. The interviewers were bilingual and were instructed to ask the respondent if he/she preferred to carry out the interview in English or in Spanish. All but 23 of the 341 first-generation immigrants preferred Spanish.[3] All but 56 of the 291 third or longer-term generations preferred English. The second generation had more variability. Two-thirds of the 338 second generation took the interview in English, one-third in Spanish. We include in the analyses only the *Mexicanos* who took the interview in Spanish (N=318), and the second/third/later generations who chose to converse in English (N=445).

The decision to use both nativity and language as the basic controls to specify *Mexicanos* and *Chicanos* reflects our judgment that these two qualities historically have been the critical markers of immigrants and other persons of Mexican descent. It could be argued, however, that we have biased the possibility of finding social identity differences by this decision, since it is well known that second- and later-generation persons of Mexican descent who do not speak English are the most likely to still hold manual laboring jobs and to live in concentrated Mexican communities, much as immigrants do (Portes and Rumbaut 1990). We checked for such a bias by testing whether or not the final Chicano social identity model fit the intercorrelations of the total U.S.-born groups as well as it fit our more restrictively defined sample of *Chicanos*. Since the fit was approximately the same, we chose to use our restrictive definition.

Defined by nativity and language preference, the *Mexicanos* and *Chicanos* differed in the ways that studies of Mexican immigration suggest that they would. The *Mexicanos*, as first-generation immigrants, have spent on average only one-fifth of their lives in the United States; the *Chicanos* on average have been in the United States 2.54 generations. The *Mexicanos* have significantly less family income (on average $4,600 less) than the *Chicanos*, as well as fewer years of formal schooling (on average 5.9 fewer years) than the *Chicanos*. A larger proportion of the *Mexicanos* (65 percent) than of the *Chicanos* (43 percent) now live in neighborhoods in which most or all are persons of Mexican descent. As would be expected from nativity alone, far more of the *Chicanos* (48 percent) than of the

Mexicanos (3 percent) grew up in neighborhoods that were either predominantly English-speaking or Spanish-English bilingual, while many more of the *Mexicanos* (89 percent) than of the *Chicanos* (18 percent) were socialized in neighborhoods where Spanish was the exclusive language.

Measures of Social Identities

The national study of persons of Mexican descent included a multidimensional measure of social identity. Here we analyze responses to thirty labels covering a variety of racial, ethnic, familial, cultural, class, and color terms that were presented to respondents in the form of a deck of cards. Respondents were asked to look through them and keep those "that describe how you think about yourself." People could choose as many as they saw fit and could present us with as complex or simple a conception of their social identities as they wished. The response to each label is dichotomous: the label was judged to be self-descriptive or not. (See Appendix A for discussion of how we handled dichotomous measures in our LISREL analyses.)

Measures of Cultural Adaptations

We focus on four dimensions of cultural adaptation, each of which indicates a type of loyalty to Mexican cultural traditions—familism, positive attitudes toward Spanish/English bilingualism, Spanish-mediated cultural preferences, and importance placed on conveying Mexican cultural traditions to children. These four dimensions of cultural loyalty have been identified by previous literature as central to distinguishing Mexicans in the United States from the dominant culture.

Mexican descendants have consistently shown a strong commitment to family, especially extended kin, in comparison not only to Anglos but to other groups as well (Keefe and Padilla 1987). The maintenance of Spanish by Mexican descendants is another important aspect of cultural loyalty; they have proven to be the most resilient Spanish speakers (Portes and Rumbaut 1990). Retaining the capacity to speak Spanish among Mexican descendants in general goes along with acquisition of English and serves crucial intragroup communication with the continuous flow of immigrants that enter Mexican communities in the United States. In this study, maintenance of Spanish is indicated by positive attitudes towards bilingualism (approval of speaking *two* languages) and towards Spanish-language entertainment and media. Finally, cultural loyalty is indicated by wanting to maintain cultural distinctiveness for themselves and their children. Cultural maintenance through the socialization of children was the last measure of cultural loyalty.

Proximal familism is measured by an index averaging responses to six questions (answered by the respondent on a three-point scale from "very important" to "not important"): "How important is it to you that the following relatives live near you? Your father, your mother, your sister(s), your brother(s), your grandparent(s), your adult child(ren)?" Scores ranged from 10 to 30, a higher score indicating greater importance that relatives live nearby. Spanish-mediated cultural preferences are measured by an index averaging the extent to which (on a four-point scale) respondents reported "liking very much" or "not liking at all" five activities: watching Spanish-language TV programs, listening to Spanish-language radio programs, going to Mexican movies, going to performances by Mexican entertainers, reading Spanish-language newspapers or magazines. Scores ranged from 10 to 40, a higher score representing stronger cultural preferences. Preference for children retaining Mexican culture is measured by responses (on a four-point scale) indicating preference from "liking very much" to "not liking at all" to a single item: "Would you like to have your children maintain Mexican traditions when they grow up?" Scores originally ranged from 1 to 4 and were then multiplied by 10 to make them comparable to the other three measures of cultural adaptation. Approval of bilingualism is measured by an index averaging responses (on a four-point scale) showing the extent of agreement from "strongly agree" to "strongly disagree" to four statements: "People of Mexican descent should know two languages," "Children of Mexican descent should learn to read and write in both Spanish and English," "All school subjects should be taught in both Spanish and English," "A person who speaks more than one language gets along better with different kinds of people." Scores ranged from 10 to 40, a high score indicating greater support for bilingualism.

Measures of Control Variables

In relating social identities to cultural adaptations, we controlled for several demographic and structural characteristics that affect adaptation of immigrants, and in particular the adaptation of immigrants from Cuba, Mexico, other Latin American countries, and of island Puerto Ricans (Dean and Tienda 1987; Chavez 1988; Keefe and Padilla 1987; Massey 1981; Pedraza 1990; Portes and Bach 1985; Portes and Rumbaut 1990). The most important controls, according to previous research on Latino/Hispanic groups, are nativity and language (already controlled by sample specification), occupation, education, income, age, married/single status, length of residency in the United States and/or sojourner, settler, citizen status, ethnic residential segregation, linguistic environment during childhood, documented and undocumented status of the immigrant, and motivations for immigrating. The measures that were available in the national study of the Mexican-descent population made it possible to control eight of these factors so we could draw conclusions about the role of social identities in cultural adaptation independent of these structural forces that also affect identities and cultural adaptations.

Family income was measured by self-report in which respondents chose one of sixteen income categories ranging from less than $2,000 annually to $30,000 or more. Number of years of schooling was measured by the respondent's self-report of years completed, which was later collapsed into eight categories ranging from less than six years to more than sixteen. Gender and marital status are dichotomous measures in which men are coded 1, women coded 2, and all currently married respondents are coded 2, all others are coded 1. Age is measured by years, with six months or more coded up to the next year. Length of residency necessary requires different measures for the *Mexicanos* and *Chicanos*. For *Mexicanos*, the measure is the percent of the respondent's life that has been lived in the United States—the number of years the respondent has lived here divided by the respondent's age. For *Chicanos*, who by definition have lived all of their lives in the United States, the measure is the number of generations that parents, grandparents, great-grandparents have lived in the United States. Residential segregation is measured by self-report, in which respondents judged how many of their current neighbors are of Mexican descent, on a scale of 1 representing "none" to 4 representing "all" of them. Linguistic environment of the childhood neighborhood is measured by the respondent's judgment of what language(s) were spoken in the neighborhood in which they grew up, on a scale of 1 representing "entirely Spanish," 2 "mostly Spanish," 3 "both Spanish and English," 4 "mostly English," and 5 "entirely English." Given the importance of manual laborer occupations for the Mexican-origin Immigrants. It is unfortunate that we do not have an adequate occupational measure. As this is a secondary analysis, we are dependent on the original coding of occupation. We found evidence of errors in the coding, and did not have access to the original interviews to re-code occupation.

RESULTS

Endorsement of the Social Identity Labels

Before testing analyses of our three sets of predictions concerning structure of social identities, content of social identities, and their role in cultural adaptation, it is useful to examine the percentage of *Mexicanos* and *Chicanos* who endorsed each of the thirty social identity labels.

Table 11.1, which gives those percentages, shows many similarities, as well as differences, between *Mexicanos* and *Chicanos*.

First, the similarities. Family and gender role labels were endorsed by at least two-thirds and generally more than three-quarters of the respondents in both groups. On these live terms ("parent," "child," "spouse," "male/female," "sibling"), the two groups differed significantly only with respect to gender. Ten percent more of the *Chicanos* than of the *Mexicanos* chose the gender label as self-descriptive, but even among *Mexicanos* this was one of the three chosen most frequently.

Three other labels were also endorsed by fairly comparable proportions of the two groups. About two-fifths of each group selected the term "raza"; half, the term "brown"; and 72 percent of the *Chicanos* and 81 percent of the *Mexicanos* the term "Spanish speaker." Despite conversing in English in this interview, nearly as many of the *Chicanos* as the *Mexicanos* thought of themselves as Spanish speakers. This finding indicates the importance of the social construction process. Self-definition goes far beyond the social realities of language competence or a language decision in a particular situation. We will show in the factor structure of social identities that even these similarly endorsed ethnic terms have different meanings for the two groups.

Mexicanos and *Chicanos* had different endorsement rates for all of the other identity labels. Some of these differences represent generational distance from Mexico. *Mexicanos* are more likely than *Chicanos* to accept the labels "Mexican," "foreigner," and "immigrant" as self-descriptive, while *Chicanos* are more likely to endorse "American of Mexican descent," "Mexican American," "American," "U.S. citizen," "U.S. native," and "English speaker." The endorsements of the two groups also reflect social class differences. *Mexicanos* are more likely to say that they think of themselves as "blue-collar

TABLE 11.1 Percentage of Chicanos and Mexicanos Who Endorsed Social Identity Labels as Self-Descriptive

Label	Chicanos (N-445)	Mexicanos (N=318)
Blue collar worker	18	54[***]
Foreigner	7	49[***]
Parent	88	83[*]
Child	69	65
Mexican	62	83[***]
Pocho	17	6[***]
Gender	91	81[***]
Middle class	69	54[***]
American of Mexican descent	80	32[***]
Sibling	73	68
Spouse	79	77
Mexican American	79	35[***]
Hispanic	41	55[**]
White	30	37[*]
Indian	26	17[**]
American	75	17[***]
U.S. Citizen	94	24[***]
Family breadwinner	51	61[**]
Brown	58	63
Poor	26	62[***]
Immigrant	5	63[***]
Farmworker	16	38[***]
Latino	37	55[***]
English speaker	83	14[***]
Spanish speaker	72	81[**]
U.S. native	75	11[***]
Working class	70	49[***]
Chicano	47	20[***]
Raza	45	38
Mestizo	17	32[***]

Notes:
[***] p<.oo1 difference between Chicanos and Mexicanos.
[**] p<.o1 difference between Chicanos and Mexicanos.
[*] p<.o5 difference between Chicanos and Mexicanos.

workers," "farmworkers," and "poor," while more *Chicanos* endorse the labels "middle class" and "working class." There is also a different political consciousness reflected in the responses of the two groups. *Mexicanos* more frequently identify with labels that indicate a broad Latin American consciousness, for example the terms "Hispanic," "Latino," and "mestizo." Some *Chicanos* see these terms as self-descriptive but, compared to the *Mexicanos*, more *Chicanos* identify with terms that were given specific political meaning in Chicano politics, for example the term "Chicano" itself and the term "pocho."

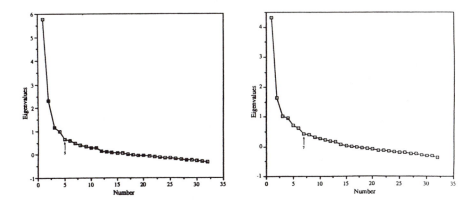

FIGURES 11.1 and 11.2 *Scree plots of eigenvalues for exploratory factory analyses*

Structure and Content of Social Identity

Our analysis of similarities and differences in the structure and content of social identities between *Mexicanos* and *Chicanos* proceeded in three stages. In the first stage, we randomly selected half of the respondents within each group from our survey data and performed an exploratory factor analysis for each group to extract preliminary structures. After theoretical consideration and refinement, we arrived at a final structure for each group. In the second stage, we performed confirmatory factor analyses of our proposed models within groups, using our survey data of those respondents not included in the first stage. Finally, in the third stage, we tested each model between groups to test how well the *Chicano* model would fit the *Mexicano* data, and vice versa.

Exploratory Factor Analyses

Our preliminary factor analyses were performed using EPAP (Joreskog and Sorbom 1986) and SAS. Half of the respondents in each group were randomly selected for inclusion in these analyses. Scree plots (Cattell 1965) of eigenvalues for each group are shown in Figures 11.1 and 11.2. From these plots, we determined that five factors should be extracted from the *Mexicano* data, and that seven factors should be extracted from the *Chicano* data. Use of these plots to determine the number of extracted factors can be very subjective but was adequate to provide some structure to our preliminary analyses. Since standard factor analysis cannot determine a unique, "best" solution, the appropriateness of each model for each group is more adequately addressed with confirmatory tests of the proposed models. Figures 11.3 and 11.4 provide diagrams of the models with results of our confirmatory factor analyses.

Confirmatory Factor Analyses

Confirmatory factor analyses were performed on the remaining data to test each model. Our results suggest that the proposed models provide a good fit for the data. Figures 11.3

TABLE 11.2 Fit Assessment of Confirmatory Factor Models

Models	df	χ^2	χ^2/df	Normed fit index
Chicano Subjects				
Chicano Factor Structure	385	839.1	2.18	.885
Mexicano Factor Structure	365	988.1	2.71	.801
Mexicano Subjects				
Mexicano Factors Struture	365	704.4	1.93	.865
Chicano Factor Structure	385	1169.8	30.4	.763

Note: The Mexicano factor structure has fewer degrees of freedom because one social identity label, pocho, was deleted due to low endorsement.

and 11.4 present the models along with estimated parameters and fit diagnostics. In addition, we tested each group using the other group's proposed model (i.e., *Mexicano* model with *Chicano* data, and *Chicano* model with *Mexicano* data). The fit statistics for these analyses are presented in Table 11.2; they suggest that the *Mexicano* model does not fit the *Chicano* respondents well, and that the *Chicano* model does not fit well with the *Mexicano* respondent. Please refer to Appendix A for a more detailed discussion of these analyses.

The Social Identities of the Mexicanos

For *Mexicanos* (Figure 11.3), all of the family and gender roles cohere to make one factor; the nationality and class terms are each driven by two latent factors. Social class is cleanly divided between the conceptions of middle class and working class. The observed variable "middle class" loads onto a separate factor from "working class" and is associated with thinking of the self as "white." The terms "poor," "farmworker," "blue collar," and "working class" converge to create a factor that represents a merger of rural and industrial workers more characteristic of the historical political economy of Mexico than of the United States. These class-based identities support the prediction that the Immigrants would show evidence of a Latin American class consciousness. This is also seen in the fact that these *Mexicanos* do not think of the working-class identity as an immigrant identity. For *Mexicanos*, identification as an Immigrant does not anchor a separate identity, as we had predicted, nor is it associated with social class. Instead, being an Immigrant is part of a family identity.

Two nationality identities emerged for the *Mexicanos*. One, a Binational identity, reflects their sense of themselves as "Mexican Americans" and "Americans of Mexican descent," along with their identification with strictly U.S. self-descriptions. As predicted, it is the U.S. labels that are particularly problematic for the *Mexicanos* and figure prominently in what it means to be an American of Mexican descent. The Binational identity does not include the term "Mexican," which is part of the family identity of the *Mexicanos*. The other nationality identity, Panraza, includes broad Latin American terms ("Hispanic" and "Latino," but also racial and color terms that have significance in Latin

Standardized Solution. All factors are free to correlate. See Phi matrix (below) for values.

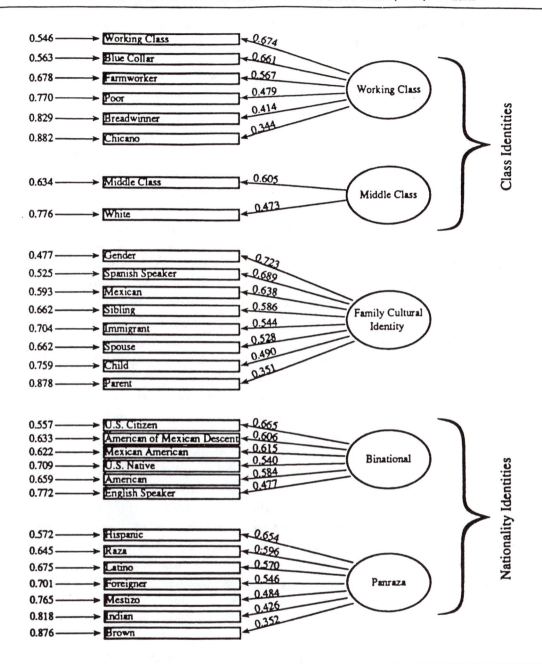

Model : N = 318, χ^2 = 708.4, df = 365, χ^2/df = 1.94, AGFI = 0.840

Phi matrix:

	Working Class	Middle Class	Fam.Cultural Id.	Binational
Middle class	0.177			
Family Cultural Identity	0.554	0.623		
Binational	0.433	0.426	0.169	
Panraza	0.678	0.544	0.652	0.435

FIGURE 11.3 Confirmatory Factor Structure of the Social Identities of Mexicanos

America). This identity shows the "homeward orientation" that was predicted to be the core of a political identity for *Mexicanos*, although the results show this identity does not specifically reflect involvement with Mexico. Instead, it reveals a sense of self as being part of something broader than either Mexico or the United States—a foreign, Hispanic/Latino self that connects with the peoples of Latin America.

The Social Identities of the Chicanos

In the *Chicano* model (Figure 11.4), we see that the identities of the *Chicano* sample are particularly differentiated with respect to social class and ethnicity. These U.S.-born English speakers have three class-tied identities that reflect the historical experience of Mexican workers in the class structure of the United States. One, the Farmworker identity, brings together labels representing the historically common position of immigrant workers from Mexico—"farmworker," "poor," "immigrant," and "foreigner." (Currently, however, nearly three-quarters of Mexican immigrants who are occupationally active work in factory, rather than rural, manual jobs [Portes and Rumbaut 1990]). The second, the Working-Class identity, involves thinking of the self as "working class" and a "family breadwinner." A third, U.S./Middle-Class identity, suggests yet a further stage of class differentiation. It is conceived of by the *Chicanos* as involving *both* class and nationality—to be part of the United States is to be middle class. This identity best supports the prediction that the *Chicanos* would show a characteristic American lack of class consciousness, and reveals the tendency in the United States to conceive of middl- class standing as an American quality. This U.S./Middle-Class identity also includes gender, showing that for *Chicanos*, the sense of the self as a woman or a man is associated with the most mainstream identity. The U.S./Middle-Class identity is an example of gaining psychological distinctiveness through individual mobility, "passing" or "exiting" from a devalued group to become psychologically part of the valued mainstream.

Nationality was also more complicated for the *Chicanos* than for the *Mexicanos*. As noted earlier, the U.S./Middle-Class identity merges nationality and class. A second nationality factor, Latino, also merges nationality and class, in "Latino," "Hispanic," and "blue collar." This identity is distinguished from a Binational identity. For *Chicanos*, the Binational identity brings together the dual terms—"American of Mexican descent" and "Mexican American"—with the term "Mexican." Thus, as predicted, it is the Mexican self that is problematic in being an American of Mexican descent for these members of the later generations.

As predicted, the Chicano respondents also produced a Raza identity that has a specifically U.S. rather than Latin American connotation. This identity is comprised of terms ("pocho," "Indian," "brown," "Spanish speaker," "Chicano," "raza," and "mestizo") that the Chicano political movement uses to describe the unique experience of Mexicans in the United States. "Raza"—the race—indicates a united racial-cultural community, and "mestizo" indicates that Mexicans are a mixture of many races. "Pocho," ordinarily a derogatory term connoting a style of speaking with a mixture of Spanish and English, became a positive identification, as did these other terms, by a reconceptualization by the Chicano movement in the 1970s. That being a Spanish speaker belongs best on this

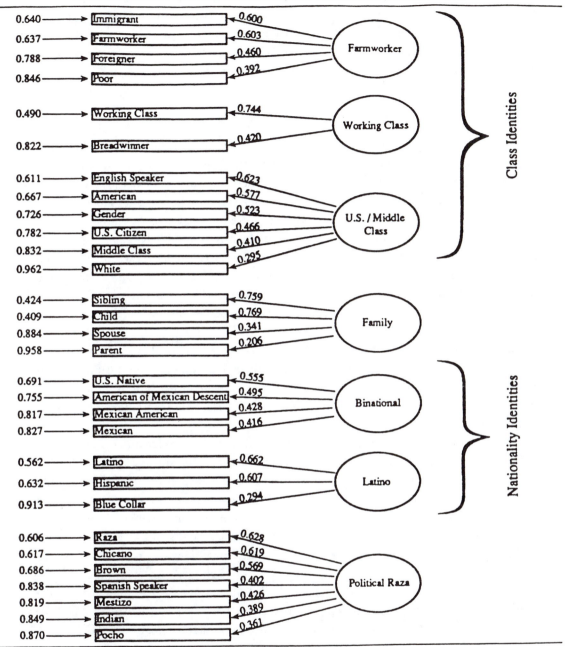

Standardized solution. All factors are free to correlate. See Phi matrix (below) for values.

	Indicator			Factor	
0.640	Immigrant	0.600			
0.637	Farmworker	0.603		Farmworker	
0.788	Foreigner	0.460			
0.846	Poor	0.392			
0.490	Working Class	0.744		Working Class	
0.822	Breadwinner	0.420			
0.611	English Speaker	0.623			
0.667	American	0.577			
0.726	Gender	0.523		U.S. / Middle Class	Class Identities
0.782	U.S. Citizen	0.466			
0.832	Middle Class	0.410			
0.962	White	0.295			
0.424	Sibling	0.759			
0.409	Child	0.769		Family	
0.884	Spouse	0.341			
0.958	Parent	0.206			
0.691	U.S. Native	0.555			
0.755	American of Mexican Descent	0.495		Binational	
0.817	Mexican American	0.428			
0.827	Mexican	0.416			Nationality Identities
0.562	Latino	0.662			
0.632	Hispanic	0.607		Latino	
0.913	Blue Collar	0.294			
0.606	Raza	0.628			
0.617	Chicano	0.619			
0.686	Brown	0.569			
0.838	Spanish Speaker	0.402		Political Raza	
0.819	Mestizo	0.426			
0.849	Indian	0.389			
0.870	Pocho	0.361			

Model : N = 436, $\chi^2 = 839.1$, df = 385, $\chi^2/df = 2.18$, AGFI = 0.850

Phi matrix:

	Farmworker	Working Class	US/Mid Class	Family	Binational	Latino
Working Class	0.085 *					
US/Middle Class	0.109	0.627				
Family	0.207	0.282	0.556			
Binational	0.151	0.529	0.807	0.493		
Latino	0.225	0.478	0.394 *	0.430	0.534	
Political Raza	0.448	0.348	0.313 *	0.424	0.604	0.650

* these elements are small in relation to their standard errors.

FIGURE 11.4 Confirmatory Factor Structure of the Social Identities of Chicanos

factor shows that Spanish maintenance has political significance to the later generations. But we were wrong to expect that the identity of being a Spanish speaker would anchor a separate identity. Language may well be problematic for these *Chicanos*, but they apparently deal with it by making Spanish a self-defining political question.

Social Identities and Cultural Adaptations

Tables 11.3 and 11.4 present regression analyses in which each of the measures of cultural loyalty is predicted from the social identity indices (five for *Mexicanos* and seven for *Chicanos*), along with the eight demographic and structural controls. Social identity scores for each factor were created through summation of the number of identity labels on each factor endorsed by the respondent. Factor scores were not used because simple multiple-group methods have been shown to be more consistently replicable (Gorsuch 1983). The standardized regression coefficients (betas) for each identity index represent the association between that identity and one of the measures of cultural loyalty after controlling for the shared variance among the identity and structural/demographic measures.

Let us look first at Table 11.3 for the *Mexicanos*. Three conclusions can be drawn from these regression analyses.

The first conclusion is that the social identities of the *Mexicanos* have little to do with their cultural adaptations. Only three of the five social identities are significantly related to *any* measure of cultural adaptation, and only one is related to *several* of these cultural measures. We will see that the social identities of the *Chicanos* are more broadly involved in their cultural adaptations.

Second, as predicted, it is the identity associated with the problematic status of manual worker, the Working-Class identity, that is the most important psychologically. The Working-Class identity is significantly related to all four measures of adapting to U.S. life by retaining elements of Mexican cultural traditions. *Mexicanos* who identify with the status of manual worker (a status that approximately 80 percent of Mexican immigrants actually hold) by accepting as self-descriptive some or most of the labels "working class," "blue-collar worker," "farmworker," "poor," "family breadwinner," and "Chicano" are also the most familistic, and most frequently want their children to retain Mexican culture, like Spanish-language media, and approve of Spanish-English bilingualism. Since structural and demographic factors are controlled in these analyses, loyalty to Mexican culture among Working-Class identified *Mexicanos* is not merely a matter of their lack of economic and structural integration. Instead, the self-construction as working class plays an independent role in the immigrant generation's commitment to preserving Mexican traditions as a mode of cultural adaptation to the American scene.

Third, two social identities of the *Mexicanos* are related in opposite ways to approval of bilingualism. The Binational identity—which in addition to the dual terms of "Mexican American" and "American of Mexican descent" includes the problematic and extremely rare identities for the immigrants of being "U.S. citizens," "U.S. natives," "Americans," and "English speakers"—is associated with *disapproval* of bilingualism. For Immigrants to deal with being or becoming Mexican Americans by embracing U.S. identities that objectively do not apply to them—something only 10 to 20 percent

TABLE 11.3 Relationships Between Mexicanos' Social Identities and Cultural Adaptations

	Proximal famillism	Pref. for retaining Mex. culture	Spanish media cultural prefs.	Approval of bilingualism
Class Identities				
Working Class	.159**	.129*	.127*	.164**
Middle Class	.000	-.090	.095	.229***
Family Identity				
Family	-.059	.007	-.075	.071
Nationality Identities				
Binational	.008	-.041	-.106	-.154***
Panraza	-.011	.092	.032	-.063

Notes: * p<.05; ** p<.01; *** p<.001; **** p<.0001.

This table presents standardized regression coefficient (betas) representing the effect of identity, controlling all other identities and structural/demographic variables.

Source: Adapted from: Aida Hurtado, Jaclyn Rodríiguez, Patricia Gurin, and Janette L. Beals (1993), "The impact of Mexican descendants' social identity on the ethnic socialization of children." In *Ethnic Identity: Formation and Transmission Among Hispanics and Other Minorities*, ed. Marta H. Bernal and George P. Knight, 131–162. New York: SUNY Press.

TABLE 11.4 Relationships Between Chicanos' Social Identities and Cultural Adaptations

	Proximal famillism	Pref. for retaining Mex. culture	Spanish media cultural prefs.	Approval of bilingualism
Class Identities				
Farmworker	.047	.040	.199****	.005
Working Class	.042	.063	-.027	.000
U.S. Middle Class	-.005	-.214***	-.196****	-.051
Nationality Identity				
Binational	-.098	-.067	-.007	-.016
Latino	-.049	.018	.031	.002
Family Identity				
Family	.142***	.054	.149***	.000
Political Identity				
Raza	.050	.160***	.156***	.208****

Notes: * p<.05; ** p<.01; *** p<.001; **** p<.0001.

This table presents standardized regression coefficient (betas) representing the effect of each identity, controlling all other identities and structural/demographic variables.

Source: Adapted from: Aida Hurtado, Jaclyn Rodríiguez, Patricia Gurin, and Janette L. Beals (1993), "The impact of Mexican descendants' social identity on the ethnic socialization of children." In *Ethnic Identity: Formation and Transmission Among Hispanics and Other Minorities*, ed. Marta H. Bernal and George P. Knight, 131–162. New York: SUNY Press.

do—seems to go along with adopting the view that "English only" is the American lin-guistic way. In contrast, the sense of self as Middle Class, comprised of the terms "mid-dle class" and "white," is associated with *positive* attitudes towards people who can speak both Spanish and English and towards school programs that teach both languages. This identity does not involve the especially problematic U.S. symbols that define the Binational identity, or the ambivalences that those symbols likely evoke for an immigrant generation. Thinking of oneself as white and middle class says nothing about being either Mexican or American, and thus this identity is not implicated in adapting to the United States through accepting cultural hostility towards bilingualism.

Table 11.4 gives the results for the *Chicanos*. It reveals that the *Chicanos'* social iden-tities are much more broadly tied to their cultural adaptations than were the social iden-tities of the *Mexicanos*. Three social identities—U.S./Middle Class, Family, and Raza—are significantly related to at least two of the cultural measures, and another identity—Farmworker—is related to one (liking Spanish-language entertainment).

Four other conclusions may be drawn from Table 11.4. First, as predicted, the identity that was made salient and problematic for *Chicanos* by the Chicano political movement, the Raza Political Identity, is the most psychologically powerful in explaining loyalty to Mexican cultural traditions. *Chicanos* who have embraced some or most of the political symbols that transformed negative characterizations of Mexican-origin people to posi-tive ones are committed to preserving elements of Mexican traditions as a mode of cul-tural adaptation in the United States. This identity is significantly related to the desire to transmit Mexican traditions to children, approval of bilingualism (which for these English-dominant speakers means retention of Spanish), and positive attitudes towards Spanish-language entertainment and media. These associations show the clear political meaning conveyed by both the Raza identity and these measures of cultural adaptation.

Second, the results further demonstrate the significance of social identities as media-tors of social experience. These *Chicanos* share long-term social experience in the United States; yet, the extent of their cultural loyalty differs greatly depending on the ways they have come to view themselves. If *Chicanos* have followed a mobility pattern and hold the U.S./Middle-class identity, they are apt to have little loyalty to Mexican cultural practices and symbols. *Chicanos* who are identified as part of the U.S. middle class do *not* support socializing children to retain Mexican cultural practices and they do not participate in Spanish-language cultural activities. In contrast, if *Chicanos* have adapted by developing a strong Family identity or a distinctively Chicano Raza sense of self, they do not assim-ilate culturally. These *Chicanos* want to retain cultural practices that involve the family, and they assert the importance of Spanish. Thus, it is critical to know how *Chicanos* have come to think of themselves, not merely how long they have resided in the United States or how structurally integrated they have become, to understand how they are apt to adapt culturally. The quite different effects of the U.S./Middle-Class identity, and the Raza and Family identities, exist independent of length of residency and other demo-graphic and structural variations that are controlled in these analyses.

Third, these results show the importance of a multidimensional conception of social identities and, in particular, the inadequacy of thinking about ethnic identity merely as identification with a nationality. In fact, the Binational and Latino identities were not significantly related to any measure of cultural adaptation among the *Chicanos*. The strongest identity-cultural adaptation relationships are found with political and family identities, and with the identity that merged class *with* nationality.

Fourth, *Chicanos'* results reveal the importance of contextual specificity. Family identity is specifically tied to a familistic social adaptation; the political identity (Raza) is specifically tied to the politicized issue of support for bilingualism. This specificity is not as evident in the results for the *Mexicanos*.

DISCUSSION

As predicted by social identity theory, the differences in the structural and historical conditions experienced by immigrants and ethnics result in a more differentiated identity structure for *Chicanos* than for *Mexicanos*. The results of the confirmatory factor analysis further support that the construction of social identities follows different models for the *Mexicanos* and the *Chicanos*. The content of the social identities of the two groups also shows important differences according to their accessibility to outgroup comparisons through mastery of the English language. Ethnicity is infused in nearly all of the social identities of both groups, but ethnicity is constructed differently by the *Mexicanos* and *Chicanos*.

The accessibility to different experiences in each successive generation in some instances results in the same identities in both groups—for example, a Binational identity, although it was comprised of different identity labels and had different meaning for adaptation. For the newcomer *Mexicanos*, the especially problematic labels involving the United States were part of what it means to be a Mexican American or American of Mexican descent, while for the later generation *Chicanos*, it was the problematic relationship to Mexico that was part of the dual identity. Moreover, the Binational identity was irrelevant for the *Chicanos'* cultural adaptations, while for *Mexicanos*, the Binational identity was associated with the view that to be an American means rejection of bilingualism.

Both groups had a Middle-Class identity, but again it was configured differently. The Middle-Class identity was merged with U.S. nationality terms for the *Chicanos* but not for the *Mexicanos*. Moreover, the merger of middle-class status with U.S. nationality is associated for the *Chicanos* with the traditional American belief that immigrants should give up their country of origin's cultural traditions. The U.S./Middle-Class identity is the most clearly assimilationist identity that emerged for the *Chicanos*.

Both groups had political identities involving a self-construction as being part of La Raza. However, this identity had a Latin American connotation for the *Mexicanos*, and was comprised of terms that have become symbols of a unique U.S. experience for the *Chicanos*. Moreover, the Latin American Panraza identity was not implicated in the cultural adaptations of the *Mexicanos*, while the U.S.-based Raza identity was the most broadly related to the cultural measures for the *Chicanos*.

Particular results from the regression analyses also support the prediction from Tajfel's theory that the most problematic social identities—those that are most devalued, that require the most negotiation for positive sense of distinctiveness, or that are politicized—are the most psychologically powerful. The strongest support for this prediction is shown by the consistently significant relationships between the Working-Class identity and cultural adaptations of the *Mexicanos*, and between the Raza identity and cultural adaptations of the *Chicanos*. These results also support Alvarez's contention that shifts in reference groups have an outcome in social comparisons that either promote acceptance of devalued social categorizations or in feelings of discontent about one's social identity. For *Mexicanos*, social class is what needs to be negotiated to achieve a sense of positive distinctiveness. These first-generation immigrants are the most economically disadvantaged of the U.S. Mexican population. They have to deal with stereotypes of the majority culture about them as manual laborers and about menial labor as "Mexican work." In this group, there is a clear Working-Class identity that reflects this problematic status, and it is the most psychologically powerful identity for their cultural adaptations. For *Chicanos*, the Raza identity has been made problematic by political and community leaders who have raised group consciousness about what it means to be a Chicano and what Raza means in the United States. It is the identity that brings together the self-constructions as Chicano and Raza with terms given positive meaning by the Chicano movement that is especially important in the *Chicanos* expressions of cultural loyalty.

Tajfel's theory is basically a psychological theory of what goes on in a reactive process of identity formation. Although it is usually depicted as a universally applicable theory, it emphasizes psychological reactions to social categorizations and comparisons that make group memberships valued or derogated. A reactive process of identity formation is one of two delineated by Portes and Rumbaut (1990) as likely to fit the adaptations of immigrants. Like Tajfel, they define a *reactive process* as coming from discrimination, categorical treatment, common labeling, and stereotypes of groups that may have shared only tenuous bonds before arriving in the United States. A *linear process*, in contrast, is shaped by cultural experiences transported from the country of origin, a linear continuation of past experience rather than an emergent reaction to the situation in the receiving country. Portes and Rumbaut argue that the reactive process is most likely to apply to immigrants who come to the United States as manual laborers and who settle in visible ethnic areas, while the linear process applies best to political refugees and to immigrant groups comprised predominantly of professional workers who live dispersed across the United States.

A reactive process ought to apply well, therefore, to Mexican immigrants. Of the largest eight contempory immigrant groups, Mexicans (along with Cambodians) are the most predominantly manual workers; they have the lowest proportions of professionals and managers; they settle primarily in four metropolitan areas (Los Angeles, Chicago, El Paso, and San Diego); they join communities that are among the most concentrated ethnic communities in the country (Portes and Rumbaut 1990). Yet, our results show that the Tajfel framework fits the *Chicanos* who have been in the United States for at least two generations better than it fits the first-generation immigrants. Social identities are more broadly implicated in the cultural adaptations of the *Chicanos* than of the *Mexicanos*. In other analyses, we have also found that social identities are more broadly related for the *Chicanos* than for the *Mexicanos* to group-conscious political attitudes (Hurtado and Gurin 1987), to intragroup and intergroup contacts (Rodriguez and Gurin 1990), and to ethnic socialization of children (Hurtado et al. 1993).

Why would the Tajfel theory of identity formation as a reactive process apply better to the *Chicanos* than to the new immigrants? A reactive process is likely to require a decision to settle in the United States. Until that decision is made, immigrants can relate to the United States as temporary sojourners for whom U.S.-based group categorizations, labeling, and common treatment are not self-defining. Several studies have found that awareness of group-based discrimination is more, not less, widespread the longer persons of Mexican descent have lived in the United States (Portes and Rumbaut 1990). The reactive process likely begins in the first-generation, but only when the aspiration of returning to Mexico recedes in the possible selves of the immigration generation. The reactive process becomes critical when the United States becomes critical; it continues to apply, generation after generation, to groups that continue to be categorized, labeled, and discriminated against in the intergroup social structure of the United States.

APPENDIX A

The remaining respondents in each group that were not selected for use in the exploratory factor analyses were used to test our proposed models in corresponding confirmatory factor analyses. Parameters were estimated using LISREL (Joreskog and Sorbom 1989). Correlation matrices used as input were created using PRELIS (Joreskog and Sorbom 1986). Our analyses were conducted using standard product-moment correlation matrices; however, since our data were dichotomous, we replicated our analyses using an input matrix of polychoric correlations estimated by PRELIS. Since our results did not significantly differ using the polychoric matrix, the results using the original product-moment correlation matrices are presented here. The standard maximum likelihood procedure was used to obtain the parameter estimates.

The standardized solution for the Mexicano model is presented in Figure 11.3. The sample size for this analysis is 318. All latent variables are permitted to correlate, but each observed variable is assumed to have only one direct effect from a latent variable. In addition, we assume that there are no correlations among the error terms of the observed variables. The estimated linkages between the substantive factors and the observed variables are reasonably strong, with the weakest between "Chicano" and the "Working Class" factor $\lambda_x = 0.344$). Correlations among the latent variables are moderate, with a few above 0.6: "Working Class" and "Panraza" (0.678), "Middle Class" and "Family" (0.623), and "Family" and "Panraza" (0.652). These are not large enough to pose any problems. All parameters λ_x, ϕ, and δ_d are highly significant. The χ^2 value obtained is high (708.4, $p < 0.00$), although χ^2/d.f. is a reasonable 1.94. The root mean square residual reports an average deviation of the correlation matrix produced by the model from the actual input matrix. For this model, it is reported at 0.067, which is low enough to suggest that χ^2 may be a biased criterion of fit for this model.

The Chicano model is presented in Figure 11.4. Our sample size here was 436. As for the Mexicano model, factors are permitted to correlate, but observed variables are permitted to have a direct link with only one latent factor. Estimated links between latent and observed variables are acceptable, although there is a noticeably low link between the "Family" factor and "Parent" ($\lambda_{x'} = 0.206$). Since we believe that there are compelling theoretical reasons why these two should be linked, we kept the "Parent" variable in the analysis. Except for the three elements of f that are indicated in Table 2, all parameters are highly significant. χ^2 is high (839.1, $p < 0.00$), but $\chi^2/\text{d.f.}$ is relatively low at 2.18. The root mean square residual for this model is 0.061.

The results suggest that both of our models fit reasonably well. Both manage to capture the original relationships among the observed variables (the input correlation matrix) while leaving out 116 and 180 possible linkages, respectively, between observed and latent variables for each model.

STUDY QUESTIONS

1. How do the results of this study show the importance of a multidimensional conception of social identities?

2. How do historical events become part of one's identity?

3. How is Tajfel's theory a reactive process of identity formation?

NOTES

1. An exception is the work of Portes and colleagues who explicitly tie features of social contexts to individual adaptations and furthermore discuss these relationships within an identity framework (see Portes and Bach 1985 and Portes and Rumbaut 1990).

2. Examples of these cycles include a period of active recruitment during the 1920s when the agricultural industry of the Southwest was expanding; then an official repatriation policy followed during the 1930s to deport Mexican-origin persons who were purportedly illegal aliens but were most often American citizens unable to prove citizenship (Schaefer 1984; Meier and Rivera 1972); later a new recruitment policy, the Los Braceros Program, agreed to by the United States and Mexican governments in 1942 and followed until 1965, that allowed migration of contracted laborers across the border; then the Operation Wetback Program (or sometimes called Special Force Operation) that was inaugurated in 1934 to send workers who could not establish legal status back to Mexico while the Bracero Program was still importing other workers from Mexico; and the continuation of deportation as one of the main strategies the United States has employed to try to halt illegal immigration even after the official Operation Wetback was formally phased out in 1956.

3. For the *Mexicanos*, this preference is closely related to self judgments of language competence. Only 18 percent felt that they had even some competence to converse in English. For *Chicanos*, language preference is not related to competence. Eighty-seven percent of these U.S.-born Mexican descendants who chose to take this interview in English said they had some ability to converse in Spanish; 69 percent thought that they could do this "well" or "very well." This finding shows a considerable amount of language resillence in a group that has been in the United States at least two generations.

REFERENCES

Alvarez, Rodolfo 1973 "The psycho-historical and socioeconomic development of the Chicano community in the United States." *Social Science Quarterly* 53:920–942.

Bean, Frank D., and Marta Tienda 1987 *The Hispanic Population of the United States*. New York: Russell Sage Foundation.

Cattell, Raymond B. 1965 "Factor analysis: An introduction to essentials." *Biometrics* 21:190–215.

Chavez, Leo 1988 "Settlers and sojourners: The case of Mexicans in the United States." *Human Organization* 47:95–108.

Connor, Walker 1992 "The nation and its myth." *International Journal of Comparative Sociology* 33:4757.

Gorsuch, Richard L. 1983 *Factor Analysis*. 2nd edition. Hillsdale, NJ: Lawrence Erlbaum Associates.

Hurtado, Aída, and Patricia Gurin 1987 "Ethnic identity and bilingualism attitudes." *Hispanic Journal of Behavioral Sciences* 9:118.

Hurtado, Aída, Jaclyn Rodriquez, Patricia Gurin, and Janette L. Beals 1993 "The impact of Mexican descendants' social identity on the ethnic socialization of children." In *Ethnic Identity: Formation and Transmission Among Hispanics and other Minorities*, eds. Marta B. Bernal and George P. Knight, 131–162. New York: SUNY Press.

Joreskog, Karl G., and Dag Sorbom 1986 PRELIS: *A Preprocessor for* LISREL. 2nd edition, Mooresville, IN: Scientific Software Inc.

———. 1987 *Analysis of Linear Structural Relationships by Maximum Likelihood Instrumental Variables and Least Squares Methods*. Scientific Software, Inc.

———. 1989 LISREL 7: *User's Reference Guide*. 1st edition, Mooresville, Ind.: Scientific Software Inc.

Keefe, Susan, and Amado M. Padilla 1987 *Chicano Ethnicity*. Albuquerque: University of New Mexico Press.

Massey, Douglas S. 1981 "Hispanic residential segregation: A comparison of Mexicans, Cubans, and Puerto Ricans." Sociology and Social Research 65:311–322.

Meir, Matt S., and Feliciano Rivera 1972 *The Chicanos: A History of Mexican Americans*. New York: Hill and Wang.

Moquin, Wayne, and Charles Van Doren 1971 *A Documentary History of the Mexican Americans*. New York: Praeger.

Olzak, Susan 1983 "Contemporary ethnic mobilization." *Annual Review of Sociology* 9:155–74.

Pedraza, Silvia 1990 "Immigration research: A conceptual map." *Social Science History* 14:43–67.

Portes, Alejandro, and Robert L. Bach 1985 *Latin Journey: Cuban and Mexican Immigrants in the United States*. Berkeley and Los Angeles: University of California Press.

Portes, Alejandro, and Ruben G. Rumbaut 1990 *Immigrant America: A Portait*. Berkeley: University of California Press.

Rodriguez, Jaclyn, and Patricia Gurin 1990 "The relationships of intergroup contact to social identity and political consciousness." *Hispanic Journal of Behavioral Sciences* 12:235–255.

Santos, Robert 1985 "A methodlogical report on the sample design of the 1979 National Chicano Survey." Stanford, Calif.: Stanford Center for Chicano Research, Working Paper Series No. 11.

Schaefer, Richard T. 1984 *Racial and Ethnic Groups*. 2nd edition. Boston: Little Brown.

Smith, A.D. 1992 "Introduction: Ethnicity and nationalism." *International Journal of Comparative Sociology* 33:12.

Tajfel, Henri 1978 *Differentiation Between Social Groups: Studies in the Social Psychology of Intergroup Relations*. London: Academic Press (European Monographs in Social Psychology).

———. 1981 *Human Groups and Social Categories: Studies in Social Psychology*. London: Cambridge University Press.

Tajfel, Henri, and John Turner 1979 "An integrative theory of Intergroup conflict." In the *Social Psychology of Intergroup Relations*, ed. W. G. Austin and S. Worchel, 33–47. Monterey, Calif.: Brooks/Cole Publishing Co.

Tiryakian, Edward A., and Ronald Rogowski, eds. 1985 *New Nationalism of the Developed West*. Winchester, MA: Allen and Unwin.

Chapter 12

Rodolfo D. Torres and ChorSwang Ngin

Racialized Boundaries, Class Relations, and Cultural Politics
The Asian-American and Latino Experience

"Race" and "ethnicity," though key concepts in sociological discourse and public debate, have remained problematic. Policy pundits, journalists, and conservative and liberal academics alike all work within categories of race and ethnicity and use these concepts in public discourse as though there is unanimity regarding their analytical value. Racialized group conflicts are similarly advanced and framed as a "race relations" problem and presented largely in black/white terms.[1] A prime example of this confusion is the analysis of the causes of the April 1992 Los Angeles riots. In the aftermath of the riots, academics and journalists analyzed the riots as a matter of race relations—first it was a problem between blacks and whites, then between blacks and Koreans, and then between blacks and Latinos, and back to blacks and whites. The interpretation of the riots as a race relations problem failed to take into account the economic changes, the economic restructuring, and the drastic shifts in demographic patterns that have created new dynamics of class and racialized ethnic relations in Los Angeles (see, for example, Davis, 1990).

The analytical status of the ideas of race and race relations has been questioned for more than a decade within British academic discussion, and it is only more recently that some U.S. scholars have begun to consider the rationale and implications of this critique. A few U.S. writers have begun to shift from treating race as an explanatory construct to

From *Culture and Difference: Critical Perspectives on the Cultural Experience in the United States.* Edited by Antonia Darder. Bergin and Garvey, an imprint of Greenwood Publishing Group, Inc., Westport, CT. (1995).

focusing on racism as a structure and ideology of domination and exclusion, and moving beyond race relations as black/white relations. David Theo Goldberg's (1993) innovative approach to mapping new expressions of multiple racism and racialized discourse; Cornel West's (1993) call for a new language to talk about race; Michael Omi's (1993) recognition of the limits of race relations theories; Tomas Almaguer's (1989, p. 24) challenge "to remain open to lines of historical interpretation that do not resonate with the nationalist sentiments"; Barbara Fields's (1990) focus on race as an ideological construction; and E. San Juan's (1992) treatment of how race articulates with power, ethnicity, nation, gender, and class all represent recent important contributions to the ongoing attempts at theorizing about racialized groups in the context of changing class relations in the United States. The parallel critique by British scholars has centered on the production and the reproduction of the concept of race within British society. Seminal writers of these works include Robert Miles (1982, 1989, 1993); Stuart Hall (1978, 1980, 1986); Paul Gilroy (1991); John Solomos (1988, 1989); A. Sivanandan (1982, 1990); and the recent works of Floya Anthias and Nira Yuval-Davis (1993).

In our analysis of the Latino and Asian American populations in California, we will move beyond the contemporary American debate by arguing for a complete rejection of the use of the terms "race" and "race relations" in academic and public discourses. We will introduce an alternative model that applies the concept of racialization to the California Asian and Latino populations and expands the concept of ethnicity to include both "ethnicity-for-itself" and "ethnicity-in-itself."

THE MUDDLES IN THE DEBATE

In everyday and academic discourse, the terms "race" and "ethnicity" are used interchangeably, creating much confusion over what is racial and what is ethnic in the designation of populations. In the U.S. tradition, the terms "race" and "ethnic" have been employed throughout as analytical categories to describe and "explain" various groups.

This muddle in the academic debate is also reflected in official governmental practices. The 1980 census, for example, listed fifteen groups in the "race" item in the questionnaire: white, black, American Indian, Eskimo, Aleut, Chinese, Filipino, Japanese, Asian Indian, Korean, Vietnamese, Hawaiian, Samoan, Guamanian, and Other. Though the Census Bureau claimed that the concept "race" as used does not denote any clear-cut scientific definition of biological stock (Loh & Medford, 1984, p. 4), by categorizing groups as "races," the Census Bureau nonetheless is suggesting that each of the listed groups including "whites" are "races." Even more complicated is the classification of peoples of Mexican, Central American, and Latin American origin. Because the census uses a "white" and "black" category, Latinos were moved back and forth from a "white" or "ethnic" ("persons of Spanish mother tongue") category in the 1930 census to a "black" or "racial" ("other non-white") category in the 1940 census. In the 1950 and 1960 censuses, the ambiguous category of "white persons of Spanish surname" was used. In 1970, the classification was changed to "white persons of Spanish surname and Spanish mother tongue." Then in 1980, Mexican Americans and Puerto Ricans, along with other Central and Latin Americans of diverse national origin, were classified as "non-white Hispanic" (Moore & Pachon, 1985, p. 3).

California, its dramatic changes in ethnic composition brought about by the liberalization of the 1965 Immigration and Naturalization Act and, more recently, by the Amnesty Bill of 1988, which legalized the residency status of Mexicans and Central Americans, has brought to the forefront the ever-increasing confusion over these categories. Are Latinos an ethnic group or a racial group? Are Asians an ethnic group or a racial group? In this debate centered on a black/white dichotomy, Asian Americans and Latinos fall through these bipolar designations. The conceptual inadequacy of this dichotomy is most evident in California as the realities and the positions of the two populations bring into question the continued use of this model. The complexity of the class character and the differential integration of Asian Americans and Latinos into the U.S.'s changing economy therefore calls for new paradigms to understand these changing populations in the post–civil rights era. To provide a critique and alternative framework of contemporary race relations, we will draw upon selected works of the innovative political economist Robert Miles.[2] As Miles's theoretical position on race and especially his advancement on the concept of "racialization" are central to our analysis, we will first outline his conceptual framework in substantial detail. This will provide a meaningful framework for analyzing the phenomena of racialized boundaries in "postmodern" capitalism.

ROBERT MILES'S DECONSTRUCTION OF RACE

Central to Robert Miles' work is the notion of the generation and the reproduction of the idea of race as a social and ideological construct. According to Miles (1982, 1989), the idea of race has changed over time. It first entered the English language in the sixteenth century to mean lineage or common descent or history (see also Banton, 1987).[3] With European colonial expansion and colonization, contacts with Others increased. This contact was structured by competition for land, introduction of private property, demand for labor, and the perceived obligation of conversion to Christianity. Miles posited that European ideas of foreigners were based on the representation of the Others generated in the context of a stronger European economic and military force. During the eighteenth century, with the scientific assertion of the existence of different biologically constituted races, the term "race" came to mean discrete categories of human beings, based on phenotypical differences, and ranked with psychological and social capacities. Later, the emergence of the science of genetics refuted this idea of race as discrete and fixed subdivisions of the human species because no such link was ever found. This scientific discourse on race, however, did not replace the earlier conception of the Other: the idea of races as biological types persisted even though proven false by the weight of scientific evidence. Miles questioned why the scientific reconception of race has little influence in everyday discourse. He maintained, moreover, that an understanding of the continuing reference to the phenotypical features suggested that "factors other than the development of biological sciences were fundamental to the formulation of the notion of 'race' and its continuing reproduction" (1982, p. 21). This use of "race" to denote phenotypical variation, which is given social recognition and which in turn structured social interaction, is what Miles referred to as the "social construction of race." Based on this historical understanding of the concept of race, Miles argues that race cannot be used descriptively to classify people in society, nor can the concept be used for either analytical or explanatory purposes.

Race itself is an ideological category that requires explanation. Thus Miles has carefully avoided the ambivalent employment of the term "race" except when he refers to its use by other writers. In challenging the analytical status of the idea of race, Miles (1982) also argues against the use of "race relations." Race relations, the central research focus of most British and American sociologists, is defined by its chief proponent John Rex as "the kinds of social relations that exist between people of the same race and ethnicity and between individuals or groups of different race and ethnicity" (1986, p. 2). Miles interpreted this conceptual transition from the social category of "race" to "race relations" as the product of the legitimation given to the belief that the "human species consists of several distinct 'races.'" This "race relation" was then objectified as an area of study. Thus, Miles (1982) stated:

> "Race relations" can only mean that "races" have social relations, one with another. So, for relations to occur, "race" must exist. Indeed, they "exist" in the sense that human agents believe them to exist, but uncritically to reproduce and accord analytical status to these beliefs is nevertheless to legitimate that process by giving it "scientific" status. (p. 33)

Following Miles, several British sociologists have also carefully placed the term "race" within inverted commas (see Williams, 1989). Susan Smith, for example, notes that the meaning of "race" is ideologically biased, and therefore is fundamentally a social construct (Smith, 1989, p. 1). Other British writers, cognizant of Miles's work, have self-consciously defended their position to use the term "race" in their analysis. Gilroy (1987), for example, retains the use of the term "race" as an analytical category. For Gilroy, race is retained as "an analytical category not because it corresponds to any biological or epistemological absolutes, but because it refers to investigation of the power that collective identities acquire by means of their roots in tradition" (1991). However, Miles (1984) rejects such an approach by arguing against the confusion of ideological and political goals with scientific rigor in methodology.

Robert Miles's rejection of the category "race" is relevant to our attempt to provide insight to the current California "race" and "ethnicity" theoretical debate. In California, Asian Americans and Latinos comprise two extremely diverse populations. The population termed "Asian American" includes at least fourteen distinct groups: Chinese, Filipino, Japanese, Asian Indian, Korean, Vietnamese, Laotian, Thai, Cambodian, Hmong, Pakistani, Indonesian, Hawaiian, and people from the Pacific Islands of Micronesia and Polynesia. Each of these Asian American ethnic categories is further divided along linguistic, religious, and especially class lines. These changing demographic realities have reshaped the ethnic and socioeconomic relations of the populations of California. The majority of the recent Asian immigrants to California from Hong Kong, Korea, Taiwan, and the Philippines are of middle-class background. The Vietnamese, Cambodians, Laotians, and Hmong, on the other hand, are mostly refugees who entered the country without much capital. But, with time, class differentiation is emerging among these newcomers. While some Asian Americans within a sub-ethnic group are entrepreneurs, professionals, or managerial workers, others are dependent on the state for welfare. In terms of generational difference, some Chinese and Japanese Americans are direct descendants of the early pioneers who immigrated to the United States in the late nineteenth century. Still others are recent immigrants who have arrived within the last few years. Segments of the Asian American population are concentrated in ethnic enclaves such as Chinatowns, Little Saigons, and Manilatowns, while others are dispersed, living in middle- and upper-middle-class suburbs. Notwithstanding, these divergent groups are categorized in the U.S. Census as one single group—Asian Americans.

The use of a single category to represent the Asian American population is also mirrored in the practice of classifying the Latino population as a single "non-white Hispanic" category. This group includes Mexican Americans of the Southwest, the colonized subjects from Puerto Rico, refugees from Cuba, and recent immigrants and refugees from Mexico, Central, and South America. These diverse Latino sub-groups are also differentiated by community, generation, and class origins. In describing the Latino community, scholars speak of the "barrio" to mean actual settlements but also in terms of the symbolic community that serves as a source of identity. The same generational difference that applies to Asian Americans and European Americans cannot be applied to Latinos, as there are Latinos who are the direct descendants of preconquest Southwest populations.[4]

The question of class and class structure is even more problematic among the Latino population. The existence of a Chicano class structure predates the Mexican American War of 1846–1848 (Barrera, 1979). This population includes the Chicano/Latino working class, petit bourgeois, recent immigrants from Mexico and Latin America, and the Chicano professional managerial class (Barrera, 1984). However, there is a paucity of studies on class divisions within the Latino community. As noted by Valle and Torres (1994), much needs to be learned about the nature and meaning of Latino class relations in a postindustrial society and the manner in which these divisions manifest themselves in the changing organization of work, urban politics, and relation with the state.

Despite these varied and complex characteristics among both Asian Americans and Latinos, a distinction can be made between the recent groups of immigrants and the earlier groups: the recent groups have not been subjected to the same harsh legal exclusionary practices and therefore do not share the lived historical memory of virulent racism. This distinction is important—it determines how ethnicity is perceived by others and how it is used by the ethnic groups involved. All immigrants, however, are connected to their native countries by transnational economic and social processes. The material forces that determine their migration, their present production relations, and their class positions are similarly determined by the larger social structure and the global economy.

This class diversity within the immigrant population makes representing them as either "race" or "ethnic" problematic. Segments of the immigrant population might conceivably be regarded as a "racial" group in the tradition of the "race-centered" theorists, as this group is subjected to hate crimes and other discriminatory practices. Others might be regarded as an "ethnic" group in the tradition of the "ethnic-centered" theorists: their middle-class status proclaimed by the neoconservatives as evidence of equal opportunities for all groups in the United States. We must be cognizant of the fact that the material success among the middle-class immigrant population should be attributed, in part, to their professional education received abroad and to the capital immigrants brought with them, and not to some inherent cultural entrepreneurial essentialism found among certain Asian Americans and "Hispanics," as argued by the new entrepreneurial cultural determinists (Kotkin, 1992).

Given the existence of class divisions within the Asian American and Latino populations, we find the key to Miles' insight—the unequivocal rejection of the notion "race"—useful in solving part of the Asian American/Latino "race/ethnic" muddle. The category "race" as applied to Asian Americans and Latinos (along with African Americans, Native Americans, and European Americans) has no heuristic value. That is, racialized social groups in the United States do not constitute "races." What about the classification of Asian Americans and Latinos as "ethnic" groups? For this, we will first briefly define the term "ethnicity" as used in the sociological literature and Robert Miles's critique of its uncritical use.

ETHNICITY

The actual term "ethnicity" (from the Greek word "ethnos," meaning "people" or "nation") has been defined by Milton Yinger (1994) as

> a segment of a larger society whose members are thought, by themselves and/or others, to have a common origin and to share important segments of a common culture and who, in addition, participate in shared activities in which the common origin and culture are significant ingredients. (p. 3)

Milton Gordon (1964) similarly defines ethnicity as "a shared feeling of peoplehood" (p. 24). The research on "ethnicity" and "ethnic group" as a dominant paradigm in contemporary British and American sociological writings has defined the "culture" of the social group as their major focus.

Miles (1982), a major critic of the use of the term "ethnicity," argues that assessing a group's beliefs and behavior in terms of its

> culturally determined distinctiveness can lead to a simple cataloguing of cultural difference (a dictionary of the "exotic") at one level, while at another it presents an analysis of the interaction between culturally distinct groups either without reference to or even in direct opposition to class relations. (p. 67)

Furthermore, "by abstracting cultural differentiation, and the notion of group identity which derives from this difference, from production relations," Miles continues, "the consequence is either a failure to identify class divisions within the culturally distinct populations . . . (or) the class position that migrants come to occupy . . . (and) the material forces which determine the migration" (1982, pp. 67–69). Thus, Miles (1982) argues that "ethnic relations" cannot be used as an analytical framework as it contains a number of "analytical, logical and empirical contradictions and/or errors." Furthermore, he argues that research of "ethnic" culture would constitute an analytical trap if it is divorced from its historical and material context (p. 70). However, Miles also recognizes there is a certain ambiguity in his work on the concept of "ethnic" and "ethnicity" (Miles, 1991, personal correspondence).

While we share Miles's rejection in assigning analytical status to "ethnic" groups, we argue for the modified use of the term. We propose the concepts "racialization of ethnic groups," "ethnicity-in-itself," and "ethnicity-for-itself" to examine the dynamics of Latino and Asian American group relations. But first, we will draw on Miles's explication of the concept of racialization.

RACIALIZATION

Miles argues that the employment of the idea of race in structuring social relations should be more appropriately termed "racialization" rather than "race relations." Writing in *Racism* (1989), racialization is referred to as

> those instances where social relations between people have been structured by the signification of human biological characteristics in such a way as to define and construct differentiated social collectivities. . . . The concept therefore refers to a process of categorization, a representational process of defining an Other (usually, but not exclusively) somatically. (p. 75)

Three characteristics are attached to the notion of racialization. First, "racialization entails a dialectical process of signification. Ascribing a real or alleged biological characteristic with meaning to define the Other necessarily entails defining Self by the same criterion" (Miles, 1989, p. 75). Thus, "the African's 'blackness' reflected the European's 'whiteness'; these opposites were therefore bound together, each giving meaning to the other in a totality of signification" (Miles, 1989, p. 75). Second, the concept of racialization should take into account "the emergence of the idea of 'race' and its subsequent reproduction and application." Third, "the racialization of human beings entails the racialization of the processes in which they participate and the structures and institutions that result" (Miles, 1989, p. 76). That is, in racialized societies, institutions and political processes, both formal and informal, are necessarily also racialized. An example of racialization would include a political process where demands are made that certain "racial" groups be represented in positions of power or be given special privileged status. In the United States, this process is commonly known as the "politics of entitlement."

The concept of racialization has been employed by U.S. scholars Michael Omi and Howard Winant (1986) in their landmark work, *Racial Formation in the United States: From the 1960s to the 1980s*. Omi and Winant use the concept "racialization" to "signify the extension of racial meaning to a previously racially unclassified relationship, social practice or group" (p. 64). Regrettably, Omi and Winant do not fully develop this concept, nor do they use it in a sustained analytical manner. The authors' concept of racialization is grounded in race relations sociology—a sociology that reifies the notion of race.[5] This reification of race implies that racial groups constitute a monolithic social category. In suggesting that race is an active subject—"an unstable and 'decentered' complex of social meanings"—the authors advance the notion that the idea of race is socially constructed. Yet they implicitly embrace and anchor their analysis of social movements and racial formation on the illusionary concept of race.[6] Omi and Winant (1986) furthermore assign analytical status to the idea of race by claiming that "the concept of racial formation should treat race in the United States as a fundamental organizing principle of social relationship" (p. 66). Whereas we maintain that racialization is grounded in class and production relations, and the idea of race need not be explicitly employed for a process of racialization to occur.

THE RACIALIZATION OF ETHNIC GROUPS

The notion of racialization set forth in Miles's writing—the representation and definition of the Others based on the signification of human biological characteristics—is particularly useful in understanding the U.S. discourse of the non-European immigrants and natives. Until recently, discourse on Native Americans, African Americans, Latinos, and Asian Americans has largely depended on a phenotypical representation and evaluation. Both color and physical appearance were given social significance. By reason of their color and physical features, these populations were perceived as bearers of diseases and as endangering European American morals and "racial" purity. This discourse based on "race" provided the ideological context, in part, for the enactment of past restrictive immigration laws and discriminatory policies. Even though fewer phenotypical characteristics are employed in contemporary discourse of the immigrant groups in formal legislative policies, the racialization process continues to inform many group practices and individual actions. We would include as instances of racialization in California the "hate crimes" directed at Asian Americans and other racialized groups; the violent attacks, vandalism, racial slurs, and hateful mail directed at immigrant institutions, churches, and individuals; and racialized code words such as "welfare queen," "Willie Horton," "illegal alien," "model minority," among others.

To understand this antipathy toward Asians and Latinos, we suggest that this is the result of categorization of immigrants and foreigners based on their physical features (skin color, mostly). Past significations of immigrant, by ascribing them with real or alleged biological or cultural characteristics, are available as part of the American culture for reinterpretation, given the existence of certain stimulus. In contemporary U.S. society, the stimuli that led to the renewed attack on Asian immigrants can be attributed, firstly, to the decline of U.S. capitalism as an economic power, particularly its economic position in relation to Japan. Much of the political debate on what's wrong with the U.S. economy focuses on Japan's unfair trade practices and acquisitions of American companies, landmarks, and cultural icons. Negative imagery of Japan in the form of "Japan bashing" is articulated by both the indigenous population and the politicians, and is often reproduced through political legitimation by the state. Second, acts of violence against racialized populations can be understood as attempts to define what is the local imagined community (Miles & Phizacklea, 1981; Anderson, 1991). The local American imagined community, a community based on the ethos of biblical foundation, republicanism, and individualism, is unable to regard those who express different values as part of the same community. This view of anti-immigrant antipathy is also echoed by sociologist Susan Smith. In her examination of working-class youth, she suggests anti-immigrant behaviors are attempts "to preserve both national exclusivity and neighborhood segregation" (Smith, 1989, p. 159).

Given these insights drawn from the works of Miles, Phizacklea, Smith, and Anderson, the bigotry and violence against racialized groups in California should be seen in the larger economic and political contexts. The authors attribute political and economic forces as having created and sustained racialized violence. These acts cannot be explained solely as the product of spontaneous violence perpetrated by psychologically aberrant gangs of white youth. The understanding of these multiple causes has enormous implications for directing effective policies designed to address and prevent racist violence against immigrants. New research needs to address the increased use of the signification of racial and cultural characteristics in political campaigns and the concurrent increase of intolerance against racialized groups in the United States.

RACIALIZATION FROM WITHIN

As immigrant groups are racialized by members outside their ethnic group, they are simultaneously engaged in defining and redefining their group identity. However, we maintain that this process of self-definition, racialization-from-within, and "ethnicity-for-itself" is but one form of ethnic activity. This is distinct from a process of activity and organization we regard as "ethnicity-in-itself." In "ethnicity-in-itself," immigrant groups are connected by their language and culture. Although it may be claimed that ethnicity is a subjective, constructed concept and cannot be defined objectively with social cultural indicators (since some with the same language/cultural characteristics may not consider themselves part of the community at all), subjective ethnic identification can often lead to creation of ethnic institutions such as newspapers and schools in order to express that sense of peoplehood. Thus, the Asians and Latinos have created separate ethnic, cultural, and economic organizations to meet their multifarious needs in functioning in an urban society. These institutions and structures provide autonomous networks separate from the institutions and structures in the dominant culture. Examples of some of these Asian groups might be the Chinese language schools, the Korean churches, and the Chinese Lions Club, in areas with a critical mass of Chinese or Korean population. These affiliations are based on the members' linguistic and cultural similarities. These associations are no different from early Italian and Polish American ethnic organizations. These ethnic activities are consistent with the traditional definition of ethnicity, where the emphasis is on a socially defined sense of peoplehood based generally on concepts of shared culture and common origin. In California, this "ethnicity-in-itself" is created in part by the ethnic enclaves that serve as buffers between their group and the dominant populations. Furthermore, the recent immigrants do not share the historical memory of older immigrants and do not see themselves as victims of discrimination.

These "ethnicity-in-itself" activities, in the context of U.S. society, are noted by the indigenous populations as the unwelcome changes in their community. This "ethnicity-in-itself" is contrasted with what we observe as "ethnicity-for-itself." We would regard "ethnicity-for-itself" as racialization from within. "Ethnicity-for-itself" includes associations with co-ethnic or other ethnic groups for the purpose of political empowerment and entitlement. The awareness of their common plight is what leads to the support of others who undergo similar experiences by emphasizing the community of memory, defining the boundary with which they can develop their own culture, and the sharing of common experience. This ethnic awareness is actively promoted to serve clearly defined ends. This racialization from within serves as a political defense strategy in the face of perceived adversity or disadvantage. It is this process of renegotiation and redefinition that defines the group's relationship with the dominant society. These groups see their existence within a larger ethnic formation. An example of "ethnicity-for-itself" is the increasing number of Asian American and Latino organizations in Southern California. These organizations are themselves conglomerates of much smaller ethnic groups. A Los Angeles Asian American organization, the Asian American Pacific Planning Council (APPACON), for example, represents thirty-three Asian American organizations. Through this collective bargaining power, it is able to exert political pressure on the local government.

The politics of "ethnicity-for-itself" can be understood by employing Benedict Anderson's (1991) concept of "imagined community." "Ethnicity" used as a basis for organization is "imagined" because it suggests potential alliances across communities of diverse national origin, cultural background, and internal hierarchies within the ethnic groups. It also suggests a significant commitment to a sense of "horizontal comradeship" in the struggle for limited state resources. This "imagined community" leads us away from the essentialist notions of cultural and biological bases for alliance. So it is not race, or ethnicity, or culture which constructs the grounds for these politics; rather, it is the way ethnicity is internally racialized to constitute group alliance.

The ethnic consciousness and the politics that develop are an important line of cleavage and an important sociopolitical force shaping contemporary society. This often leads to pan-ethnic movements. An example is the multicultural movement that attempts to incorporate into the curriculum and the campus environment the wide range of cultures that coexist in the United States.

Some of the "ethnicity-for-itself" members who engage in ethnic activities, speak in their native language, or celebrate ethnic cultural festivities, for example, might be considered "unassimilated" when judged from an assimilationist perspective. However, we are arguing that the question is not whether members of the group have assimilated, in the way Gordon (1964) uses the term, where he refers to it as "a kind of ethnic change where people become similar to the dominant group." We argue, instead, that the way members continue to associate with one another is a conscious attempt to use ethnicity for the purpose of empowerment and entitlement. Most members of "ethnicity-for-itself" are in fact fully assimilated. Even if they are not, their distinctive cultural difference is not considered a handicap insofar as they are relating to other co-ethnic members. The "fully assimilated" may support "ethnicity-in-itself" activities because it is perceived as empowering the ethnic "cause." Others may support ethnic activities because they see these as opportunities to reinvent their own culture.

The attacks on expression of ethnicity are attacks on the activities of "ethnicity-in-itself." These activities are perceived by others as leading to the balkanization of American society. It represents a sort of social anxiety that Stuart Hall and his colleagues (1978) refer to as "moral panic." It is precisely these attacks or racialization from without that lead to the political consciousness of the members engaging in "ethnicity-in-itself." In response to the attacks, members see the need for associating and supporting other ethnic groups for political empowerment. In the process, the apolitical nature of "ethnicity-in-itself" gains a political consciousness, as minorities within a dominant society, and becomes "ethnicity-for-itself."

It is this political character of "ethnicity-for-itself" that we wish to retain. Therefore, we have departed from Robert Miles in that we recognize "ethnicity" as a powerful concept in understanding ethnic organization and group relations. We agree, though, with Miles that ethnicity cannot be used as an analytical category for research on ethnic groups, for it often leads to "a catalogue of the exotic" and can constitute an "analytical trap" if "divorced from its historical and material context" (Miles, 1982, p. 70).

CONCLUSION

In applying Miles's argument, we have rejected the employment of "race" and "ethnic" groups as analytical categories, and the social relations between groups as "race relations." As discussed in our introduction, we found the traditional race relations approach grounded in the black/white paradigm incapable of providing insights into the complex nature of multiple racisms in an increasingly diverse society. We referred to the instances of racialization of Asian and Latino/Chicano populations as those social processes whereby social groups are singled out for unequal treatment on the social significance attached to physical or genetic differences. The significance of employing this theoretical approach is its application for examining any social group outside of the black/white categories. Furthermore, the process of racialization should be equally applicable in the examination of racialization within and between groups: the racialization of recent Southeast Asian immigrants by more established Asian Americans, the racialization of Central and Latin Americans by Mexican Americans, and the racialization of one ethnic group by another ethnic group, regardless of color. We have also made the distinction between "ethnicity-in-itself" and "ethnicity-for-itself" to account for the apolitical cultural practices of recent immigrants in the former, and the use of ethnicity for self-racialization and political alliance across ethnic lines in the latter. This distinction provides us with the analytical framework for understanding the dynamics of ethnic politics and multiple cultural identities within the context of a changing political economy.

Clearly, there are major areas where further research and theorizing are needed to move us forward in understanding the expression and consequences of racism(s). The first area is the need for comparative studies of racialized groups in the United States. As suggested in this chapter, this will require a radical break with the dominant race relations paradigm that assigns analytical status to the idea of race and frames racial matters in black and white terms. Second, more studies are required that treat with analytical specificity the nature and meaning of class divisions within racialized populations and communities, and the manner in which these changing class relations manifest themselves in community politics, and the relations with the state in a "postindustrial" political economy. Third, while different racisms have been hegemonic, they have always been the object of resistance and struggle. Studies of resistance must be undertaken, in particular, to demonstrate the complexities and contradictions that arise from the struggle against racism.

STUDY QUESTIONS

1. Discuss the concept of racialization. How is the concept used to study contemporary "race relations?"

2. How is the analysis developed by Robert Miles used by the authors to deconstruct the idea of "race" and its relevance to the study of Asian Americans and Latinos in the United States?

3. What is meant by positing that "race" is an ideological construct and that it does not have either an analytical or explanatory value?

NOTES

1. A survey of recent book titles indicates the ubiquitous employment of the term "race" and the biracial theorizing. This uncritical theorizing and obsession with race only objectifies, obfuscates, and reproduces what is merely a social construct. Examples of some of these recent titles include *Two Nations: Black and White, Separate, Hostile, Unequal* (Hacker, 1992); *Chain Reaction: The Impact of Race, Rights, and Taxes on American Politics* (Edsall & Edsall, 1991); *Race in America: The Struggle for Equality* (Hill & Jones, 1993); and *Race Matters* (West, 1993).

2. In addition to the works of Robert Miles, there has been a growth of British literature that moves forward the debate beyond race and its expression and significance in contemporary society. Other seminal writers of these works include the recent edited volume of articles drawing upon postmodernist, poststructuralist, and feminist concerns by James Donald and Ali Rattansi (*"Race," Culture, and Difference*, 1992); John Solomos (*Black Youth, Racism and the State*, 1988; *Race and Racism in Contemporary Britain*, 1989); the liberal sociology of Michael Banton (*Racial Theories*, 1987; *Racial Consciousness*, 1988); John Rex (*Theories of Race and Ethnic Relations*, 1986; *The Ghetto and the Underclass*, 1988; *Race and Ethnicity*, 1986); and the Marxist-influenced work of the Center for Contemporary Cultural Studies (CCCS) of the University of Birmingham under the leadership of Stuart Hall (*The Empire Strikes Back*, 1982). Stuart Hall's seminal essay, "Race, Articulation and Societies Structured in Dominance," is a result of the UNESCO debate on race and racism (*Sociological Theories: Race and Colonialism*, 1980). Other important works included Stephen Castle's *Here for Good* (1984), Tuen Van Djik's *Racism and the Press* (1993), and the writings of A. Sivanandan, the director of the Institute of Race Relations (*A Different Hunger* [1982], and his recent *Communities of Resistance: Writings on Black Struggles for Socialism* [1990]).

3. Michael Banton (1987) has traced the entry of the word in the English intellectual thought to the beginning of the sixteenth century (p. 1), and the use of the term "race" through its several distinctive senses and the several changes. The most common use of the term speaks of the human "races" in the sense of subspecies, the common being the division of the humankind into Negroid, Mongoloid, and Caucasoid. Over the last few decades, it became clear that no meaningful taxonomy of human races was possible. A second common use of the term refers to a group of people who are *socially* defined in a given society as belonging together because of physical markers such as skin color, stature, and so on. The same social label may cover people with very different genetic relatedness and ancestry, for example, "blacks" in South Africa and "blacks" in Australia. In the United States, a person of black and European ancestry is labeled black, whereas the same person would be classified as white in Brazil.

4. This Latino "race" problematic and the social and political context of racial labels in the U.S. Census are explicated in the work of Lee (1993).

5. Miles (1982) refers to the term "reification" as the elevation of an idea, or concept, to the status of an object.

6. In their second edition (1994), the authors continue to assign analytical status to the concept of race despite its "uncertainties and contradictions" (p. 55).

REFERENCES

Almaguer, T. (1989). "Ideological distortions in recent Chicano historiography: The internal colonial model and Chicano historical interpretation." *Aztlan, 18*(1) (Spring).

Anderson, B. (1991). *Imagined communities*. Rev. ed. London, England: Verso.

Anthias, F., and N. Yuval-Davis. (1993). *Racialized boundaries: Race, nation, gender, colour and class and the anti-racist struggle*. London, England: Routledge.

Banton, M. (1988). *Racial consciousness*. New York, NY: Longman.

———. (1987). *Racial theories*. Cambridge, MA: Cambridge University Press.

Barrera, M. (1984). "Chicano class structure." In Eugene E. Garcia, Francisco A. Lomeli, & Isdro D. Ortiz (eds.), *Chicano studies: A multidisciplinary approach*. New York, NY: Teachers College Press.

———.(1979). *Race and class in the Southwest*. Notre Dame, IN: University of Notre Dame Press.

Castle, S. (1984). *Here for good—Western Europe's new ethnic minorities*. London, England: Pluto Press.

Center for Contemporary Cultural Studies (1982). *The empire strikes back: Race and racism in 70s Britain*. London, England: Hutchinson Library.

Davis, M. (1990). *City of Quartz*. London, England: Verso.

Donald, J., and A. Rattansi (1992). *"Race," culture, and difference*. London, England: Sage.

Edsall, T., and M. Edsall (1991). *Chain reaction: The impact of race, rights, and taxes on American politics*. New York, NY: W.W. Norton & Co.

Fields, B. (1990). "Slavery, race and ideology in the United States of America." *New Left Review, 181* (May/June).

Gilroy, P. (1991). *There ain't no black in the union jack*. Chicago, IL: University of Chicago Press.

Goldberg, D.T. (1993). *Racist culture*. Cambridge, MA: Blackwell.

Gordon, M. (1964). *Assimilation in American life: The role of religion, race, and national origin*. New York, NY: Oxford University Press.

Hacker, A. (1992). *Two nations: Black and white, separate, hostile, unequal*. New York, NY: Scribner's.

Hall, S. (1986). "Gramsci's relevance for the study of race and ethnicity." *The Journal of Communication Inquiry, 10*.

———. (1980). "Race articulation and societies structured in dominance." In *Sociological theories: Race and colonialism*. Paris, France: UNESCO.

Hall, S., C. Critcher, T. Jefferson, and B. Roberts. (1978) *Policing the crisis: Mugging, the state, and law and order*. London, England: Macmilian.

Hill, H., and J. E. Jones, Jr. (1993). *Race in America: The struggle for equality*. Madison, WI: University of Wisconsin Press.

Kotkin, J. (1992). *Tribes: How race, religion and identity determine success in the new global economy*. New York, NY: Random House.

Lee, S. (1993). "Racial classification in the U.S. census: 1890–1990." *Ethnic and Racial Studies, 16*(1) (January).

Loh, E., and R. Medford. (1984). *Statistical sources on California Hispanic population 1984: A preliminary survey*. Chicano Studies Research Center, University of California, Los Angeles, CA.

Miles, R. (1993). *Racism after "race relations."* New York: Routledge.

——— (1991). Personal correspondence.

——— 1989). *Racism, key ideas series*. London, England: Routledge

——— (1984). "Marxism versus the sociology of "race relations'?" *Ethnic and Social Studies*, 7(2) (April).

———. (1982). *Racism and migrant labor*. New York, NY: Routledge and Kegan Paul.

Miles, R., and A. Phizacklea (1981). "Racism and capitalist decline." In Michael Harloe (ed.), *New perspectives in urban change and conflict*. London, England: Heinemann Educational Books, pp. 80–100.

Omi, M. (1993). "Out of the melting pot and into the fire: Race relations policy." *The State of Asian Pacific America*. Los Angeles, CA: UCLA Asian American Studies Center.

Omi, M., and H. Winant. (1994). *Racial formation in the United States: From the 1960s to the 1990s*. 2d ed. New York, NY: Routledge.

———. (1986). *Racial formation in the United States from the 1960s to the 1980s*. New York, NY: Routledge and Kegan Paul.

Moore, J., and H. Pachon. (1985). *Hispanics in the United States*. Englewood Cliffs, NJ: Prentice-Hall.

Rex, J. (1988). *The ghetto and the underclass: Essay on race and social policy*. Brookfield, VT: Gower.

———. (1986). *Race and ethnicity*. Milton Keynes, England: Open University Press.

San Juan, Jr., E. (1992). *Racial formations/critical transformations: Articulations of power in ethnic and racial studies in the United States*. Atlantic Highlands, NJ: Humanities Press.

Sivanandan, A. (1990). *Communities of resistance: Writings on Black struggles for socialism*. London, England: Verso.

———. (1982). *A different hunger: Writings on Black resistance*. London, England: Pluto Press.

Smith, S. (1989). *The politics of "race" and residence*. Cambridge, England: Polity Press.

Solomos, J. (1989). *Race and racism in contemporary Britain*. London, England: Macmillan.

———. (1988). *Black youth, racism and the state: The politics of ideology and policy*. Cambridge, MA: Cambridge University Press.

Valle, V., and R. Torres. (1994). "Latinos in a 'postindustrial' disorder: Politics in a changing city." *Socialist Review*, 23(4).

Van Djik, T. (1993). *Racism and the press*. London, England: Routledge.

West, C. (1993). *Race matters*. Boston, MA: Beacon.

Williams, F. (1989). *Social policy: A critical introduction*. Cambridge, MA: Polity Press.

Yinger, M. (1994). *Ethnicity: Source of strength? Source of conflict?* Albany, NY: State University of New York Press.

Politics, Policy, and Community

Introduction

Policy issues relating to immigration have become increasingly contentious in recent years as corporate profits soar while large numbers of workers are thrown out of work. The resurgence of nativism, hate groups, and thinly veiled racist rhetoric form the backdrop of recent political referenda and public policy discussion, culminating most dramatically with the triumph of Proposition 187 in the State of California. Lost in the rancorous debate, however, are the historical reference points and empirical studies that describe and analyze the structural problems in the U.S. economy and labor market.

While a slim majority of Asian Americans and Mexican Americans voted in favor of Proposition 187, the attack of restrictionist forces has had the effect of mobilizing these internally diverse communities. Moreover, the mounting campaign against both legal and nonlegal immigration has forced many Asian American and Latino organizations to confront the class divisions, intra-ethnic tensions, and linguistic differences that fragment the respective communities. At this pivotal moment in U.S. history, it remains to be seen whether existing social divisions will be exacerbated by the new immigration or, alternately, whether enlightened social policy can bring about a "common good" shaped from the diversity, difference, and mulitiplicity represented by Asian and Latino groups.

Chapter 13

Abel Valenzuela, Jr.

Compatriots or Competitors?
Job Competition Between Foreign- and U.S.-Born Angelenos

The influx of Latino and Asian immigrants to Southern California has transformed the region's demographic composition; the changing population has redefined the meaning of race relations, particularly as it pertains to labor-market issues facing minority groups. This is a more nuanced and complicated framework, encompassing multiracial and ethnic configurations and new forms of conflicts among minorities, and certainly between majority and minority groups. Economic conflict has become a source of tension among different factions, aiding a conservative backlash against civil rights and a nativist movement bent on stopping immigration. Perhaps the most volatile and contentious factor in this conflict is the notion of job competition among various groups of low-skilled workers, usually between an immigrant and a U.S.-born minority group.

The notion of job displacement of native-born workers by foreigners is one of the most emotionally polarized debates surrounding issues of immigration to the United States. This fear fluctuates with national and regional economic cycles, particularly those of high immigrant population states such as California and New York. Since 1965 the large wave of immigration to this country has been blamed for increases in American urban poverty, particularly to the growth of its urban underclass and the high jobless rate of African-Americans.[1] While the contemporary and popular interest in immigration stems from a growing nativist backlash and rises in ethnic conflict, its perceived contribution to the increasing rates of poverty during the past two decades and effect on the composition and location of the poor are equally compelling.[2,3]

This selection originally appeared in *The New England Journal of Public Policy*, Vol. 11, No. 1. © 1995 by *The New England Journal of Public Policy*. Reprinted by permission.

As research on poverty and the underclass has expanded, studies, and especially policies of immigration, have multiplied.[4] This increased attention is also attributable to the large influx of legal and illegal immigrants during the past two decades.[5] Students of immigration are interested in understanding the causes and consequences of international migration, the assimilation and integration of immigrants into society generally and labor markets in particular, and the possible economic impact that immigrants may have on earnings, employment, and welfare expenditures. These issues are at the forefront of U.S. immigration research because of two other important factors, namely, the composition and geographic location of the "new immigration."[6,7] Because the country-of-origin composition of immigrants has changed from European to Asian and Latin American stock, and immigrants continue to concentrate in urban centers, concern over their economic impact has increased. Congruent with this change is speculation that the skills composition of recent immigrants is lower than that of earlier waves and, as a result, contributes to worsened labor-market opportunities and job competition with other low-skilled immigrants and minorities in inner cities.[8]

Given the increase in urban poverty, the underclass, and immigration during the 1970s and 1980s, two questions emerge: Are these phenomena related to each other? If so, how are they related? More specifically, does the increase in low-skilled immigrants worsen labor-market opportunities for native underclass residents? If opportunities are curtailed and native workers are being displaced by immigrants, is this displacement related to the formation of an urban underclass, and if so, how?

This article analyzes the relationship between the labor-market concentration of Mexican, Latino, and Asian immigrants and the employment opportunities of U.S.-born white, black, and Mexican workers in Los Angeles from 1970 to 1980. I address the question of whether native workers are adversely affected by the industrial and occupational concentration of immigrants and whether this contributes to the emergence of a Latino and black underclass. My study departs from a conventional analysis of immigrant and native-born labor-market competition in that I analyze shifts in industry concentration of immigrants after controlling for the size of competing labor pools and the growth in each industry in a standard metropolitan statistical area (SMSA). Past studies assessing the economic well-being of immigrants and their impact on U.S.-born labor are based on national samples that inadequately examine economic integration processes in regional or local areas. Because immigrants tend disproportionately to settle in certain parts of the country, regional and local impacts are significant in understanding labor-market changes. This study, by focusing on one region, specific industries and occupations, and particular samples of racial and ethnic groups, reveals several dimensions of job competition offering new insights into the labor-market impacts of immigration.

In addition, my study is important to the underclass literature for several reasons. Evidence that immigrants curtail the employment opportunities of U.S.-born workers, particularly U.S.-born Mexicans and such other minority groups as African-Americans, addresses a major issue in the underclass literature: whether job opportunities for African-Americans and other minorities have lessened over the course of the decade as a result of immigration. Minority U.S.-born laborers, particularly African-Americans, have increasingly experienced worsening labor-market opportunities. Black unemployment increased steadily from 9.8 percent in 1974 to 11.4 percent in 1979 to 16.4 percent in 1984. The labor-force participation rate of African-Americans also has shown a steady decline between these years, from 72.9 percent in 1974 to 71.3 percent in 1979, to 70.8 percent, respectively.[9] If immigrant labor can be substituted for U.S.-born labor, immigrants may be reducing the wages of minority and other native labor, increasing American unemployment, and lowering labor-force participation. If, however, evidence suggests that immigrants do not function simply as competitive substitute sources of labor, other explanations for declining job opportunities for domestic labor will be necessary.

Job Competition: Old Question, New Context

Historically, there has always been nativist concern over job competition between immigrants and U.S.-born labor; immigrants were blamed for the country's worsening economies during the 1930s, 1950s, and 1970s. The concern that immigrants are displacing American workers has once again become an extremely volatile topic in California and other states and cities with immigrant concentrations. As U.S. economic fortunes continue to deteriorate and jobs become scarce or shift into part-time or poorly paid service occupations, immigrants become easy prey for shifts in joblessness among U.S.-born workers. The overtones of today's debate, which seems to be driven by emotion, fear, xenophobia, and politics, are strikingly similar to those of the past. A plethora of actors, from California's Governor Pete Wilson to journalists, advocacy groups such as the Federation for American Immigration Reform, and state- and city-sponsored reports, have contributed to this fear.[10] However, the present debate on job competition takes on new overtones because it singles out African-Americans and other native-born minority groups as the primary victims of immigration's "negative costs" in the form of fewer jobs, reduced services, and a lower quality of life.

Theories on the Impacts of Immigration

The debate over the effects of immigration on the U.S. labor market has lasted almost sixty years, since the U.S. Immigration Commission concluded in 1935 that "immigration was responsible for many of the poor working conditions then evident in the United States."[11] Two major theories describe immigrants' participation in and economic effects on the U.S. labor market, commonly known as the displacement and segmentation hypotheses. Paradoxically, they make opposite assumptions about the labor market and hence reach disparate conclusions about the impact of immigrant labor.

In general, the neoclassical displacement hypothesis argues that immigrants arrive in the United States in the face of declining wages. An increased supply of foreign workers, in turn, further pushes domestic wages down by expanding the aggregate supply despite a stable demand for labor. Immigrants displace native-born workers because the former are assumed to be perfect substitutes for the latter and skill differences are ignored.[12]

The segmentation theory, on the other hand, argues that the U.S. labor market is sufficiently divided between immigrant and nonimmigrant jobs to insulate domestic workers from direct displacement effects by migrants.[13] Proponents of this theory argue that immigrants are hired into a low-wage sector of the labor market where few nonimmigrants are employed, owing partly to differences in skill. Native workers, likewise, may be employed in unskilled jobs but are nevertheless protected from job competition because their jobs may be covered by union contracts, an institutional barrier that prevents the employment of immigrant workers. Under this view, immigrant and domestic labor may complement each other in different sectors of the economy.

Related to the segmentation hypothesis is the argument that immigrants take jobs that native workers no longer want; that is, a job ladder, or queue, for immigrant workers exists. Over time, U.S.-born laborers move on to better occupations, vacating "lower-rung" and less desirable jobs that various groups of newcomers then fill. Once hired, immigrants employ social networks to recruit other immigrants and, in this way, certain industries become reserved exclusively for them.[14] Employers also have a queue in which certain groups may be preferred over others. In this instance, immigrants may be valued more than black or other U.S.-born labor, perhaps because the former are perceived as harder working, cheaper, and more docile than the latter. To the extent that such a queue is developing in secondary occupations or peripheral industries in which immigrants and other disadvantaged groups are concentrated, immigrants may work at the expense of black or U.S.-born labor.

Empirical Evidence

The empirical evidence on the market impact of increased immigration on native labor can be divided into three categories: production function models that estimate across national samples of individuals; industrial and occupational sectoral studies that employ large numbers of immigrants; and analyses of labor-market outcomes across regions or SMSAs, which contain a large number of immigrants.

Production Function Models on National Samples

Production function models determine the relationship between the output of goods—wages or employment—and relevant inputs—factors of production such as immigrant labor. Econometric research based on production function models has attempted to estimate the aggregate effect of immigration on natives' wages. Based on the conclusion of several researchers in this field, the aggregate negative effect of increases in the supply of immigrants on the earnings and employment of natives is either small or nonexistent and mostly falls on other recent immigrants.[15]

Borjas, in a series of studies, concludes that immigrants have minimal, if any, adverse impact on the wage rates, earnings, and participation rates of different groups of native workers.[16] For example, he estimates, in one study using multivariate analysis, that male migration increased the earnings of both young and older black males in 1970.[17] A similar estimate for 1980 also provided no statistically significant evidence that black male earnings were reduced either by recent or past immigration. Here, immigrants appear to be complementing the black labor force.

Rivera-Batiz, Sechzer, and Grang, using a translog production function model, argue that, depending on the amount of skills, education, and experience a person commands, a "disturbance in the rates of return to these three inputs will result in a change in wages."[18] Thus, an influx of immigrants affects the native-born by changing the returns to education, experience, and skills. In another study, Borjas argues that immigrants tend to be substitutes for low-skilled native labor and complements for high-skilled natives.[19] Based on labor demand's elasticity and regression analysis, he asserts that any negative effect immigrants may have on natives, if any, is negligible and may at most have a slight impact on earlier immigrants. For example, Borjas asserts that a 10 percent increase in immigration appears to decrease the wages of residents born abroad by between 2 and 9 percent.[20] In a similar study, Stewart and Hyclak, using data for central cities of the largest U.S. SMSAs in 1970, examine the effects of recent immigrants (ten or fewer years) on the relative earnings of black males in comparison with white males.[21] They find some degree of substitutability between black males and recent immigrants from countries other than Mexico, Cuba, and the West Indies. According to this study, if any competition takes place between immigrants and domestic laborers, it occurs only with other minorities or recent immigrants of similar backgrounds.

Bean, Lowell, and Taylor extend Borjas's work to analyze the effects of illegal immigration on the annual earnings of native workers.[22] They show that the undocumented Mexican population has no depressive effect on the annual earnings of black males or females and that legal Mexican immigrants and native Mexicans actually complement blacks in the labor market.

Industrial and Occupational Sectoral Studies

Sectoral studies examine the relationships between immigrant and native workers in particular labor markets rather than throughout the nation as a whole. A few of these studies focus on the impact of immigration on the employment and earnings of natives. Studies that address this issue rely on census data or are based on specific case studies. It is important to review research on specific industrial and occupational labor markets to see if these studies corroborate or negate existing aggregate multivariate analysis on immigration impact, and the case studies reveal factors not captured in multivariate studies. The following is a brief summary of the literature in a few selected industries and occupations in which immigrants are concentrated. Based on this review of the literature, I conclude that the effects of immigration on U.S. workers, specifically in industries and occupations with a large number of immigrants, are varied.

Agriculture is one of the most thoroughly researched industries in sectoral studies of immigration and labor markets, probably because of its historical reliance on cheap labor and its appeal to immigrant labor, legal and illegal. Most of these studies evaluate immigration effects on particular crops and regions. One study concludes that the loss of immigrant workers leads to an increase in crop prices insofar as native labor is unwilling to perform agricultural labor at immigrant wages.[23]

De Frietas and De Frietas and Marshall claim that heavy concentrations of immigrant labor affect the wages of less-skilled workers in manufacturing.[24] They conclude that in industries with concentrations of immigrants exceeding 20 percent, a 1 percent increase in immigration results in about a 1.2 percent decrease in the rate of wage growth. However, this evidence can also be interpreted differently. As immigrants become absorbed or replace workers in the lower-paying occupational sectors, domestic workers move to better-paying industries and occupations. Waldinger, in his study of the garment industry in New York City, argues that "to some extent immigrants may have displaced domestic workers, but [only] to the extent that complementary jobs were available elsewhere."[25] Thomas Bailey's analysis of New York City's restaurant industry provides convincing evidence that immigrant men do not compete with native black workers but may compete with other immigrants, specifically recently arrived women and teenagers.[26] Research on the service industry indicates an increasing concentration of immigrants in a variety of service sector occupations.[27] Based on interviews with more than a thousand Hispanic and black unemployed workers seeking positions through two local Los Angeles service centers of the California Employment Development Department, Maram and King conclude that more than 51 percent of the Hispanics and blacks interviewed would be willing to work for lower wages than those presently being paid in most service-sector occupations.[28] Thus, the authors conclude that the downward pressure exerted by immigrants on the wages of current legal workers has caused some job displacement.

Most industry studies on the impact of immigration are largely based on a qualitative approach with some limited quantitative analysis. Those most affected by immigrants seem to be earlier immigrant cohorts or low-skilled native workers employed in occupations and industries with high concentrations of women, teenagers, and minorities. But these sectoral studies lack the explicit connection to other sectors in the economy and cannot be taken as conclusive evidence regarding the impact of immigration on native workers. Native workers may in some instances be moving to better-paying jobs, as suggested by Waldinger and Maram and King.[29]

The effects of immigration on specific industries and occupations seem to vary. They depend on the size of the firm and its vitality, the type and market area of the industry, and the skills and other characteristics of the immigrants. A large firm that employs many workers in an area with a large surplus of immigrant laborers could easily exert downward wage pressures because immigrants would be willing to work for less pay than natives. Likewise, a growing industry with strong internal labor markets and a union presence would insulate native-born labor from any wage or employment downswing as a result of increased immigration.

Regional and Metropolitan Studies

Regional and metropolitan studies focus on the local distribution of immigrants and their aggregate effects on their location patterns, regional labor forces, and "immigrant cities" such as Los Angeles and New York. These studies of immigration and its economic impact fall into two broad categories: regional, which usually looks at four major U.S. geographical areas—Northeast, North Central, South, and West—and metropolitan, which examines several "immigrant" cities and their metropolitan areas—New York, Los Angeles, Miami, Houston, and Chicago.

It is important to review this research because of immigration's uneven regional distri-bution and differences in economic development. Immigrants' uneven distribution prob-ably means that their regional economic effects will also vary. Morever, their distribution may be influenced by patterns of regional economic development. For example, it is no coincidence that the growth of immigration to Los Angeles during 1970 and 1980 occurred during a time when the city was experiencing manufacturing growth. In addi-tion, the geographic distribution of the foreign-born is shifting toward the Sunbelt and the West, areas that also have sustained economic growth.

Data about the regional distribution and characteristics of immigration provide a recent, yet preliminary, picture of immigrants in labor markets. Immigrants contribute to regional labor forces differently. For example, 20 percent of the West's overall labor-force growth between 1970 and 1980 came through immigration. This pattern differs from the Northeast (13%), the South (9%), and the North Central region (4%). Immigrants' labor-force characteristics, such as occupational concentration, human capital character-istics, labor-force participation, and earnings, also differ significantly by region. For example, Lowell, using census data for 1970 and 1980 by region, shows how Mexican-origin migrants tend to have lower human capital characteristics—education, skills, job experience —than other foreign-born persons, particularly Asians, in the West.[30] Lowell also shows that time of arrival is correlated with human capital character-istics and variations in occupational concentration and earnings.[31] For example, half of all immigrants in the West arrived since 1970, meaning that they, on average, have fewer years in the labor market than the native born. Immigrants in the West are also younger, less likely to complete high school, and less apt to speak English than the native-born.[32] But what do these differences signify in regard to a regional economic impact on native wages and employment?

New York City, the gateway for many of our nation's immigrants, is a rich source of research on the roles of immigrants in metropolitan labor markets. Some of the major works on New York include Waldinger and Lapp, Bailey and Waldinger, and Sassen, Waldinger, and Bailey.[33] They provide an assortment of data that for the most part focuses on immigrant economic mobility as a result of industrial restructuring rather than on the specific impact of immigrants on native workers' job opportunities. Immigra-tion research on Chicago, as on New York, has for the most part addressed the issue of group mobility and industrial restructuring.[34] Studies on Miami focus on the Cuban enclave as an example of largely self-contained social and economic environments that provide for successful mobility patterns and labor market integration.[35] Research on Los Angeles suggests that immigrants have a negative effect on wages in selected low-skill industries.[36] This effect is primarily concentrated on Hispanic recent arrivals with simi-lar education, skills, age, sex, and ethnic-origin characteristics.[37]

Two broad conclusions emerge from regional and metropolitan studies: the economic effects of immigration on natives, regionally, are small, and metropolitan studies suggest that some level of displacement occurs in several low-skill occupations and between ear-lier and later immigrant groups that share similar human-capital and job qualifications.

When analyzed separately or as a whole, production function models, sectoral, and regional and metropolitan studies provide us with some answers as to the overall economic impact immigrants have on native earnings and employment. It is generally not adverse, though immigration may result in slight wage depression and displacement for some groups of workers.[38] Immigrants also expand employment opportunities for complementary workers.[39]

The displacement and segmentation hypotheses propose an either-or situation that does not correspond to available empirical evidence. The issue then becomes: Under what circumstances does displacement occur, and under what circumstances does it not? The key to further specifying immigrant impact on natives is to document in greater detail which groups of workers and industries and occupations are affected. A more thorough analysis of the economic impacts of increased immigration depends on numerous factors, including the following: the size and composition of the domestic labor supply; the education, experience, and other human capital characteristics of immigrants; the growth or decline of the firm or industrial segment in which immigrants are employed; the race, ethnicity, and gender of immigrants; the regional and metropolitan location of the industrial segment; and the protected or unprotected nature of the labor markets in which immigrants work. The impact of immigrants on the domestic labor force is largely mediated by regional, occupational, and industrial change. A more complete examination must incorporate the changing occupational and industrial structure into labor-market analysis.

RESEARCH METHOD

In undertaking this study I compiled data on Los Angeles showing the extent of immigrant and native concentration in industrial and occupational labor markets. To test for actual competition between groups of workers, I adapted Waldinger's shift-share model and applied it to industries and occupations categorized according to three different typologies or tests, which are explained below.[40] Using shift-share allows me to test factors contributing to industrial and occupational employment changes between two time periods.

Waldinger first applied this method to measuring employment differentials between several racial and ethnic immigrant and U.S.-born groups in New York during 1970 and 1980.[41] He found that the composition of the work force is a crucial factor in the occupational position of nonwhites, and changes in the size of the white population set the stage for an upward realignment of nonwhite workers. New York's economic shift from goods to services was primarily responsible for the decline in the availability of white workers who left for better-paying jobs in outlying areas, which in turn created a replacement demand for nonwhite workers; that is, a process of job succession or "musical chairs," in which immigrants replace departing white labor, took place in New York during the 1970s.[42] Waldinger concludes by suggesting that the impact of compositional change was blunted by a trend toward ethnic competition, as reflected in a declining employment total and share for U.S.-born blacks.

Waldinger's study analyzed only eleven major industrial categories.[43] Such a broad, aggregated study may mask important differences in the employment of immigrant and U.S.-born workers in industries and occupations that are not aggregated or analyzed as one regional economy. Thus, my research expands on Waldinger's by disaggregating industrial categories according to whether they are at the core or periphery and are experiencing growth or decline. In addition, I apply this method to occupations organized according to fifteen broad categories and four occupational segments—for example, independent primary, craft, subordinate primary, and secondary.[44]

Shift-share allows me to analyze for any given region whether the number of immigrants, when compared with other groups in the same labor markets, grew or declined over time in industrial and occupational concentration as a result of changes in the relative size of the labor supply of different ethnic groups; changes in the size of an industry or occupation—industry/occupation effect; and changes in a group's employment in an industry or occupation net of group size and industry/occupation effect. This last variable reflects the extent to which a group in concentrating or "deconcentrating" in a specific labor market.[45] Adding group size and industry/occupation change reveals whether the two factors undercut or reinforce the trends to concentrate or deconcentrate in a particular industry or occupation.

A positive figure in share represents an increasing group share of all industries/occupations in a particular sector. For example, if a particular immigrant group in an industry or occupation shows a positive total group share, it is being employed in that sector at rates higher than those at which it is entering other sectors and is thus becoming more concentrated in that sector. A negative share signifies the opposite; that is, a particular group is entering that sector at rates lower than those at which it is entering other sectors and is becoming less concentrated or deconcentrated.[46]

Job Competition

This research is primarily concerned with the displacement of U.S.-born workers in industries and occupations owing to an increase in the supply of immigrant labor. More specifically, I assess the employment shares of three native groups—whites, African-Americans, and Mexicans—to see how they respond to changes in the employment share of three immigrant groups—Mexicans, Latinos, and Asians.[47] After I analyzed the results of the model, five possible job competition patterns emerged. These patterns distinguish between various job competition scenarios that are not easily identifiable or clear-cut when analyzed only as raw shift-share results, that is, absolute figures. Therefore, each native group in every industrial and occupational category is analyzed and coded with one of these five possible patterns to correspond to the model results as follows:

- Complete Displacement (CD) takes place when all native groups lose jobs while all immigrant groups gain.

- Displacement (D) occurs when some native groups and some immigrant groups lose jobs in the same industry during the same time period. Because both native and immigrant groups are losing jobs, I attribute this pattern to factors other than immigration, such as industrial restructuring.

- Partial Displacement (PD) happens when one or two native groups lose jobs while one or two immigrant groups gain. In this pattern, particular attention is paid to the native Mexican group, because it is a closer substitute for the immigrant groups analyzed here and consequently may be especially vulnerable to displacement.

- Complete Complementarity (CC) occurs when native groups gain jobs simultaneously with all three immigrant groups' gains. The gain in native and immigrant jobs is a factor not only of increase in immigration but also of industrial growth, a robust economy, and other structural factors.

- Native Complementarity (NC) takes place when native groups gain jobs while immigrant groups lose.

RESEARCH DATA

Recent immigrants comprise a small proportion of the U.S. population at any given time. The data set I utilized had to be large enough to include the different subpopulations by race, ethnicity, and gender among native-born and foreign-born Angelenos. In addition, the data set had to be comparable between two time periods, 1970 and 1980, to assess shifts in the labor market resulting from immigration. The best data for this task are the Public Use Sample (PUS) of the 1970 census and the Public Use Microdata Sample (PUMS) of the 1980 census. These data are large stratified samples of housing units enumerated in the U.S. census; they contain sociodemographic information on housing units—household records—and each person residing within them—person records. Specifically, I gathered my data from the 1 percent sample of the PUS from the 1970 census and the 5 percent sample of the PUMS from the 1980 census. The 1990 PUMS decennial census was not available at the start of this study at the necessary disaggregated level.[48]

FINDINGS

Industrial Repositioning (Test 1)

As Table 13.1 shows, between 1970 and 1980 total employment for Los Angeles grew by more than 349,960 jobs, a 9 percent increase. A large portion of this increase came from the growth of the health, education, finance, insurance and real estate, and business industries, which together accounted for more than two-thirds of the total growth rate. There was also substantial growth in the restaurant, apparel, high-technology, transportation, and public administration industries. However, Los Angeles also experienced major losses in several industries, for example, personal services, miscellaneous manufacturing, air and ordinance, and specialty retail stores.

The core and periphery for this region grew at 13 percent and 2 percent, respectively. In the periphery, major losses were experienced by the miscellaneous manufacturing, utilities and sanitation, specialty retail, personal service, and domestic service industries. However, these losses were offset by large increases in the business, entertainment and recreation, apparel, and eating and drinking establishment industries. When the total industrial population is divided according to nativity, an interesting trend emerges. Immigrants show no losses in their industrial employment in the periphery and two insignificant losses in the core, in tobacco manufacturing and in rail service. Indeed, in those industries which experienced losses, they were felt almost exclusively by the U.S.-born laborer.

TABLE 13.1 Industrial Change by Core and Periphery, Los Angeles, 1970–1980

	1970	1980	Change	%Chg.
Core Industries	2,319,400	2,632,180	312,780	0.13
Periphery Industries	1,629,500	1,666,680	37,180	0.02
Total Employment	3,948,900	4,298,860	349,960	0.09
Immigrants				
Core Industries	279,500	543,980	264,480	
Periphery Industries	256,000	488,640	232,640	
Total Employment	535,500	1,032,620	497,120	
U.S. Born				
Core Industries	2,039,900	2,088,200	48,300	
Periphery Industries	1,373,500	1,178,040	-195,460	
Total Employment	3,413,400	3,266,240	-147,160	

Sources: U.S. Bureau of the Census, 1970; and 1980 Public Use Microdata Samples.

When I further divided industrial data by race and ethnicity for 1970 and 1980, whites were the primary losers in both the core and periphery.[49] Blacks also suffered job losses in several industries in the core and periphery but in much fewer numbers and as a lower percentage of total loss per industry. Latinos and Asians, on the other hand, showed large job gains.

Table 13.2 organizes the population according to five racial and ethnic groups and shows the number of industrial jobs per sector held by each group in Los Angeles in 1970 and 1980. Its fourth column shows the number of jobs each group would have gained had its gains been proportional to the growth in the overall Los Angeles economy during this period, when industrial employment grew by 9 percent, from 3,948,900 jobs in 1970 to 4,298,860 in 1980. Table 13.2 then indicates how many jobs the group actually gained or lost and the difference between expected and actual employment losses.

This table allows us to glimpse the different dynamics affecting the process of job change in Los Angeles during 1970 and 1980. Here we can see that the biggest losers of jobs were whites, losing close to 400,000 jobs in the core and peripheral industries. However, this loss is offset by the large job gain experienced by nonwhite groups, both native- and foreign-born, in both sectors, providing Los Angeles with an overall job growth rate of 9 percent. What accounts for the white job loss and the nonwhite job gain? Is job competition, in the form of displacement between immigrants and nonimmigrants or between whites and nonwhites, partly to blame for mostly white and some black loss? In the following section I attempt to answer these questions.

To assess the impact of industrial and occupational compositional change, I used shift-share analysis, classifying all 46 industries to dual labor-market theory (see note 44) as are listed according to Tolbert, Horan, and Beck's typology.[50] I extend the authors' matrix and further classify the industries according to those which grew and declined between 1970 and 1980 per sector. In Los Angeles' core sector, 18 industries grew and 9 declined, while in its periphery, 11 grew and 8 declined. These two patterns alone show

Politics, Policy, and Community

TABLE 13.2 Changes in Industrial Employment for Selected Ethnic Groups,
Los Angeles, 1970–1980

Groups in Core Industries	1970	1980	Employment Expected	Actual	Job Change Actual Expected	Act-E/ 1970 Emp.
NB White	1,615,200	1,452,280	209,976	-162,920	-372,896	-23.09%
NB Black	205,400	316,860	26,702	111,460	84,758	41.26%
NB Mexican	141,700	200,320	18,421	58,620	40,199	28.37%
FB Mexican	64,500	188,640	8,385	124,140	115,755	179.47%
FB Latino	32,000	71,100	4,160	39,100	34,940	109.19%
FB Asian	19,500	103,420	2,535	83,920	81,385	417.36%
Groups in Periphery Industries						
NB White	1,060,500	840,160	21,210	-220,340	-241,550	-22.78%
NB Black	156,600	147,180	3,132	-9,420	-12,552	-8.02%
NB Mexican	99,300	114,660	1,986	15,360	13,374	13.47%
FB Mexican	74,400	210,620	1,488	136,220	134,732	181.09%
FB Latino	30,600	74,640	612	44,040	43,428	141.92%
FB Asian	22,200	70,880	444	48,680	48,236	217.28%

Sources: My estimates are based on data from the U.S. Census Bureau's 1970 PUS (1%) and 1980 PUMS (5%, sample) files.

Note: NB = native-born, FB = foreign-born.

that during the 1970s, Los Angeles' economy, especially in the core sector, was quite robust in terms of industrial change.

The share results show several combinations of both native and immigrant losses and gains in industrial employment. These reflect different instances of displacement and complementarity that, in part, are attributable to immigrant growth and other factors such as industrial restructuring, the general economic climate, and other variables not tested in this model. To make better sense of the share results and their implication for job competition, I coded different immigrant employment-share patterns that assist in identifying industries in which job competition possibly is occurring between immigrant and native-born workers. I coded the patterns for each industry which, unfortunately, provides few recognizable patterns with which to analyze job competition. To ameliorate this problem, I created summary Tables 13.3 and 13.4 showing job competition patterns according to industrial change—growth and decline—for the three native-born groups at issue.

DOES COMPETITION EXIST?

Table 13.3 provides a general summary of job competition patterns for the three native-born groups in the core and peripheral sectors in Los Angeles. The data in the two

TABLE 13.3 Immigrant Job Competition Patterns for Los Angeles Native Workers

Pattern	Whites No. Indust.	Whites % of Total	Blacks No. Indust.	Blacks % of Total	Mexicans No. Indust.	Mexicans % of Total
Complete Displacement	7	0.15	3	0.07	6	0.13
Partial Displacement	16	0.35	12	0.26	10	0.22
Overall Displacement	23	0.50	15	0.33	16	0.35
Displacement Owing to Other Factors	5	0.11	6	0.13	7	0.15
Complete Complementarity	2	0.04	6	0.13	8	0.17
Complementarity Owing to Immigration	16	0.35	19	0.41	15	0.33
Overall Complementarity	18	0.39	25	0.54	23	0.50
Total	46	1.00	46	1.00	46	1.00

Source: My estimates are based on data from the U.S. Census Bureau's 1970 PUS (1%) and 1980 (5%) files.

Note: Totals do not include overall displacement and overall complementarity.

columns for each of these groups indicate the number of industries that fall into each job competition pattern. The first column provides the actual number of industries that fall under one of the five patterns, and the second column provides the percentage total of this figure.

The data in this table indicate that, indeed, both job displacement and complementarity exist in Los Angeles. However, more industries show complementarity rather than displacement for blacks and Mexicans, the two groups most vulnerable to job competition with immigrants because of their substitutability. Combining complete displacement with partial displacement yields an overall displacement trend, and combining complete complementarity and complementarity owing to immigrant job loss produces an overall complementarity trend.[51] Comparing the job competition trends of overall displacement with overall complementarity shows that immigrants complement native-born groups in much larger proportions than they displace them.[52]

Of particular note in Table 13.3 is pattern 5, which shows the number of industries in which immigrant groups were displaced by native-born workers. This finding suggests that, just as native-born workers are displaced as a result of increased immigration, immigrants are displaced in particular industries as a result of native-born employment gains. As the regional labor market fluctuates through cycles of growth and decline, different groups compete for different jobs, but displacement can harm either immigrants or the native-born.

DOES INDUSTRIAL CHANGE MATTER?

The second inquiry of this section is whether industrial change—growth or decline—matters in stimulating or thwarting job competition. Table 13.4 lists the number of industries for each sector in which native-born workers were displaced or complemented by the employment of immigrants; it also separates the displacement and complementarity categories based on whether the industries grew or declined during the 1970s.[53] Industrial growth or decline may influence whether job displacement or complementarity occurs in an industry. In declining industries, displacement is more likely than in a robust growing industry.

In Los Angeles, more industries in the core grew—18 of 27—than declined, and complementarity was more likely to occur in those industries which grew than in those which declined. However, no clear patterns emerged to show that job displacement was more prevalent in the declining industries and complementarity was concentrated in the growth industries. This finding suggests that both instances of immigrant displacement and complementarity occur, regardless of whether an industry is declining or growing. Industrial change makes no difference in patterns of job competition caused by increased immigration.

In general, this first test shows data to be inconclusive for blacks and Mexicans; that is, I cannot conclude one way or the other that immigrants systematically displace or complement black and Mexican workers in Los Angeles. Test 1 does not signify that increases in immigration lead to the displacement of native-born labor. In fact, the only group that experienced instances of displacement was the white population. However, such displacement was concentrated only in the core. This finding is important because it suggests that (1) displacement may be occurring in high-skill as opposed to low-skill industries, contrary to what is usually argued, and (2) immigrants may be preferred over or be close substitutes for whites in high-skill industries. In either case, job displacement in industries is not occurring between immigrant and minority workers in Los Angeles.

Furthermore, the following findings suggest a higher incidence of complementarity to the native-born as a result of increased industrial employment of immigrants:

- Blacks and Mexicans had more industries (54% and 50%, respectively) with instances of complementarity than whites (39%).
- Whites, blacks, and Mexicans gained in employment share in several industries, while immigrants lost in those same industries, suggesting that immigrants may be losing in their industrial employment share as a result of native gain.
- Instances of immigrant displacement and complementarity occur regardless of whether an industry is declining or growing. Industrial change makes no difference in stratifying complementary or displacement effects of increased immigration.

OCCUPATIONAL REPOSITIONING

The foregoing data indicate the extent of immigrant and native access to various sectors of the economy, but they say little about the levels at which these workers are employed. Here, I examine occupational repositioning for the same ethnic groups. I employ two

TABLE 13.4 Effect of Immigrant Job Competition Patterns on Los Angeles Industries

Growth/Decline Patterns	Number of Industries Affected	Number of Industries Affected	Number of Industries Affected
CORE INDUSTRIES			
Displacement			
Growth	12	8	9
Decline	4	5	5
Total	*16*	*13*	*14*
Complementarity			
Growth	6	10	9
Decline	5	4	4
Total	*11*	*14*	*13*
PERIPHERY INDUSTRIES			
Displacement			
Growth	10	5	6
Decline	2	3	3
Total	*12*	*8*	*9*
Complementarity			
Growth	1	6	5
Decline	6	5	5
Total	*7*	*11*	*10*

Source: My estimates are based on data from the U.S. Census Bureau's PUS (1%) and 1980 PUMS (5%) files.

tests that correspond to two occupational typologies according to fifteen categories and four segments. I have chosen to look at fifteen census-defined broad categories divided between growth and decline to assess, as in the previous test, whether occupational change—growth and decline—makes a difference in stratifying occurrences of job competition. The latter test divides all the census-defined occupations into four broad categories—independent primary, craft, subordinate primary, and secondary (see note 44 for a description of job characteristics for each of these categories). The test's primary purpose is to measure whether institutional barriers such as unions or credential (certificate) jobs make a difference in stratifying instances of job competition.

Between 1970 and 1980, the Los Angeles economy, like the national economy, shifted from producing goods to services, resulting in expanded white-collar and service occupations. Los Angeles showed a net growth of 350,000 jobs concentrated in the managerial, sales, goods-producing, and service occupations.

Table 13.5 provides data on the number of jobs per occupation for the total populations and by nativity. Immigrants gained in employment share in every occupation. Their largest gains were concentrated in the semiskilled, craft, and clerical occupations, which coincidentally also had the largest employment losses for the native-born population. Almost half a million immigrants gained in occupational employment while natives lost more than 145,000 jobs.

An alternative method to classify occupations is by segmentation analysis.[54] The lower portion of Table 13.5 provides data on the number of jobs per occupational segment for the total population and by nativity. As the data for the four occupational segments show, the largest employer in 1970 was the subordinate primary, followed by the secondary, independent primary, and craft. This order changed in 1980, when the independent primary became the second largest employer. During the 1970s, occupations that are characterized in the subordinate primary declined by 2 percent. When disaggregated by nativity, the data show that native workers experienced the largest loss of jobs in the subordinate primary, secondary, and craft occupations. However, these losses were offset by the large growth of immigrant employment in each of the four segments.

Similar to industries in Los Angeles, occupational growth was concentrated among the immigrant and minority populations, while whites and the natives showed a loss. What can shift-share methodology tell us about the occupational employment change for these population groups? Is competition a factor in white and native occupational job loss? In the following section I attempt to answer these two questions.

Shift-Share Model, Fifteen Categories (Test 2)

Data for changes in occupational employment for the total population in Los Angeles and for each ethnic group show that U.S.-born whites suffered significant job loss in Los Angeles while the other racial and ethnic groups offset that loss by phenomenal growth. These latter groups exceeded the expected job growth rate, in some cases by over 2,000 percent![55] These data reveal a different set of dynamics affecting the process of job change and concentration. As the Los Angeles economy grew, it absorbed large numbers of immigrants, mostly in the services and some white-collar jobs. White employment declined for the same reasons cited in an earlier study of New York City by Waldinger: the decline in white employment there was caused primarily by the older age, higher death rate, lower birth rate, and greater outmigration to the suburbs or other regions of the United States of whites in comparison with nonwhites.[56] In addition, Waldinger notes that a large cohort of European immigrants who arrived between 1900 and 1915 reached retirement age during the 1970s.[57] I address the extent and type of occupational job competition.

After I implemented the shift-share model on the fifteen occupational categories, several combinations of occupational gains and losses appeared for native and immigrant workers. For example, both natives and immigrants gained in employment share in the managerial and administration occupations but showed losses in the semiskilled occupations. As with the analysis of industrial repositioning, these gains and losses reflect different instances of native displacement and complementary that can partially be attributed to immigrant employment-share gain. Other factors such as occupational change, each region's general economic climate, and other variables not tested in this model can also affect both native and immigrant job loss in an occupation.

In Los Angeles, the occupations that suffered the severest decline in providing employment also produced the largest job losses for immigrants and natives. For example, semi-

TABLE 13.5 Occupational Change in Los Angeles, 1970–1980 by Total Employment, Nativity, and Segments (in thousands)

| Occupations | Total Employment | | | | Nativity | | | | | |
| | | | | | Immigrant | | | U.S. Born | | |
	1970	1980	Chg.	% Chg.	1970	1980	Chg.	1970	1980	Chg.
Management & administration	308	460	152	.49	37	79	42	271	380	109
Professional	604	646	42	.07	66	106	40	537	539	2
Sales	322	449	127	.40	37	78	41	284	370	86
Clerical	883	850	-33	-.04	86	136	50	796	713	-83
Craft	456	502	46	.10	68	143	75	388	359	29
Semiskilled	557	437	-120	-.22	128	216	88	428	220	-208
Transport	108	120	12	.12	9	20	11	98	99	1
Laborers	162	221	59	.36	24	71	47	137	149	12
Household service	59	36	-23	-.38	10	19	9	48	17	-31
Protective service	39	55	16	.39	1	4	3	37	50	13
Food & food preparation	175	195	20	.11	28	63	35	147	131	-16
Health service	55	71	16	.30	5	16	11	49	55	6
Janitorial service	85	109	24	.29	12	36	24	72	73	1
Personal service	114	89	-25	-.22	11	18	7	102	71	-1
Farm, forestry, fisheries	17	53	36	2.10	5	20	15	12	32	20
Total	3,944	4,293	349	0.09	527	1,025	498	3,406	3,258	-148

OCCUPATIONAL SEGMENTS

	1970	1980	Chg.	% Chg.	1970	1980	Chg.	1970	1980	Chg.
Independent	858	1,132	274	.32	93	193	100	765	938	173
Primary Craft	356	393	37	.10	54	107	53	301	285	-16
Subordinate										
Primary	1,688	1,658	-030	-.02	211	354	143	1,477	1,304	-173
Secondary	1,044	1,114	070	.07	175	376	201	869	0737	-132
Total	3,946	4,297	351	.09	533	1,030	497	3,412	3,264	-148

Source: U.S. Bureau of the Census, 1970 and 1980 Public Use Microdata Samples.

skilled occupations experienced the largest job loss—close to 120,000 jobs. Both immigrant and native employment shares in this occupation were negative and large, suggesting that job losses are attributable to factors other than job competition between immigrants and native-born workers. As Table 13.6 shows, the white population experienced partial displacement in more occupations than the black or Mexican popula-

TABLE 13.6 Effect of Immigrant Competition Patterns on Los Angeles Occupations

	Number of Occupations		
Patterns	*Whites*	*Blacks*	*Mexicans*
Complete Displacement	2	2	1
Partial Displacement	7	3	2
Overall Displacement	*9*	*5*	*3*
Displacement Owing to Other Factors	2	1	2
Complete Complementarity	1	4	5
Native Complementarity Owing to Immigration	3	5	5
Overall Complementarity	*4*	*9*	*10*
Total	15	15	15

Sources: My estimates are based on data from the U.S. Census Bureau's 1970 PUS (1%) and 1980 PUMS (5%) files.

Note: Totals do not include overall displacement or overall complementarity.

tion. This table then aggregates these patterns into two simple categories of either displacement or complementary.[58] Los Angeles displayed more instances of complementarity than displacement for its black and Mexican populations; its white population, however, experienced more displacement than complementarity. Most whites in most occupations were partially, not completely, displaced, suggesting that the aggregated overall displacement subcategory is not as fraught with native displacement as its title implies. In general, Los Angeles immigrants complement natives in occupations more than they displace them, and displacement, when it occurs, is typically partial.

Shift-Share Model, Four Segments (Test 3)

My final analysis assesses the shift-share model results of four occupational categories derived from segmentation theory. Data on changes in occupational segment employment for selected racial and ethnic groups provide a glimpse of the changing employment composition for each group. The data show that whites were the primary losers of jobs in the craft, subordinate primary, and secondary segments. However, they gained by more than 81,000 jobs in the independent primary segment, suggesting that some of their losses in the other segments may have been the result of their upward mobility into this segment.

Table 13.7 presents the shift-share model results for each racial and ethnic group by occupational segment. These data measure the employment-share gain or loss for each group and provide some insights into the different job competition patterns described earlier. On the basis of the shift-share results on the occupational segments, whites were

TABLE 13.7 Occupational Segment Shift-Share Model Results for Selected Ethnic Groups, Los Angeles, 1970–1980

	Employment			Change Owing to				
	1970	1980	Change	Industry Change	Inter-active Effect	Group Size	Share	Job Com. Patt.
Groups in Independent Primary								
NB White	675,900	756,940	81,040	216,288	81,108	135,180	-68	PD
NB Black	39,500	85,220	45,720	12,640	45,425	32,785	295	CC
NB Mexican	24,300	49,180	24,880	7,776	24,786	17,010	94	CC
FB Mexican	6,200	30,140	23,940	1,984	23,932	21,948	08	
FB Latino	6,200	20,000	13,800	1,984	13,764	11,780	36	
FB Asian	8,600	49,180	40,580	2,752	40,506	37,754	74	
Groups in Craft								
NB White	241,600	204,260	-37,340	24,160	-24,160	-48,320	-13,180	PD
NB Black	26,600	33,580	6,980	2,660	6,916	4,256	64	CC
NB Mexican	21,700	30,480	8,780	2,170	8,680	6,510	100	CC
FB Mexican	12,900	43,920	31,020	1,290	30,960	29,670	60	
FB Latino	7,800	15,600	7,800	780	7,800	7,020	0	
FB Asian	3,700	15,020	11,320	370	11,285	10,915	35	
Groups in Subordinate Primary								
NB White	1,173,400	900,700	-272,700	-23,468	-246,414	-2,818		PD
NB Black	145,950	196,790	50,840	-2,919	49,623	52,542	1,217	CC
NB Mexican	101,100	125,920	24,820	-2,022	25,275	27,297	455	CD
FB Mexican	45,900	118,830	72,930	-918	72,522	73,440	408	
FB Latino	25,150	48,440	23,290	-503	23,138	23,641	152	
FB Asian	16,200	69,510	53,310	-324	53,298	53,622	12	
Groups in Secondary								
NB White	584,800	430,540	-154,260	40,936	-152,048	-192,984	-2,212	PD
NB Black	149,950	148,450	-1,500	10,497	-1,500	-11,997	-1	CC
NB Mexican	93,900	109,400	15,500	6,573	15,024	8,451	476	CC
FB Mexican	73,900	206,370	132,470	6,173	130,803	125,630	1,667	
FB Latino	23,450	61,700	38,250	1,642	38,224	36,583	27	
FB Asian	13,200	40,590	27,390	924	27,324	26,400	66	

Sources: My estimates are based on data from the U.S. Census Bureau's 1970 PUS (1%) and 1980 PUMS (5%) files.
Notes: To maintain consistency with the study emphasis on the native-born labor force, the Job Competition Pattern column provides data only for the native-born group of each segment.
NB = native-born; FB = foreign-born.

the only group that experienced instances of displacement as a result of increased immigrant employment share. Both native-born blacks and Mexicans complemented the presence of immigrants in each of the four segments, except for Mexicans in the subordinate primary segment. The subordinate primary sector was the only one that experienced a loss of jobs between 1970 and 1980, making it more vulnerable than the other segments to instances of job competition.

The job competition patterns for the occupational segments show overwhelmingly that immigrants played a minimal role in the displacement of native-born groups in each of the four segments. While whites did lose in each segment, these losses could very well be the result of their upward mobility into the independent primary segment, a situation suggested by the data results of the shift-share model. The nonwhite native groups gained in employment share, suggesting that immigrants do not displace them but rather complement their employment.

In general, the data indicate that blacks and Mexicans were complemented by increases in immigration in growing occupations. However, no discernible impact could be found on whites, blacks, and Mexicans in the occupations that declined—that is, even in a declining labor market, Los Angeles immigrants were not responsible for black, white, and Mexican job loss. Thus, Test 2 shows that increases in the occupational employment of immigrants do not lead to displacement of native-born labor. In fact, this situation arose only for whites in the growth occupations.

Test of this study focused on all the census-defined occupations classified into four segments. Data show that blacks and native-born Mexicans in the three primary and in the secondary segment were complemented by the presence of immigrants; that is, minority workers, with the exception of Mexicans in the subordinate primary segment, did not lose jobs in the four labor-market segments as a result of increased immigrant employment. The data also suggest that whites were partially displaced in every segment. Thus, to the extent that displacement between immigrants and natives is occurring in Los Angeles, it is primarily relegated to native-born whites and, to a lesser extent, Mexicans, but only in the subordinate primary. This finding is consistent with earlier data that showed whites to be the primary victims of occupational-segment job loss between 1970 and 1980.

POLICY IMPLICATIONS

After carefully summarizing the main findings and discussing the hypotheses for each of the three tests, I conclude that the segmentation/queuing theory best describes what is occurring in Los Angeles's labor markets. While the results of this study are complex and many, several major findings are evident. One is that, overall, immigrants are not displacing native-born labor in disproportionate numbers. Instances are found, however, of sporadic or isolated job displacement between immigrants and native-born whites and Mexicans in some occupations and industries. However, the data show that complementarity is more frequent than displacement and that the white labor force has decreased significantly owing to factors other than immigration. These two findings taken together suggest a process of queuing, whereby whites vacate jobs that are filled by immigrant and minority labor. These findings suggest that immigrants do not contribute to or perpetuate an urban underclass.

The concern over the effects that immigration may have on the employment of natives, particularly other Latinos and blacks, was of primary interest in this study. The job competition question, as argued in the underclass debate, postulates that low-skilled Latino immigrants may be a closer substitute for low-skilled U.S.-born Latinos and blacks than for other U.S.-born groups such as women, teenagers, and whites. As a result, competition in specific labor markets between immigrants and minority groups may result in the displacement of low-skilled U.S.-born Latinos and blacks, thus contributing to their already higher-than-average rates of unemployment. This formulation, however, fails to capture the structural attributes and changes that have occurred in the secondary and primary labor markets and their growth or decline.

Immigration, especially during economic boom periods, is often seen as a positive economic stimulus. Increased inflows of immigrants during boom and bust times can be complementary units of production to other nonimmigrant groups, as this research has shown. As immigration increases, the employment opportunities of U.S.-born workers also improve because of the rising demand for complementary workers and the increased demand for goods and services. That the entry of immigrants into local labor markets has a negligible and, at worst, mixed effect on U.S.-born workers' employment prospects is echoed by several prominent immigration scholars.[59]

Los Angeles Latino immigrants may serve as substitutes for some low-skilled groups and as complements to other workers. What accounts for some of the sporadic displacement evident in some of the occupations and industries in Los Angeles? It may be that employers prefer immigrant or other types of workers over black and white workers. Indeed, Kirshenman and Neckerman, Kirshenman, and Neckerman show that employers regard black workers, especially males, as more devious, argumentative, intimidating, and uncooperative than women or immigrants.[60] Employers may be relocating to suburban areas, thus relying on informal recruiting and transportation systems that exclude black workers from employment. Another good possibility is that employers may be excluding blacks and whites from jobs in particular industries because they prefer to hire recent immigrants who are more vulnerable to employer exploitation and not apt to complain. Because the data in this research suggest that an ethnic succession or job-queuing process is taking place in Los Angeles, I believe that employers may selectively choose immigrants over white and some black workers for labor markets in which their skills are tangible. Because these markets are rare, immigration is not a major contributor to a black and Latino underclass.

The immigration debate in California and other high immigrant-receiving states has mostly focused on the immigrant impact on labor supply rather than on structural problems in the U.S. economy and labor market. The primary concern in this debate is the cost associated with providing education, health care, welfare services, and employment to a burgeoning immigrant population, both legal and undocumented. As a result, policies that deny immigrants a public education, a driver's license, or even citizenship status for their children have been proposed to curb their flow. These solutions are shortsighted at best, because they do not address the fundamental reason why immigrants come to this country: to work and make better lives for themselves, not to become dependents of a state.

The misguided Band-Aid policies being debated in California's capitol, rather than stymieing the movement of immigrants into this country, will have the unintended effect of further marginalizing a major portion of the population. The net effect of not providing education and health care to thousands of school-age children and adults will be an uneducated, unhealthy, and unemployed populace that will, in the long run, cost dearly. Public policies should instead focus on structural solutions, such as maintaining and expanding our industrial job base and increasing employment and training programs. Additionally, policy analysts and social scientists need to further analyze the magnitude of and relationship between immigrant and native labor markets.

Present industrial policy or lack thereof serves as a magnet for cheap immigrant labor. The continued demand for cheap labor not only attracts immigrant labor, legal or otherwise, but also serves as a catalyst for poor labor-market conditions that in turn are more conducive to job competition between immigrants and other marginalized workers. The same industries demanding cheap or immigrant labor also have the largest number of workplace hazards, low wages and few benefits, and a poor environmental record. These deficiencies translate into substandard conditions of working poverty, especially for a family of four in 1992, when the poverty threshold was approximately $14,350. The burden of impoverishment falls not only on a family or individual but also on the state in terms of such expenses as future welfare rolls and unemployment benefits. Industrial policies that increase the minimum wage favor the employment of native-born workers, and the implementation of a national health care plan will make jobs, which previously did not provide medical and other benefits, more attractive to U.S.-born labor. While immigrants will still be attracted to these jobs, knowing that there is a well-established native labor force will discourage, to some extent, immigration for work purposes.

Job displacement for California workers, indeed the entire country, is attributable less to job competition with immigrants than to the massive exodus and closure of firms that the state suffered in the middle to late 1980s. Los Angeles provides a case in point. During the 1970s, the area actually showed an expansion in its manufacturing base when, according to the Bureau of Labor Statistics, Los Angeles accounted for approximately one-fourth of the net growth in manufacturing jobs for the entire country. By the 1980s, however, the Los Angeles economy, which was highly dependent on its defense and associated industries, began the rapid decline that persists. Though the area continues to maintain a readily available and cheap supply of labor, the adoption of somewhat tougher environmental laws, improved labor standards, and other "hostile" regulations throughout the state and regional areas such as Los Angeles, San Diego, and the Bay Area has been blamed for the departure of industries to more "friendly" environments and even cheaper labor.

Finally, because undocumented immigrants are such a small proportion of the legal immigrant population—fewer than 14 percent—and an even smaller proportion of the total population of California—fewer than 4 percent—their negative impact is negligible or marginal at best. An analysis of several of California's largest revenue-producing industries, such as agriculture and wine, reveals that the largest number of their employees are immigrants. These industries are vital to the state's economy and rely on immigrant workers because other types of labor are unwilling or unable to work in this area. Historically, immigrant labor has always been vital to California's growth and economy. Implementing shortsighted policies that hurt the employability of immigrants will in turn hamper the contributions they can make to the state's future economy.

STUDY QUESTIONS

1. To what extent are public policies that focus on immigration and the issue of job competition misguided?

2. The large body of literature (studies) on the issue of job competition between immigrants and nonimmigrants concludes that immigrants impact the employment and wages of nonimmigrants in what manner?

3. Why is it important to account for industrial growth or decline and to look at cities such as Los Angeles and New York in conducting studies on the impacts of immigration?

NOTES

1. Job competition is one of several "costs" being argued in the California immigration debate. Other equally volatile immigration issues such as border patrol enforcement and undocumented immigration, federal reimbursement to state coffers for federal immigration policies, and medical and health benefits to legal and undocumented immigrants, also at the forefront of the immigration debate, led to California's passage of Proposition 187. This proposition makes it illegal for undocumented immigrants and their children to participate in California's publicly funded education system, procure public health services, except for emergency care, and partake in other government-sponsored social services.

2. During the late 1980s, poverty rates were much higher than in the 1970s, especially for African-Americans and Hispanics. For Hispanics, the poverty rate increased from 28 percent to 39 percent between 1972 and 1987; for whites, it was 9.9 percent in 1970, 10.2 percent in 1980, and 10.5 percent in 1987; and for African-Americans, the percentages were 33.5, 32.5, and 33.1, respectively. While the poverty rate for the population as a whole has been stable around 13 percent since the early 1980s, young families have experienced a steadily increasing chance of being poor. Whereas one-quarter of those sixty-five or older had an income below the poverty line in 1970, only one-eighth did in 1987 (U.S. Department of Commerce, Bureau of the Census, *General Social and Economic Characteristics*, Summary Report, Vol. 1, Chapter C [Washington, D.C.: U.S. Government Printing Office, 1983]).

3. According to the U.S. Bureau of the Census, poverty has shifted from rural areas to the inner cities, particularly in New York, Chicago, Boston, Detroit, and Los Angeles: In 1960, 28 percent of rural households were poor compared with 13.7 percent in the central cities and 10 percent in the suburbs. By 1987, the rate had decreased to 14 percent in rural areas and 6.5 percent in the suburbs but climbed to 15.4 percent in the central cities. See U.S. Bureau of the Census, *Census of Population*: 1970, Subject Reports, "Low Income Areas in Large Cities," PC(2)-9B (Washington, D.C.: Government Printing Office, 1973); U.S. Bureau of the Census, Census of Population: 1980, Subject Reports, "Poverty Areas in Large Cities," PC-80-2-8D (Washington, D.C.: Government Printing Office, 1989).

4. The term "underclass," used sporadically during the last three decades, was first introduced in this country by Gunnar Myrdal in *Challenge to Affluence* (New York: Pantheon, 1962), and in his influential "The War on Poverty," *The New Republic* 150, no. 6 (1964): 14–16. For a thorough historical summary of its origins and varied definitions, see R. Aponte, "Definitions of the Underclass: A Critical Analysis," *Sociology in America*, ed. H. J. Gans (Newbury Park, Calif.: Sage Publications, 1990).

5. The rate of legal immigration to the United States in the 1980s was among the highest in its history, surpassed only by the flows of the first two decades of this century. Immigration during the first eight years of the 1980s averaged 575,000 admissions per year; the 1980 decennial census, in an estimate by J. Passel and K. Woodward, "Geographic Distribution of Undocumented Aliens Counted in the 1980 Census by States," U.S. Bureau of the Census (Washington, D.C.: Government Printing Office, 1984), enumerated nearly 2 million undocumented immigrants.

6. In the 1960s, nearly two-thirds of the legal immigrants who entered the United States annually came from Europe and Canada (45 percent and 12 percent, respectively). In the 1970s, the rate was cut in half; fewer than one-third of the new arrivals came from European nations and Canada, 28 percent and 3 percent, respectively. See L. Maldonado and J. Moore, "Urban Ethnicity in the United States: New Immigrants and Old Minorities," *Urban Affairs Annual Review*, 1987, 20. This shift was labeled the "new immigration" because of the centuries-long monopoly Europe had held on immigration to the United States. Between 1961 and 1981, legal immigrants from South America, Asia, and Africa numbered approximately 733,000, compared with 505,000 from Europe. See M. G. Wong, "Post-1965 Immigrants: Demographic and Socioeconomic Profile," in *Urban Ethnicity in the United States: New Immigrants and Old Minorities*, ed. L. Maldonado and J. Moore (Beverly Hills: Sage Publications, 1985). Like country-of-origin characteristics, the composition of immigrant skills also has changed during the past two decades. Borjas, employing the Public Use Samples of the 1940, 1960, 1970, and 1980 censuses, shows that the gap between the skills and labor market—educational attainment, labor-force participation and unemployment rates, hours worked per year, and hourly wage rates for immigrants and natives—is growing over time, suggesting that immigrants of earlier years were more skilled than today's. See G. J. Borjas, *Friends or Strangers: The Impact of Immigrants on the U.S. Economy* (New York: Basic Books, 1990).

7. Recent immigrants locate primarily in a few metropolitan cities. In 1980, 40 percent of immigrant newcomers lived in either New York or Los Angeles. The 1980 census data for all ten metropolitan areas with the largest new immigrant populations reveal that New York City, Los Angeles, and Chicago received the largest numbers of documented and undocumented arrivals from the Third World.

8. Borjas, *Friends or Strangers*.

9. Figures are from the U.S. Department of Labor, *Handbook of Labor Statistics, Employment and Earnings 1985, Bulletin* 2217 (Washington, D.C.: Government Printing Office, June 1985).

10. See J. Miles, "Blacks vs. Browns: The Struggle for the Bottom Rung," *Atlantic Monthly* 270, no. 4 (October 1992); R. LaVally, *California Together: Defining the State's Role in Immigration* (Sacramento: Senate Office on Research, 1993), Report no. 717–2; M. Moreno-Evans, *Impact of Undocumented Persons and Other Immigrants on Costs, Revenues, and Services in Los Angeles County*, report prepared for the Los Angeles County Board of Supervisors, 1992; R. Louis and R. Parker, *A Fiscal Impact Analysis of Undocumented Immigrants Residing in San Diego County: Costs and Revenues of Significant State and Local Government Programs*, Report by the Office of the Auditor General (San Diego: Rea and Parker, 1992); R. Louis and R. Parker, *Illegal*

Immigration in San Diego County: An Analysis of Costs and Revenues, Report to the California State Senate Special Committee on Border Issues (San Diego: Rea and Parker, 1993).

11. M. J. Greenwood and J. M. McDowell, *The Labor Market Consequences of U.S. Immigration: A Survey* (Washington, D.C.: Immigration Policy Group, U.S. Department of Labor, 1988).

12. V. M. Briggs, Jr., "Illegal Aliens: The Need for a More Restrictive Border Policy," *Social Science Quarterly* 56, no. 3 (1975): 477–491.

13. M. J. Piore, *Birds of Passage: Migrant Labor and Industrial Societies* (Cambridge: Cambridge University Press, 1979).

14. R. Waldinger, "Changing Ladders and Musical Chairs: Ethnicity and Opportunity in Post-Industrial New York," *Politics and Society* 15, no. 4 (1987): 369–401.

15. Borjas, *Friends or Strangers*; D. G. Papademetriou, *The Effects of Immigration on the U.S. Economy and Labor Market*, Immigration Policy and Research Report 1, Bureau of International Labor Affairs, U.S. Department of Labor, 1989; Greenwood and McDowell, "The Labor Market Consequences of U.S. Immigration."

16. G. J. Borjas, "Substitutability of Black, Hispanic, and White Labor," in *Economic Inquiry* 21 (1983): 101; G. J. Borjas, "The Impact of Immigrants on the Earnings of the Native-Born," *Immigration: Issues and Policies* edited by V. M. Briggs and M. Tienda (Salt Lake City: Olympus, 1984); G. J. Borjas, "Immigrants, Minorities, and Labor Market Competition," *Industrial and Labor Relations Review* 40, no. 3 (1987): 382–392.

17. Borjas, "The Impact of Immigrants."

18. F. L. Rivera-Batiz, S. L. Sechzer, and I. N. Gang, *U.S. Immigration Policy Reform in the 1980s: A Preliminary Assessment* (New York: Praeger, 1991).

19. Borjas, "Immigrants, Minorities, and Labor Market Competition."

20. Ibid.

21. J. Stewart and T. Hyclak, "An Analysis of the Earnings Profiles of Immigrants," *Review of Economic Statistics* 66 (1984): 2.

22. F. Bean, L. Lowell, and L. J. Taylor, "Undocumented Mexican Workers and the Earnings of Other Workers in the United States," *Demography* 25 (1988): 35–52.

23. R. Mines and P. L. Martin, "Immigrant Workers and the California Citrus Industry," *Industrial Relations* 23, no. 1 (1984): 139–149.

24. F. De Freitas, "Hispanic Immigration and Labor Market Segmentation," *Industrial Relations* 27, no. 2 (1988): 195–214; F. De Freitas and A. Marshall, "Immigration and Wage Growth in U.S. Manufacturing in the 1970s," *Proceedings of the Thirty-Sixth Annual Meeting*, 148–560, Industrial Relations Research Association, Madison, Wisconsin, 1984.

25. R. Waldinger, "Immigration and Industrial Change in the New York City Apparel Industry," *Hispanics in the U.S. Economy*, edited by G. J. Borjas and M. Tienda (Orlando: Academic Press, 1985).

26. T. Bailey, *Immigrant and Native Workers: Contrasts and Competition* (Boulder, Colo.: Westview Press, 1987).

27. S. Sassen, *The Mobility of Labor and Capital: A Study in International Investment and Labor Flow* (Cambridge: Cambridge University Press, 1987); Waldinger, "Changing Ladders and Musical Chairs."

28. S. L. Maram and J. C. King, "The Labor Market Impact of Hispanic Undocumented Immigrants: An Analysis of the Garment and Restaurant Industries in Los Angeles," study prepared for the Rockefeller Foundation, New York, 1983.

29. Waldinger, "Immigration and Industrial Change"; Maram and King, "The Labor Market Impact of Hispanic Undocumented Immigrants."

30. B. L. Lowell, "Regional and Local Effects of Immigration, Chapter 3," *The Effects of Immigration on the U.S. Economy and Labor Market*, Immigration Policy and Research Report 1, 47–95, Bureau of International Labor Affairs, U.S. Department of Labor, 1989.

31. Ibid.

32. F. D. Bean and M. Tienda, *The Hispanic Population of the United States* (New York: Russell Sage, 1987).

33. R. Waldinger and M. Lapp, "Immigrants and Their Impact on the New York Garment Industry," and T. Bailey and R. Waldinger, "Economic Change and the Employment of Immigrants and Native Minorities in New York City," papers presented to the U.S. Department of Labor Conference on Immigration, Washington, D.C., September 1988; Sassen, *The Mobility of Labor and Capital*; R. Waldinger, *Through the Eye of the Needle: Immigrants and Enterprise in New York's Garment Trades* (New York: New York University Press, 1986); Waldinger, "Changing Ladders and Musical Chairs"; Bailey, *Immigrant and Native Workers*.

34. B. L. Lowell, "Regional and Local Effects of Immigration."

35. A. Portes and R. L. Bach, *Latin Journey: Cuban and Mexican Immigrants in the United States* (Berkeley: University of California Press, 1985); A. Portes and A. Stepick, *City on the Edge: The Transformation of Miami* (Berkeley: University of California Press, 1993).

36. T. Muller and T. Espenshade, *The Fourth Wave: California's Newest Immigrants* (Washington, D.C.: Urban Institute Press, 1985); K. F. McCarthy and R. B. Valdez, *Current and Future Effects of Mexican Immigration in California* (Santa Monica: Rand Corporation, 1985); W. A. Cornelius, L. R. Chavez, and J. G. Castro, *Mexican Immigrants and Southern California: A Summary of Current Knowledge*, Center for U.S.-Mexican Studies Research Report, Series No. 36, La Jolla (San Diego: University of California, 1982); Maram and King, "The Labor Market Impact of Hispanic Undocumented Immigrants."

37. Muller and Espenshade, *The Fourth Wave*.

38. G. J. Borjas and M. Tienda, "The Economic Consequences of Immigration," *Science* 235 (1987): 645–651.

39. Greenwood and McDowell, "The Labor Market Consequences of U.S. Immigration."

40. Waldinger, "Changing Ladders and Musical Chairs."

41. Ibid.

42. Ibid.

43. Ibid.

44. Dividing industries into core and peripheral sectors and occupations into segments is derived from dual labor-market theory, which proposes that the economic system is characterized by the existence of two distinct industrial sectors and four occupational segments. In the core sector, firms have oligopoly power in their product markets, employ large numbers of workers, have vast financial resources, are favored by government regulations and contracting, and employ workers who are likely to be union members. Firms in the periphery are smaller, have less influence over product markets, lack access to financial resources, and usually depend on subcontracting or retailing for larger firms. Jobs characterized in this category are low paying, nonunion, and exhibit high levels of turnover. Occupations are similarly categorized into four segments: (1) independent primary, (2) craft, (3) subordinate primary, and (4) secondary. Independent primary market jobs, which are characterized by educational credentials or state licensing of the occupation, offer a clear path for advancement, better pay, and a well-defined occupational structure. Subordinate primary jobs are characterized by the presence of unions and a technical or "machine-paced" system of labor control. Craft falls somewhere between these two categories. Secondary jobs are described as

the worst, employing poorly educated workers, with high turnover, low pay, bad working conditions, and little upward integration.

45. Deconcentration refers to the departure of a group of workers from a specific segment of the labor market.

46. For a detailed explanation of shift-share methodology, see A. Bendavid-Val, "Relative Regional Industrial-Composition Analysis," in *Regional and Local Economic Analysis for Practitioners* (New York: Praeger, 1983), 67–78.

47. Latino refers to all the census-defined Hispanic subgroups—Puerto Ricans, Cubans, Central and South Americans—in the aggregate, except for Mexicans, who are analyzed separately and referred to as such.

48. I am limited to these two data sets because although other data, e.g., the Current Population Survey, may be more current, they do not have a large enough sample to analyze Latinos or Asians in specific labor markets in single SMSA regions. The decennial census, despite well-known and documented criticisms, is nonetheless unique for the detailed data it provides on ethnic, industrial, and occupational characteristics.

49. This is, of course, true in absolute numbers and proportionally because whites are by far the largest employed group in Los Angeles.

50. C. Tolbert, P. M. Horan, and E. M. Beck, "The Structure of Economic Segmentation: A Dual Economy Approach," *American Journal of Sociology* 85, no.5 (1980): 1095–1116.

51. It is important to distinguish between complete and partial displacement because the former is an instance in which all three native groups have been displaced in a particular industry while the latter includes the displacement of one or two native-born groups. Nonetheless, I combine these two patterns to get an overall displacement trend while acknowledging that this combination is not as accurate—some native-born groups in an industry in this category may actually be gaining jobs—as if it were analyzed individually.

52. The exception to this pattern is for native-born whites in Los Angeles.

53. I aggregated the displaced row category to include the three displacement patterns (1–3), and the complementarity row category includes the two complement patterns (4 and 5) as discussed above.

54. D. M. Gordon, R. Edwards, M. Reich, *Segmented Work, Divided Workers: The Historical Transformation of Labor in the United States* (Cambridge: Cambridge University Press, 1982).

55. "Expected" growth rate calculates the number of jobs each group would have gained had gains been proportional to the growth experienced by the overall regional economy during this period, when Los Angeles employment grew by about 9 percent, from 3,948,900 jobs in 1970 to 4,298,860 in 1980.

56. Waldinger, "Changing Ladders and Musical Chairs."

57. Ibid.

58. Individual analysis of the five job competition patterns is important because it describes different types of displacements and complements. For example, the partial displacement category underemphasizes the overall displacement subcategory because it describes a situation in which only one or two native groups have experienced loss in their employment share, while one, two, or three immigrant groups have gained. Likewise, complete complementarity describes a situation in which both the native and immigrant populations gain in their employment share while the complementarity owing to immigration describes a situation in which natives gain in their employment share while immigrants lose. It is important to distinguish between these two complementarity scenarios because the latter shows that immigrants can also be displaced in the job competition debate.

59. Borjas, *Friends or Strangers*; Greenwood and McDowell, "The Labor Market Consequences of U.S. Immigration"; L. J. Simon, *The Economic Consequences of Immigration* (Boston: Basil Blackwell, CATO Institute, 1989); R. D. Reischauer, "Immigration and the Underclass," *Annals of the American Academy of Political and Social Science* 501 (1989): 120–131.

60. J. Kirschenman and K. M. Neckerman, "We'd Love to Hire Them, But . . . The Meaning of Race for Employers," in *The Urban Underclass*, edited by C. Jencks and P.E. Peterson (Washington, D.C.: Brookings Institution, 1991); J. Kirschenman, "Gender Within Race in the Labor Market," paper presented to the Urban Poverty and Family Life Conference, University of Chicago, October 1991; K. Neckerman, "What Getting Ahead Means to Employers and Disadvantaged Workers," paper presented to the Urban Poverty and Family Life Conference.

Chapter 14

Bill Ong Hing

Immigration Policy
Making and Remaking Asian Pacific America

Asian Pacific Americans will continue to be the fastest growing ethnic group in the United States into the next millennium principally because of immigration. The demographic predictions for the year 2020 show that 54 percent of Asian Pacific Americans will be foreign-born. This is consistent with census figures in 1980 and 1990 which revealed that, except for Japanese Americans, every group was mostly comprised of those born abroad (e.g., Chinese, over 60 percent; Koreans, 80 percent; Asian Indians, 80 percent; Filipinos, over 70 percent; Vietnamese, 90 percent). These predictions also find support from current annual levels of immigration (e.g., Filipinos 60,000, Chinese 55,000, Koreans 30,000, Asian Indians 30,000, Pakistanis 9,700, Thais 8,900). In 1992, 50,000 Southeast Asian refugees were admitted. And a trend in increased immigration from Japan has developed as well. During the 1980s, Asian Pacific immigration totaled about two million to help account for the 108 percent increase during the decade (from approximately 3.8 million to 7.3 million).

Beyond numbers, there is every reason to believe that immigration and refugee policies will continue to shape the Asian Pacific American profile in terms of where people live, gender ratios, employment and income profiles, and even social and political life.

UNDERSTANDING HOW IMMIGRATION POLICY SHAPES ASIAN PACIFIC AMERICA

The 1965 amendments to the Immigration and Nationality Act set the stage for the development of Asian Pacific America as we know it today.[1] Its emphasis on family reunification

From *The State of Asian Pacific America*, LEAP Asian Pacific American Policy Institute and UCLA Asian American Studies Center (1993).

(ironically not intended to benefit Asian immigration) provided the basis for growth. Family categories offered many more visas (80 percent of all preference and 100 percent of immediate relative, nonquota visas were designated for family reunification) and less stringent visa requirements. A relationship as spouse, parent, child, or sibling is all that was necessary. In the occupational categories, on the other hand, a certification from the Department of Labor was needed to show that no qualified American worker could fill the position an immigrant was offered. Today, 80 to 90 percent of the immigration from most Asian Pacific nations is in the family categories. But that was not always the case.

Filipinos, Asian Indians, and Koreans are the best examples of how the 1965 amendments were used to transform Asian immigration. In the late 1960s, about 45 percent of Filipino immigrants entered in the professional and 55 percent in the family unity categories. Within a few years, however, family networks developed that enabled naturalized citizens to take advantage of reunification categories. By 1976 Filipino immigration in the occupational categories dropped to about 21 percent. And by 1990, just over 8 percent came from the occupational categories compared to 88 percent in the family categories. About 64 percent of all Koreans entered in family categories in 1969 compared to over 90 percent by 1990. For Asian Indians, the figures were 27 percent in 1969 and about 90 percent in 1990. In the late 1960s and early 1970s, Koreans and Asian Indians also took advantage of the nonpreference investor category. About 12 percent of all Koreans and 27 percent of Asian Indians entered as investors at that time. Investor visas became unavailable in 1978.

Here are some examples of how many Asians eventually used the family categories under the 1965 amendments:

Under the 1965 reforms, immigrants essentially were categorized as immediate relatives of U.S. citizens or under the preference system. As immediate relatives they were not subject to quotas or numerical limitations. The category included the spouses and minor, unmarried children of citizens, as well as the parents of adult citizens. The preference system included seven categories. First preference: adult, unmarried sons and daughters of citizens. Second preference: spouses and unmarried sons and daughters of lawful permanent resident aliens. Permanent residents (green card holders) could petition for relatives only through this category. Third preference: members of the professions or those with exceptional ability in the sciences or the arts. Proof from the Department of Labor that the immigrant would not be displacing an available worker was required for third and sixth preference. Fourth preference: married sons and daughters of citizens. Fifth preference: siblings of adult citizens. Sixth preference: skilled or unskilled workers, of which there was a shortage of employable and willing workers in the United States. Seventh preference: persons fleeing from a communist-dominated country, a country of the Middle East, or who were uprooted by a natural catastrophe. Seventh preference was eliminated in 1980, but not until after about 14,000 Chinese from mainland China entered in the category.

Here are some examples of how the immigration system worked between 1965 and 1990:

- A Korean woman who had married a U.S. serviceman (presumably a citizen) could immigrate in the immediate relative category, thereby becoming a lawful permanent resident of the United States. After three years of marriage, she could apply for naturalization and become a citizen. She could then petition for her parents under the immediate relative category, and also for siblings under the fifth preference. Once her parents immigrated, they, as lawful permanent residents, could petition for other unmarried sons and daughters under the second preference. Married siblings entering under the fifth preference could be accompanied by spouses and minor, unmarried children.

- A doctor or engineer from India could immigrate under the third preference as a professional. He/she could be accompanied by a spouse and unmarried, minor children. After five years of permanent residence, the doctor/engineer could apply for naturalization, and upon obtaining citizenship could petition for parents under the immediate relative category, siblings under the fifth preference, and married sons and daughters under the fourth preference (who could also bring their spouses and minor, unmarried children). The same scenario is possible even if the first Indian immigrant in this family had entered as a nonpreference investor when such visas were available.

- A nurse from the Philippines might be able to immigrate under the third preference. After qualifying for citizenship five years later, she could petition for her parents. Her parents could petition for other unmarried sons and daughters under the second preference or the nurse could petition for these siblings under the fifth preference. If the son or daughter married on a visit to the Philippines, that spouse could then be petitioned for under the second preference.

- A Chinese American citizen might marry a foreign student from Taiwan. The student would then be able to become an immigrant under the immediate relative category. After three years of marriage to a citizen, naturalization opens immigration possibilities for parents under the immediate relative category and siblings under the fifth preference.

Gender ratios are affected by immigration as well. Today, more women than men immigrate from the Philippines, China, Korea, and Japan. For example, about 60 percent of Filipino and 55 percent of Korean immigrants in 1990 were women. This has contributed to census findings that the Chinese, Japanese, Filipino, and Korean American communities are predominantly female. The Asian Indian community has a very even gender ratio, in part because about the same number of men as women immigrate each year from India.

There is every reason to believe that many Asian women (particularly Koreans, Filipinos, and Japanese) immigrate because they perceive relatively progressive views on gender equality in the United States. This is interrelated to the fact that many women from Korea and the Philippines were able to qualify for employment categories as nurses and in other medical fields. Marriages between women and U.S. servicemen in these countries also contributed to a larger share of immigrant women.

The employment profile of various Asian Pacific communities also has its roots in immigration policy. The fifth of the preference visas that were set aside for employment categories under the 1965 amendments provided a window for many Asians to immigrate who did not have specific relatives in the United States. The proportion of professionals in every Asian Pacific community increased as a result. And even after more began using the family categories, the actual number of immigrants who identified themselves as professionals or managers remained high.

Some observers, who note fewer professionals among Chinese immigrants for example, contend that after the initial influx of professionals in the late 1960s and early 1970s, poorer, working-class Chinese began entering. But this is only part of the story. The proportion who enter in professional and occupational categories did decrease over time in part because a 1976 law required all professionals to first secure a job offer from an employer. The absolute number of professionals and executives, however, has increased. In 1969, for example, a total of 3,499 immigrated from mainland China, Taiwan, and Hong Kong. In 1983 the total had jumped to 8,524. Thus, the smaller percentage merely reflects the increased use of family categories. The proportion of those who enter in professional and occupational categories from Taiwan is also much higher than for those from mainland China (28 percent to 5 percent in 1989). And though more than twice as many born in mainland China entered in 1989 (32,272 to 13,974), Taiwan had more occupational immigrants (3,842 to 1,599). Large numbers of professionals continue to enter from the Philippines, Korea, and India as well. Over 6,500 Indian immigrants who designate their prior occupation as professionals or managers enter annually.

Immigration policies influence residential preferences as well. Historical recruitment of Asian and Pacific immigrants to work in the fields, on the railroads, and in service industries in the West Coast established a residential pattern that has continued for some time. However, in recent years, more and more Asian immigrants are settling in other parts of the country. Since 1967, New York City has attracted more Chinese immigrants than San Francisco and Oakland combined, and more than 17 percent of Chinese Americans reside in New York State. Almost 23 percent of Korean Americans live in the Northeast, 19.2 percent in the South, and 13.7 percent in the Midwest. Thirty-five percent of Asian Indians live in the Northeast and about 24 percent in the South. Asian Indians and Filipinos are the largest Asian American communities in New Jersey and Illinois. Relatedly, working-class immigrants who are able to enter in the family categories have helped to sustain Chinatowns and develop residential enclaves among Koreans, Filipinos, and Asian Indians. Koreans have also established small business enclaves in places like New York, Chicago, Washington, D.C., and, of course, Los Angeles.

The 134.8 percent growth rate of Vietnamese Americans between 1980 and 1990 (from 261,729 to 614,547) makes them the fastest growing Asian Pacific group. The development of Southeast Asian communities in the United States is related more to refugee policies than to standard immigration admission criteria. Take its current size. Of the 18,000 who immigrated by 1974, many were the spouses of American businessmen and military personnel who had been stationed in Vietnam. But a dramatic upsurge in new arrivals began after 1975, with 125,000 admitted immediately after the troops pulled out of Southeast Asia. By 1980 more than 400,000 additional refugees were welcomed from Vietnam, Laos, and Cambodia, approximately 90 percent of whom were from Vietnam. Although the 1980 Refugee Act established new controls, the flow of refugees continued due to persistent humanitarian pressure on the United States. After a second, sizable wave entered in 1980, the flow of new entries declined steadily. In 1984, 40,604 Vietnamese refugees entered, then the average dropped to about 22,000 annually until 1988 when 17,626 were admitted. So by 1988, 540,700 Vietnamese refugees had arrived. By October 1991, 18,280 Amerasians (mostly from Vietnam) arrived along with another 44,071 relatives. Eventually as many as 80,000 to 100,000 Amerasians and their relatives may enter. As a result of these entrants, over 90 percent of the Vietnamese population is foreign-born, the highest percentage of all Asian American groups.

Refugee policies also affect gender ratios. In 1980 there were 108.5 Vietnamese men per one hundred Vietnamese women, compared to 94.5 per one hundred in the general population. This ratio is not as skewed as those for initial waves of Filipinos and Chinese, which were much more male dominated. The refugee policy that enabled Vietnamese to enter after 1975 under unique circumstances contributed to greater balance. Rather than fleeing individually, those departing Vietnam have done their best to keep their families intact. Roughly 45 percent of recent arrivals are women.

Another policy was to resettle refugees across the country in order to lessen the economic and social impact on just a few areas and to avoid ghettoization. Although many refugees moved after their initial placement, refugees have become widely dispersed. By 1990, over 54 percent of the Vietnamese resided in the West, but 27.4 percent were in the South, almost 10 percent in the Northeast, and 8.5 percent in the Midwest. More of them lived in the South and Midwest than Filipinos and Japanese.

The goal of preventing ethnic enclaves ignored the dynamics of Vietnamese culture and perhaps even basic psychology. The need for ethnically based social, cultural, and economic support among refugees was either seriously misjudged or coldly ignored. Although enclaves provided an historical means for the mainstream to keep an eye on Asian immigrants, those established by Chinese, Filipino, and Japanese immigrants played key roles in easing their adjustment to American society. The need for a stable support system may be even more crucial for Southeast Asians, whose experience has been profoundly unsettling. Politically persecuted, unexpectedly driven from their homes, their hopes dashed, these refugees not surprisingly turned to the past for sustenance.

In doing so they turned to each other, and despite numerous obstacles have been remarkably successful in developing their own communities. They have, for example, transformed San Francisco's red-light district near Union Square into a bustling hub of Vietnamese hotels, residences, and small businesses. Vietnamese Americans have likewise helped to develop a "booming" wholesale district out of Skid Row in Los Angeles and altered the downtown areas of San Jose and Santa Ana, California, as well as a section of the Washington, D.C., suburb of Arlington, Virginia.

Nationwide, 64 percent of all Southeast Asian households headed by refugees arriving after 1980 are on public assistance, three times the rate of African Americans and four times that of Latinos. Not surprisingly, groups such as the Vietnamese have been accused of developing a welfare mentality, and the government has responded in knee-jerk fashion. Their relatively low rate of labor-force participation has in fact led many Vietnamese refugees to depend on government assistance. But much of this dependency is due to a system that creates disincentives to work. Policy makers have urged state and local resettlement agencies to expeditiously assist refugees with job placement. Under the 1980 Refugee Act, refugees were given 36-month stipends of special refugee cash, medical assistance programs, and other support services. But in 1982 amendments to the act reduced the stipends to 18 months to pressure refugees to become economically independent more quickly. These changes came with the entry of the poorer, less-educated, and more devastated second wave of refugees. After 1982, most programs stressed employment-enhancing services such as vocational, English-language, and job development training. Most refugees are unable to acquire the skills that would qualify them for anything other than minimum-wage jobs in 18 months. They were, nonetheless, constrained to take these positions in the absence of continued public assistance.

Restrictions on federal assistance thus help to account for increased Vietnamese American concentration in entry-level, minimum-wage jobs requiring little formal education or mastery of English. For many refugees, in fact, these types of jobs and the poverty that results are unavoidable. Indeed, figures show that in 1979, a striking 35.1 percent of Vietnamese families were living below the poverty level. And by 1985 the figure had risen to an astonishing 50 percent for all Southeast Asian refugees.

AMENDMENTS TO THE LAW IN 1990

After 1990 reforms, immigration visas are distributed under two preference systems, one for family reunification and the other for employment. The immediate relative category (spouses, unmarried children, and parents of adult citizens) continues to remain unlimited and outside of any of the numerically restricted preference systems. In the family preferences, first preference is for unmarried adult sons and daughters of citizens. Second preference is the only category under which lawful permanent residents of the United States can petition for relatives. There are two subcategories: (1) the 2A category for the spouses and children (unmarried and under 21), and (2) the 2B category for unmarried sons and daughters (age 21 and over). Third preference is reserved for the married sons and daughters of United States citizens. And fourth preference is for brothers and sisters of adult citizens. Only United States citizens, not lawful permanent residents or noncitizen nationals, can petition for married sons and daughters and for siblings.

The law now provides several categories for employment-based immigrant visas. First preference is for immigrants with extraordinary ability (such as in the sciences, arts, education, business, or athletics), outstanding professors and researchers, and certain executives and managers of multinational companies. Second preference is for members of the professions holding advanced degrees or for those of exceptional ability. Third preference is for skilled workers, professionals, and other workers. Fourth preference is for special immigrants (except returning lawful permanent residents and former citizens). Fifth preference is a category for investors whose investments are to each create at least ten new jobs.

Persons who immigrate to the United States under the preference systems are subject to two types of numerical limitations: a worldwide numerical cap and a country or territorial limit.

At least 226,000 family preference category visas are available annually on a worldwide basis. While in theory the worldwide quota can be increased to a cap of 465,000 annually through 1994, and 480,000 thereafter, the level will not likely be much more than 226,000. This is because the family preference category level is determined by sub-tracting the number of immediate relative entrants—generally well over 200,000 annu-ally—from the cap (465,000 or 480,000), with an absolute floor of 226,000. Assuming that 226,000 is the operative figure, this means that in a given year, a maximum of 226,000 persons can immigrate to the United States under the first, second, third, and fourth preferences. A separate worldwide numerical limitation of 140,000 is set aside for employment-based immigrants.

In addition to the worldwide numerical limitations, the law also provides an annual limitation of visas per country of 7 percent of the worldwide quotas. Thus, assuming a 226,000 worldwide family visa numerical limitation and 140,000 for employment visas, 7 percent of the total (366,000) is 25,620 for each country. But 75 percent of the visas issued for spouses and children of lawful permanent residents (family second preference "2A") are not counted against each country's quota.

Note that the visa of any immigrant born in a colony or other dependent area of a country is charged to that country. However, Hong Kong, which will become part of the People's Republic of China in 1997, is treated as a separate foreign state for purposes of its annual visa allotment (i.e., 25,620), except that through the end of fiscal year 1993 its annual quota is set at 10,000 preference visas.

CONSIDERATIONS FOR THE FUTURE

The confluence of social, political, and economic conditions in Asia and the Pacific region will continue to drive immigration to the United States for many more decades. And U.S. policies will continue to shape the profiles of Asian and Pacific communities here. As the prospects of immigration during the next several decades are appraised, these are the types of issues that have to be kept in mind:

- *Impact of 1990 reforms.* Asian Pacific immigrants comprise almost half of all legal immigrants today, mostly entering in the family reunification categories. The 1990 reforms did not reduce the number of visas available to family immigrants. In fact it added some numbers for families and added large numbers for employment cate-gories. Asian Pacific immigrants are likely to continue taking advantage of the family preference system. And as in the late 1960s and early 1970s, they will likely use the employment categories and new investor category to create further bases for future family migration. For example, interest in emigration remains high among Chinese professionals. Taiwan's politically volatile environment has contributed to the desire of the educated class to look for residential options elsewhere, and the stability of the United States and its longstanding anti-communist philosophy appeals to them. Similarly, the impending return of Hong Kong to mainland China's jurisdiction in 1997 has provided a strong impetus for its elite to look to the United States. And the Tiananmen Square massacre in June 1989 significantly accelerated emigration from Hong Kong. But there are analogous sociopolitical considerations for Filipinos, Asian Indians, and Koreans. And Japanese have also demonstrated a slow but steady increase in immigration in recent years, particularly among women.

- *Gender ratios.* The special interest in immigration that has been demonstrated by Korean, Filipino, Chinese, and Japanese women is likely to continue, especially because of the increase in employment-based visas and the perception of gender equality in the United States.

- *Working-class immigrants.* A continued influx of working-class and service-class immigrants will also continue to enter in family preference categories. This will continue to impact not only the employment profile of communities, but also such things as the viability of residential enclaves—not only Chinatowns, but also Koreatowns, Little Manilas, and Asian Indian ghettos.

- *Southeast Asians.* In spite of large numbers of refugees that continue to flee Southeast Asian and occupy refugee camps in Asia, the United States has gradually reduced the number of refugee slots to Southeast Asians since the Refugee Act of 1980. The admission of up to 35,000 refugees from Southeast Asia was allocated in 1990, and another 22,000 spots were reserved for relatives of refugees already in the United States under the Orderly Departure Program. But this is a far cry from the 525,000 that were admitted between 1975 and 1980. Following the pattern set by other Asian Americans, small but increasing numbers of Vietnamese are entering in family reunification categories. In order to take full advantage of these categories, U.S. citizenship is required, and most Vietnamese have been residents long enough to qualify. Some do so to demonstrate allegiance, others recognize that, as citizens, they may petition for more relatives. Though about 38 percent of the first wave of Vietnamese were naturalized by 1984, the rate for the second wave is significantly lower. In 1983 roughly 3,300 entered in the family categories, and by 1988 more than 4,000 had. These figures do not approach those of the other large Asian American communities for family category admissions (with the exception of the Japanese). Non-refugee admission is likely to remain low because in the absence of normal diplomatic ties between the United States and Vietnam, Vietnamese nationals attempting to obtain exit permits face tremendous difficulties. After an immigration petition is filed by a resident on behalf of a relative in Vietnam, the Vietnamese government must approve it. In 1984 only 3,700 immigrants were allowed under the Orderly Departure Program. More than half a million cases are currently backlogged. As a result, sizable growth of the Vietnamese American community exclusively through existing nonrefugee categories is unlikely.

- *Other Asians.* Aside from the larger Asian Pacific groups mentioned—Chinese, Filipinos, Japanese, Koreans, Vietnamese, and Asian Indians—as well as other groups alluded to, such as Laotians and Cambodians, other Asian Pacific countries send at least a few thousand immigrants to the United States each year. Annual admissions of Indonesians (3,500), Malaysians (1,800), Pakistanis (9,700), Thais (8,900), Tongans (1,400), and Samoans (700) contribute to growing communities that have become part of the Asian Pacific patchwork.

- *Political backlash.* As always, immigration and refugee policies in the near and distant future will respond to economic and social pressures. The 1990 reforms put into place the concept of a ceiling on preference visas, which could be extended to the immediate relative category given strong xenophobia or nativism. While some might label as extreme the anti-immigrant of color sentiment of someone like presidential candidate Patrick Buchanan, are his views really that different from those of the mainstream's, given the popularity of English-only initiatives across the nation? We also kid ourselves if we think this sentiment is aimed solely at Latin immigration. Consider only the experiences of Chinese in Monterey Park and the widespread upsurge in anti-Asian violence. Public opinion polls reveal that the general population does not hold Asian Americans in very high esteem. In one national survey that ascertained attitudes towards 15 different ethnic groups, no European ethnic group received lower than 53 percent positive rating, and no Asian group received higher than a 47 positive rating. Conducted before recent Japan bashing, Japanese were considered to be the minority group that had contributed the most (47 percent), followed by African Americans, Chinese, Mexicans, Koreans, Vietnamese, Puerto Ricans, Haitians, and Cubans. In a separate poll that focused on refugees, only 21 percent believed that Southeast Asian refugees should be encouraged to move into their community. Nearly half believed that Southeast Asians should have settled in other Asian countries, and one-fourth believed that "America has too many Asians in its population." Other polls continue to show that much of the public regards Asians as sinister, suspicious, and foreign. Thus, the threat of a serious backlash against Asian Pacific Americans that could negatively impact immigration laws is always real.

Asian Pacific America has been shaped by immigration and refugee policies. The profiles of the communities we know today are reflective of the 1965 amendments and a variety of refugee policies. The reforms in 1990 in all likelihood will continue the opportunities of the past 27 years, particularly in family reunification categories, but also open new doors with the expansion of employment-based numbers and the renewed availability of an investors category. Only if anti-immigrant, or specifically anti-Asian, sentiment carries the day will the course set in 1965 be obstructed.

STUDY QUESTIONS

1. How did the 1965 reforms shape Asian migration?

2. How did the family preference categories produce more Asian female immigrants?

3. What was the impact of the 1990 reforms?

NOTE

1. A much more detailed analysis of how immigration and refugee policies shape the demographic and social profiles of various Asian Pacific communities can be found in my book *Making and Remaking Asian American Through Immigration Policy* (Stanford: Stanford University Press, 1992).

Chapter 15

Philip Martin

Proposition 187 in California

On November 8, 1994, California voters approved Proposition 187, the "Save Our State" (sos) initiative, 59 to 41 percent. If implemented Proposition 187 would create a state-run system to verify the legal status of all persons seeking public education, health care, and other public benefits, and add public education to the list of services for which unauthorized aliens are ineligible. As of March 1995, the only sections of Proposition 187 in effect are those that make the manufacture, distribution, or use of false documents to obtain employment or public benefits a state felony.

Proposition 187 may mark the beginning of efforts to reduce legal and illegal immigration, much as Proposition 13 in 1978 arguably laid the basis for the Reagan-era tax cuts of the early 1980s. On the other hand, Proposition 187 may turn out to be a largely symbolic expression of frustration with illegal immigration, much as was Proposition 63, which made English the state's "official language" in 1986, proved to be.

MAJOR PROVISIONS

Proposition 187 primarily creates a state-mandated screening system for persons seeking tax-supported benefits. In the language of Proposition 187, no person—citizen, legal immigrant or illegal immigrant—"shall receive any public social services to which he or she may otherwise be entitled until the legal status of that person has been verified."

Proposition 187 has five major sections. First, it bars illegal aliens from the state's public education systems from kindergarten through university, and requires public educational

From *International Migration Review*, Vol. 29, No. 1, 1995.

institutions to begin verifying the legal status of both students (effective January 1, 1995) and their parents (effective January 1, 1996).

California educational institutions today verify residence but not legal status of elementary school pupils and university students. There are no tuition charges for K–12 education. One of California's three higher education systems—the state university system—charges resident illegal aliens lower in-state tuition, while community colleges and the University of California charge them higher out-of-state tuition (almost 1 in 7 college/university students in the United States attends a public institution in California).

Second, Proposition 187 requires all providers of publicly paid, non-emergency health care services to verify the legal status of persons seeking services in order to be reimbursed by the State of California. Persons seeking emergency care must also establish their legal status, but all persons, including unauthorized aliens, must be provided emergency health services.

Third, Proposition 187 requires that all persons seeking cash assistance and other benefits verify their legal status before receiving such benefits. Unauthorized aliens are generally not eligible for these benefits, so this provision adds a state-run verification system on top of the current federal screening system.

Fourth, all service providers are required to report suspected illegal aliens to California's Attorney General and to the Immigration and Naturalization Service (INS). This means that parents enrolling children in school, or clerks determining eligibility for public benefits, are required to report persons requesting education or benefits if they suspect that applicants are unauthorized aliens. State and local police must also determine the legal status of persons arrested and report unauthorized aliens.

Fifth, the making, distribution, and use of false documents to obtain public benefits or employment by concealing one's legal status is now a state felony, punishable by fines and prison terms. Proposition 187 does not affect, for example, teenagers who buy or use false documents to obtain alcohol.

Proposition 187 is an initiative statute whose provisions remain state law unless disapproved by a two-thirds vote of the California legislature or by another initiative. Sections of Proposition 187 can be implemented individually. On November 9, 1994, Governor Wilson ordered that state-reimbursed health services for prenatal care be stopped as soon as possible, and that unauthorized aliens no longer be enrolled in state-reimbursed long-term health care programs (nursing home care). Even though federal and state courts have blocked the implementation of Proposition 187, the state continues to prepare regulations to implement it.

CURRENT STATUS

Citing serious constitutional questions, a federal judge in Los Angeles on December 14, 1994, barred the enforcement of Proposition 187's requirement that public schools and agencies verify the legal status of all persons seeking education, health, and other services until the constitutionality of the Proposition is determined by the courts. Judge Pfaelzer expressed concern that implementation of the Proposition 187's screening system could prompt immigrants who are currently entitled to services under federal law to leave the United States. Her injunction blocks enforcement of all but two of the initiative's provisions—those dealing with higher education and the use of false documents—until well into 1995.

Judge Pfaelzer cited "a balance of hardship that decidedly tips in favor of" continuing to provide services to unauthorized immigrants. Specifically, the judge said that the initiative may not be constitutional because it does not provide due process or a hearing before an individual is denied benefits such as schooling or health care. The section dealing with public education does provide 90 days of continued schooling while legal status questions are sorted out.

The denial of public education to illegal alien children is likely to be the most controversial section of Proposition 187 to be resolved by the courts. The 1982 *Plyer v. Doe* U.S. Supreme Court decision declared that the equal protection clause of the Fourteenth Amendment protects everyone within a state's borders, regardless of immigration status. However, the court split 5–4 on whether "equal protection" for illegal alien children included the same education available to U.S.-citizen children.

In *Plyer v. Doe*, the majority emphasized that education is especially needed to prevent the development of an underclass. The minority noted that education was not a fundamental constitutional right and argued that the court was making social policy when it said that Texas could not deny public education to illegal alien children because, in the majority view, not educating them would prove more costly in the long run.

Public education is the most costly service used by illegal aliens in California—providing education for the estimated 300,000 to 400,000 illegal alien children in California schools accounts for about half of the estimated $3 billion annual costs of services provided to the estimated 1.7 million illegal aliens in the State. (California's State budget is $40 billion annually.)

Several school districts joined in suits seeking to have the denial-of-public-education part of Proposition 187 declared unconstitutional. This in turn prompted protests and, in a few instances, threats to initiate recall campaigns against public officials who vote to spend taxpayer dollars to fight Proposition 187.

In Los Angeles, where 51 percent of the voters supported Proposition 187, there have been threats of recall campaigns against school board members who voted to file a lawsuit seeking to overturn the Proposition 187 public school provisions. The State Board of Education, on November 21, 1994, ordered the preparation of emergency regulations to implement Proposition 187 in the event the courts lift the injunction that currently prevents its implementation.

THE CAMPAIGN

The Proposition 187 SOS initiative began with a huge lead in opinion polls—it had a 37-point lead in July 1994, and led among likely voters by 62 to 29 percent in mid-September 1994. However, by early November, polls indicated that as many likely voters opposed as supported SOS. Most politicians and opinion leaders argued that voters should reject Proposition 187 because it was too blunt an instrument to deal with the complex issue of illegal immigration; no major California newspaper supported the SOS Proposition.

In the week before the election, Governor Wilson, who was re-elected with 55 percent of the vote, asserted that if Proposition 187 became law, he would require state and local government employees to report suspected illegal aliens as required by the initiative. California Attorney General Dan Lungren, who was also re-elected, promised to develop emergency regulations to implement the initiative immediately, but noted that there was no penalty for persons who do not report suspected illegal aliens.

Wilson's campaign bought the only pro-Proposition 187 television ads that were aired, while the anti-Proposition 187 campaign used contributions from doctors and teachers to run opposition television ads. Democratic gubernatorial challenger Kathleen Brown ran out of money for television ads at the end of her campaign, and toured high school and college campuses urging students to work to defeat Proposition 187.

President Clinton argued strongly against Proposition 187. According to Clinton, "It is not wrong for you [Californians] to want to reduce illegal immigration. And it is not wrong for you to say it is a national responsibility to deal with immigration." Clinton said that "the federal government should do more to help to stop illegal immigration and to help California bear the costs of the illegal immigrants who are there," but urged California voters to reject Proposition 187 and allow the federal government to "keep working on what we're doing—stiffening the border patrol, stiffening the sanctions on employers who knowingly hire illegal immigrants, stiffening our ability to get illegal immigrants out of the workforce, increasing our ability to deport people who have committed crimes who are illegal immigrants." Clinton promised that the federal government would do more to "help California, and other states, deal with incarceration, health and education costs of illegal immigration."

Some pundits predicted that Clinton reduced his chances to carry California in the 1996 Presidential race by campaigning so vigorously against Proposition 187. The "white male backlash" against illegal immigration may, these observers say, also manifest itself in attacks on affirmative action and similar programs. A California civil rights initiative that would eliminate state affirmative action programs is already being prepared.

The final days were marked by large numbers of Hispanic students walking out of high school to protest Proposition 187. In the opinion of many Proposition 187 opponents, these protests were counterproductive; the Mexican flags students waved reportedly convinced many undecided voters to support Proposition 187.

The closing days of the campaign were also marked by charges of hypocrisy between U.S. Senate candidates Feinstein and Huffington. Both took tough stands against illegal immigration, and both charged that the other employed an illegal alien housemaid. Feinstein hired an illegal housekeeper in the early 1980s—before it was unlawful for a U.S. employer to knowingly hire illegal alien workers—and Huffington hired an illegal alien for childcare in the late 1980s and early 1990s when such hiring was unlawful. Some Huffington supporters alleged that illegal aliens voted for Feinstein, who was narrowly re-elected.

THE VOTE

A majority of voters in 50 of California's 58 counties supported Proposition 187—the exceptions were eight San Francisco Bay Area counties. According to exit polls, 64 percent of whites, 57 percent of Asian Americans, 56 percent of African Americans, and 31 percent of Latinos voted in favor of Proposition 187. Some 78 percent of those voting in favor of Proposition 187 agreed that "it sends a message that needs to be sent" and 51 percent agreed that "it will force the federal government to face the issue." Some 40 percent of voters in one exit poll said that they voted primarily because Proposition 187 was on the ballot. Of those voting against the measure, 60 percent agreed with the statement that it "doesn't solve the problem" and about 40 percent agreed that "it would throw children out of school" and that "it is racist/anti-Latino."

California's population in 1990 was 57 percent white, 25 percent Latino, 9 percent Asian American, and 7 percent African American. However, voters on November 8 were 75 to 80 percent white, 8 to 10 percent Latino, 4 to 5 percent Asian American, and 10 percent African American.

REACTIONS TO PROPOSITION 187

Proposition 187 was based on the theory that changes in immigrant policy can affect immigration. According to Governor Wilson, denying public services to unauthorized aliens would discourage them from coming to the United States, and encourage some who are here to leave.

There were conflicting reports after November 8 about the behavior of unauthorized immigrants. Some hospitals and clinics reported sharply fewer patients, and there were scattered reports that some of the estimated 300,000 to 400,000 unauthorized alien children in California schools were not going to school. However, most health facilities and schools reported business as usual.

In one widely reported case, illegal alien parents supposedly did not seek medical care for their 12-year old son for fear of deportation to Mexico; the boy subsequently died. Many service providers printed up materials in their clients' language explaining that nothing had changed and that patients and students would not be asked to prove legal status before they received services.

There were numerous workshops on campuses, in churches, and in ethnic communities in which speakers decried the passage of Proposition 187 and urged opponents to get politically involved. Some speakers denounced the racism that, they asserted, motivated the vote, and some asserted that unauthorized immigrants reported feeling hatred in the streets.

Activists in several other states threatened to boycott California in retaliation for the approval of Proposition 187. Denver's mayor urged city residents to boycott California, and the 110,000-member League of United Latin American Citizens said that most of its December 1994 conference would be devoted to planning a California boycott. Several other Hispanic organizations announced that they would not hold conventions in California, and some Hispanic leaders urged a boycott of Disneyland to send a signal of their dissatisfaction with the California vote.

Dealing with illegal immigration has been a bipartisan issue—the Immigration Reform and Control Act of 1986, for example, was carried largely by a Republican Senator and a Democratic Representative. Proposition 187 was opposed by most Democrats and split

Republicans. Among the putative Republican contenders for president in 1996, Wilson and Patrick Buchanan have campaigned for the measure, while William Bennett and Jack Kemp, former Cabinet Secretaries with more libertarian philosophies, opposed Proposition 187 for fostering an "anti-immigrant climate." Immigrants, they argued, are likely to be Republican voters since they have the "entrepreneurial spirit and self-reliance, hostility to government intervention, strong family values and deeply rooted religious faith." According to Bennett, "it's assimilation, stupid"—meaning that the major problem is not the number or type of immigrant entering the United States but how soon and success-fully they integrate into American society. Bennett argues that programs such as bilingual education impede integration by promoting multiculturalism. Kemp reportedly acted to prevent the 1996 Republican platform from having a nativist or anti-immigrant plank.

Governor Wilson responded that the Republicans should hew to a law and order line and emphasize the sharp distinction between legal and illegal immigrants. According to Wilson, the U.S. Border Patrol has a "mission impossible" task trying to keep people from entering the United States illegally, but the federal government guarantees services and benefits "to everyone who succeeds in evading the Border Patrol." House of Repre-sentatives Speaker Gingrich assured Wilson that he believes the federal government should either fully reimburse states for the costs they incur to provide services to illegal aliens, or eliminate the requirement that the states provide services to them.

Denying public services to unauthorized aliens may not be easy, because many Cali-fornia households include persons with different legal statuses. In so-called mixed fami-lies, family members include U.S. citizens, legal immigrants, and unauthorized persons. Some fear that if a U.S. citizen or legal immigrant seeks services to which they are enti-tled, they may expose an unauthorized family member to immigration authorities. To prevent such detection, many public employees pledged not to comply with Proposition 187 verification requirements.

MEXICAN REACTIONS

Many commentators were surprised by the active opposition of the Mexican govern-ment to Proposition 187 and the extensive coverage of the campaign for and against Proposition 187 in the Mexican media. In his final state-of-the-nation address, Mexican president Carlos Salinas de Gortari asserted that "Mexico affirms rejection of this xeno-phobic campaign, and will continue to act in defense of the labor and human rights of our migrant workers," although he acknowledged that Mexico could not hope to use economic sanctions against the United States or California to protest the approval of Proposition 187.

Ernesto Zedillo, who becomes Mexico's president on December 1, asserted during his November trip to Washington, DC, that Mexico "cannot object to legitimate enforcement of U.S. laws," but Mexico objects to "enforcement [that] might lead to deprivation or violation of basic human rights. . . [including] education and health care." The Mexican government promised to contribute attorneys and funds to fight Proposition 187 in U.S. courts.

A week after Proposition 187 was approved, President Salinas called on the United States to discuss a bilateral agreement that would permit Mexicans to work legally in the

United States under a guestworker program. According to Salinas, the movement of Mexican workers to the United States "is inevitable, and it is better to order and regulate it than to confront it with administrative measures that are not going to stop it because the force of the economies is greater." Governor Wilson, in a widely reported November 18, 1994, speech to the Heritage Foundation, announced his support for a program to import Mexican guestworkers.

Knowledgeable U.S. observers are skeptical, doubting that the Zedillo administration will make the enactment of what would be a controversial guestworker program a top priority. Indeed, some advise the Mexican government that any guestworker proposal in the current U.S. political climate could be counterproductive. The Mexican government does not want to have the United States close the safety valve on which several million of its citizens depend. Mexico sees no significant lessening of emigration pressures during the 1990s.

The scenario for Mexico requesting and the United States negotiating a guestworker program in 1995 runs something like this. Labor shortages develop, perhaps in the May 1995 Oregon strawberry harvest. The INS meanwhile, concludes that border operations such as Gatekeeper have succeeded in reducing the influx of illegal aliens, and discusses ways to make legal border crossings easier. U.S. employers argue that the current H-2 programs, under which foreign workers may be imported to the United States in the event of labor shortages, are too inflexible, and Mexico asks for a bilateral program that recognizes its proximity and the tradition of U.S. employers hiring Mexican workers.

In such a scenario, the discussion could very quickly shift from whether there should be a guestworker program with Mexico to what kind of program. Given Proposition 187, it is already clear that any guestworkers would have little access to U.S. public services while here, and that a significant portion of their wages would be likely to be withheld to encourage their return.

OUTLOOK

Proposition 187 has slipped from the front pages of California newspapers. The state of California continues to develop regulations to implement Proposition 187, but federal and state trials on the constitutionality will not begin until June 1995.

Newspapers report that the lives of unauthorized immigrants in California are returning to normal. Health care clinics report the usual number of patients, and immigrant activists report that they do not know of any unauthorized immigrants who have left California due to Proposition 187. As before the election, reports of mixed families illustrate how difficult it would be to enforce Proposition 187's provisions. For example, if the father is a legal immigrant, the baby is U.S.-born and a U.S. citizen, and mother and older children are unauthorized, who gets which services, and do privacy laws protect the unauthorized members of the family when legal members seek services?

Many of the grassroots supporters of Proposition 187 have become vocal supporters of the California Civil Rights Initiative (CCRI), an initiative planned for the 1996 ballot, that would "prohibit the state or any of its political subdivisions from using race, sex, color, ethnicity, or national origin as a criterion for either discriminating against, or granting preferential treatment to, any individual or group in the operation of the state's system of public employment, public education, or public contracting." Governor Wilson has endorsed the CCRI, which has become the focus of national media attention.

Immigration to California is slowing, which should make it easier for employment growth to keep up with population growth in the 1990s. Some argue that Proposition 187 was simply an overreaction to extraordinarily high net immigration between 1988 and 1990. In addition, when recession hit California in 1990–1991, the taxes paid by immigrants flowed to a federal government that was sharply reducing defense spending in California, while the costs of services provided to unauthorized aliens was borne by state and local taxpayers.

The seven states with the most illegal immigrants—California, New York, Texas, Florida, Illinois, New Jersey, and Arizona—have two-thirds of the electoral votes needed to elect a U.S. president. Hispanic activists opposed to Proposition 187-type measures have announced that they are working hard on what they consider the next great civil rights movement—preserving the rights of legal and unauthorized aliens.

STUDY QUESTIONS

1. What role have school districts played in the implementation of Proposition 187?

2. What relationship was suggested between President Clinton's position on Proposition 187 in 1994 and his campaign for re-election in 1996?

3. How did those affected by Proposition 187 respond in terms of demand for services?

Chapter 16

Robert L. Bach

Recrafting the Common Good
Immigration and Community

Certain events characterize their times. The Watts riots in the 1960s, the hostage crisis in the late 1970s, the Mariel boatlift in 1980, and certainly the fall of the Berlin Wall in 1989 all left indelible images of their social and political contexts. The events themselves were not historically decisive, but they remain the anchor of memories, emotions, and opinions about the problems they represent.

The 1992 Los Angeles riots may be a similar event for the current decade. After years of neglect, they symbolize a renewed interest in the well-being of urban communities. But they have also rekindled concern about the impact of immigration. The aftermath of the riots has changed public discourse about the last two decades of high levels of immigration to the United States. After years of positive reporting on immigrants' economic contributions, national media such as the *Wall Street Journal* and *Business Week* have refocused on the growing social and cultural impact of immigrants. Rhetoric about riots and rioters has returned to popular discourse and, this time, included immigrants. Perhaps the most graphic reaction included these warnings about the role of immigration in Los Angeles's decay: "When the barbarians sacked Rome in 410, the Romans thought it was the end of civilization. You smile—but what followed was the Dark Ages."[1]

This new popular voice goes beyond efforts of organizations such as the Federation for American Immigration Reform that have long supported more limited immigration. It includes growing segments of the environmental movement and fragments of the conser-

From *ANNALS*, AAPSS, 530, November 1993. Reprinted by permission of Sage Publications, Inc.

vative coalition that throughout the 1980s supported large-scale immigration. A split in the conservative ranks became most visible during the presidential primaries as David Duke, Patrick Buchanan, and California Governor Pete Wilson campaigned against new-comers. Most of this new conservative opposition to immigration rests on its alleged social and cultural impacts.[2]

Much of the scholarly literature on immigration is ill prepared to respond to this current popular assault on the impact of newcomers on established communities. Most immigration research has focused primarily on individual and group differences in rates of assimilation or on structural barriers to economic advancement. Policy discussions have focused almost exclusively on questions about the volume and criteria for admissions. Questions about group advancement, ethnic identity, and empowerment obviously are critical issues for understanding the unequal patterns of immigrant incorporation in the United States. Still, these approaches are limited in their understanding of the full recomposition of community life that has resulted from the political and economic restructuring of the 1980s and the new cultural diversity that large-scale immigration has created.[3]

REDIRECTING IMMIGRATION RESEARCH

Refocusing immigration research to include community transformation as a whole requires attention to three primary issues. First, attention to broad social transformations challenges ethnic categories that have become well entrenched in both scholarly and public policy discussions. The new immigration, with all its ethnic, class, linguistic, and religious variations, has changed the composition and relationships between members of groups in urban communities. Class divisions within immigrant groups are now at least as great as between established residents. Immigrants often share more with members of other ethnic or racial groups within their social strata than with individuals of different strata within their own national-origin groups.

Within-group heterogeneity also complicates ethnic identification. One result of the multiplication of national origins of new immigrants throughout the 1970s and 1980s is that newcomers often have little in common with those with whom they are categorized. For instance, the ethnic label "Hispanic" obscures the ways in which immigrants from El Salvador differ significantly from waves of Mexican immigrants who settled before them.[4] Popular media also continue to reduce much of this new social complexity to simple spinoffs of black and white differences. *Time* magazine, for instance, has treated the intertwining of ethnic, linguistic, national, and cultural differences as merely a middle ground between black and white, not quite black and not quite white. Preoccupation with racial differences, of course, is understandable; it still remains the American dilemma. Yet ethnic and racial diversity has changed qualitatively from the concerns established during the civil rights movement, when group-conscious empowerment strategies and identities became well established.

Second, immigration research neglects established communities. The focus on characteristics of different immigrant groups and their structural positions systematically ignores relationships that newcomers form with established residents within certain social spheres. Research often overstates the extent to which sources of change and lack of advancement are due to characteristics of immigrant groups and differences between them, rather than to broad political and economic restructuring that affects all groups. Very little research has taken as its point of departure the "commonality between immigrants and minorities in the U.S. economy"[5] and the difficulties that immigrants share with established residents living in the same or neighboring communities. General conditions in local communities, whether related to housing, jobs, schools, crime, or recreational facilities, constrain not only how immigrants are able to adapt to their host community but also how communities respond to newcomers.

Research also understates the extent of change in many established communities. For many immigrants who live in communities in which the primary, dominant group is Chicano or African American, Anglo conformity, long considered the reference point for assimilation, is simply no longer salient. African Americans now face large numbers of racially similar Haitian immigrants, who bring a different language, culture, and class background. Latino communities, long dominated by residents of either Mexican or Puerto Rican heritage, now find as much difference between groups that speak Spanish as between Spanish speakers and long-established, English-speaking residents. In Miami, for instance, Haitian immigrants enter and adapt to predominantly African American schools, while in San Diego, Mexican immigrants and Southeast Asian refugees face well-established Chicano communities. Immigrants' adjustments to U.S. life are adaptations to the dominant subcultural patterns in local schools and neighborhoods and to the perception of the place of minorities in U.S. society as a whole.

Ironically, even the Anglo reference point has changed. Turn-of-the-century European immigration was as heterogeneous and contentious as the contemporary influx. Settlement often created social tensions that took on an ethnic character. As historian Arthur Schlesinger points out, European immigration "itself palpitated with internal hostilities, everyone at everybody else's throats."[6] Only the distortions of historical hindsight and the lens of contemporary politics have blurred and transformed these differences and vibrant diversity into a mythical, homogeneous Euro-ancestry.

Third, the theoretical foundations of much immigration research miss opportunities to identify cooperative efforts between newcomers and established residents, especially those that lead to community-wide activities. Little attention is given to the everyday activities, organized and unorganized, that bring people together and form the foundations for community stability and change. When the popular media turned to ask why communities were in conflict, few studies could offer evidence of common interests and shared activities amid the social and cultural diversity within urban areas. Unchallenged, the media report pervasive images of intergroup conflict.

In the mid-1980s, a similar flurry of media reports about conflict between immigrants and established residents, primarily between Korean shopkeepers and African American customers, stimulated the creation of a nationwide project to explore the character of relations between newcomers and established residents.[7] Among other things, the project sought to determine the extent to which newspaper accounts about conflicts between immigrants and established residents reflected the true character of community relations. What was happening in the quiet, day-to-day activities that the media never examined? Who was at work bringing people together? Was the nation fragmenting and polarizing, or were there possibilities for democracy and community?

Overall, the project's results show a much more complex and subtle story than that reported by the press. Tensions certainly exist between immigrants and established residents. Korean shopkeepers and their African American neighbors are not the only examples. Still, in the communities studied, the incidence of conflict is much less than the media report. Rather, communities contain myriad everyday encounters that bring about coexistence, accommodation, and change in quiet but stark contrast to the dramatic portraits of conflict. Possibilities also exist for converting pervasive social tensions into creative strategies of accommodation, working together to reconstruct community. The National Project Board concludes that

> there is a common experience of crisis in many of America's communities which limits interactions and possibilities for cooperation [between immigrants and established residents]. Yet, these same problems also create shared interests and compatible goals. Many of the most promising signs of leadership and intergroup organization focus on local issues of community standards, including the availability, cost, and value of housing, social services, schools, education, law enforcement, and safety.[8]

This study and others[9] offer potential, promising responses to the growing concern about relations between new immigrants and established residents and the viability of urban communities. They direct attention to two critical questions. What are the conditions and activities that create social tensions and conflicts and ultimately threaten communities, and what are the social and human bonds that hold people and places together?

IMMIGRATION, DIVERSITY, AND SOCIAL CONFLICT

The new diversity of major U.S. cities now divides groups along lines of language, race, culture, identity, and history. Demography and economic restructuring have combined to drive whites into suburbs, blacks into separate neighborhoods, and, now, new, diverse immigrants in among them. In these areas, immigrants and established residents live in socially divided worlds. Residential and institutional separation, of course, is not new in the United States or to newcomers. African American novelist Richard Wright described his discovery of an earlier etiquette of intergroup relations as he, too, crossed a border—that from the black South to the white North: black and white were " 'each seemingly intent upon his private mission. There was no racial fear. Indeed, each person acted as though no one existed but himself.' "[10]

Many immigrants and established residents have carved out distinct social arenas, including the differential use of service agencies, businesses, and community organizations. Labor markets have become sharply separated. In the office buildings of many large cities, the daytime white and black work force gives way to a night-time immigrant, and often undocumented, service corp. This social distance is so clear and well defined that some groups find it easy to claim ownership over particular areas and activities. In Houston, researchers recorded two examples: "When blacks were asked why they did not participate in other general education classes (in which Latinas participated), the usual response was 'those classes are for Mexicans' or 'everyone speaks Spanish in those classes.'" Another informant said that "Blacks expect Mexicans to go to LULAC while Blacks go to the NAACP."[11] The impact of assertions of cultural ownership, of course, is to dominate activities in a way that blocks the participation of other groups from potentially shared projects.

Paradoxically, it is this segregation and separation that create tensions when and where groups come into contact. Groups interact in only a few special places, including schools, workplaces, churches, and playing fields. These are rare places, and each faces the excessive strain of absorbing and responding to the demographic diversity that characterizes America's communities. Few of them are capable of continuously withstanding the strain.

Still, social tensions do not simply explode as the summer heat rises or the number of newcomers grows or the volume of rock music increases. Riots, such as those that followed the Rodney King verdict in Los Angeles, do not happen just because of economic decline, intergroup tensions, and social neglect, although these, of course, are essential ingredients. Rather, tensions ignite into conflict through abuse and opposition; someone or something makes them happen. In the 1960s, various national commissions concluded that many civil disorders resulted from "police riots." Recent disorders involving immigrant communities in Miami, Washington, D.C., and Los Angeles also resulted from clear miscarriages of justice.

Conflict also results when established groups and leaders resist change and take a hard-line approach to traditional community standards. For example, in Monterey Park, a suburb of Los Angeles, negative reactions to immigrants resulted from English-only advocates' attempts to ban Chinese shopkeepers from using both English and Chinese characters on their signs.[12] The signs posed no safety hazards, and they clearly met acceptable community norms. Opposition to them created hostility where there could have been receptiveness, and resentment when there should have been cooperation.

Much less dramatic social tensions than the all-too-familiar hate crimes and abuses that plague contemporary U.S. life can also lead to conflict. Today's demography creates a social context for misinterpretation of even the most routine interpersonal tensions by turning clashes between individuals into intergroup conflict. The greater the mix of groups, the more likely it is that normal tensions and conflicts will express, by numerical chance, intergroup antagonisms. The rise in conflict between different minority groups, for instance, may result as much from the increase in the number of opportunities to have these encounters as from a significant increase in motivations to harm each other. Under the new demographic diversity, the same number of interpersonal incidents as before can produce a greater number of incidents between different groups.

The response and interpretation of interpersonal and intergroup tensions can themselves become sources of conflict. Professional mediators or the media often mistakenly represent interpersonal incidents as intergroup conflict. Community dispute resolution efforts can bring into a neighborhood mediators who work with models of group membership that force residents to seek out appropriate group representatives to satisfy the required rules of formal negotiations. This representational model transforms neighborly disputes into conflicting claims about distributive justice among groups. When mediators are not present, social tensions are often worked out between the individuals involved.[13]

ECONOMIC RESTRUCTURING

The primary source of social separation and the tensions that it fosters lie deeply rooted in the restructuring of the U.S. economy. After all, it is the economy that brings immigrants to the United States and distributes the resources to settle in new communities. Economic demand brings groups together, but it also pushes them apart. It changes the ways in which established residents as well as immigrants have learned to accommodate to each other and adds uncertainty and competition to their perceptions of each other.

The increase in social inequality and the general weakness of the U.S. economy in the 1980s had strong consequences for both immigrants and established residents. It rekindled the central debate between economic growth and social fairness that haunts much of democratic politics in America. In the last decade, market-based competition and antigovernment rhetoric supported efforts to promote unfettered, aggregate economic growth, lower taxes, and increased corporate flexibility.[14] The emphasis on aggregate growth, however, ignored or obscured the underlying issues of fairness and an awareness of persistent poverty and marginalization. Excessive privatization also undermined civic participation, leaving many with a strong sense of decline. Neglect made many problems seem even more intractable than before.

Higher levels of immigration and less regulated use of newcomer and established labor were inextricable parts of these national trends.[15] Yet political attention to the legislative battle over the levels of admissions misrepresented the interplay of immigration with those general conditions. Economic restructuring accounts for one of the most misunderstood issues of contemporary relations between immigrants and established residents —the extent to which immigrants compete with and displace U.S. workers. Historically, the workplace was one of the most important locations for interactions between newcomers and established residents and for the creation of shared interests and goals. After two decades of the decline of unions, the collapse of large-scale manufacturing and, with them, large production facilities, and the growth of service industries, the work force is fragmented. Individual workers are isolated, laboring away in smaller service-oriented firms or connected only by new technologies designed to make the exchange between humans faster and more efficient but less personal. Much of this separation corresponds to deep divisions in the work force by race, ethnicity, and gender.

Although many observers have tried to dismiss it, the connection between this economic restructuring and the perception and experience of job loss is real enough.[16] Typical reactions from communities throughout the nation are reflected in these observations recorded by researchers from Houston: "The same is true for Blacks who used to work at the ship channel. Many Blacks lost their jobs because of mechanization and also as a result of the downturn in the economy in the 1980s . . . if you go to the channel today you won't see many Blacks but, you will see a number of Latinos. It is believed, by the people inside and outside the community, that racism has prevented many Blacks from being rehired at the channel." "Many Blacks in the city note that at one time you could see black women standing at bus stops around the River Oaks area waiting to go home; now one sees Latino immigrant females at these stops."[17] Similar experiences of restructuring and loss are not limited to African Americans. They can be recorded among whites who have witnesses the movement of wealthy Taiwanese into Monterey Park and among Anglos watching the influx of Cubans to Miami.[18]

The problem in understanding the nature of economic relations between immigrant and established groups is that restructuring, by definition, creates new job openings while destroying others. The openings and closings do not occur in an orderly manner, and there is often little displacement because there is little competition. New workers, including immigrants, often fill the opening jobs precisely because employers seek additional workers as they expand. During much of the 1980s, the business cycle drew many new workers into the labor force. But, as the economy faltered and firms were moved or closed, established residents watched as the jobs they held disappeared and those employing immigrants remained.

This continuous fluctuation within the labor market leads simultaneously to two apparently contradictory conclusions. As various studies have shown, the net result of immigration in a dynamic economy is virtually zero.[19] But the gross movements of workers within the labor market, with some established workers losing jobs while others gain, have the consequence of creating abundant experiences and accurate accounts of job displacement due to immigration. Communities do not live in the aggregate, nor do people perceive net or balanced outcomes. The continual neglect of the large gains and losses in the labor market leads to an excessively benign account of the impact of economic restructuring on workers in general and, in some cases, of immigration on established residents.

LINGUISTIC DIVERSITY

Intergroup tensions also result from the use of different languages in the same social activities. Political battles over bilingualism in the last two decades polarized the debate about language usage and distorted its importance to everyday encounters in local communities. Communities throughout the nation continue to demonstrate the need for active pursuit of language training and protection from forced loss of native, non-English languages, a loss that harms educational progress and adjustment in general. They also demonstrate a pervasive desire among immigrants to learn English.

Yet language is a complex and contradictory force in social relations. Sharing a language binds some people together while separating others. The use of several languages in a shared social arena, such as in neighborhoods, playgrounds, and community meetings, can create clear intergroup tensions.[20] The reasons, though, are complex. For example, the Philadelphia team of the Changing Relations Project reported instances in which the militant push for Spanish-English bilingual programs was resented and opposed by Korean and Polish groups moving into the same area.[21] Immigration has produced many more of these multilingual communities than is generally realized. For instance, the 1990 U.S. Census revealed that Los Angeles County has at least ten languages spoken by significantly large numbers of people within its borders.[22] In these new diverse communities, older models of English-Spanish bilingual programs, like traditional models of race relations based solely on black-white interactions, no longer remain applicable.

Language use also means something very different depending on the class and power of each group. For low-wage immigrants, speaking a language other than English means survival. On the other hand, learning English is a necessary route to upward mobility. Yet, for upper-class Cuban or Chinese immigrants, language use can be a source and symbol of power, and the social clash a test of who dominates a community. For elite non-English-speaking groups, public and private demands to use English are often interpreted as a threat to their privilege and status, a loss for those who are used to commanding their own social worlds.

CRAFTING A NEW PLURALISM

Unquestionably, intergroup tensions are rooted in deeply entrenched social, economic, and political trends that separate and divide. Yet efforts to cross these dividing lines are made daily. Newcomers and established residents do not coexist simply by avoiding each other. Active, conscious decisions to organize around common issues—not just for the sake of integration but when diverse people perceive similar interests—exist throughout U.S. cities. Today's failures to recognize and build upon them grow more out of an inability to craft ways to work together than from overwhelming resistance among either established residents or newcomers.

Over a century ago, observers noted that efforts to continuously reinvent democracy in the United States begin with the "little associations" of voluntary participation. Voluntary associations, organized formally or informally, provide the energy, resources, and direction for community building. They mobilize private and group values into community standards, obligations, and responsibilities and are especially important in shaping culture and discourse. Even as early as deTocqueville's travels, observers recognized that voluntary associations reinforced the value of diverse interests to community life.[23]

Most theoretical perspectives on community change predict that government monopolization of social policy and community programs inevitably diminishes the role of the voluntary sector. Historically, however, the voluntary sector expands during periods of increased immigration. Voluntary organizations serve as critical intermediaries between immigrants and established residents. They form the basis of association and social trust that cement local relationships, then become the foundation for participation in regional and national political, social, and economic life.

In the last two decades, expansion of government activities has coincided with an increase in voluntary sector activities, including those serving immigrants. As one observer has remarked, "What is new is that [growth in] both immigrant and ethnic associations [has taken] place in countries with large institutionalized social welfare programs and professional social work bureaucracies."[24] Youth organizations, informal business and commercial groups, community-improvement leagues, immigrant associations, and charitable associations, among others, have all proliferated. Their activities include assistance offered by established residents to help resettle newcomers, neighborhood cleanups that involve both newcomers and established residents, expansion of selections in community libraries to provide learning space for all groups, and youth sports clubs that bring together both children and their parents. The persistence and even revival of these voluntary associations and activities challenge the value of both bureaucratized programs and laissez-faire, market-oriented policies toward immigrant settlement.

Voluntary associations also provide a context for crafting informal social rules that organize and ultimately control community problems when they arise. For instance, part of the problem that arises between Korean shopkeepers and African American consumers is that employers draw only from family and friends for their workers. They establish few connections to the people in the neighborhood who at some time shop in their stores. The result is that no one in the store has the trust or informal authority forged through familiarity and extensive social connections to negotiate and confine a misunderstanding before it becomes a larger social conflict.[25]

MOVING FORWARD

The voluntary sector faces two profound challenges in responding to the contemporary settlement of immigrants and the renewal of interest in community reconstruction. During the 1980s, voluntary organizations adopted an increasingly direct role as primary agents of immigrant and refugee settlement. Voluntary organizations expanded and shifted their programs to serve newcomers in large part because of the rapid increase in the availability of federal resources through the Refugee Act of 1980 and the State Legalization Impact Assistance Grants (SLIAG) that accompanied the 1986 Immigration Reform and Control Act. By the late 1980s, though, the government had reduced its commitment to new immigrants and the communities in which they settle. The Immigration Act of 1990, which is only now becoming operational, expands the number of new immigrants and their geographical and occupational backgrounds. Yet the act offers no significant government resources to respond to the new volume or composition.

Similar reductions in funding for refugee resettlement have created problems for voluntary agencies serving local communities. After a decade of increasing refugee admissions, substantial declines in per capita support for resettlement finally resulted in such a deep cut in available funds that it required fundamental restructuring of the federal program. Privatization became a rallying call and a mechanism for disinvesting the federal government from refugee resettlement and responsibility for its immigration policy. Proposed changes shift greater control and authority over settlement activities to local voluntary agencies. But unless the Clinton administration reverses course, these changes leave local areas and organizations without a matching increase in resources.

The Refugee and SLIAG programs, however, are part of a general crisis in the relations between different branches of government that has resulted in huge gaps between federal authority and local capacities. In a March 1993 speech at the Kennedy School of Government, Governor Ann Richards of Texas characterized this crisis of federalism as an "adversarial combat between different levels of government: between state and local governments and the Federal Government. The power to mandate," she emphasized, "has become separated from the power to pay." One way to respond to this crisis, of course, is to increase the financial resources available to local governments to pay for federally mandated programs. To a large extent, this is the aim of a new lobbying effort that seeks to gain additional federal resources by constructing an immigrant policy for the United States. The idea borrows heavily from the 1980s model of refugee resettlement and its structure of reimbursing states for federally mandated programs in local communities.

The problem with this strategy is that the adversarial battle that Governor Richards identified requires, by way of counterattack, a restructuring that is not completely acceptable to those advocating a national immigrant policy. By following federal dollars, an immigrant policy could undermine community efforts at reform and, through targeting newcomers as a separate, special group, further reinforce community divisions. Such a policy could also promote exactly what anti-immigrant groups charge—that immigrants have needs that require special programs because there are too many of them for communities to absorb.

An alternative strategy of local mobilization begins with the recognition that the problems most immigrants face are shared by the entire community. Just as immigrants are not to blame for community problems, neither should they become an excuse for state and local governments to seek federal money to solve general fiscal woes. Voluntary agencies that work at the community level will, by their nature, be the fuel for the fire that energizes a new push for restructuring local programs. Established programs themselves must change to incorporate immigrants' and refugees' needs by changing established methods of defining priorities, recruiting members, and providing assistance. Local activities and coalitions need a degree of independence from government mandates, especially those that target only particular groups, to craft programs that work in the interests of everyone in the community.

The voluntary sector's second profound challenge results from its indirect involvement in newcomer settlement activities. Many established community organizations face a potential mismatch in their ability to respond to the needs and diversity of new immigrants. The ethnic and racial diversity of recent immigration has posed an especially difficult dilemma for established organizations initially organized around group rights and empowerment. The need to promote group solidarity and identity remains, especially at a time when attempts to overturn previous gains have increased. Yet some of these organizations have now become sources of separation and exclusion. Their group-based empowerment strategies may not be organizationally effective, and attempts to reach out may conflict with immigrants' own political strategies.

Tensions between groups in a period of large-scale settlement are not new. Still, established groups and institutions may not be well suited to respond to these new demands. Historically, trade unions were a primary mechanism for integrating diverse newcomers into a common work force. Yet these same unions also excluded women, African Americans, and unskilled workers. In addition, although unions have been historically one of the most important voluntary sector organizations in receiving new immigrants, the recent decline in membership and the impact of government reforms have weakened their capacities to respond to diverse newcomers. Immigration reform in the last four or five years has driven a wedge between the interests of many immigrant advocacy groups and unionized workers, pitting groups whose political focus is employment standards and social protections against those seeking larger numbers of immigrants.[26] Yet, when local unions, such as those representing maintenance workers and hotel employees, alter existing practices to respond to the language issues and health needs of immigrants, they can succeed in effectively encouraging the participation of both their established and newcomer members.[27]

One of the new challenges of this local diversity involves civil rights groups. Especially in cities in which the white majority is no longer numerically or politically dominant, the axis of group interactions has shifted. Increasingly, inter-racial, interethnic tensions and conflicts are between "minority" groups all seeking access and participation in the city's established institutions.

These organizations have not necessarily excluded anyone from membership. Rather, as ethnic and racial diversity expands, the appeal of established civil rights groups for reform and assistance often refers to increasingly narrow definitions of constituents and their interests. By simply maintaining an established membership and focus while community issues and composition have diversified, these groups represent less of the local population. Community members who experience these changes often mention the need for more flexibility for existing community organizations to respond to newcomers. For other observers, the problem lies in the redirection of public resources or in simply not being responsive to the changing diversity. For example, in Miami, the public resources claimed by a growing immigrant population challenged American-born blacks and strengthened resistance to Haitian newcomers.[28] Ironically, some observers in Miami are also concerned that "as Cubans come to dominate elite institutions, they may emulate the earlier exclusionary practices of established residents, particularly with regard to minorities. This became dramatically evident when the Cuban American Bar Association decided to exclude a Mexican from its ranks."[29]

Many of the groups and organizations that were born during the civil rights movement are now established community institutions. The new challenge is to organize civil rights, empowerment-based strategies, and the desire of many new immigrant groups to forge their own community associations into efforts that expand cooperation and search for shared goals that redefine the public order and common good.

TAKING UP THE GLOBAL CHALLENGE

Concern about the social implications of immigration reflects a familiar response to urban unrest. Twenty-five years ago, former Vice President Hubert Humphrey voiced similar worries about riots, conflicts, and commitment to community. When announcing his campaign for the presidency, he said, "Either we turn backward into a continually increasing polarizing of the nation and a widening spiral of fear—or we continue to go forward into a new day of justice and order. Which way: Apartheid or democracy? Separation or community? A society of ordered liberty or a society of fear and repression?"[30]

After the Los Angeles riots of 1992, the new discourse about immigration and community renewal is fundamentally rooted in a revival of discussions about the common good and a clear shift away from the assimilation of individual immigrants and distribution of benefits to separate groups. Yet recent commentators have noted generally that efforts to define and articulate the common good have become increasingly difficult. Some have even suggested that the United States has lost its civic culture,[31] including the core values that have been essential for forging a national culture out of successive waves of diverse immigrants.[32]

The rise and dominance of government, the argument goes, may have created alternative ways of thinking about public responsibility. Rather than feeling personally responsible for neighbors and communities, individuals turn to centralized agencies, and to the professionals employed by these agencies, as a more effective means of addressing complex problems. The market ideology of the 1980s also carried negative implications for the spirit of voluntarism. As social service agencies adopted market-based principles of assessing outcomes, paid professionals were more likely to make decisions according to financial considerations than according to the traditional values of caring and helping embodied in volunteer work.

Despite these changes, recent public opinion studies show that altruism and the spirit of voluntarism remain high in the U.S. population. Voluntary associations remain actively engaged as contributors to the new debates about local culture. They often serve as the fundamental building blocks of public debate about social standards. They are, as Berger and Neuhaus have described, them, "important laboratories of innovation in social services . . . (that) sustain the expression of the rich pluralism of American life."[33] They work on a daily basis with programs in schools, churches, youth and recreational groups, and employer and worker organizations, and certainly among direct service providers. Many local associations have consciously recrafted their membership and programs to mirror the full diversity of local ethnic residents. This strategy creates and reinforces new visions of the nation's culture, a grassroots multiculturalism, that may be emerging from efforts to respond to the incredible ethnic diversity of many of the communities in which immigrants have settled.

These social, cultural, and political pressures on established communities that accompany immigration are not unique to the United States.[34] The internationalization of U.S. communities is part of a global shift that involves closer integration among diverse peoples. Regional economic integration, free trade, and common markets are establishing and expanding bonds between peoples of the world that further encourage large-scale immigration. Family connections, even transnational communities, have emerged that now fuel self-propelled, large-scale immigration.

This is also a period of dramatic disintegration of established communities and the making of new political entities. Disintegrating pressures are closely connected to migration issues that seem to lead to an endless string of crises. The images are all too familiar: Kurdish rebels in Iraq, Haitian boat people, Hong Kong detention camps, asylum seekers attacked in Marseilles and Berlin, and ethnic cleansing in Yugoslavia. Now, according to some, Los Angeles, Washington Heights, Mt. Pleasant, and Liberty City join the list of communities at risk where immigrants have settled in large numbers.

Public reactions to the Los Angeles riots are not the first or last time that calls to curb immigration will be offered as an antidote to America's social ills. Taking care of one's own is a natural response to difficult times. But millions of immigrants are already a settled part of hundreds of communities throughout the United States. They reflect the nation's success and commitment to shared values of family reunion and humanitarian spirit.

Community renewal in those areas in which immigrants have settled requires a fundamental shift in perspective among the popular media, policymakers, and researchers. A new focus is called for that examines community and national transformation. An initial conceptual step is to recognize that immigrants are neither strangers nor outsiders to their new communities. The nation frequently forgets its responsibility for immigration. Migration to the United States occurs primarily by invitation. What most established Americans have never fully understood, but which immigrants never forget, is that America is deeply implicated in the migration flow and its destiny. U.S. employers fuel the immigration, U.S. foreign policy embraces it, and U.S. family values maintain it.[35]

STUDY QUESTIONS

1. How has economic restructuring affected the concept and practice of public responsibility?

2. How has the post-1992 discussion of immigration and community moved away from the notion of assimilation?

3. What is a strategy of "local mobilization"?

NOTES

1. Jack Miles, "Black-Brown Relations," *Atlantic Monthly*, p. 42 (OCT. 1992).

2. Peter Brimelow, "Time to Rethink Immigration?" *National Review*, 22 June 1992, pp. 30–46. See also the exchange in "Why Control the Borders?" *National Review*, 1 Feb. 1993, pp. 27–34.

3. Robert L. Bach, "Immigration: Issues of Ethnicity, Class, and Public Policy in the United States," *The Annals of the American Academy of Political and Social Science*, 485:139–52 (May 1986).

4. Nestor P. Rodriguez, "Undocumented Central Americans in Houston: Diverse Populations," *International Migration Review*, 21:4–26 (Spring 1987).

5. Bach, "Immigration."

6. Arthur Schlesinger, Jr., *The Disuniting of America: Reflections on a Multicultural Society* (Knoxville, TN: Whittle Communications, 1991), pp. 70–71.

7. The Changing Relations Project was developed in 1986, organized in 1987, and carried out from 1988 to 1991. A national board organized the research, which involved ethnographic fieldwork by six teams of over 50 researchers working in Philadelphia, Miami, Chicago, Garden City (Kansas), Houston, and Monterey Park (California). For the board's final report, see National Project Board, *Changing Relations: Newcomers and Established Residents in U.S. Communities* (New York: Ford Foundation, 1993).

8. National Project Board, *Changing Relations: Newcomers and Established Residents in U.S. Communities*, technical report (New York: Ford Foundation, 1991), pp. 23–24.

9. For example, see Lawrence Fuchs, *The American Kaleidoscope: Race, Ethnicity, and the Civic Culture* (Hanover, NH: University Press of New England, Wesleyan University Press, 1991).

10. Quoted in James R. Grossman, *Land of Hope: Chicago, Black Southerners and the Great Migration* (Chicago: University of Chicago Press, 1989).

11. Houston Research Team, as reported in *Changing Relations*, by National Project Board (1991).

12. Monterey Park Research Team, as reported in *Changing Relations*, by National Project Board (1991).

13. Sally Engle Merry, *Urban Danger: Life in a Neighborhood of Strangers* (Philadelphia: Temple University Press, 1981).

14. Ralf Dahrendorf, *The Modern Social Conflict: An Essay on the Politics of Liberty* (London: Weidenfeld & Nicolson, 1988).

15. Julian Simon, *The Economic Consequences of Immigration* (New York: Basil Blackwell, 1989).

16. George Borjas, *Friends or Strangers: The Impact of Immigrants on the U.S. Economy* (New York: Basic Books, 1990).

17. Houston Research Team, as reported in *Changing Relations*, by National Project Board (1991).

18. National Project Board, *Changing Relations* (1993).

19. Richard Freeman, *Immigration and the Work Force: Economic Consequences for the United States and Source Areas* (Chicago: University of Chicago Press, 1992).

20. National Project Board, *Changing Relations* (1993).

21. Philadelphia Research Team, as reported in *Changing Relations*, by National Project Board (1991).

22. U.S. Department of Commerce, Bureau of the Census, 1990 *Census of Population and Housing Summary Tape File 3A, Los Angeles County.*

23. Robert Wuthnow, "The Voluntary Sector: Legacy of the Past, Hope for the Future?" in *Between States and Markets: The Voluntary Sector in Comparative Perspective*, ed. Robert Wuthnow (Princeton, NJ: Princeton University Press, 1991), pp. 3–29.

24. Shirley Jenkins, "Introduction: Immigration, Ethnic Associations, and Social Services," in *Ethnic Associations and the Welfare State: Services to Immigrants in Five Countries*, ed. Shirley Jenkins (New York: Columbia University Press, 1988), pp. 3–29

25. An example is provided by the Chicago Research Team in *Changing Relations*, by National Research Board (1991).

26. Robert L. Bach, "Settlement Policies in the United States," in *Australia and U.S. Immigration Policies*, ed. J. Jupp and G. Freedman (New York: Oxford University Press, 1992).

27. Robert L. Bach and Howard Brill, *Impact of IRCA on the U.S. Labor Market and Economy*, final report to the U.S. Department of Labor, 1991.

28. Miami Research Team, as reported in *Changing Relations*, by National Project Board (1991).

29. National Project Board, *Changing Relations* (1993), p. 68.

30. Speech before B'nai B'rith, New York City, 1968.

31. Daniel Kemmis, *Community and the Politics of Place* (Norman: University of Oklahoma Press, 1990); Harry C. Boyte, *Commonwealth: A Return to Citizen Politics* (New York: Free Press, 1989).

32. Fuchs, *American Kaleidoscope*.

33. Peter L. Berger and Richard John Neuhaus, *To Empower People: The Role of Mediating Structures in Public Policy* (Washington, D.C.: American Enterprise Institute for Public Policy Research, 1977), p. 36.

34. Frank Bovenkerk, Robert Miles, and Gilles Verbunt, "Racism, Migration and the State in Western Europe: A Case for Comparative Analysis," *International Sociology*, 5(4):475–90 (Dec. 1990).

35. Rephrased from National Project Board, *Changing Relations* (1993), p. 21.

Selected Bibliography on Asian and Latino Immigration

Asian Immigration

Barringer, Herbert et al. *Asians and Pacific Islanders in the United States*. New York: Russell Sage Foundation, 1995.

Chan, Sucheng. *Asian Americans: An Interpretive History*. New York: Twayne Publishers, 1991.

Fong, Timothy P. *The First Suburban Chinatown: The Remaking of Montery Park, California*. Philadelphia: Temple University Press, 1994.

Freeman, James. *Hearts of Sorrow, Vietnamese American Lives*. Palo Alto: Stanford University Press, 1989.

Hing, Bill Ong and Ronald Lee, eds. *The State of Asian Pacific America: Reframing the Immigration Debate*. Los Angeles: LEAP Asian Pacific American Public Policy Institue and UCLA Asian American Studies Center, 1996.

Horton, John. *The Politics of Diveristy: Immigration, Resistance, and Change in Montery Park, California*. Philadelphia: Temple University Press, 1995.

Knoll, Tricia. *Becoming Americans: Asian Sojourners, Immigrants, and Refugees in the Western United States*. Portland: Coast to Coast Books, 1982.

LEAP Asians Pacific American Public Policy Institute and UCLA Asian American Studies Center. *The State of Asian Pacific America: Policy Issues to 2020*. Los Angeles: LEAP Asian Pacific American Public Policy Institute and UCLA Asian American Studies Center, 1993.

Ong, Paul et al., eds *The New Asian Immigration in Los Angeles and Global Restructuring*. Philadelphia: Temple University Press, 1994.

Rutledge, Paul James. *The Vietnamese Experience in America*. Palo Alto: Stanford University Press, 1992.

Takaki, Ronald. *A Different Mirror: A History of Multicultural America.* Boston: Little, Brown and Company, 1993.

————. *Strangers from a Different Shore: A Story of Asian Americans.* Boston: Little, Brown and Company, 1993.

United States Commission on Civil Rights. *Civil Rights Issues Facing Asian Americans in the 1990s.* Washington, D.C.: U.S. Government Printing Office, 1992.

LATINO IMMIGRATION

Calavita, Kitty. *Inside the State: The Bracero Program, Immigration, and the I.N.S.* New York: Routledge, 1992.

Chavez, Leo R. *Shadowed Lives: Undocumented Immigrants in American Society.* Orlando, Florida: Holt, Rinehart and Winston, 1992.

Cordasco, Francisco. *The New American Immigration: Evolving Patterns of Legal and Illegal Immigration: A Bibliography of Selected References.* New York: Garland, 1987.

Delgado, Hector. *New Immigrants, Old Unions: Organizing Undocumented Workers in Los Angeles.* Philadelphia: Temple University Press, 1993.

Gutierrez, David G., ed. *Between Two Worlds: Mexican Immigrants in the United States.* Wilmington: Scholarly Resources Inc, 1996

Hayes-Bautista, David E., et al. *The Burden of Support; Young Latinos in an Aging Society.* Stanford: Stanford University Press, 1988.

Hondagneu-Sotelo, Pierrette. *Gendered Transitions: Mexican Experiences of Immigration.* Berkeley: University of California Press, 1994.

Mahler, Sarah J., *American Dreaming: Immigrant Life on the Margins.* Princeton: Princeton University Press, 1995.

NACLA. "Coming North: Latino and Caribbean Immigration." *Report on the Americas,* Vol. 26, No. 1 (1992).

Portes, Alejandro, ed. *The Economic Sociology of Immigration: Essays on Networks, Ethnicity and Entrepreneurship.* New York: Russell Sage Foundation, 1995.

————. *City on the Edge: The Transformation of Miami.* Berkeley: University of California Press, 1993.

Repak, Terry A. *Waiting on Washington: Central American Workers in the Nation's Capital.* Philadelphia: Temple University Press, 1995.

Rodriguez, Clara. *Puerto Ricans: Born in the U.S.A.* Boulder, Colorado: Westview Press, 1991.

Sanchez Korrol, Virginia. *From Colonia to Community: The History of Puerto Ricans in New York City.* Berkeley: University of California Press, 1994.

Siems, Larry., ed. *Between the Lines: Letters between Undocumented Mexican and Central American Immigrants and Their Families and Friends.* Hopewell, New Jersey: Ecco Press, 1992.

Torres, Andres. *Between Melting Pot and Mosaic: African Americans and Puerto Ricans in the New York Political Economy.* Philadelphia: Temple University Press, 1995.

United States Senate, Committee on the Judiciary, Subcommittee on Immigration and Refugee Affairs. *Central American Migration to the United States.* Washington, D.C.: U.S. Government Printing Office, 1990.

Contributors

ROBERT L. BACH is a professor in the Department of Sociology, State University of New York, Binghamton.

EVELYN BLUMENBERG is a graduate student in the Department of Urban Planning, University of California, Los Angeles.

NORMA STOLTZ CHINCHILLA is a professor in the Department of Sociology, California State University, Long Beach.

ROGER DANIELS is a professor in the Department of History, University of Cincinnati.

YEN ESPIRITU is a professor in the Department of Ethnic Studies, University of California, San Diego.

M. PATRICIA FERNÁNDEZ-KELLY is a professor in the Department of Sociology, Johns Hopkins University.

PATRICIA GURIN, is a professor in the Department of Psychology, University of Michigan.

DARRELL Y. HAMAMOTO is a professor in the Department of Asian American Studies, University of California, Davis.

NORA HAMILTON is professor in the Department of Political Science, University of Southern California.

BILL ONG HING is a professor in the School of Law, Stanford University.

AÍDA HURTADO is a professor in the Department of Psychology, University of California, Santa Cruz.

PETER KWONG is a professor in the Department of Urban Affairs and Planning, Hunter College, City University of New York.

DAVID LOPEZ is a professor in the Department of Sociology, University of California, Los Angeles.

PHILIP MARTIN is a professor in the Department of Agricultural Economics, University of California, Davis.

CHORSWANG NGIN is a professor in the Department of Anthropolgy, California State University, Los Angeles.

PAUL ONG is a professor in the Department of Urban Planning, University of California, Los Angeles.

TIMOTHY PENG, is a graduate student in the Department of Psychology, University of Michigan.

MARIFELI PÉREZ-STABLE is a professor in the Department of Sociology, State University of New York, College of Old Westbury.

RUBÉN G. RUMBAUT is a professor in the Department of Sociology, Michigan State University.

RICHARD SCHAUFFLER is a graduate student in the Department of Sociology, Johns Hopkins University.

MAURA I. TORO-MORN is a professor in the Department of Sociology and Anthropology, Illinois State University, Normal.

RODOLFO D. TORRES is a professor in the Graduate Center for Public Policy and Administration, and the Department of Comparative Latino Studies, California State University, Long Beach.

MIREN URIARTE is a professor in the College of Public and Community Services, University of Massushetts, Boston.

ABEL VALENZUELA, JR. is a professor in Chicano Studies and Urban Planning , University of California, Los Angeles.

TAMAR DIANA WILSON is an anthropologist currently conducting research in Baja California.